Religion: The Social Context

Religion: The Social Context

Meredith B. McGuire
Montclair State College

Wadsworth Publishing Company
Belmont, California
A Division of Wadsworth, Inc.

Sociology Editor: Curt Peoples
Production Editor: Diane Sipes
Designer: Patricia Dunbar
Copy Editor: John Eastman
Cover Design: Patricia Dunbar and Maureen O'Lone

Printed in the United States of America

2 3 4 5 6 7 8 9 10 — 85 84 83

Library of Congress Cataloging in Publication Data
McGuire, Meredith B
    Religion, the social context.

    Bibliography: p.
    Includes index.
    1. Religion and sociology. I. Title.
BL60.M27   306'.6   80-21807
ISBN 0-534-00951-4

ISBN 0-534-00951-4

Contents

Preface

Religion exists in a social context, is shaped by that social context, and, in turn, often influences it. To convey this complex relationship, I have selected key issues in the sociology of religion, rather than writing a comprehensive text. My primary aim is to present an integrated interpretation of religion in society, while describing different interpretive approaches. Since the field of sociology is not unified, the book's integrative approach offers the reader a useful basis on which to evaluate the issues. The book is best used as a core of essays around which instructors can build a course and assign related articles, monographs, or readings to complement their own emphasis. This material is aimed at college students taking a first course in sociology of religion, and I hope it will prove useful to seminary and graduate students and to interested general readers.

Chapter 1 serves as an introduction, defining sociology of religion. Chapter 2, which outlines the main theoretical approaches used in this book, follows the theories of Berger (and, to a lesser extent, Luckmann and Geertz) in emphasizing the ability of religion to provide both meaning and belonging. I agree with Greeley (1972a) that this synthesis of the theories of the classical sociologists of religion clarifies many important issues in the field. This theoretical approach is balanced in later chapters by other perspectives, but I believe that a guiding interpretive framework is useful at the outset.

Subsequent chapters of the book, though presented in an orderly sequence, may be used in any order. Each chapter introduces relevant key concepts and a limited number of sociological theorists or researchers. For reasons of practical flexibility, I have reiterated explanations of a few key terms in more than one chapter. The authors mentioned by name in the text have been generally selected for the importance of their theoretical contributions to the specific theme of the chapter or for their general sociological significance. Other important authors are cited in the references and recommended readings, which have been included not only to acknowledge my intellectual debts but to provide students with useful references for further research.

Most chapters also include an extended example in addition to the main explicative portion. The purpose of such examples is to illustrate a sociological

interpretation of relevant religious phenomena, such as new religious movements
and the conflict in Northern Ireland. Some of these essays reflect interpretations
of phenomena on which I have done extensive empirical research: faith healing,
new religious movements, and religion in Ireland. All of the extended examples
represent a more personal stance than the discussions in the main text and, as
such, invite the reader to encounter the sociological issues intellectually and
perhaps disagree. These interpretations are intended to illustrate useful sociological concepts in a stimulating and provocative way and to show how sociological
theories are relevant to interesting aspects of social life. Several of these interpretive essays are far from neutral; my sympathies clearly lie with the exploited and
oppressed (specifically women, blacks, and natives of colonized lands), and my
personal concern is to explore the role of religion in their oppression and liberation.

Ending each chapter is an annotated list of recommended readings—articles,
books, and selections from recent books of readings. Two appendices suggest
further useful materials. Appendix A outlines major resources for a literature
search in sociology of religion. Students preparing term papers or theses will find
these resources essential. Appendix B is an annotated film resources list. I have
found good films to be almost essential in teaching sociology of religion because
they provide concise glimpses into religious situations beyond the often limited
experiences of students. Field learning experiences can also help, but films are
typically more manageable and broadly informative.

In writing this book, I have received help from many people, whose assistance I gratefully acknowledge: Ken Aman, Jim Beckford, Ken Brook, Pat Brown,
Barbara Chasin, Peter Freund, Laura Gordon, Gail Lynch, David McGuire, Linda
Mai, Ben Mariante, George Martin, Evelyn Savage, and William Swatos. I also
thank students in sociology of religion classes at Montclair State College and
Stonehill College for their thoughtful comments on an earlier draft of several
chapters. I appreciate the suggestions and insights provided over several years by
participants of the Society for the Scientific Study of Religion's "teaching"
sessions, especially Ted Mills and Ed Lehman. Also very welcome were the advice
and encouragement of my editors, Curt Peoples and Steve Rutter, and reviewers,
M. Kenneth Brody, of Drake University; Jere Cohen, of the University of Mary-
land, Baltimore County; Charles C. Langford, of Oregon State University; Douglas B. McGaw, of Emporia State University; Patrick H. McNamara, of the University of New Mexico; Howard L. Sacks, of Kenyon College; and Charles M. Tolbert,
of Baylor University. I want to express my special appreciation to Susan Gos-
cinski, Eneida Gonzalez, and June Lindeman for their care in the preparation of
the manuscript. Finally, I want to thank Daniel, Rachel, and Kieran McGuire for
their patience, for pleasant (if not always immediately appreciated) diversions
from my writing tasks, and for helping to keep this entire project in perspective.

Meredith B. McGuire

CHAPTER ONE

The Sociological Perspective on Religion

Religion is one of the most powerful, deeply felt, and influential forces in human society. It has shaped people's relationships with each other, influencing family, community, economic, and political life. Religious beliefs and values motivate human action, and religious groups organize their collective religious expressions. Religion is a significant aspect of social life, and the social dimension is an important part of religion.

The Nature of the Sociological Perspective

Sociologists are interested in studying religion primarily for two reasons. First, religion is very important to many people. Religious practices are important parts of many individuals' lives. Religious values influence their actions, and religious meanings help them interpret their experiences. Sociologists seek to understand the meaning of religion to believers themselves. Second, religion is an important object for sociological study because of its influence upon society and society's impact upon religion. Analysis of this dynamic relationship requires examining the interdependence of religion and other aspects of society. Often this means questioning taken-for-granted ways of understanding social action. From the earliest foundations of the discipline, sociologists have sought to understand the larger society through examining religion and its influence.

Because religion is so intensely personal and reverently held, some people have difficulty in grasping a **sociological perspective** on it. The sociological perspective is a way of looking at religion that focuses on the human (especially social) aspects of religious belief and practice. Religion is both individual and social. Even the most intensively subjective mystical experience is given meaning through socially available symbols and has value partly because of culturally established interpretations of such experiences. A personal religious experience such as conversion is voluntary and subjective, yet is situated in social circumstances and given meaning by social conventions. When the individual communicates that religious experience, the symbols used to interpret it are socially determined.

Two characteristics of the sociological perspective separate it from nonscientific approaches to religion: It is *empirical* and *objective*. As much as possible, sociologists base their interpretations upon empirical evidence. They seek to verify their images and explanations of social reality by experimental or experiential evidence. And they look for generalizations about a larger societal, historical, and cross-cultural picture, continually asking: Of what larger phenomenon is this particular situation an example? Objectivity means that sociological interpretations of religion do not attempt to evaluate, accept, or reject the content of religious belief. Sociological researchers set aside, for purposes of the study, their personal opinions about religion and try to be as objective as possible in observing and interpreting the religious phenomenon under study. From a sociological perspective, one religion is not superior to another. Indeed, the sociological perspective does not even presume the merits of religious over nonreligious groups.

These aspects of the sociological perspective on religion may discomfort students who find their cherished beliefs and practices dispassionately treated as objects of study. It may be disturbing to have one's own religion treated as comparable to other religions and not as superior or uniquely true. The perspectives of the religious believer and the sociologist are necessarily quite different, but neither perspective represents the whole reality of religion.

Let's use the analogy of another object of attention. In looking at a flower, for example, several people could view the same one, yet each employ a different perspective. A botanist could employ a scientific perspective, analyzing in great detail the flower's physical properties, comparing it with other plants, and classifying the flower accordingly. An artist could interpret the flower onto the canvas, abstracting those visual qualities that convey its image. A mystic could use the flower as a focal point for meditation, perhaps experiencing a sense of oneness with the flower and the rest of the natural environment. And a child could examine the flower to consider its suitability for a daisy chain. The point is that none of these perspectives has a monopoly on the reality of the flower; what is discovered from the perspective of the botanist does not disconfirm what the artist's perspective has revealed.

Similarly the religious perspective on human life often produces a very different picture of that reality than a sociological perspective. What is relevant to the religious believer may be irrelevant or inadmissible evidence to the sociologist. What is central to the sociologist may be irrelevant or uninteresting to the religious believer. The reality perceived from the sociological perspective cannot disprove that of the religious believer; it is not possible for a sociologist to prove, for example, whether or not a religious prophecy or vision is from God. Furthermore, the perspective of the religious believer does not disprove that of the sociologist. If, for example, a religious "revelation" contradicts sociological evidence, the fact that the believer considers the "revelation" to be from God does not disprove the sociological observation.

These two different perspectives are, however, often difficult to reconcile. The sociological perspective, by definition, lacks a key religious quality—faith.

The believer accepts certain beliefs and meanings on faith. Faith implies taking certain meanings or practices for granted, implicitly trusting, not questioning. By contrast, the sociologist does not take the believer's meanings for granted but takes them as an object of study.

The sociological perspective sometimes implies that people believe for reasons other than the truth value of the belief system. For example, sociologists have observed that upper-class persons are likely to belong to different Christian denominations than lower-class persons. A 1964 sample of church members showed that 64 percent of Congregationalists had annual incomes of $10,000 or more, compared with 39 percent of American Baptists and only 22 percent of members belonging to various sects such as Pentecostal, Holiness, or Adventist groups (Stark and Glock, 1968:96). These substantial differences suggest that not only the "truth" of the denomination's belief system, but also social class variables, account for why people belong to one or the other group.

The more causality that believers attribute to supernatural sources, the less their interpretation can be reconciled with a sociological perspective. The very fact of treating certain interactions like conversion as human behavior, as an object of sociological study, is often incompatible with the basic beliefs of some religious groups. Sociology must necessarily "bracket" (i.e., methodologically set aside) the crucial religious question: To what extent is this action *also* from God? This does not mean that sociology treats religious behavior and experience as "merely" human. Important dimensions of religion may not be accessible to sociological interpretation. Nevertheless, whatever else they may be, religious behavior and experience are also human and are therefore proper subjects for sociological research and understanding. With these limitations of the sociological perspective in mind, let us explore some definitions of religion within this perspective.

Defining Religion

The purpose of a sociological definition is to bring order to a vast array of social phenomena. The definition of any concept establishes (somewhat arbitrarily) boundaries around those phenomena to be considered as instances of that concept. Thus in order to focus our attention on phenomena to be considered "religion," we must establish a working definition of religion.

Before reading the various scholars' definitions, try writing your own sociological definition of religion. It should be broad enough to include all kinds of religion but narrow enough to exclude what is similar to, yet not the same as, religion. One way to construct your definition is to think of specific instances of "religion" or "nonreligion" and see whether your definition includes or excludes them. For example, does your definition include the religions of Asia or Africa? Does your definition use terms (e.g., "church" or "god") that, unless clarified, may apply only to some religions? Is your definition narrow enough? Does it distinguish between religious commitment and other commitments such as allegiance to a social club, an ethnic group, or family? There are several phenomena that only some sociologists define as religion (e.g., magic, superstition, witchcraft, astrology, spiritualism). Does your definition account for these phenomena? Why? How do the phenomena of nationalism, Marxism, atheism, or humanism fit into your definition? Does your definition include or exclude them? Why? Do you consider psychotherapy, sports, or rock music to be "religion"? Some sociological definitions of religion are so broad as to include all of these phenomena; others exclude some or all of them. We will examine some of these definitions and some arguments for excluding or including certain characteristics within a definition of religion.

Definitions of religion are an issue of serious debate, not just academic wrangling, in sociology. How one defines religion shapes one's explanation of its role in society. Different definitions of religion result in different interpretations of issues such as social change (see Chapter 7), secularization (see Chapter 8), and nonchurch religion (see Chapter 4). Indeed, part of the problem in determining a definition of religion that is satisfactory for analytical purposes is that the issue of what is "properly religious" is a continuing controversy in modern societies. In recent years, for example, the courts have examined several cases in which their verdicts hinged upon deciding whether or not a given phenomenon was or was not a valid instance of religion. If the definitive boundaries of religion are not very firm for everyday social and legal purposes—as they are not—then producing a neat sociological definition may be counterproductive and misleading (Fenn, 1978:29).

Definition as Strategy

It is useful to approach sociological definitions as strategies rather than as "truths." A definitional strategy narrows the field under consideration and suggests ways of thinking about it. Definitions can be evaluated according to how useful they are for a given task. What interpretive tasks does any given definition help to accomplish? Pragmatically, then, it is sometimes helpful to use different, even opposing definitional strategies to approach a phenomenon.

Two major strategies used by sociologists of religion are **substantive** and **functional** definitions. Substantive definitions try to establish what religion *is*; functional definitions describe what religion *does*. These approaches can be illustrated by analogy with definitions of the concept "chair." A substantive definition might state that a chair is an object of furniture that usually has four legs and a back; the definition might add further physical details to distinguish a chair from a sofa, bench, or toilet. A functional definition of "chair" might state that it is a seat, usually for one person. This functional definition is somewhat broader, allowing objects that various cultures use as seats but that may have no legs at all. Defining "chair" is easier than defining "religion," however, because one can point to various physical objects called "chair" and then derive a set of distinguishing characteristics from observing them. Religion does not have clear-cut physical properties, nor are its characteristics readily ascertained and agreed upon.

Substantive Definitions

A substantive definition defines what religion *is*. It attempts to establish categories of religious content that qualify as religion and other categories specified as nonreligion. Spiro (1966:96) offers a straightforward substantive definition of religion: "An institution consisting of culturally patterned interaction with culturally postulated superhuman beings." By "institution," this definition refers to socially shared patterns of behavior and belief. All institutions include beliefs, patterns of actions, and value systems; the critical feature of religion is that the beliefs, patterns of action, and values refer to "superhuman beings" (Spiro, 1966:98).

Spiro's definition of religion is a good example of a sociological definitional strategy because all of the categories in the definition—"institution," "culturally patterned," "culturally postulated"—are sociologically relevant. His explication of the concept of "superhuman beings" is also sociologically significant because it emphasizes the sense of *power*. "Superhuman beings" are defined as those having greater power than humans, beings who can help or hurt humans but can be influenced by human action (Spiro, 1966:98). Power is one of the most important concepts in the sociology of religion, and a definition that emphasizes power can be useful. Other substantive definitions of religion use similar concepts, including "nonhuman agencies," "supernatural realm," "super-empirical reality," "transcendent reality," and "sacred cosmos" (several representative substantive definitions are appended at the end of this section).

In addition to these theoretical approaches to religion, many empirical studies of institutional religion implicitly use substantive definitions for a different reason: They are easier to adapt to survey research. A somewhat oversimplified example is seen in the questionnaire that asks the respondent's religion, then lists the following alternative choices: "Protestant," "Catholic," "Jew," "other," "none." The underlying assumption of such a question is a substantive definition of religion as a specific Western religious institution.

The major advantage of substantive definitions is that they are more specific than functional ones. They are more explicit about the content of religion. Substantive definitions tend to be narrower and neater than functional definitions; using them, one can specify whether a phenomenon is or is not religion. Substantive definitions also tend to correspond more closely than functional definitions to commonsense notions of religion because they are generally based upon Western—especially Christian—ideas about reality. For example, the distinction between "natural" and "supernatural" is a product of Western thinking, such as the elaborate medieval cosmographies (i.e., pictures of the universe) that classified natural and supernatural beings on numerous levels. Although hierarchies of archangels and seraphim may not be relevant in contemporary society, the division of natural from supernatural still seems familiar.

Substantive definitions are appropriate for studying religion in relatively stable societies, which present few problems with issues of social change and cross-cultural applicability. Substantive definitions are problematic precisely because they are historically and culturally bound, based upon what was considered religion in one place and time. Because of their basis in Western historical experience, substantive definitions are often too narrow to account for non-Western religious phenomena. Substantive definitions are sometimes deceptively neat. Without specifying the functions of supernatural beings, for example, it is impossible to distinguish the gods from ghosts, Santa Claus, and the tooth fairy.

Some sociologists identify religion with church-oriented religiosity; relatively few non-Western societies, however, have formal organizations like churches.

Does this mean that such societies therefore have no religion? If supernatural, nonempirical, or nonrational entities do not figure importantly in a society, does that society lack religion? Confucianism (the state religion of China from about 200 B.C. until the early twentieth century A.D.) is essentially a set of principles of order, especially regarding social relationships surrounding authority and kinship. It does not include the worship of any gods, although nature and ancestors receive much ritual reverence. If supernaturalism is a key criterion of a substantive definition, then Confucianism and some strains of Buddhism (in which there is no deity but only reverence and imitation of holy men) would not be considered religions. A current also exists within contemporary Christian thinking toward leveling this-worldly and other-worldly distinctions (e.g., the theologies of Pannenberg, Metz, Solle, and Moltmann). Would Christianity without supernaturalism cease to be a religion?

Substantive definitions have difficulty accounting for religious change. If religion is identified only in terms of religious expression in one historical period, any change from that form of expression looks like nonreligion. Many theories of religious change, for example, start from a notion of a time when people were "really religious." In Christian history, the thirteenth century is usually identified as the period when religion was a powerful force in the entire society and thoroughly interwoven with other aspects of life—work, education, politics, family, and so on. If one equates that image of religion with "real religion," any change from that pattern is viewed as a trend toward nonreligion ("secularization"). A parallel problem occurs in studies of the family. If "family" is defined in terms of its historical manifestations (e.g., concrete blood or marriage ties), many contemporary living arrangements do not qualify as family. Do two unmarried people and their offspring constitute a family? What about a single woman and her adopted children? What about six unmarried persons sharing sexual partners and collectively caring for their offspring? Since cultures constantly and sometimes rapidly change, it is difficult to create a substantive definition that applies through time. On the other hand, it is difficult to document historical changes in religion's place in society if we lack a sufficiently specific definition of religion. If we compare, for example, the situation of religion in the French Revolution with the religious situation of the American Revolution, we must be able to identify exactly which aspects of social life we mean by "religion."

As a definitional strategy, substantive definitions have advantages: They are more specific and amenable to empirical studies of religion. On the other hand, they tend to be more historically and culturally bound than functional definitions. Substantive definitions, in short, produce a very different interpretation of social change than functional definitions (for essays promoting substantive definitional approaches, see Berger, 1967: 175–178; 1974; Robertson, 1970: 34–51; Spiro, 1966).

Functional Definitions

A functional definition of religion emphasizes what religion *does* for the individual and social group. Accordingly religion is defined by the social functions it fulfills. The content of religious belief and practice is less important for this definitional strategy than the consequences of religion.

Geertz's definition of religion is a useful example of a functional definition: "A *religion* is: (1) a system of symbols which acts to (2) establish powerful, pervasive, and long-lasting moods and motivations in men by (3) formulating conceptions of a general order of existence and (4) clothing these conceptions with such an aura of factuality that (5) the moods and motivations seem uniquely realistic" (Geertz, 1966:4).

This definition emphasizes several sociologically important concepts. The most important element is the provision of meaning, since the establishing of shared meanings (i.e., symbols) is an essentially social event. The definition also accounts for social structural and social psychological functions through the concepts of "moods, " "motivations," and "factuality" (which also relate to the notion of "institution," as Spiro uses it). The distinguishing features of this definition are the "conceptions of a general order of existence" and their realism. According to Geertz, people interpret events and experiences as meaningful by linking them with a larger sense of *order*. This larger sense of order is perceived from a religious perspective as entirely real—even more real than mundane events and experiences. Empirically this distinction means that the content of religious beliefs and practices does not matter so long as it serves to symbolize some transcendent order to believers (Geertz, 1966:12ff).

Some of the functions identified by various sociological definitions of religion include the provision of ultimate meaning; the attempt to interpret the unknown and control the uncontrollable; personification of human ideals; integration of the culture and legitimation of the social system; projection of human meanings and social patterns onto a superior entity; and the effort to deal with ultimate problems of human existence. Some of these functions are described further in later chapters.

One distinction used in many functional definitions is the social attribution of the **sacred**. Whereas the natural/supernatural distinction of some substantive definitions refers to the intrinsic quality of the *object* of worship, the sacred/profane distinction refers to the *attitude* of worshippers. The realm of the sacred refers to that which a group of believers sets apart as holy and protects from the "profane" by special rites and rules (Durkheim, 1965:62). The sacred is regarded as especially powerful and serious. for example, a communion wafer may be regarded as nothing but a piece of bread by nonbelievers, but Christian worshippers regard it as special and treat it differently from ordinary bread. Natural objects such as candles, beads, books, water, oil, and wood can be regarded as sacred. Thus nonsupernatural cultural systems (e.g., nationalism) could be viewed as sacred systems because of the attitude of their followers. Nationalist groups often treat the state and its symbols—flags, national holidays, shrines—as sacred.

Functional definitions of religion include all that substantive definitions identify as religion, but they are usually much broader. Both substantive and functional approaches would define the phenomena of Calvinism, Roman Catholicism, Methodism, Mormonism, and Reform Judaism as "religion." The inclusiveness of some functionalist approaches, however, extends to some phenomena that substantivists identify as nonreligion: ideologies, ethos, value systems, world views, interpersonal relations, leisure activities, voluntary associations, and so on. Geertz (1966:13) points out that his definition of religion would include, for example, golf—not merely if a person played it with a passion, but rather if golf were seen as symbolic of some transcendent order.[1] Functional definitions often include as "religion" phenomena such as nationalism, Maoism, Marxism, humanism, psychologism, the Human Potential movement, spiritualism, and even atheism. The religious qualities of less comprehensive human activities, such as sports, art, music, and sex, are incorporated into some functionalist definitions as well.

The primary advantage of a functionalist definitional strategy is its breadth. Functional definitions tend to be better than substantive definitions for encompassing cross-cultural, transhistorical, and changing aspects of religion. Functional definitions encourage the observer to be sensitive to the religious quality of many social settings.

A drawback of some functional approaches to religion, however, is their assumption that society has certain functional requisites. This assumption implies that society requires certain social functions, some of which are uniquely fulfilled by religion. Some theories, for example, assume that society requires cultural integration (i.e., a common core of beliefs, values, and commitments). If religion is then defined as that which provides cultural integration, the theory implies that religion is a requisite for society's existence (Parsons, 1944:86). Such an argument is circular, describing religion as that which provides that which is defined as religion. The assumption that religion is necessary is unproven.

The breadth of functional definitions is a mixed blessing. While functional definitions are less culturally and historically bound, this inclusiveness makes it difficult to use them for empirical studies requiring neat, quantifiable categories. Some critics say that functional strategies result in all-inclusive categories, defining virtually everything human as religion.

Sociologists using functional definitions need to show why they include phenomena that participants themselves do not consider to be religious. From a functionalist standpoint, a good case could be made for considering sensitivity and psychotherapeutic groups as essentially religious phenomena. Members of these groups, however, often do not recognize their own beliefs and behavior as religious; they may even intensely disavow the religious label. On the one hand, it seems fair to accept the participants' notion of what they are doing; on the other, it is an honorable sociological tradition to point out the facades behind which people mask their activities. Few sociologists would accept at face value prison staff members' assertions that prisons are mainly for the purpose of rehabilitating prisoners. Similarly there may be good sociological reasons for questioning whether vehemently nonreligious groups are actually nonreligious. Representatives of Transcendental Meditation have argued strongly in court that TM is not religion and therefore should be allowed in the public schools. The religious aspects of TM's beliefs and practices are downplayed because the desired image of TM is as technique rather than religion. The fact that a movement's desired image

[1]Geertz, 1966:13. Geertz was probably not surprised by the actual development and international expansion of Japanese "golf religion," the Church of Perfect Liberty. One minister of this church explained that golf is "a little miniature of life. We can learn about ourselves through golf. Our teachings say that in life, anger, worry, and sorrow destroy success, just as in golf. Like golfing, life is an individual game, where you seek individuality; in golf, as in life, it's always the next shot, another chance for perfection" (quoted in the *New York Times*, May 30, 1975).

may be promoted by denying its religious qualities is worth studying, but sociologists need not accept a group's self-definition (for essays promoting functional definitional approaches, see Geertz, 1966; Lemert, 1975; Luckmann, 1967; 1977).

The choice between substantive and functional definitions is finally a matter of strategy. Each approach has advantages that may recommend it to certain sociological tasks. The two strategies, however, result in very different interpretations of various issues such as social change, secularization, the relationship between religion and other institutions in society, and new forms of religion. An awareness of the limitations and scope of each definitional approach will enable us to evaluate these other issues more critically. This book draws largely on examples that would be defined as religion by both substantive and functional definitions. At the same time, however, it explores phenomena such as civil religion and various new forms of religion that only functional approaches would consider as religion. This approach seems fruitful for two reasons: It allows us to consider an interesting range of phenomena from a sociology of religion perspective; and it raises broader theoretical issues.

The following section includes additional definitions representative of these definitional strategies. These definitions from the works of several major figures in the sociology of religion exemplify the definitive categories described above.

Representative Definitions of Religion
Emile Durkheim:

> A religion is a unified system of beliefs and practices relative to sacred things, that is to say, things set apart and forbidden—beliefs and practices which unite into one single moral community called a Church, all those who adhere to them (1965:62).

Ludwig Feuerbach:

> Religion, at least the Christian, is the relation of man to himself, or more correctly to his own nature (i.e., his subjective nature); but a relation to it, viewed as a nature apart from his own. The divine being is nothing else than the human being, or, rather the human nature purified, freed from the limits of the individual man, made objective—i.e., contemplated and revered as another, a distinct being. All the attributes of the divine nature are, therefore, attributes of the human nature (1957[1841]:12–14).

Karl Marx and Frederick Engels:

> *Man makes religion,* religion does not make man. In other words, religion is the self-consciousness and self-feeling of man who has either not yet found himself or has already lost himself again. But *man* is no abstract being squatting outside the world. Man is the *world of man,* the state, society . . . [Religion] is the *fantastic realization* of the human essence because the *human essence* has no true reality (1964:41).

Talcott Parsons:

> A religion we will define as a set of beliefs, practices, and institutions which men have evolved in various societies, as far as they can be understood, as responses to

those aspects of their life and situation which are believed not in the empirical-instrumental sense to be rationally understandable and/or controllable, and to which they attach a significance which includes some kind of reference to the relevant actions and events to man's conception of the existence of the "super-natural" order which is conceived and felt to have a fundamental bearing on man's position in the universe and the values which give meaning to his fate as an individual and his relations to his fellows (1951:2).

Robert Bellah:

Religion [is] a set of symbolic forms and acts which relate man to the ultimate conditions of his existence (1964:359; used by permission).

J. Milton Yinger:

Religion, then, can be defined as a system of beliefs and practices by means of which a group of people struggles with these ultimate problems of human life (1970:7).

Thomas Luckmann:

The world view, as an "objective" and historical social reality, performs an essentially religious function and [we may] define it as an *elementary form of religion*. This social form is universal in human society. . . . The world view is an encompassing system of meaning in which socially relevant categories of time, space, causality and purpose are superordinated to more specific interpretive schemes in which reality is segmented and the segments related to one another (1967:53; used by permission).

Peter Berger:

Whenever the socially established nomos attains the quality of being taken for granted, there occurs a merging of its meanings with what are considered to be the fundamental meanings inherent in the universe. Nomos and cosmos appear to be co-extensive. . . . Religion is the human enterprise by which a sacred cosmos is established. Put differently, religion is cosmization in a sacred mode (1967:24–26).

Roland Robertson:

Religious culture is that set of beliefs and symbols (and values derived directly therefrom) pertaining to a distinction between an empirical and super-empirical, transcendent reality; the affairs of the empirical being subordinated in significance to the non-empirical (1970:47).

Max Weber:

To define "religion," to say what it *is*, is not possible at the start of a presentation such as this. Definition can be attempted, if at all, only at the conclusion of the study. The essence of religion is not even our concern, as we make it our task to study the conditions and effects of a particular type of social behavior (1963[1922]:1).

Aspects of Religion

There are many facets of religion that are important for the sociologist to recognize. In Western society, much emphasis is placed upon formal beliefs. Religious education consists of informing children of what one's group believes; children read religious textbooks of explanations, learn catechisms (i.e., statements of propositions to which a believer should assent), study scripture, hear sermons. Christianity and Judaism place relatively great emphasis on intellectual and formal belief. In other cultures, however, formal beliefs are relatively unimportant. Other important aspects of religion include ritual, religious experience, and community. Children learn all that is relevant to their faith by participating in group ceremonies and imitating their elders' experiences. The following aspects of religion refer not only to the individual's religion but more generally to the ways in which the religious group organizes itself to focus its shared meanings.

Religious Belief

Every religion has an essential **cognitive** aspect. The religion shapes what the adherent *knows* about the world. This cosmic knowledge organizes the individual's perceptions of the world and serves as a basis for action. If I believe, for example, that active, powerful evil spirits surround me, I will perceive "evidence" of their activity, and I will take actions to protect myself from them. My belief in evil spirits helps me explain other aspects of my life, such as why I cannot get a job and why I feel depressed and anxious. The same belief suggests appropriate actions, such as necessary prayers to ally myself with good spirits or use of amulets to ward off the influence of these evil spirits.

There is a tendency in modern Western societies to treat religious beliefs as "mere opinion" opposed to empirical beliefs, which are treated as "knowledge." This distinction hides the fact that both types of belief are "knowledge" to the individual who holds them. If a person considers evil spirits to be real, they *are* real in their consequences; they shape the person's experience and actions. The individual who believes that evil spirits cause illness and the individual who believes that germs cause illness are both acting according to their "knowledge."

Most of us are quite familiar with formal religious beliefs, the statements to which adherents of a given religion are supposed to assent, such as a catechism or a creed. The entire enterprise of theology out of which formal beliefs are developed represents a highly specialized and intellectualized approach to religion. But religion also includes less formal kinds of beliefs such as myths, images, norms, and values. Myths of creation and rebirth, for example, are told and enacted in dance and song. These other kinds of symbolization are often more potent influences on behavior than intellectualized beliefs.

Religious beliefs are not mere abstractions that are irrelevant to everyday life. People use their beliefs to make choices, interpret events, and plan actions. Myths, one form of religious belief, are paradigms of human existence. There are myths about all major aspects of human life: birth and rebirth, creation and transformation, one's people and place, marriage, work, fertility, sterility, and death. Myths are stories that provide a rationale for a group's actions. They can be metaphors for concrete social structure and for real human events. Individuals draw upon these interpretations to give meaning and direction to their own actions. Indeed, the very language in which beliefs are expressed structures believers' perceptions of the world.

Religious beliefs also inform the individual what action is good and desirable or bad and to be avoided. They may tell the individual that marriage is good and right because the holy marriage of the gods is to be copied by humans. Religious beliefs may inform the individual that eating other people is wrong because the gods value people and therefore do not define them as appropriate food. Thus an entire range of values, norms, and attitudes derive from religious beliefs.

Religious Ritual

Ritual consists of symbolic actions that represent religious meanings. Whereas beliefs represent the cognitive aspect of religion, ritual is the enactment of religious meaning. The two are closely intertwined. Beliefs of the religious group give meaning and shape to ritual performances. Ritual enactments strengthen and reaffirm the group's beliefs. They are ways of symbolizing unity of the group and, at the same time, of contributing to it. Ritual helps generate religious conviction. By ritual action, the group collectively remembers its shared meanings and revitalizes its consciousness of itself. This has important consequences both for the group and the individual member. The group renews its fervor and sense of unity, and individual members come to identify with the group and its goals (Durkheim, 1965:420; Geertz, 1966:28).

Various religious groups place different emphasis on ritual. Eastern Orthodox, Roman Catholic, and Episcopalian Christians emphasize overt ritual more than Baptists or Methodists. The use of symbolism, such as processions, sacraments, candles, ikons, and chanting, aids the collective remembering of the group's shared meanings. Even groups that do not consciously use rituals repeatedly symbolize their unifying beliefs. "Revival" meetings often emphasize spontaneity in worship and downplay formal ritual. Nevertheless, though the words of their prayers may not be formally set, members respond especially fervently to prayers that fit a familiar formula, and their responses are often equally stereotyped and expected. These periodic reenactments are just as much ritual as the "high church" ceremonies of Episcopalians.

As these examples suggest, the *content* of an act is not what makes it a ritual act; rather it is the symbolic meaning attached to the act by participants. This symbolic value is what distinguishes, for example, lighting a candle to beautify one's dinner table and lighting a candle of the menorah to commemorate the Feast of Lights (the Jewish holiday of Hanukkah). There are also ritual acts that have, over time, become remote from their symbolic significance. For example, Roman Catholic priests wear different colored vestments to celebrate Mass on various holidays, but many people in the congregation may not even know what the symbolism of pink or green vestments means, and thus the ritual significance of the vestments is empty for them. Ritual performed for its own sake, empty of meaning for participants, had led to the notion that ritual itself is deadening.

It is not that ritual per se is dead but rather that the relationship between the symbolism and the group's shared meanings is weak or severed. Events or beliefs that a given ritual has symbolized may, over time, become less important or even forgotten. Perhaps the group may have moved on to new ways of symbolizing itself and its beliefs. Or perhaps the empty ritual may be symptomatic of weak ties in the group itself, that it has no essential unity to celebrate. By contrast, ritual that is a vital symbolic expression of important meanings for the group can be a sustaining, strengthening, and enlivening experience of unity.

The dynamic potential of religious ritual suggests its link not only with religious belief but also with religious experience. Religious symbols, expressed in beliefs and rituals, have *real* power, which can be experienced personally by the individual. Ritual words and ceremonies can evoke experience of awe, mystery, wonder, and delight. Religions often emphasize the power of ritual words, as exemplified by the seriousness surrounding the pronouncement of the words, "This is my body," in Christian communion services; or by the expectation surrounding the exclamation "Heal!" in a faith healing service. Ritual has the potential to produce special religious experiences for the group and its individual members.

Religious Experience

Religious experience refers to all of the individual's **subjective involvement** with the sacred. Although such experience is essentially private, people try to communicate it through expression of beliefs and in rituals. A communal ritual may be the setting for a personal religious experience. Thus a person receiving communion (i.e., a communal ritual) in a Christian worship service may also experience an intensely subjective awareness of God. Similarly even a private experience has a social element because socially acquired beliefs shape the individual's interpretation of religious experience. The symbolism of various religious traditions shapes the interpretations of even highly mystical experiences through such images as the pilgrimage, perfect love and marriage, and rebirth or transformation (Underhill, 1961:125–148).

Individual religious experiences vary considerably in intensity. They range from momentary senses of peace and awe to extraordinary mystical experiences. Different religions place different emphases on religious experience. In America, most denominations do not actively encourage highly emotive religious experiences; whereas in some Pentecostal groups, these experiences are central and eagerly sought. In many religions, extraordinary and intense experiences are segregated, appropriate only for certain members or on certain occasions. Thus among the peoples of the northern Asian arctic region (e.g., Eskimos), extraordinary religious experiences are expected of certain members called "shamans." Shamans are religious specialists who have undergone an intense encounter with sacred forces, emerging with special powers to effect good or evil on behalf of the rest of the group (see Castenada, 1968; Eliade, 1964). Another example is the segregation of occasions for special religious experiences (e.g., initiation rites).

The content of religious experience varies. It may include pleasurable aspects such as a sense of peace, harmony, joy, well-being, and security. Religious experience may also produce terror, anxiety, and fear. While the content of the experience partly depends upon the group's beliefs about what is being encountered, both the pleasurable and frightening experiences are related to the sense of power or force with which the sacred is believed to be endowed. The individual who experiences a sense of security does so because of the power of the sacred to impart security; the individual who experiences great fear does so because of the power of the sacred to cause grave harm. The notion of the sacred thus entails both harmful and helpful aspects. Personal experiences of this power can be overwhelming.

William James (1958:67) quotes an account of a religious experience that illustrates the intensity of some of these aspects:

> I remember the night, and almost the very spot on the hilltop, where my soul opened out, as it were, into the Infinite, and there was a rushing together of the two worlds, the inner and the outer. It was deep calling unto deep,—the deep that my own struggle had opened up within being answered by the unfathomable deep without, reaching beyond the stars. I stood alone with Him who had made me, and all the beauty of the world, and love, and sorrow, and even temptation. I did not seek Him, but felt the perfect unison of my spirit with His. The ordinary sense of things around me faded. For the moment nothing but an ineffable joy and exaltation remained. It is impossible fully to describe the experience. It was like the effect of some great orchestra when all the separate notes have melted into one swelling harmony that leaves the listener conscious of nothing save that his soul is being wafted upwards, and almost bursting with its own emotion. The perfect stillness of the night was thrilled by a more solemn silence. The darkness held a presence that was all the more felt because it was not seen. I could not anymore have doubted that *He* was there than that I was. Indeed, I felt myself to be, if possible, the less real of the two.

This kind of religious experience represents an "alternate state of consciousness"—a situation in which the individual's consciousness is relatively remote from the sphere of everyday reality. The person may experience being out of one's body or being one with something or someone else. For example, one person described such an experience as follows: "I came to a point where time and motion ceased. . . . I am absorbed in the light of the Universe, in Reality, glowing like fire with the knowledge of itself, without ceasing to be one and myself, merged like a drop of quick-silver in the Whole, yet still separate as a grain of sand in the desert" (quoted in Happold, 1970:133).

Alternate states of consciousness are not necessarily religious. Substances such as peyote, for example, can produce alternate states of consciousness, but the context in which they are taken (e.g., ritual) and the meanings attached to taking them (i.e., symbolism) determine whether they produce religious experiences. "Alternate states of consciousness" or "peak experiences" are only one extreme of a continuum of religious experiences (see, for example, Maslow, 1964). Less dramatic religious experiences include a sense of the presence of God, a moving conversion experience, or a deeply absorbing ritual experience.

American society often ignores or discourages such experiences. Peak experiences such as those described, however, may be more common than generally acknowledged. Approximately 35 percent of a national sample of Americans (N-1,467) had at some time experienced feeling "very close to a powerful, spiritual force that seemed to lift you out of yourself" (McCready and Greeley, 1976:132; see also Greeley, 1974; Hood, 1973; Hood, 1976). Perhaps a self-fulfilling prophecy may operate in a culture's encouragement or discouragement of such experiences. In those cultures that value and encourage special religious experiences, members have felt and acknowledged these experiences; in cultures that devalue or discourage these experiences, members neither seek nor recognize them.

While a sizable proportion of Americans have had some special spiritual experience, American culture in general does not particularly value such experiences. This culture places great emphasis upon rational, intellectual, "objective" ways of knowing. Religious experience, by contrast, is a way of knowing by subjectively apprehending a reality. One woman described her own experience as follows: "I felt a deep sense of warmth and security and a startling awareness of how much the Lord cares for me personally." This kind of knowledge, while it may correspond with the official belief system of a religious group, is not simply learned, deduced, theologically debated, or received from church authorities.

Religious Community
Religious experience may also include the awareness of belonging to a group of believers. Rituals often remind the individual of this belonging, creating an intense sense of togetherness. The community of believers may be formally or informally organized. Formal specialization of a group into an organization such as a church is a relatively recent historical development. The religious group—formal or informal—is essential for supporting the individual's beliefs and norms. And the nature of the religious community illustrates the social context of religious meaning and experience. We will explore this aspect further in the next two chapters.

The Development of the Sociology of Religion

The very development of sociology and the sociology of religion in particular is rooted in some of the social processes we will examine (especially the process of secularization). Only as beliefs and social practices were perceived as something other than taken-for-granted realities could a scientific study of these "social facts" become possible. The development of Enlightenment rationality and paradigms of scientific thought encouraged examination of religion as human action (see Birnbaum and Lenzer, 1969; Robertson, 1970: 7–33).

Ironically these same developments also acted upon religion, possibly changing it fundamentally. Thus sociology has some complicity in this alteration; to a certain extent, popularization of the sociological perspective on religion has the effect of altering the nature of religion itself. The social sciences, as heirs to Enlightenment humanism, have interpreted religion as a human construction, undermining its claims to transcendence. Some recent sociologists have called attention to this perspective and questioned whether the social sciences can validly claim to be value free if their very choice of an interpretive stance implies certain value judgments. They ask whether it is possible to have a social science of religion that allows for the truth of religion (see Anthony and Robbins, 1975; Bellah, 1970; Greeley, 1972b; and especially B. Johnson, 1977).

An important strand of classical sociology of religion has a prophetic ring. Weber's doubts about the future of a fully "rationalized" society, Durkheim's concern about the impact of social change upon the cohesion and moral unity of society, Simmel's insights into the threat to the individual of increasing societal controls, and Marx's questioning the continued legitimacy of capitalistic modes of organization, all contain strong critical themes (see Durkheim, 1965; Marx, 1963; Simmel, 1971; Weber, 1958a). These theorists saw their contribution to a sociology of religion as part of a larger examination of the nature of modern society. They asked questions such as: In what direction is modern society going? How did it develop to this point, and what factors influence its further development? What is the place of the individual in modern society, and what is the impact of these broader social changes on the individual? These classical contributions are emphasized in several chapters of this book.

Later developments in sociology, especially in America, did not continue these themes of concern. The sociology of religion was largely ignored until the late 1940s and 1950s, when an upswing in church membership and participation, combined with increasing interest of religious leaders in institutional research, provided an impetus for sociologists to focus again on religion. The dominant theoretical perspectives on religion then current in sociology were, however, very narrow (see Berger and Luckmann, 1963). Religion was defined strictly in terms of its formal organizational setting: the institutional churches. Much of the research was circumscribed by the needs and interests of these organizations. Demographic features of parishes were studied, for example, in order to predict future building and staffing needs. The standard methodological approaches of that period were similarly restricting; survey research techniques were best suited for measuring clearly definable institutional behavior or opinions. A survey interviewer could more readily ask a respondent to name a denominational preference than to describe fully an entire personal meaning system.

This stage in the development of sociology of religion was characterized by several assumptions, notably the identification of "church" as "religion." Another general assumption of this phase was that individual religiosity could be equated with individual participation in religious institutions. A corollary assumption was that the subjective aspects of religion could be tapped by identifying the individual's religious opinions or attitudes (see Luckmann, 1967:20–23; some criticisms of these assumptions are developed further in Chapter 4).

Beginning in the mid-1960s, the sociology of religion greatly expanded its theoretical focus and research interests. New developments in Western religion spurred this expansion. Following publication of Anglican Bishop John Robinson's provocative book *Honest to God* (1963), theologians debated the viability of culturally bound Christian theology, and a school of theology proclaiming the "Death of God" developed. Simultaneously Catholic theologians explored new interpretations of their tradition, and the Second Ecumenical Council (Vatican II) established far-reaching structural changes in that church. Religious participation in various human rights movements, the articulation of various national "civil religions," and the emergence of numerous new religious movements raised important sociological questions that pressed the discipline to expand its interpretive scope.

Recent sociology of religion is characterized by its broader emphasis. It encompasses not only Western but also non-Western religious expression; it sees parallels between religious behavior in this society and simpler societies; it is interested in both institutional and noninstitutional religious behavior. Its theoretical concerns reflect both a thoughtful return to classical themes and an ability to go beyond the classics. This development is part of a generally larger interest within sociology in building critically upon classical theory. Recent sociology of religion is more central to the larger sociological enterprise than before, asking what can we understand about the nature of society through examination of religion? This focus leads current sociology of religion to themes that are central in contemporary theory, such as the legitimation of society, the individual-to-society link, and the impact of social change (Robertson, 1977).

Summary

This chapter has examined key features of the sociological perspective on religion: its objectivity and empirical focus. Definitions of religion are matters of serious academic debate, and the choice of definitional strategies (i.e., substantive or functional) influences the observer's conclusions about the place of religion in contemporary society. In order to understand how religious groups organize themselves around shared meanings, it is necessary to examine several aspects of religion: religious belief, ritual, experience, and community.

The development of the sociology of religion is itself rooted in some of the social processes that have influenced religion's role in society. Only as beliefs and social practices lost their taken-for-granted quality could a scientific study of them proceed. Sociology of religion was central to the focus of classical sociology—its concern about the emerging forms of societal legitimacy, social controls, and the place of the individual in modern society. Recent sociological thought examines these issues with renewed fervor.

The Focus of This Book

These theoretical themes are the basis of the organization of this book. Chapter 1 has described the scope of the field and illustrates how different strategies for defining religion result in different interpretations of the location of religion in contemporary society. Chapter 2 discusses the ways in which religion provides meaning and belonging for the organization of individual lives and social groups. The capacity of religion to provide meaning and belonging are further illustrated in Chapter 3, which explores how the individual's religion is socially acquired, maintained, or changed. The individual's religion cannot be narrowly equated with participation in specifically religious organizations, as

Chapter 4 shows; rather it comprises a complex array of beliefs and practices organized (sometimes not very coherently) into a personally meaningful and useful way of thinking and doing—a world view. People do, however, affiliate themselves with groups to express and maintain their religions, and specifically religious organizations have identifiable characteristic patterns, as described in Chapter 5 on religious collectivities. These patterns are dynamic, resulting from tensions within the religious group and between the religious collectivity and the larger society. Chapter 6 explains the dual potential of religion to promote social conflict and to enhance social cohesion; these aspects of religion are also related to religion's role in social change. Chapter 7 examines the conditions under which religion is likely to promote or inhibit social change. Various social changes also influence religion and its social location. Chapter 8 discusses several interpretations of such changes connected with the controversial "secularization" thesis. These theories are directly related to some of the broader issues of modern sociology.

Because of this focus, this book de-emphasizes much of the respectable but narrow material from the sociology of institutionally specialized religion. There is relatively little discussion of the clergy and its roles or of congregational polity. For the same reason, methodological issues discussed in this volume suggest ways of exploring nonchurch religiosity and other aspects of noninstitutional religion. Yet much of this emphasis is relatively new, so not many research results exemplify this broader focus, and whole areas of relevant information remain untapped. The sociology of religion has produced much excellent work, but some of the weaknesses of data, methodology, and theory pointed out in this book suggest areas for further development. The implications of contemporary sociology are far-reaching, and I hope to share with the reader the intellectual excitement of pursuing some of these issues.

Recommended Readings

Articles

Robert N. Bellah. "Christianity and Symbolic Realism." *Journal for the Scientific Study of Religion* 9 (2), 1970:89–96; reprinted in Newman reader (1974).

Peter Berger and Thomas Luckmann. "Sociology of Religion and Sociology of Knowledge." *Sociology and Social Research* 47 (4), 1963:417–427; reprinted in Birnbaum and Lenzer (1969), Newman (1974), and Robertson (1969) readers.

Clifford Geertz. "Religion as a Cultural System." *Anthropological Approaches to the Study of Religion,* Michael Banton, ed. London: Tavistock, 1966:1–46: reprinted (abridged) in McNamara (1974) reader.

Talcott Parsons. "The Theoretical Development of the Sociology of Religion." *Journal of the History of Ideas* 5 (April), 1944:176–190; reprinted in Bobbs-Merrill reprints and in Faulkner (1972) and Robertson (1969) readers.

Melford Spiro. "Religion: Problems of Definition and Explanation." *Anthropological Approaches to the Study of Religion,* Michael Banton, ed. London: Tavistock, 1966:85–126.

Books

Two collections of readings particularly emphasize theories of religion. They are:

Norman Birnbaum and Gertrud Lenzer, eds. *Sociology and Religion: A Book of Readings.* Englewood Cliffs, N.J.: Prentice Hall, 1969. This collection includes excerpts from both "classical" and contemporary theorists.

Roland Robertson. *Sociology of Religion.* Harmondsworth, England: Penguin, 1969. Robertson includes some excellent selections from a cross-cultural perspective together with good theoretical essays.

Materials about non-Western religion are particularly helpful in conjunction with this chapter. Two highly readable sources are:

Huston Smith. *The Religion of Man.* New York: Harper & Row, 1965.

Colin Turnbull. *The Forest People.* New York: Simon & Schuster, 1961.

Religion and Systems of Meaning
    Meaning for the Social Group
    The Individual's Meaning System
Crisis of Meaning
    Theodicies
    Anomie
    Mazeway Disintegration
Community and Religious Belonging
    Religion as the Expression of Social Unity
    Plausibility Structures of Meaning
    Subsocietal Plausibility Structures
        Sectarianism
        Tribalism
        Localism
Extended Application: Millenarianism and Dualism in Contemporary Social Movements
    Two Opposing Principles: Good and Evil
        Dualism as a Response to Anomie
        Dualism as Theodicy
    The Imminence of the Millennium
        Religious Millenarianism
        Social and Political Millenarianism
    Dualism and Millenarianism in Social Movements
Summary
Recommended Readings

CHAPTER TWO

The Provision of Meaning and Belonging

*R*eligion represents an important tie between the individual and the larger social group, both as a **basis of association** and as an **expression of shared meanings** (cf. Greeley, 1972a). In this chapter, we will examine the provision of meaning for the individual and for the larger social group. This provision of meaning is linked with the communal aspect of religion; a community of believers maintains a meaning system and mediates it to the individual. The religious processes described in this chapter are interesting in themselves, but we must ask the broader question: What does our understanding of religion tell us about society itself? Comprehending how the individual and the larger social group are linked in a community of shared meanings is important for the larger issue of how society is possible.

Religion and Systems of Meaning

The capacity of religion to provide meaning for human experience has been a major theme in the sociology of religion since its early emphasis in the works of Weber (1958a). **Meaning** refers to the interpretation of situations and events in terms of some broader frame of reference. For example, the experience of losing one's job is given meaning when it is interpreted as "bad luck," "market forces," "the boss is trying to get rid of pro-union workers," "job discrimination," or "God's will." As this example shows, meaning here refers to ordinary, everyday interpretations of experience. Sometimes meaning is expressed in grand, theoretical terms, such as elaborate theories of meaning formulated by philosophers and theologians. Most of what is meaningful to people in their everyday lives, however, is less complex.

Have you ever tried to write your autobiography? The ways in which you interpret your experiences and the events, persons, and experiences you choose to remember, as well as how you explain them, reflect the meanings you apply to events in your own life. This chapter discusses how that kind of meaning is attached to individual and social life.

21

People typically choose their interpretations from a larger meaning system, a broad, interpretive framework. Although the meanings that constitute this personal system are all interrelated, they are not necessarily coherent or internally consistent. People may believe in the idea of germs and also in the seemingly contradictory idea of evil spirits as explanations for illness. They may simply use the concept of germs to interpret some illnesses and evil spirits to explain others.

Most historical religions are comprehensive meaning systems that locate all experiences of the individual and social group in a single general explanatory arrangement. A comprehensive meaning system such as these is called a **world view** (Berger and Luckmann, 1966). We shall use the concepts of "religious world view" and "religious meaning system" more or less interchangeably, because most historical religious meaning systems have been comprehensive. Nevertheless in modern society, religious meaning systems compete with many other world views. Individuals are less likely to use any single comprehensive meaning system but may apply religious meanings to segments of their lives. For example, some meaning systems (e.g., astrology) explain only certain spheres of their adherents' lives, and believers find other meanings elsewhere.

According to some sociological definitions of religion (especially functional definitions, described in Chapter 1), any comprehensive meaning system is fundamentally religious, regardless of its content. For the purposes of this discussion, however, it is sufficient to say that comprehensive meaning systems that are not overtly religious (e.g., psychotherapeutic or political meaning systems) share most characteristics of specifically religious meaning systems. The process of conversion from one comprehensive meaning system to another is comparable, regardless of the belief content of either meaning system. We must also keep in mind that meaning systems are not abstract but are created and held by people.

According to Berger (1967), the provision of meaning is particularly important for an understanding of religion because of the ways in which meaning links the individual with the larger social group. *Meaning is not inherent in a situation but is bestowed.* The example of how one interprets losing one's job shows the wide variety of possible meanings that could be attached to the event. Although the individual may examine the event itself for clues as to which meaning "fits" best, the final choice of meaning is *applied to* the event. The person fired might conclude that, although the boss cited uncooperative attitudes, the "real" meaning of the event points to a greater mission as an organizer of workers elsewhere. The experience is given meaning by this choice of interpretations. Attaching meaning to events is a *human* process (Berger, 1967:19).

Geertz (1966:40) suggests that religion serves as a template in establishing meaning. It not only interprets reality but also shapes it. The template of religion "fits" experiences of everyday life and "makes sense" of them; in turn, this meaning shapes the experiences themselves and orients the individual's actions. A meaning system in which Satan is prominent can explain past events and experiences (e.g., temptation or illness) as evidence of Satan's effects and can shape future experiences (e.g., by warning believers to avoid certain places or activities where Satan is likely to ensnare them).

By examining how this meaning-giving process occurs, we can understand some of the ways by which religion links the individual with the larger social group.

Meaning for the Social Group

Meaning systems interpret an entire group's existence. Thus the group's ways of doing things and its very existence are assigned meaning. The group, for example, may explain its moral norms as instituted by God; its pattern of family life may be interpreted as copying the family of the gods; and its history may become meaningful as the story of the gods' relationship with their people. As Berger (1967:29–33) points out, the meaning system is both *explanatory* and *normative*; that is, it explains why things are the way they are and prescribes how things should be. The meaning system of the group "makes sense" of its *social order*—the present/existing and future/desired social arrangements of a group, such as its form of authority and power, its stratification system and allocation of roles, its distribution of resources and rewards, and so on. These qualities make the meaning system a strong legitimation for the social order of the group.

A **legitimation** is any form of socially established explanation that is given to justify a course of action. Legitimations include any explanation of social practices: Why do we do things this way? Why should we behave according to that norm? Why do we have this position in society? Particularly important are those legitimations that establish authority in the group (Berger, 1967:29 ff.).

Legitimations are expressed in a wide variety of forms. Myths, legends, proverbs, folktales, and history are all invoked to justify certain social arrangements. Taken together, these legitimations may be viewed as the "story" out of which a group lives. These examples show that legitimations are seldom intellectual in form. Intellectual legitimations, such as those developed in philosophy, theology, and political and economic theory, are a highly specialized form of legitimation. Nonintellectual forms are far more common.

Legitimations explain the ways in which the social group has behaved, but they also shape future action by justifying the norms of appropriate or desirable action. Religious legitimations make especially strong claims for the bases of order and authority and for the specific arrangements of the social order by their references to a higher authority. Thus the social order is represented as more than human convention. The European idea of the "divine right of kings," for example, implied that the king ruled not merely as a political arrangement but as a permanent, God-given right. Contemporary examples of social arrangements that are religiously legitimated include the sanctity of marriage, the right to own and defend property, and the moral rightness of waging certain kinds of war.

The effectiveness of these legitimations often involves a certain amount of *mystification* (Berger, 1967:90). Anything suggesting that the social arrangements are purely human convention is allowed to be forgotten or is deliberately masked. The present way of doing things is promoted as the "true tradition," and contrary evidence is not emphasized in the group's tale of its own history. For example, the Christian ideal of the institution of marriage is often represented as being exactly the ideal held during the whole history of Christianity. Actually, however, both the ideals and practices of marriage have changed considerably, and current religiously legitimated arrangements, such as the practice of church weddings, are relatively recent. Until the sixteenth and seventeenth centuries, ordinary people typically wed by private self-marriage (later formalized as "common-law" marriage). This was the acceptable pattern through the Middle Ages, though couples sometimes went to the church steps for a blessing. Only in the sixteenth century was church marriage declared a sacrament, but during the subsequent Reformation, many Protestant groups denied that marriage was a sacrament. Most Protestant groups did, however, keep the practice of church weddings, and they developed their own rituals for these ceremonies. (Noonan's 1965 analysis of Roman Catholic marriage and family norms and Nelson, 1949, provide further examples of how Christian ideals of marriage and other social institutions have changed considerably over the years.) Thus we see how the effectiveness of legitimations of present-day marriage practices depends upon treating these practices as traditional and upon forgetting or de-emphasizing those parts of history that are inconsistent with present norms and practices.

Although religious legitimations are generally used to justify existing social arrangements, they are also potent forms of criticism of the existing social order, as Chapter 7 shows in some detail. The Old Testament prophet Amos legitimated his denunciation of people's ways by reference to their God. Religious legitimations may be invoked to justify even revolutionary action. Thus religious legitimations are not solely a tool of the dominant group but may justify actions of subordinant and dissenting groups as well.

The Individual's Meaning System

The individual does not construct a personal meaning system from nothing. An individual's meaning system is learned, for the most part, during the process of socialization. The interpretations that seem most plausible to a person are likely to be those that are familiar and held by others who are important to that individual. So although each individual operates with a highly personal meaning system, that set of meanings is greatly influenced by family, friends, institutions (e.g., education), and the larger society. While the individual comes to accept some of the meanings communicated during socialization, the resulting meaning system is not, however, an inevitable product of socialization. The individual can reject or modify meanings communicated by others. When several competing meaning systems are presented as alternatives (which happens especially in modern society), the individual can choose which meanings to accept. The individual may accept the meaning system presented by a subgroup in society and not that of the larger society. Yet all personal meaning systems gain effectiveness by their link with some community in which they are shared.

Meaning and individual identity are intertwined. People locate themselves and their personal actions in a larger social order by means of their meaning systems. The individual selects an interpretation of events and experiences from the larger interpretive scheme provided by the meaning system, and that personally accepted meaning system becomes the individual's point of reference. The applied meaning system informs the individual what "kind" of person one is, the importance of the roles that one performs, the purpose of the events in which one participates, and the significance of being who one is. A meaning system, in other words, *makes sense* of one's identity and social being.

People can bestow meaning on a situation in various ways. Beliefs are important in this process. Ideas can help locate an experience in a meaning system, but a meaning system cannot be reduced to its formal belief content. Miracles, magic, ritual, and symbols also contribute to a pervasive sense of meaning. The individual can apply meaning to a situation by performing an appropriate ritual for the event. Similarly, by interpreting an event as miraculous or magical, the individual places special meaning upon it. The application of meaning to human experience entails social processes. Through everyday conversation, the individual tries out interpretations of experiences. Interaction with others—especially with persons whose response "counts" to the individual—is a significant part of the process of bestowing meaning upon a situation.

At the same time, the meaning system informs the individual of the values and norms of the larger group. The following interpretive statements illustrate the variety of ways in which norms and values can be embodied in a meaning system:

—"Cleanliness is next to godliness."

—"Masturbation is likely to lead to insanity."

—"Most of the problems with youth nowadays are due to bad mothers who go out to work instead of taking care of their children."

—"Doctors should make a lot more money than others because they had to work so hard and long to become qualified, and their skills are more important to society."

—"People who commit adultery will be punished by God."

—"He brought his illness on himself by his bitter and hateful outlook on life."

—"Hard work and patience are always rewarded."

Even though you may personally disagree with some or all of these statements, you can see how each statement can be used to *interpret* situations or experiences and to *evaluate* general kinds of behavior. Meaning systems embody norms, social evaluations of behavior. To the extent that one applies these norma tive interpretations to one's own behavior, the meaning system brings an evaluative element to one's identity. Thus in terms of the interpretive framework, one may conclude: "I am a sinner," "I am a good mother," "I am a successful warrior," "I am ill-fated," or "I am a virtuous person."

The individual's meaning system makes possible the evaluation of past actions and the motivation of future actions. The ability to perceive events as ordered in some way enables one to plan and orient one's actions. If things are experienced as "just happening" in a chaotic, meaningless string of events, the person literally does not know what to do. If, however, these events are given meaning, their interpretation implies an appropriate course of action (even if that action consists in seemingly passive responses such as "suffering through it" or "praying over it"). By relating mundane social life to the realm of the transcendent, religion is particularly effective in motivating the individual's participation in the larger social group. The classic example of such motivation is the concept of "vocation," the idea that one is "called" to an occupational or economic status by God. This idea gives special meaning to everyday work. By understanding such work in terms of "vocation," individuals gain a sense of purpose and value to their labor, and society gains the willing contribution of its members (see Weber, 1958a:Chapter 3).

Both the individual and the social group draw upon religion for meaning of their existences. The meaning system provides interpretation for their experiences, locating human lives and events in terms of a larger framework. Religion also serves as an important form of legitimation, or justification, for both the individual and the social order. Religion interprets and evaluates the "way things are to be done" in the social group. These legitimations provide meaning for individual members of the group who accept these explanations and incorporate them into their ways of thinking about the world.

Crisis of Meaning

The meaning system of the individual or group is able to integrate most routine events into an understandable pattern, a meaningful whole. Some events and experiences, however, are not so easily interpreted within the existing meaning system. The individual who experiences the death of a loved one, a painful illness, or serious economic misfortune may not be helped by the existing personal meaning system. An entire group can undergo similar meaning-threatening experiences: oppression by an enemy, famine, earthquake, or economic depression. Such events are particularly meaning-threatening if they appear to contradict important aspects of the existing meaning system. Groups who believe in a loving, personal god have more difficulty reconciling disastrous events with their meaning system than do groups whose god is remote and capricious.

Another situation that creates a problem of meaning is serious discrepancy between the ideal that a group promulgates and the actual practice. Inequality and injustice can be especially meaning-threatening when they are inconsistent with the group's ideals. Because the threat of the meaninglessness of such events is so great, individuals and groups try to build special legitimations into their meaning systems to justify these apparent contradictions or discrepancies. In other words, part of the meaning system itself interprets events and experiences that would seem to contradict the meaning system. These meanings are responses to the *problem of theodicy* (Weber, 1963:Chapter 9).

Theodicies

Theodicies are religious explanations that provide meaning for meaning-threatening experiences. Most religions, for example, offer theodicies of suffering and death. The content of these explanations differs among the various religions, but the desire to find meaning for such experiences appears virtually universal. Disaster and death create a problem of theodicy not because they are unpleasant, but because they threaten the fundamental assumptions of order underlying society itself (Berger, 1967:24). Theodicies tell the individual or group that the experience is not meaningless but is rather part of a larger system of order. Some successful theodicies are, in fact, nothing but assertions of order. A woman discussing her personal meaning crisis after her husband's premature death said: "I finally came to understand that it didn't matter whether *I* understood why he died when he did, but that God had a reason for it, and that was all that mattered." For this believer, knowing that an order exists behind events was more important than knowing *what* that order is.

Similarly theodicies do not necessarily make the believer happy or even promise future happiness. A person suffering poverty and disease may be satisfied with
the explanation that the situation has resulted from sins committed by the ancestors. Such an interpretation offers little hope for overcoming the poverty or disease,
but it does offer meaning. It answers the question, "Why do I suffer?"

The capability of religion to provide meaning can be illustrated by how a society
handles the especially meaning-threatening situation of dying and death. There is
an inherent problem of meaning in the prospect of one's own or a loved one's death.
Death seems to negate the individual's or group's sense of order. For this reason,
the way in which a society handles the process of dying is revealing of its larger
meaning system. Long before most individuals face death, their religion has been
providing meaning for their various life stages (e.g., by rites of passage into
adulthood or by legitimating the norms and prerogatives of old age). In many
societies, the meaning system somewhat normalizes dying as a further stage of
human development. Some meaning systems affirm an afterlife or a rebirth; others
emphasize that people live on through their offspring or tribe.

In American society, dying and death have become particularly meaning-
threatening. This problem of meaning partly results from the undermining of
traditional theodicies; formerly used explanations have become less satisfying to
many persons. The problem of the meaning of death is especially acute in this
society because its value system assigns comparatively great worth to individual
lives. Numerous social arrangements contribute to the problem. The dying person is typically segregated from one of the foremost meaning-providing social
supports—the family. Furthermore, the specialized roles of those tending the
dying seldom include the provision of meaning. Unlike their counterparts in
traditional medical systems, modern doctors do not consider as part of their role
helping the patient assign meaning to illness or death (Kleinman, 1978). Death
and dying have become generally secularized processes, and the problem of their
meaning has become acute.

Anomie

Sometimes a meaning system is completely unable to absorb a crisis experience. The theodicies applied may not be effective in reintegrating the experience
into the meaning system, or the group supports of the entire meaning system may
be so weakened by the crisis that people are unable to restore a sense of order and
meaning. When an individual or group has lost its fundamental sense of meaning
and order, ongoing social life becomes virtually impossible. Why should one want
to do anything if everything seems senseless? When a meaning system is so
weakened, the moral norms it supports are also undermined. And with no
underlying order to existence, there is no apparent basis for distinguishing between "right" and "wrong" ways of behaving.

It becomes necessary, if social life is to continue, to establish a new basis of
order and a new meaning system. If a group's way of life has been thoroughly
disrupted by military conquest, for example, the group might reorganize itself
around a social movement (e.g., followers of a new prophet) that offers a new
basis of order and meaning for group members. The new meaning system sometimes consists of embracing new meanings (e.g., those of the conquerors), a
rearrangement and reaffirmation of old meanings (e.g., in nativistic movements),

or syncretism—the interweaving of new meanings into the traditional meaning system. Regardless of the source of elements for the new meaning system, its importance lies in its ability to reorganize the basis of order for the group. Social life is given new meaning.

The situation of crisis in the group's meaning and order is described in Durkheim's concept of **anomie** (or "anomy"). The word *anomie* means literally "without order." Durkheim applied this concept to social situations in which there was a deregulation of the public conscience. Anomie means a crisis in the moral order of a social group (Durkheim, 1951:246–257; see also Berger, 1967:22ff). Although anomie has serious consequences for the individual (e.g., it might lead one to suicide), it is primarily a social situation referring to the inability of the social group to provide order and normative regulation for individual members. Religion's capability of providing meaning and order suggests that religion functions as a protection from anomie in two ways: A firm religious basis of order is a buffer against the occurrence of anomie in the first place; and if the group does experience an anomic situation, religion can potently respond to the crisis of moral meanings. Meaning is fundamental to a sense of order—without it, there is chaos. Indeed, Berger suggests that the opposite of "sacred" *is* "chaos." He states, "The sacred cosmos, which transcends and includes man in its ordering of reality, thus provides man's ultimate shield against the terror of anomy" (Berger, 1967:27; see also Geertz, 1966:14).

Mazeway Disintegration

Another way of understanding social life in such crises is by examining the parallels between peoples' reactions to major physical disasters and their responses to cultural crises. Wallace (1956, 1957) calls both of these responses **mazeway disintegration**. The cultural mazeway is the socially constructed and learned patterns and rules for interaction that a given group has developed over many generations as "the way" to achieve their wants. Wallace suggests that people in such crises are initially unable to act because their cultural mazeway has fallen apart. The crisis of mazeway disintegration is resolved by reaffirming their identification with some cultural system—traditional, new, or syncretic. For this reason, religious movements that arise to accomplish this reaffirmation may be considered "revitalization movements"; that is, they enable the social group to come alive again.

Although massive disruptions in a group's way of life (e.g., conquest and famine) are obvious starting points of such crises, less dramatic change is more common and the sense of crisis is less profound. Members of the group may feel only a vague sense of malaise, a discomfort with the way things are going and a general ambiguity about what they as individuals should do. Rapid social change often leaves people unsure as to where they "stand." Norms become open; while the old regulations no longer hold, new ones have not been crystallized. Examples of such ambiguities are found in the whole area of gender role expectations in contemporary American society.

An important reason why rapid social change is so threatening to a group's meaning system is that the very *fact* of change undermines many legitimations of the existing social order. It temporarily humanizes the established rules and patterns of interaction by showing them to be changeable products of human convention. Before such change, the group's ways of doing things may have appeared immutable, but the very fact of change belies this perception. In this context it is possible to understand, for example, the exasperation of a Roman Catholic who, during the period immediately after Vatican II, exclaimed, "How can it be that last year eating meat on Friday was a terrible and grave sin, and this year it is merely an optional and private sacrifice?" Even more threatening are the perceived changes in a social group's fundamental norms and values, such as patterns of family life. Periods of dramatic social change seriously challenge the existing meaning system of a group. Often these periods are marked by the rise of new religious movements that affirm an "improved" meaning system, typically claiming that its own ways are not changeable because they stem from a higher authority than that of the old meaning system.

To summarize, then, crises of meaning may occur on the personal level or for an entire social group. The impact of crises of meaning on groups and individuals highlights the significance of the meaning-providing capabilities of religion. Nevertheless we should not assume an overly intellectualized image of humans. Although a strong case can be made that meaning is a fundamental social requirement (Luckmann, 1967; see also Berger, 1967), we must keep in mind that all people do not necessarily equally desire to find meaning for all aspects of their lives. Similarly some people are more tolerant than others of inconsistencies in their meaning systems. Some people desire more intellectually elaborate systems of meaning; others are satisfied with quite simple views. Yet historical religions and quasi-religions address similar problems of meaning: discrepancies between the ideal and actual practices in the society; personal suffering and death; and group crises such as war, conquest, and natural disasters. By providing meaning in the face of meaning-threatening situations, religion enables the individual or group to cope with the situation. If the meaning-threatening situation can be successfully reintegrated into the group's sense of order, social life can continue.

Community and Religious Belonging

There is a direct relationship between the community of believers and the strength of the meaning system. The unity of the group is expressed and enhanced by its shared meanings. The group's meaning system, in turn, depends upon the group as its social base for its continued existence and importance. The idea of the "church" (i.e., community of believers) is not merely an organizational feature of religions but expresses a fundamental link between the meaning system and the community that holds it.

Religion as the Expression of Social Unity

Durkheim recognized the essentially communal quality of religion and made it definitive (see Chapter 1 of this book for his full definition). The collective nature of religion was central to Durkheim's analysis. He concluded that religious rituals and symbols are, at root, representations of the social group. These *collective representations* are the ways by which the group expresses something important about itself to its own members. Thus by participating in group rituals, individual members renew their link with the group, and they learn and reaffirm shared meanings (Durkheim, 1965:257). We will explore Durkheim's theories of religious belonging further in Chapter 6. It is sufficient for our immediate purposes to note his emphasis upon religion's dual role: It both expresses and contributes to social unity.

Plausibility Structures of Meaning

Berger emphasizes that meaning systems require social "bases" for their continued existence. These social bases are called **plausibility structures**—specific social processes or interactions within a network of persons sharing a meaning system. As the term implies, the meaning system continues to be plausible (i.e., believable) within these social structures. Berger asserts that *all* religious traditions require specific communities of believers for their continuing plausibility (1967:46). A sound plausibility structure allows the meaning system to be held as a common, taken-for-granted entity. Likewise it strengthens the ability of individuals to believe, for the group gives them social support and reinforcement in their world view.

Historically most religious world views were coextensive with the societies that held them. Relatively simple societies exemplify especially well the link between the group's meaning system and networks of fellow believers. If one were born and socialized into a Malay tribe, for example, the religious meanings and rituals of the group would be taken for granted. Simply belonging to the tribe would make one a part of the religion, and the whole tribe would serve as social support for one's belief and practice. Indeed, it would be difficult if not impossible for a member isolated in such a tribe to conceive of any other meaning system.

A society-wide plausibility structure still exists in many relatively complex societies. In many parts of Latin America, religion is pervasive in all aspects of life, and a single, particular world view dominates the society. Most people spend their daily lives solely in the company of people who share their entire world view. Such massive social support for shared religious beliefs and practices makes it relatively easy for believers to take them for granted.

The significance of plausibility structures can also be seen in situations where believers of a world view are separated from the social group that serves as its basis of plausibility. Missionaries typically went out in closely knit bands among the "unbelievers" (i.e., people with a different world view from their own). This arrangement was not merely for mutual physical protection but—more importantly—for mutual protection of their view of reality. A meaning system shared even with only a few significant others is stronger than one held alone and surrounded by persons who do not share that meaning. In this context, we can appreciate how grave a punishment it was for some societies to exile a member. Exiles were cut off both from other members of the society and from the social support for their meaning system.

Subsocietal Plausibility Structures

Pluralistic societies, by contrast, characteristically lack a single, comprehensive world view. Instead, several different meaning systems compete for adherents. Pluralism itself makes the maintenance of a meaning system problematic because it undermines its taken-for-granted quality. In pluralistic situations, the religious group must organize itself to serve as its own plausibility base because the society as a whole does not support its meaning system. Thus in pluralistic societies such as the United States, religious groups often emphasize their communal ties. Three common manifestations of emphatic belonging are sectariansim, tribalism, and localism (all of which characterize many religious and nonreligious groups in this society).

Sectarianism. An orientation by which a group tries to maintain its distinctive world view by emphasizing primary, face-to-face relationships with fellow believers and high levels of commitment and loyalty to the group is **sectarianism**. These close-knit, intense relationships provide a structure within which the group's world view is plausible; whereas outside the group, that world view is disconfirmed. Frequent interaction within this primary group, together with a distancing from nonbelievers' views, helps support members' world views in the face of real or perceived opposition from the "world." The more dramatically the group's distinctive world view differs from those prevalent in the society, the more important becomes huddling together in the sectarian enclave.

Sectarian strategies also include physical or symbolic withdrawal from the "world," limiting outside influences (e.g., television or unapproved books) and restricting members' social contacts. Especially important is the socialization of children; the group protects its children from exposure to competing world views, perhaps by running its own schools. Also important is the selection of spouses. The plausibility of a person's meaning system is more likely to be undermined by interaction with an unbelieving spouse than with a co-worker. Thus a group trying to defend its plausibility often prohibits members from marrying outside the group and arranges social events to encourage marriageable members to meet and marry each other. Groups such as the Amish or Hassidim exemplify extreme sectarian plausibility structures; they are entirely self-contained communities, cut off from the "world." Even large established religious groups, such as Roman Catholics, Lutherans, and Baptists, have used some of these sectarian strategies to defend the plausibility of their world views in face of a society that does not generally support them. This sectarian quality of religion in contemporary pluralistic societies is developed further in Chapter 5.

Tribalism. Another orientation that protects the group's distinctive world view is **tribalism**—which, in the United States and other ethnically pluralistic societies, refers to locating oneself within a specific ethnic community and its perspective. Several observers have noted the close link between religion and ethnicity among American immigrant peoples. Religious groups provided important resources to newly arrived immigrants, especially during the great waves of immigration in the nineteenth and twentieth centuries. They provided informal networks of association through which the immigrant could obtain a job, help with housing, and other mutual assistance. They also provided protection from the dominant society, keeping alive the old ways, educating children in "safe" environments where their backgrounds would not be held against them, and providing mutual protection from the hostility of those who did not accept the immigrants. The historical need for many of these functions is muted or gone, but the ethno-religious community is still a source of mutual aid, friendship, and a sense of belonging for many Americans. For these individuals, the ethno-religious group as a set of relationships—not the fact of ethnicity itself—provides a stable source of belonging.

Herberg analyzed the relationship between religion and ethnicity, specifically asking why Americans tended to identify themselves in terms of one of three religious "communities": Protestant, Catholic, or Jew. He suggested that as the immigrant became assimilated into the dominant American culture, ethnic ties superseded localistic ties that characterized one's self-identity and self-location in the old country. The ethnic church was an important expression of these new ties. According to Herberg, however, ethnic differences are residual and disappearing. As assimilation proceeds even further, religious identity assumes even greater significance—not as actual affiliation with a particular religious group, participation in church activities, or even affirmation of the group's belief system—but rather as a basis of identification and social location. According to Herberg, self-identification in ethnic terms was not altogether satisfactory because it implied incomplete integration into American life. By contrast, religion in America is an acceptable way for people to differentiate themselves and thus becomes a way for people to define and locate themselves in the larger society. For this reason, according to Herberg's interpretation, people will identify themselves with one of the three legitimate religious "communities"—Protestant, Catholic, or Jewish—even though they do not necessarily practice that religion or believe its tenets (Herberg, 1960: 6–64).

Greeley emphasizes that American ethnicity is not merely a vestige of old country ways but is rather a dynamic, special way of negotiating the transition to American culture. Ethnic communities provide a shelter in which immigrants can assimilate at their own pace, unobtrusively. Ethnicity enables them to legitimate their new identities by reference to their traditions (Greeley, 1977). Belonging to the ethnic community thus promotes a smoother transition to a new identity and sense of belonging.

Herberg's prediction of ethnicity's disappearance as a basis of personal identity may have been premature (Greeley, 1971:82). There is some evidence from research on marriage and friendship choices that ethnicity continues to be a significant factor. Nevertheless higher levels of education, urban residence, and longer residence in the United States reduce the significance of ethnic ties (Abramson, 1973:66, 98; Laumann, 1969). Evidence from these studies suggests that religious and ethnic identification are, for some Americans, subtly intertwined.

Localism. A similar but broader network of social ties supporting belief is **localism**, an orientation to the local residential community as a source of identity and involvement. In contrast to persons with cosmopolitan orientations, locals focus on their immediate community and their attachments to family, local social groups, and community associations. The localist orientation is parochial and narrow; the cosmopolitan is more open, identifying with wider communities of national or international scope (Merton, 1957:387–420). Mobility, advanced education, exposure to mass media, and urban life appear to diminish localism.

Recent studies corroborate this interpretation of the relationship between localism and religious plausibility. Localistic factors such as length of residence in a community, belonging to community organizations, having most of one's closest friends residing locally, and having one's network of friends attending one's own religious group contribute to the likelihood that a person will belong to, and participate in, a church or synagogue (see Gallup Poll and Princeton Religious Research Center, 1978:16). Another study, using an index of localism, found that "declining community attachment, *more so than the erosion of traditional belief per se*, is the critical factor in accounting for the declines in church support and participation" (Roof, 1978:136). Persons with local group identification have a structure of social support to maintain the plausibility of their meaning system.

When a religious group holds a world view not supported by the larger society, it must construct its own plausibility structures. Sectarianism, tribalism, and localism are three orientations that serve this purpose. Other processes that illustrate the way in which religious belonging supports a meaning system include socialization, conversion, and commitment, discussed further in Chapter 3.

Extended Application: Millenarianism and Dualism in Contemporary Social Movements

Many of the concepts presented in this chapter are particularly relevant to an understanding of contemporary meaning systems. The last part of this chapter is an extended example that applies some of these concepts to modern social movements. We begin by noticing certain themes common to many contemporary movements: millenarianism and dualism. What do these themes imply about the movements' responses to problems of meaning? More importantly, what does the attraction of such movements imply about people's relationship to the existing social order? This essay is one interpretation of the significance of millenarianism and dualism in contemporary social movements.

These two themes appear regularly in the world views promulgated by many developing religious movements in America. A **dualistic world view** holds that reality consists of two irreducible modes—Good versus Evil. The theme of dualism permeates the belief systems of such diverse groups as the Jesus People, the Unification Church, Catholic Pentecostalism, and Satanism. **Millenarianism** is the expectation of an imminent collapse of the entire social order and its replacement with a perfect new order. The millenarian vision is also a theme in many contemporary religious and quasi-religious movements. The occurrence of movements that emphasize these two elements reveals some of the problems of meaning in contemporary society.[1]

These two elements of belief are not merely quaint characteristics of the movement but are central to their appeal. The appeal of the dualistic interpretation of reality and of millennial expectations results from a need for a new, firmer order in a

[1]Because this essay is presented as an example, it is necessarily somewhat oversimplified. See referenced sources for some of the complexities of interpreting social movements. The essay suggests only that dualistic and millenarian theodicies are effective responses to problems of meaning posed by anomie. That does not mean that these movements are "caused" by anomie. A full explanation of these phenomena would need to show that recruits had experienced anomie. It would also need to analyze the sources of problems of meaning in contemporary society.

time when the old basis of order appears to be collapsing. The elements of dualism and millenarianism represent the assertion of order in the face of felt disorder.

Two Opposing Principles: Good and Evil

A dualistic world view depicts all reality as consisting of two fundamental modes or opposing principles—one Good and the other Evil. This dualistic perspective is especially important in the belief systems of groups growing from Western religious perspectives (e.g., Islam, Judaism, and especially Christianity). A spokesperson of the Catholic Charismatic Renewal stated:

> It is characteristic of the Pentecostal movement that, along with renewed faith in the Holy Spirit, there comes a greater awareness of the evil spirit. . . . experience has taught people in the Pentecostal movement to take very seriously that aspect of the Christian life that has to do with warring against the evil one. . . . it has been a common practice within the movement to exorcise Satan any time there seems to be reason to fear his influence (O'Connor, 1971:79,80).

The idea of warring forces of Good and Evil has been recurrent in Christian ideologies, and contemporary expressions of this idea can be traced to enthusiastic religious movements of the sixteenth and seventeenth centuries. Some form of dualism is used by many Christian groups to explain the nature of humankind, the presence of evil, temptation, sin, suffering, and the need for God's help.

Many emerging religious movements in America particularly emphasize dualistic interpretations of the world (see, for example, Anthony and Robbins, 1978; Bird, 1978, 1979; Fichter, 1975; Richardson et al., 1978; Robbins et al., 1976; Westley, 1978a). Through a new emphasis on mystery, magic, and miracle, believers perceive their world as full of evidence of the action of Good and Evil forces. Believers experience the world as remystified by the presence of God's spirit; it is also remystified by the presence of Satan in numerous forms. Just as God is influential in their world, so too is Satan immediate and active. Believers see the direct influence of God in the beneficial and pleasant events of their lives; at the same time, they see the Evil One as the source of doubts, temptations, dissension, sickness, and other troubles. This remystification of everyday life is in marked contrast to the usual, more secular interpretation of events.

Some dualistic belief systems identify and personify the forces of Evil in movements, issues, or people that threaten the values of the group. Dualism in the early ideology of Black Muslims identified the forces of Evil with the white oppressors (Washington, 1972:128–139). Similarly various fundamentalist Christian groups identify communism with the forces of Evil. One recent variant of this type is the Unification Church of Rev. Sun Myung Moon. This belief system holds that the fundamental struggle is between communism and the "God-fearing world" of which America is the center (Anthony and Robbins, 1978). The cosmic opposition implied in dualism provides a ready explanation for felt opposition to one's own belief system. Numerous religious movements identify their own beliefs and practices as on the side of Good and decry competing religious movements as on the side of Evil. Often, however, Evil is identified with vague general forces that seem to work against the commitments of the religious group. Thus one neo-Pentecostal member stated:

I think Satan does his best. I think it's time we recognized that the power of evil lives in the world and that we as individuals have to cope with the evil that's in the world today. And again that's another thing, another advantage of having a prayer community. It's because we gather together for strength and you sort of get to be invincible in a group. If you try to hit it out on your own, I mean obviously, you just can't with those devils. You just don't stand a ghost of a chance. You know, I know a lot of people don't believe the devil exists, but I really don't think things would be as bad as they are, the evil in us, the evil in man. The evil that's in man is the evil that's an extension of possession of the devil. The devil is using that person just like God can use us. . . . I do believe that a lot of evil, a lot of sadness and sickness in this world is brought out by Satan. I think it's in his scheme of things to turn us against God.

The persistence and strength of belief in dualism suggest that it is not merely one characteristic of these movements but may indeed be central to their appeal.

Dualism as a Response to Anomie. Dualistic interpretations are useful to both the group and the individual, especially as a response to anomie, which results in a sense of normlessness and powerlessness. Being out of touch with the source of moral power means being powerless in the face of the nameless terrors of the disordered universe. Only a firm reordering can provide an effective protection against such terror (Berger, 1967:27). A new order must be established and maintained continually against the occurrence of further order-threatening phenomena. Even a firmly established new order is threatened by occurrences such as suffering and death, which perpetually raise the problems of "meaning" and "order."

A dualistic world view provides both a framework for the *construction* of a new order and legitimation for its *maintenance*. Religious dualism is particularly effective in this reordering, since it holds that both the sources of all problems and the "real" solutions to these problems derive from a transcendent realm (see Lofland, 1966:36). Dualism enables believers to name the sources of their anxieties, fears, and problems. This identification is in itself an important source of believers' sense of order and control. Identifying certain difficulties as caused by Evil forces also implies a clear-cut course of action. Believers locate their personal courses of action within a cosmic struggle, a continual battle between the forces of Good and the forces of Evil. This identification provides explanations of all events—good or bad—that occur in their lives, and it gives meaning to everyday existence. Even trivial aspects of daily life become part of the order implied in the dualistic world view.

This order-giving potential of dualism is partly responsible for believers' sense of spiritual opposition. The believer perceives frequent, regular evidence of the immediacy and influence of both good and evil spirits. This evidence, it should be emphasized, is usually in the form of actual events in everyday life. A dualistic world view contains a built-in tendency to ascribe all good events to God and all bad ones to the devil. The tidiness and order of the dualistic interpretation of the world are part of the basic appeal of such movements. Dualistic figures of ultimate Good and Evil simplify the world to people who are overwhelmed by the ambiguity and complexity of modern life.

In facing the perceived opposition, the group gains cohesion and strength.

This sense of opposition is also a useful legitimation for maintaining the new order because it enables believers to see significance in subsequent events, even those that would otherwise threaten their new beliefs. The dualistic world view heightens the sense that the opposition is a conspiracy against believers and their group (cf. Barkun, 1974; Beckford, 1975b; and Westin, 1964). In one group a leader witnessed:

> We became aware at the [leaders'] meeting of how Satan is really alive today. He is trying to get at the leaders of the movement, trying to disintegrate our unity. He's really powerful, and he's working hard to hurt our movement. One of the ways he's working is trying to disunite the leaders' families. He is really alive today. Bind him! Bind him in Jesus' precious blood.

There are two sides to the believer's sense of order. On the "negative" side is a sense of fearsome powers bent on a conspiratorial attack on believers and their values. On the "positive" side, the same sense of order provides the believer with a feeling of harmony and symmetry. Both positive and negative aspects involve the forming of patterns and imposing of a sense of order (Weil, 1973:178–179). The believer's world view is founded on the expectation that everything *is* ordered; therefore order and patterns in the world are subsequently perceived. The "positive" side of this spiritual order can be seen in the believer's constant discovery of "holy coincidence," "providence," and other evidences of the pattern of God's work in everyday life. The dualistic world view gives form and a "cast of characters" to the patterns that believers perceive in the world around them.

Dualism as Theodicy. Dualism also offers the believer an explanatory system for reinterpreting order-threatening events. As such, it functions as a theodicy. The theodicy provides meaning but not necessarily happiness, informing the believer, "You may be miserable, but be comforted that there is, at least, meaning to your suffering."

Dualism is a particularly effective form of theodicy because it is a closed system of legitimation; that is, built into the legitimating system itself is an "explanation" of every argument against the system. Thus the same theodicy can explain both good and bad events, opposition and confirmation. It also provides a basis for self-justification and for the moral condemnation of others (cf. Rokeach, 1960:69).

Religious groups often use the dualistic theodicy to explain the doubts and uncertainties experienced by new believers: "Your doubts and anxieties are because the devil is trying to confuse and tempt you back to your old way of life." This theodicy gives meaning to the natural doubts and sense of uncertainty encountered by the new believer in the resocialization process. Armed with a concrete identification of the source of these difficulties, the new believer has a greater sense of power in facing such problems of belief. The theodicy that fears and doubts are planted by Satan is a welcome explanation.

The foremost function of dualism is the reshaping of believers' interpretations of everyday events. Believers reinterpret even their own roles. Dualism bestows significance on events that formerly seemed meaningless. Human failure, suffering, social problems, personal difficulties, and death are all given meaning.

Events that formerly appeared to be random, haphazard, and disorderly come to be perceived as part of a clear pattern. One's sense of ambiguity and insecurity is resolved by perceiving one's personal role as part of "something big"—a great cosmic struggle in which one gains power and purpose by siding with the good forces. By contrast, in the case of Satanism, members side with the evil forces, figuring them to be more powerful; nevertheless the same sense of power is gained by Satanists' dualistic stance (see Moody, 1974).

Dualism enables the group to create order out of chaos. The source of threat is not only the external chaos of the anomic social world; intragroup problems constitute a threat, too. Internal conflict is especially disruptive because it undermines those interpersonal relationships that support the believers' world view. Problems of "disorder" are inherent in the establishment of any new group, and there is much ambiguity during the developing stages of a movement. Also, if members perceive their new belief system to be a departure from their previous one, the fact of change may cause some uncertainty. Emphasizing the group's role in a cosmic dualistic confrontation enables the group to resolve its problems of uncertainty and ambiguity (Slater, 1966). Dualistic beliefs affirm the boundaries between the group and "the world," and they provide mechanisms (e.g., exorcism, confession, and healing) for dealing with internal conflict.

The dualistic theodicy enhances the individual believer's sense of security. Recruits to these movements often express a strong desire to know for sure where they "stand" before God. This desire for certainty is fulfilled by a secure sense of order, which affirms a clear duality between the forces of Good and Evil and shows a distinct path for the believer who would side with Good. This simplified course of action informs the member that, having sided with the Good, one is safe and secure.

The Imminence of the Millennium

A dualistic theodicy is particularly forceful if combined with a millenarian theodicy. **Millenarianism**, the expectation of an imminent disintegration of the entire social order and its replacement with a perfect new order, is a recurring theme in religious movements. The millenarian theodicy informs the believer that the present chaotic social order, with its misery and deprivations, is transient and that in the coming new order the believer will have a better life and no longer experience the turmoil and malaise of the present. Millenarianism offers both an explanation of the wrongness of the present social order and a hope for future change; as such, it is a potent source of change-oriented behavior.

The millennial dream that the perfect new order is imminent is also a response to anomie. When the old order is seen as nearly defunct, the new order must be near (see Barkun, 1974; Vlachos, 1975). A member of a "Jesus movement" group said, "America is on the road to Hell! The conditions described in Revelation and in Acts paint a pretty clear picture of America today" (quoted in Peterson and Mauss, 1973:268). Similarly, Reverend Moon warned:

> But today America is retreating. It's not just an accident that great tragedy is constantly striking America and the world, such as the assassination of President Kennedy and the sudden death of Secretary-General Hammarskjöld of the

United Nations, both in the same decade. The spirit of America has declined since then. Unless this nation, unless the leadership of the nation lives up to the mission ordained by God, many troubles will plague you. God is beginning to leave America. This is God's warning (quoted in Anthony and Robbins, 1978:84).

People who view this society as badly out of order and consider the established religions impotent to do anything about the "problems" are likely to hope for dramatic change. The ultimate religious "solution" is the end of the world. The coming of the millennium will not only destroy the old problematic order but will also vindicate the faith of the believers.

Religious Millenarianism. The idea of an apocalypse—a dramatic end of the world—is not a new religious theme. Many religious groups have anticipated the imminent end of the social order they define as ungodly. Some have expected a total physical cataclysm in which the world would end; others have awaited a god-sent revolutionary end in which the existing social order would cease and be replaced by a perfect new order. This latter hope was frequently combined with the anticipation of a messiah who would bring about the new order. Such themes are particularly prominent in Western religions, especially Christianity (see Barkun, 1974; Cohn, 1970; Festinger et al., 1956; Talmon, 1966; and Wilson, 1970).

Millenarian movements were widespread in America in the nineteenth century, sometimes combined with a messianic vision of a special destiny for the American people. The Mormons, Millerites (and their offshoot, Seventh Day Adventists), Christadelphians, and Jehovah's Witnesses are examples of groups in which the millenarian expectation was or is central (see Wilson, 1970). Nativistic religious movements, which envisioned the millennium as the dramatic restoration of a traditional "native" way of life, arose in the nineteenth century among several American Indian tribes, whose social and economic plight was desperate. The Ghost Dance,[2] Handsome Lake, Indian Shakers, and the peyote cult exemplify these movements by which native Americans responded to the profound disruption of their traditional way of life wrought by white settlers, government policy, and the army (see Aberle, 1966; Barnett, 1957; Mooney, 1965; and Myerhoff, 1974). A black syncretic movement, the Lost Found Nation of Islam (i.e., Black Muslims) appealed to both the millennial possibilities in Islam and American blacks' familiarity with Christian millenarian themes. Its early teaching was that 1914 ended the 6,000 years of the "white devils'" rule, after which the lost Nation of Islam would finally realize its destiny (Lincoln, 1973; later, however, the movement de-emphasized this prophesy).

Belief in the imminence of the millennium is widespread among new religious movements as well as in traditional sects and some of the more fundamentalist denominations. A study of Catholic Pentecostals found that 71 percent believed that the Second Coming of Christ is near (Fichter, 1975:44). Similarly the Jesus movement among youth has a strong millenarian theme, as have some strains of its less countercultural evangelical successor (Ellwood, 1973). A syncretic move-

---

[2]The Ghost Dance was a highly traditionalistic movement that foresaw the destruction of the white man. Although the movement itself was pacifist, its appeal and potential for uniting diverse tribes frightened the frontier army, culminating in the Battle of Wounded Knee, in which over 200 Indian men, women, and children were killed.

ment, the Unification Church, has explicit millenarian expectations, identifying Rev. Moon as the Lord of the Second Advent (see Anthony and Robbins, 1978; Kim, 1977). An Eastern inspired movement, the Divine Light Mission of Guru Maharaj Ji celebrated "Millennium '73," at which devotees expected extraordinary apocalyptic events. Peculiarly modern forms of millenarianism include groups that base their millennial expectations on UFOs and extraterrestrial communications (see Balch and Taylor, 1976, 1977; Festinger et al., 1956).

Social and Political Millenarianism. Not only specifically religious movements, but also many other social and political movements, have dominant millenarian themes. Several "isms" of the nineteenth and twentieth centuries project a secular millennium. Thus many forms of nationalism are based upon a vision of a people realizing their destiny in the destruction of the old social order. The millenarian and messianic appeal of the Russian Revolution is another example (Murvar, 1971). Indeed, a persuasive case can be made that the major revolutions of this century (Nazism, Soviet and Chinese communism) were millenarian movements. The potential for modern movements to create and sustain a sense of urgency and imminent disaster in a larger mass population can be partially attributed to the impact of mass media (see Barkun, 1974; Cohn, 1970). Even without reference to a supernatural realm, these belief systems are millenarian responses to problems of order and meaning.

Dualism and Millenarianism in Social Movements

Expectation of the millennium is not merely an incidental item of belief; rather it is a significant part of the group's response to the problem of anomie. If people have experienced anomie, the solution *par excellence* is not only to affirm a new order for the present but also to believe in a future reordering that will reintegrate all problematic aspects of the present situation into an overall, meaningful perfect order.

The imminence of this dramatic reordering creates a sense of urgency and makes the mundane business of daily life "in the world" seem trivial. Millennial expectations, therefore, enhance members' commitment to the group through which they will help usher in the new order. The idea that the end of this world is near makes it much easier for members to give up possessions, jobs, education, and other things that have value only in the nearly defunct world. Like the dualistic theodicy, millenarianism encourages pattern forming. Believers interpret seemingly random events as evidence for the imminence of the millennium. For example, a leaflet distributed before the Divine Light Mission's "Millennium '73" event stated:

WHY NOW?
War has erupted in the Mideast.
. . . . *why now?*
UFOs in increasing numbers are being sighted especially in southern states.
. . . . *why now?*
The Kohoutek Comet is blazing across our solar system and will be clearly visible in early November.
. . . . *why now?*

Astrologers predict a rare Cardinal Cross in the sky November 8–10.
. . . . *why now?*
MILLENNIUM '73 announces 1,000 years of peace at the Houston Astrodome,
November 8–10.[3]

The millenarian vision is likewise a theodicy for the discrepancies within the present order. Even after conversion, members are likely to have difficulties— friends and relatives "not understanding," prayers seemingly not answered, doubts and uncertainties, and the society still not on the "right track." The belief in the coming of the millennium relativizes the problems and opposition of the present by the knowledge that all of these will be overcome in a glorious future. Members can feel that although "things" are really bad now and will probably get worse, they are not personally threatened by the disorder and ambiguity since they know that they are allied in the present with the source of perfect order and will have a privileged position in the unknown glorious future.

Although infinite possible meanings could be attached to any given event, the themes of millenarianism and dualism illustrate how meaning systems interpret events and locate them in some larger framework. We have seen how individuals and groups use their belief systems to bestow meaning on the social world; and how elements of belief such as imminence of the millennium, messianic expectations, and dualism are responses to a social situation that appears chaotic, ambiguous, or hopeless. Individuals who hold dualistic or millenarian world views relate to their social world accordingly. Their world view organizes their experiences and influences their associations and their very identities.

Summary

This chapter has outlined some of the ways in which the meaning-providing and belonging components of religion are linked. Religion is both a basis of association and an expression of shared meanings, the importance of which depends largely upon the social support of a community of believers.

Religious meaning systems are ways of interpreting events and experiences. They assign meaning to a group's existence and to an individual's identity. The meaning system of a group interprets its social order, serving as a legitimation of social arrangements. Meaning systems also locate human lives and events in terms of a larger framework, identifying the individual with an overarching order. The significance of meaning in individual and social life is illustrated by situations in which meaning is threatened. Theodicies are religious explanations that offer meaning for meaning-threatening experiences such as suffering and death. Some crises of meaning profoundly disrupt the social order. The concepts of anomie and mazeway failure describe the impact of such crises on the individual and group.

Analysis of the themes of millenarianism and dualism in contemporary social movements illustrates how groups bestow meaning on the social situation. These two themes can be interpreted as responses to problems of meaning and order.

[3]Interestingly, Christian Pentecostal groups in which I was a participant-observer during this same period also testified about the war in the Mideast, UFOs, and the comet as evidence of their millennial expectations.

They represent an effort to posit a new order in response to the ambiguity and confusion of meanings produced by social change. Millenarianism and dualism are theodicies that locate believers' experiences in terms of a larger framework of order and meaning.

Religious belonging is a natural outcome of shared meaning systems. At the same time, a community of believers (however small) is necessary for maintaining the plausibility of a meaning system. Where a particular world view has monolithic status in a society, these plausibility structures pervade the entire society. In pluralistic societies, by contrast, world views are in competition. Each group of believers must structure itself to maintain the plausibility of its distinctive meaning system. Three such strategies characterize many religious groups in the United States: sectarianism, tribalism, and localism—all forms of protective enclaves. The interrelationship of the meaning-providing and belonging aspects of religion are well illustrated in the social processes of religious socialization, conversion, and commitment, to be explored in Chapter 3.

Recommended Readings

Nonfiction

Peter L. Berger. *The Sacred Canopy: Elements of a Sociological Theory of Religion.* Garden City, N.Y.: Doubleday, 1967. Berger's interpretation of the contemporary religious situation is based upon a carefully developed theory of identity.

Thomas Luckmann. *The Invisible Religion: The Problem of Religion in Modern Society.* New York: Macmillan, 1967. Luckmann develops a theory of modern religion, interpreting nonofficial religion, privatization, and individual religious forms.

Wade Clark Roof. *Community and Commitment: Religious Plausibility in a Liberal Protestant Church.* New York: Elsevier, 1978. This empirical study uses sophisticated methodological tools to apply some of Berger's concepts in an analysis of the bases of community and commitment among Episcopalians.

Max Weber. *The Sociology of Religion.* Trans. E. Fischoff. Boston: Beacon, 1963. This book contains Weber's mature thinking on several important aspects of religion, including theodicy, the idea of salvation, asceticism and mysticism, the role of the prophet, and the religion of nonprivileged classes.

Fiction

Issues of religious meaning and belonging are often well illustrated in fiction. The following sources are useful:

Walter M. Miller, Jr. *A Canticle for Leibowitz.* New York: Harold Matson, 1959. Describes the role of religion in regenerating civilization following nuclear war, how the Albertian Order of Leibowitz was founded, and how it struggled against the Dark Ages that followed the nuclear holocaust. The few artifacts upon which the new knowledge was built included sacred texts written by the Blessed Leibowitz, such as the following fragment: "Pound pastrami, can kraut, six bagels. . . ."

Kurt Vonnegut, Jr. *Cat's Cradle.* Baltimore: Penguin, 1963. A science fiction account of the end of the world and the ultimate religious movement, Bokonism. Serious humor about the construction of sacred texts, symbols, and meaning.

Elie Wiesel. *Night.* New York: Pyramid, 1960. A moving personal journal of the author's experience as a child in a Nazi concentration camp. The issue of meaning is implicit and powerful.

CHAPTER THREE

The Individual's Religion

Sociology of religion emphasizes religious groups and social expressions of religion. The individual members of religious groups are, however, social *actors*—that is, persons with motives and meanings of their own. While the individual actor's attitudes, conceptions, and behavior may be strongly influenced by social groups, there is no neat or deterministic correlation between what the group believes and what the individual member personally holds central. In order to understand religious behavior, we must know how religion shapes and is expressed by the individual actor. Chapter 2 suggested some of these ways. Religion provides meaning for the individual's life, enabling one to interpret, evaluate, and project experiences in everyday life. Also, social groups are essential in shaping, maintaining, or changing the individual's world view.

This chapter examines the processes by which the individual adopts and becomes committed to a religious world view and community. First, following a life cycle model, we will explore the social forces shaping and maintaining the individual's world view. Second, we will analyze the process of conversion by which the individual dramatically changes that world view. Finally we will examine the process of commitment, by which old and new believers alike commit themselves to the group of fellow believers. These social processes illustrate the link between the meaning-providing and communal features of religion described in Chapter 2. The individual's meaning system is socially acquired, socially maintained, or socially changed.

Shaping the Individual's Religion

The individual's religion is not a static entity. It develops and changes over the course of one's life. A person is not born with a full-blown set of religious beliefs and practices; religion is developed and nurtured (or ignored) in the socialization of the child. Although one may have reached an identifiable religious perspective or commitment by young adulthood, it would be a mistake to consider this the end of one's religious development. The individual's religion continues to develop and change, perhaps less dramatically, throughout the rest of life. Indeed the very meaning of "being religious" changes in different periods of life, and the place of religion in the individual's life also changes. In keeping with this dynamic perspective on religious development, this section follows the life cycle of the individual believer. It focuses (as does religious practice itself) upon certain critical periods: early childhood, adolescence, marriage and procreation, and old age and dying. One intermediate period, for which there are no special religious rituals or events, is included: middle age.

One of the difficulties in describing an adequately complex picture of religious development in modern societies is that much of the research in this area has focused upon narrowly defined church-oriented religion. There are several studies, for example, about the effect of religious affiliation upon fertility rates but little information about how religion shapes the individual's idea of parenting. Likewise we have considerable data about the correlation between religious affiliation and attitudes toward premarital sexual relations; but we know relatively little about what religious meanings people attach to all aspects of human sexuality. The following description, then, suggests a line of reasoning that future studies might pursue in exploring the relationship between religion and family, community, identity, life cycle, and human development.

Childhood, Family, and Community

Early childhood is a critical period in the development of the individual's religion. The child begins to learn what it means to be "one of us" (our society, our ethnic group, our religion, our family, our tribe, and so on). Specifically in socialization, the individual internalizes the social group's moral norms and basic values. Socialization also accounts for the development of the individual's attitudes and values, such as attitudes about authority or the relative value of acquiring material possessions. These attitudes and values are closely linked with religious belief, and they vary according to the type of religiosity that individuals acquire through socialization into their group.

In relatively simple societies, there is no distinction between socialization into the larger group and religious socialization. Becoming religious—however defined in that society—is simply part of gradually becoming an adult, responsible member of society. Religious roles in simple societies are not differentiated from other roles such as mother, healer, or chieftain. Similarly the child's religious roles simply involve the child's participation in ongoing social activities. The child might assist the father in his work and observe the father praying over his tools. Or a child might learn, in helping the grandmother, that one should bless the hearth and fire each morning upon rekindling the fire. He or she might learn the central myths of the tribe from sitting beside a storyteller after a meal. The pervasiveness of religion in simple societies enables the religious socialization of children to occur informally and continuously.

The emphasis upon intellectual learning and formal religious knowledge, which characterizes religious socialization in many complex societies, is atypical. The idea of going to Sunday School to learn specialized religious knowledge is, for example, foreign to most religions because their emphasis is upon learning by doing. What the child needs to know can be best learned by accompanying adults and imitating them. By contrast, Western religions have emphasized the importance of formal religious knowledge. Their relatively complex belief systems are presented to the child as a body of knowledge to be mastered. Sunday Schools, Vacation Bible Schools, catechism classes, parochial schools, Confraternity of Christian Doctrine (after-school classes), yeshivot (intensive programs of Jewish religious education), and Hebrew schools (usually weekend classes in religion) are outcomes of this interest. The society's differentiation of religious knowledge from other relevant formal knowledge complicates the child's acquisition of religious knowledge.

Learning the content of the meaning system of one's group is, however, not sufficient. Children need to internalize this meaning system, to make it their own. A computer could teach a child an entire catechism, but that knowledge of itself would probably have very little significance in the child's life. Internalization of the group's meaning system occurs through interaction of the child with specific other members of the group who mediate the group's way of thinking and doing to the child. In early socialization, the child's family is the foremost influence.

Meaning, Belonging, and Identity. The significance of specific human others in conveying the group's meaning system to the child emphasizes the connection between the meaning-providing and belonging aspects of religion, as described in Chapter 2. The child does not (indeed cannot) internalize the group's meaning system without having a sense of belonging to the group in which that meaning system is grounded. Typically, in societies with relatively homogeneous meaning systems, belonging to the group means coming to take its world view for granted.

In societies with competing world views, socialization into one's own group includes some awareness of the existence and differences of other groups around one's own. The child's identity includes an important sense of belonging to a specific religion, ethnic group, or nation as well as a feeling of contrast with others not of that religion, ethnic group, or nation. More importantly, individual identity includes a set of symbols by which the person can socially locate and focus feelings toward the self (i.e., "I like myself," "I am a worthless person") and assert personal identity to the self and others (Klapp, 1969:viii).

The individual's identity and social location are closely intertwined. Often the question "Who am I?" is answered in terms of "This is where I belong." Thus a woman might describe herself as "a mother, a wife, a Catholic, a Polish-American, a member of the town volunteer ambulance squad, in the church choir, and vice-president of the P.T.A." These roles represent not merely formal memberships but—more importantly—social locations of her identity. Religion pervades all such social roles in relatively undifferentiated societies. In modern, highly differentiated societies, however, religion is only one significant source of the individual's sense of belonging; it is also intertwined with most other important sources of belonging: family, ethnic community, friendship groups, and nationality.

The Family. The first, perhaps most enduring source of the individual's sense of belonging is the family. In the child's socialization, the family is something of a "boundary structure," connecting the borderline between the foundations of personality and the child's beginning participation in society (Parsons, 1969:424). The very young child is not *in* society but is a part of the family, only indirectly participating in society. Later full participation in society is organized according to the values, motivations, and attitudes incorporated during socialization into the individual's personality.

Rituals and symbols allocate identity even in early childhood. One of the most significant and widespread of these is the naming of the child. The choice of given names, the affirmation of kinship networks (e.g., naming the child after a grandparent), and the bestowing of the family name (or refusal to bestow it) are highly symbolic acts. Many groups have special ritual occasions for giving a new family member this initial identity. Other occasions of childhood (e.g., birthday celebrations) also affirm the child's identity. The status of the child is relatively clear in most societies; thus major rituals and symbols of identity are often used to make important transitions, such as the change from childhood to adulthood, in identity.

Most Americans believe they should provide religious training for their children (Marty et al., 1968:208). Children's religious training is a major consideration in adults' decisions to reestablish their church attendance (Gallup Poll and Princeton Religion Research Center, 1978:41) and in choosing a church to attend (Berger and Nash, 1962). A substantial drop has occurred in the proportion of children receiving specifically religious training. In 1952, only 6 percent of adult Americans had received no religious training as a child; this figure had risen to 9 percent in 1965 and to 17 percent in 1978 (figures cited in Gallup Poll and Princeton Religion Research Center, 1978).

The family is more than an agent of religious socialization. It is often, indeed, a primary religious group, a fundamental unit of the institution of religion. The trite adage "the family that prays together stays together" is probably reversed in its reasoning. It is entirely likely that any cohesive family expresses, rather than originates, its unity in rituals and symbols that, in most cultures, are also fundamentally religious. At the same time, religion has historically legitimated the family, established rituals to celebrate family unity, and provided norms and social controls to protect the institution of the family. The scope of the family unit in modern society is greatly narrowed from the extended family and large kinship networks of earlier periods. As a result, the primary agents of socialization in the family are fewer, usually only the parents and older brothers and sisters.

The Community. Another major source of identity is based on the individual's sense of belonging to a distinctive group—tribe, nation, ethnic group. America's history of immigration makes ethnicity an important factor in many people's experience. The degree of affiliation with an ethno-religious group varies considerably. Ethnicity may be an important basis for a person's choices of neighborhood, friends, job, marriage partner, leisure time activities, and organizational memberships. For another person, ethnicity may be irrelevant to such choices.

The process by which the child is socialized into the family and ethno-religious group is gradual. It begins with the child's simple experiencing of group membership as a taken-for-granted part of life. Later the child may learn terms for identification with the group (i.e., "I'm a Catholic," "My people are Korean"). This simple identification proceeds from a confused usage of these terms to a clearer conceptualization of their meaning and of belonging to one or another group. One study found that young children (ages 5 to 7) had a vague impression of their religious affiliation as a kind of family name. One six-year-old responded that it was impossible to be a Protestant and an American at the same time because "you can't have two names," unless perhaps you moved. Somewhat older children (ages 7 to 9) understood religious belonging in terms of wearing particular symbols or of characteristic behaviors (e.g., wearing religious medals or having a Christmas tree). Only much later, usually in adolescence, did children have conceptions of religious belonging that included nonobservable qualities such as faith or belief. Also in later stages of development, some children explained their own identification in terms of contrast to other religious groups (Elkind, 1964; see also Strommen, 1971).

Such studies unfortunately focus upon too narrow a definition of religious identity and belonging. Although the individual's gradual self-identification in terms of official religious affiliation is one component of religious identity, we need to know more about the development of other aspects, especially commitment and loyalty. The relationship between identity and values, attitudes, and behavior also needs further exploration without narrow restriction to church-oriented religion. The communities of family, neighborhood, friendship, and ethno-religious group provide an initial sense of belonging and a foundation for identity; subsequent communities provide a base of support for maintaining that identity or for changing it (as our later discussion of conversion will show). They are also the social base for the continued plausibility of the group's entire meaning system (Berger, 1967:45–47). Thus the meaning-providing and belonging aspects of religion are directly connected.

Social changes and developments such as pluralism (i.e., the coexistence of competing world views) seem to have undermined some of the cohesiveness of these communities (as Chapter 8 will further describe). As children emerge from the taken-for-granted small communities of family and neighbors, they will probably encounter a bewildering variety of other groups with other belief systems and ways of life. Some individuals remain immersed in the initial network that supported the plausibility of early beliefs and identity; other individuals detach themselves from these bonds and seek elsewhere a social base for their beliefs and sense of who they are. The very existence of this element of choice in identity and belief system characterizes only certain kinds of society. The possibility of detaching oneself from the taken-for-granted beliefs and social groups into which one has been socialized provides greater freedom—and simultaneously makes both belief and identity problematic (Berger, 1967:137, 151; see also Klapp, 1969).

Problems of Family and Community in Contemporary Society. Many processes in contemporary society have seriously weakened the ability of family, community, and religion to offer the individual a stable source of belonging and identity. Neighborhood communities are decreasingly characterized by face-to-face intimacy and personal, affective bonds. Furthermore, family, neighborhood, and religion alike have been undermined by **privatization**—the process by which certain spheres of life become removed from effective roles in the public sphere (especially in the arena of economic production and power). Chapter 8 will examine the impact of privatization upon religion in greater detail, but it is important here to note the link between privatization of the family and religion.

The power of religion to legitimate other institutions such as the family has been undermined. There is little support for the family from public institutions. What support exists is largely due to the family's significance as an economic unit of consumption (witness the sales appeal of television shows such as "The Waltons" and "Little House on the Prairie") and to the family's symbolic importance (e.g., in the rhetoric of politicians). These processes, together with the pluralism of society, have weakened the norms governing family interaction. At the same time, however, greater demands are made on the family. The weaknesses of the neighborhood and community in providing support for members' identities result in greater pressure upon the family to be a complete repository of identity (Brittan, 1977:58, 59).

As the individual's control over life in the public sphere diminishes—and as the institutions of the public sphere become less and less concerned with providing meaning for their participants—the individual seeks more fulfillment, security, control, and meaning in the private sphere. The family and other institutions of the private sphere are expected to provide a haven from the public sphere and to compensate for what their members are deprived of in the public sphere (Berger, 1967; Luckmann, 1967:106–114). Privatization thrusts the search for personal identity out of the public sphere. The nature of work and division of labor in modern societies makes it difficult for people to derive their primary sense of identity from their work role. Yet the family cannot sustain the burden of providing all personal identity for its members. One critic of contemporary modes of familism states, "This new emphasis on one's personal feelings and inner needs, one's 'head' or 'life-style', to use contemporary formulations, gives a continued meaning to family life and at the same time threatens to blow it apart" (Zaretsky, 1976:34).

The local community (as a social unit, not just a political or geographical one) has also been undermined. Religion has traditionally been inextricably intertwined with community; the boundaries of one were frequently coextensive with the boundaries of the other. Social and geographical mobility, together with the general acculturation of waves of immigrants, have changed the patterns of community in American society. Local communities are increasingly voluntaristic, segmented, and irrelevant to institutions of the public sphere. The voluntary nature of community has the advantage of freeing individuals to choose their community of identification (Cox, 1965), but it also reduces their power relative to institutions of the public sphere and their ability to provide stable sources of identity for members. The process of privatization is not inexorable, but its impact on family and community is already evident.

Alternative Modes of Family and Community. One historical alternative to the dominant mode of family and community has been the ethno-religious group that withdraws from the society in order to preserve its distinctiveness. Examples of this kind of community include the Jewish Hassidim, the Amish, Doukhobors, and Hutterites. The Hassidim are particularly interesting because their withdrawal is not to a rural refuge; instead, they have organized their life within urban areas to sustain their religious identity.

The Hassidim are an ultraorthodox group of Jews, mostly first- and second-generation immigrants who fled persecution in central and eastern Europe (see Mintz, 1977; Poll, 1969; Shaffir, 1974). There are relatively few American converts to Hassidism, although the largest branch (Lubavitcher) proselytes among less Orthodox Jews. An estimated 100,000 Hassidim live in the United States, and large Hassidic communities also exist in Canada. The Hassidic community is carefully organized to enable members to follow the 613 rules regulating everyday life for Orthodox Jews. Members must live close enough to the synagogue to be able to walk there for services on the Sabbath. Food that passes the highest levels of kosher regulations must be available. Outside the home, men and women are segregated at all times, partly because of religious rules designed to protect men from defilement by contact with a menstruating woman. Thus the men of the community arrange their work so that they have no interaction with women (e.g., by working in the neighborhood or in an all-male trade). The men further arrange their work time to be free for frequent daytime religious services.

The Hassidic community has its own system of law and its own shops, trades, and schools. The rebbe (i.e., chief rabbi) is the final authority in both spiritual and secular matters. Indeed, there is no distinction between spiritual and secular issues; religion pervades all spheres of life. The socialization of children into the group's approved way of life is relatively unproblematic because of the group's success in limiting outside influences. Children attend religious schools, are heavily occupied with their studies and (in adolescence) with their own religious duties, and are seldom exposed to outside media such as television or movies. The community enclave makes the Hassidic way of life a taken-for-granted reality to the child. Personal identity and a sense of belonging are similarly unproblematic. Roles and norms for appropriate behavior are fixed, with roles available to males varying considerably from those for females. Boys clearly learn their roles as men, and girls learn clear-cut expectations of women; both are rewarded by the close-knit community for meeting these role expectations.

A related kind of local community, the **intentional community**, is one in which members choose to live together communally. This arrangement turns the voluntary nature of its commitment into a virtue. Religious communalism has a long tradition in Western society; monastic communalism dates back to the sixth century A.D. A wide variety of groups dissatisfied with the values and structures of contemporary society have adopted a communitarian form of organization. Intentional communities are potential alternatives to the modes of both family and community life of the larger society. The intentional community allows the group to alter all aspects of social interaction—work, leisure, marriage, family, decision making, education, and so on. Thus a group can integrate the spheres of work and religion for its members because, in the separate community, these spheres need not be segregated as they are for most members of society. The intentional community also provides a potentially stronger base of personal identity and a stronger sense of belonging than the privatized family and community can. Communitarian groups often resemble traditional communities with their close-knit, affective interpersonal relationships; they differ, however, in being essentially voluntary. Members cannot take their belonging for granted, although certain practices of the group may make it difficult for the member to consider leaving. The group's continual point of reference is the dominant society from which its way of life departs.

The recent commune movement in America illustrates some of these themes. Communes such as Twin Oaks, The Farm, Ananda, Brotherhood of the Spirit, and the Lama Foundation organized themselves as alternatives to the dominant mode of personal, family, and community life. Other intentional communities were outgrowths of specifically religious movements; these include the Jesus People, Hare Krishnas (Krsna Consciousness), Unification Church, Catholic Pentecostalism (later called Catholic Charismatic Renewal), and the Bruderhof (Society of Brothers). Most Catholic Pentecostal prayer groups, for example, consist of persons who live in typical middle-class neighborhoods and maintain ordinary middle-class family styles. Their prayer group attempts to provide additional sources of community support, bolstering families and individual members in their distinctive beliefs and practices. This movement has also spawned a number of "covenant communities"—intensive groups whose living arrangements, finances, childcare, and other family functions are communally shared. Such communities enable members to have a much stronger base of social support for their way of life than would be otherwise possible.

Contemporary religious communalism can be interpreted both as a celebration of, and protest against, privatization of religion, family, and community. On the one hand, communitarian groups attempt to restructure social organization to allow religion, family, and community to influence other spheres of their lives such as work, education, decision making, and so on. Their protest is against the fragmentation of social life in society. At the same time, however, they are a celebration of privatization because they have removed themselves from society, presenting little challenge to the institutions of the public sphere. Privatization robs communitarian groups of their impact. Establishing a commune, no matter how dissident, is a somewhat expanded way of "doing your own thing" in the private sphere of family, religion, and community.

Adolescence

While childhood is a period of initial socialization into a group's way of life and meaning system, the transition to adulthood is a critical transformation in most cultures. Childhood is important in establishing identity and group belonging in a general way, but the transition to adulthood means passage to a new identity involving responsibility, knowledge, ritual and symbolic roles, and acceptance into adult circles. The dramatic quality of this transition is ritually expressed in many cultures by **rites of passage** for adolescents.

Rites of passage are rituals that accompany a change of place, state, social position, and age. One interpretation suggests that rites of passage enable societies to effect an orderly, meaningful transition for individuals and groups who move from one socially recognized stable state (e.g., childhood) into another (e.g., adulthood). The stable statuses have clearly defined rights, obligations, and roles. The transition between them, however, is dangerous because rights, obligations, and roles are temporarily ambiguous and disordered. Both the social group and the individual member are thus served by these rituals that express, yet circumscribe, the ambiguity and disorder of this period.

These rites consist of three phases: separation, marginality, and aggregation. In the separation phase, ritual actions symbolize detachment of the individual from the previous stable state; the individual metaphorically dies to the old self. The phase of marginality symbolizes the ambiguity of the transition. It represents a structureless realm in which previously taken-for-granted roles and relationships are brought into question. The phase of aggregation unites the individual with others in the new status group. It includes the transmission of knowledge needed by the individual in the new role together with the symbolic features of the new role (e.g., clothing representing the new self). Rites of initiation in simple societies illustrate these processes (Van Gennep, 1960; see also Eliade, 1958; Turner, 1974a, 1974b, 1979).

Contemporary religious groups have rituals that are remnants of earlier rites of passage; baptism, for example, has many features of initiation rites. Confirmation among Christians and bar (bat) mitzvahs among Jews also represent the transition from childhood to adulthood in the religious group. These rituals are, however, relatively weak in effecting such transition in American society. This weakness is partly because religious groups allow ritual adulthood to members whom they do not consider fully socially adult. A thirteen-year-old boy who had recently become a full member of the Presbyterian church (having attended communicants' classes, made a profession of faith, and received his first communion) wrote to the elders (governing board) of the church suggesting changes in church activities. His letter was received with mirth: "Isn't that cute that he thinks he's old enough now to be telling us what to do." A stronger example of the ambiguity of adult status is the recent emergence of forcible "deprogramming," in which parents of legally adult "children" refuse to accept their offsprings' choice of religious identities.

Another more serious basis of this weakness is the quality of adolescence in this society. There is no clear-cut event that confirms adult status. Puberty marks the end of biological childhood, but social adulthood is many years away. The economic structure requires years of preparation for adulthood. A student of twenty who is not fully self-sufficient and independent of parental and school control is no longer a child but is not socially recognized as fully adult. Demarcation events such as leaving home, a first self-supporting job, and marriage are recognized as the beginning of adulthood for some individuals but not for others. Some observers suggest that the forms taken by adolescent rebellion against adult authority are themselves attempts to symbolize a transition (B. Berger, 1969).

Rather than the *medium* by which transition to adulthood is structured, religion in this society often ends up as the *content* over which adolescent rebellion is staged. Adolescence is often a time of identity crisis because the ambiguity is not culturally resolved. The assertion of one's identity (separate from the child's identity, which is defined by family and community values) sometimes takes the form of religious rebellion. The young person tries to assert an adult self by denying those aspects of life perceived as symbolic of the childhood self and tie to parents or family. An obvious example of this rebellion is the youth who joins a religious group that appears diametrically opposed to his or her childhood religion. A very different pattern—the young person who becomes superreligious in the childhood religion—is another way of expressing rejection of the family's "low level" of religiosity and their "hypocrisy." A holier-than-thou stance is comparable to changing religions as a way of asserting an independent identity and rejecting parental values (Greeley, 1979). These seemingly dissimilar adolescent strategies may account for a number of contemporary religious expressions: the attraction of youth to countercultural religious movements, the seemingly fanatical adherence to both old and emerging religious groups, and the agonizing, often bitter struggles between parents and youth over a newly asserted religious identity.

Marriage, Sexuality, and Procreation

Marriage marks a status passage and the beginning of a new family of procreation. Especially for women in most cultures, marriage is the entry to full adulthood. A wealth of ritual and symbolism accompanies and defines this status passage. Religion often directly promotes the ideal of marriage by setting the norms for marriage and establishing the appropriate behavior of members before, during, and after the marriage ceremony. In societies where several religious or ethno-religious groups coexist, religious groups also delimit the pool of acceptable spouses; members are not supposed to marry "outside the fold."

Images evoked in the marriage rituals of historic religions symbolize this status passage. The traditional transition of the woman from her father's possession to her husband's is symbolized by the father "giving away" the bride. Some denominations have attempted to change this symbolism to fit the realities of contemporary American family life—for example, by having both parents escort the bride to the groom or by allowing the bride to present herself. Nevertheless the symbolism represents a fundamental transition of status for both bride and groom. Other symbols (e.g., wedding bands, ceremonial binding of hands, exchange of ceremonial crowns) represent the unity of the new social group—husband and wife.

Although historically religion has been closely linked with family life and the regulation of marriage and sexual behavior, its impact in contemporary American family life appears to be more indirect and perhaps weakened. Unfortunately the data available are narrowly limited to the impact of religion on marriage in four particular areas: endogamy (i.e., marrying within one's ethno-religious group), sexual norms (e.g., restrictions of premarital, extramarital, homosexual, or "deviant" sexual activities), divorce, and fertility. Furthermore, these data describe only relatively recent attitudes and behavior. We have no comparable information about the impact of religion on family life in, say, 1830 or 1600. These data are also generally based upon a narrow consideration of the term *religion*; correlations usually refer only to "religious affiliation."

Although all Jewish and Christian groups emphasize the ideal of permanent marriage, divorce rates and attitudes toward divorce have been changing. It is difficult to assess the impact of religion in these changes. While lack of religious affiliation is correlated with marital disruption (i.e., divorce and separation), this correlation results largely from differences in socioeconomic status between religiously affiliated and nonaffiliated persons. There is also considerable diversity among various denominations and ethnic groups in rates of marital disruption (e.g., the divorce rate among Baptists is higher than among persons with no religious affiliation). The overall rate of marital disruption for Roman Catholics and Protestants is roughly the same (although Roman Catholic divorces may be somewhat underreported because of the church's restriction on formal divorce). Jewish marriages are the least likely to end in divorce (Bumpass and Sweet, 1970). The rate of marital disruption of all three groups is rising, as is the proportion of members who approve of divorce (and remarriage of divorced persons). Although the official teachings of the Roman Catholic church are strongly against divorce and remarriage, fewer than 50 percent of Roman Catholics disapprove of divorce (Marty et al., 1968).

These and similar data on fertility rates, marriage rates, and attitudes toward sexual permissiveness are interesting but much too narrow. It would be useful to know how religion (defined more broadly than religious affiliation) influences the extent to which people perceive themselves as having choices in life (e.g., the choice not to stay married). How does religion influence the individual's general orientation toward life (e.g., fatalism or hopefulness) and toward others (e.g., are others perceived as basically good or bad)? What impact, if any, does religion have on the individual's sense of self-worth and independence; does the individual's religion contribute to the sense of self outside the marriage or family? These broader influences of religion are probably more critical for our understanding of marriage and divorce then are formal moral norms of specific religious organizations.

Likewise it would be fruitful to explore what kinds of marriages result from different kinds of religious orientations. For example, are the religious orientations and perspectives of the spouses important in determining the power relationships between them? Their ideals of married love? The degree of interpersonal communication in their marriage? The allocation of tasks, resources, decision making, and rewards in the marriage and family? Probably religion is one important factor in shaping the quality of marriage relationships, but the precise nature of its influence has yet to be documented.

A related correlation is the influence of religion on gender roles. Various religious perspectives lead to different images of maleness and femaleness. Gender roles are extremely important in marriage, as in other institutional settings. What a man expects of himself and what others expect of him as a man directly influence the kind of activities and relationships in which he engages. If it is considered unmanly to care for babies, a man is likely to avoid situations in which he would do (or be seen doing) this. Religious beliefs, myths, images, and symbols have been important forces in shaping gender roles, as illustrated in the Extended Application section of Chapter 4. Religious groups also maintain a system of social support for appropriate gender role behavior and social control for "deviant" gender role behavior. In recent years, for example, a Mormon feminist was taken before a church court for her open support of ERA (i.e., the Equal Rights Amendment to the U.S. Constitution).

Similarly a broader approach to the influence of religion on childbearing, childbirth, and family life is needed. Numerous studies have correlated religious affiliation and fertility (see, for example, Ryder, 1973). In general, Roman Catholics tend to have more children than Protestants, who have more children than Jews. Most of these differences, however, also partly result from differences in social class, education, and ethnicity. With more Roman Catholics approving of "artificial" birth control and gaining educational and socioeconomic statuses comparable to those of Protestants, their fertility rates will also probably approximate those of Protestants.

Studies of comparative fertility rates, however, have focused too much on the differences between religious organizations in relating their norms of assumed control over the reproductive behavior of members. Far more interesting would be information about how religion shapes the attitudes of men and women toward children. The meaning of having children is different for men than for women, for older couples than for younger ones, for Italians than for Germans, for Jews than for Hindus, and so on. What exactly is the impact of the individual's religion on his or her attitude toward children—especially one's own children? Also, what is the impact of religion on attitudes toward reproductive events per se? How does religion shape the individual's ideas of and feelings about menstruation, intercourse, pregnancy, and childbirth? How does religion influence the person's experience of these events?

Finally the narrow focus of research on attitudes toward sexual norms has failed to tap the broader issue of sexuality itself. All religions have attempted to interpret sexual themes or experiences. Religious symbolism frequently deals directly with themes of sexuality. Important parallels exist between spiritual and sexual ecstasy; sexual images are linked with religious images in the writings of many great mystics such as Saint John of the Cross and Saint Theresa of Avila.

Religion's link with human sexuality is understandable because both are direct, personal experiences of *power*, which evokes a sense of chaos and need for control, pollution and need for purification, danger and need for protection (Douglas, 1966). Religion, with its capacity to give meaning and order, offers control, purification, and protection from the chaotic power of sexuality. The establishment of moral norms to regulate sexual behavior is only one aspect of this control. Other important aspects include religious interpretation of sexual experiences and events (e.g., interpreting marital intercourse as imitative of the marriage of the gods). Religion also provides rituals and symbols to deal with some of the more potent and awesome aspects of sexuality. Many religions have a ritual of purification for women after childbirth (e.g., the "churching" of women in some Christian groups). And religion offers ways of channeling sexual energies into spiritual energies. Many religious groups (including a number of "new" religious movements) believe that sexual activity reduces one's spiritual energies; thus, norms of abstinence from intercourse are based not on notions of right and wrong but upon the ideal of heightening one's spiritual powers.

These reflections about the interrelationship of religion and sexuality suggest some of the directions that further study could take. Existing research on religion and marriage, sexuality, and procreation is much too narrow in both its use of the concept "religion" and its definition of what is relevant in the study of these important human experiences.

Middle Age

Significantly there are no rites of passage to middle age. In earlier times, fewer people lived in relatively good health much beyond the time their children became adults. Thus there was no major gap between the years of active childrearing and support and the years of relative retirement from work and old age. Now, however, with increased longevity and smaller families, a gap of twenty or more years between the time children leave home and parents reach retirement age is not uncommon.

Middle age is often a period of "identity crisis" for both men and women. Many women discover that they have invested their entire sense of purpose in serving their families, but their status as "mother" means little in middle age. The correspondence of this social loss with the time of biological change (i.e., menopause) can be doubly traumatic because some women consider their reproductive capacity a basic part of their sense of self and personal worth. Although the existence of a male biological equivalent to menopause is debated, the social transitions of men in middle age are often as pronounced as those of women. A man may have invested much energy and time into his career and, in middle age, begins to realize that his career goals are unlikely to be achieved. Or he may come to doubt the goals and values that had motivated him in earlier years of his career. Precisely at the stage when his children are becoming more independent of their parents, he often begins to want a closer relationship with them. The structure of family and work in this society make middle age a problematic time: One's chances of achieving socially desirable goals in family and job are considered past or severely reduced, but one is not yet free to quit striving for those goals.

In Western societies, chronological age is a key criterion by which social roles are linked together. It becomes an evaluative criterion when the individual or social group measures the age appropriateness of the person's achievements and activities. A student of twenty-five who returns to college after several years of apparent disinterest in educational goals is called a "late bloomer"; and statements such as "He is too young to be married" or "She is too old to be working full-time" exemplify the social basis of these definitions of age appropriateness. The person may be physically capable of full-time work or marriage and childbearing, but the society has established its criteria of the appropriate ages for these roles (Kearl, 1980; see also Berger et al., 1973:73).

Age is also a key criterion in comparing oneself with others. Many social institutions encourage and even formally organize these comparisons. Schools compare the individual's achievements with others of the same age or grade; businesses compare the achievements of age cohorts of workers. Self-evaluation is also often based upon the individual's comparison of self with others of the same age. As age progresses, however, opportunities for comparing favorably with others of one's cohort decrease. By middle age, many people sense that their number of remaining years and resources for competition severely limit their likelihood of "getting ahead." Middle age brings the peak of socioeconomic mobility; for many individuals, it may mark the beginning of the downward mobility characteristic of old age. Institutions, especially in the sphere of work, further solidify this sense; often workers' job statuses remain relatively static in later years of employment. Retirement marks the worker's entry into "old age"—again, a socially defined threshold of age-appropriate behavior.

Contemporary religious groups do little to smooth this status passage with ritual or symbolism. Some groups give some special status to middle-aged persons (e.g., by making them elders of the church). Overall, however, the main impact of religion upon this status passage is not its interpretation of the meaning of the status through a symbol system but its offering of potential significance to the middleaged through participation in the religious community. Middle age is generally a period of increasing church involvement for many Americans. The overall age pattern in adult church attendance shows a steady increase from late teens to a peak in the late fifties to early sixties, followed by a slight decline in later old age (Atchley, 1980:330–340). These figures do not necessarily reflect greater religiosity of middle-aged and old-aged persons but should be viewed as changing patterns of involvement in voluntary associations (involvement in work-related, sport-related, and school service associations drops dramatically during these same years). This associational involvement may indirectly influence the member's beliefs and practices.

Generally, however, middle age is not a valued life period in our culture, the dominant values of which emphasize youthfulness: youthful standards of beauty, energy, bodily functioning, and carefree life-style. Middle age is, by contrast, a time of increased awareness that one has begun aging, both biologically and socially, and is on the verge of an even less valued period of life in this culture—old age.

Old Age

Popular imagery holds that religion is more important in the lives of old people. Thus one study asserts that the holding of orthodox beliefs (such as certainty in the existence of God), the evaluation of oneself as religious, and the degree of satisfaction received from religion all increase in later years of life (Gray and Moberg, 1977). Other, possibly contradictory evidence shows that the elderly tend to become disaffiliated from religious and other voluntary organizations (Bahr, 1970). Most of these data refer only to church-oriented religiosity, and little information exists about the place of individuals' personal religion in their older years. While physical limitations might prevent an older person from attending church-related activities, it is possible that the person might pray more frequently, remember religious experiences or events more intensely, or base more everyday activity upon religious values.

Problems of meaning and belonging may be particularly acute for older persons. Difficulties of financial and physical limitations may compound the broader problem of the society's general devaluation of old age. A 1974 survey found that only 6 percent of American adults consider the "best years of life" to be one's fifties, sixties, or seventies. By contrast, 34 percent felt that one's sixties and seventies were the "worst years of life" (Harris and Associates, 1975). At the same time, elderly persons become increasingly aware of the imminence of their own death and must often cope with the reality of the deaths of their spouse and friends. To the extent that important aspects of the individual's identity are supported by relationships with such relatives and friends, these deaths may mean real losses in the individual's own life.

Popular notions also suggest that the greater religiosity of old age is something of a last-chance "cramming for the final exam." Although there may be some validity to this conception, the religiosity of the elderly is probably more of a reflection of their social situation. Old people may emphasize spiritual and human relationship values in their lives because the society has relegated them to the private sphere—out of the world of work. Our society places great value upon one's work role (especially for men, but increasingly also for women) throughout the individual's adult life, and old age brings the often abrupt end of that role. Retirement effectively means, for many people, leaving the public sphere. Thus the elderly person must find all bases of identity and self-worth in the private sphere—family, leisure time activities, religion, neighborhood. Perhaps because they have been characteristically confined to the private sphere, women often adjust better than men to old age. They have already developed more social roles in the private sphere, and society has not expected them to invest themselves in their employment roles (if any) as heavily as men (Myerhoff, 1978).

Increased emphasis upon religious bases of individual identity may thus represent an attempt to transform the previous (i.e., culturally encouraged) valuation based on work and parenthood to a new valuation based upon spiritual status. Because this represents a fairly dramatic change in self-evaluation, however, it probably does not succeed for many people in our society.

By contrast, some societies provide recognizable spiritual roles for elderly persons to assume. Hindu men who have raised and supported their children to adulthood are allowed to retire in honor to a life of contemplation and spiritual exercises. Elderly women in other cultures often have spiritual roles as healers and midwives—positions of culturally recognized spiritual power. American society, characteristically, does not provide such roles. Individuals may be recognized and honored for their "holiness" or "goodness" within their own immediate religious group, but such roles are privatized. The honor an elderly woman may receive at her Wednesday night prayer meeting does not carry over to her treatment by the Social Security bureaucracy, hospital clinic, or other tenants in her apartment building.

One of the critical problems of meaning in middle and old age is modern society's sense of time. Primitive religions integrate all human action into cosmic time; the events of one's life can be interpreted as part of a larger cosmic drama. The individual's passage through the life cycle repeats and imitates the deities' birth, adolescence, marriage, childbirth, parenting, work, play, fighting, aging, and death. In this religious perspective, time has sacred significance. It collapses past and future into an eternal present.

Historic religions such as Christianity and Islam also give sacred significance to time. The past is full of the deities' self-revelation to humans; the present is important in the working out of the deities' will for humans; the future will bring the full realization of that will and celebration of a glorious reward. In this perspective, time promises immortality. Old age has sacred meaning, both as a fulfillment of divine will and as a threshold to higher levels of spiritual rewards.

Modern society, by contrast, encourages a profane image of time. Time "passes," and its passage signifies decay or entropy. Time is a resource to be used but contains no special meaning; when the resource is depleted, life ends. In this context, old age has no special significance with reference to past accomplishments (e.g., social rewards for living a good life) or to future rewards (e.g., heaven, nirvana). Old age means merely the end of full life opportunities (Kearl, 1980).

U.S. society values economic roles especially highly. The individual's occupational role shapes the society's evaluation of that person and his or her own identity. Consumer roles are equally important. Social status is based partly upon evaluations of the individual's ability to maintain a certain standard of consumption (e.g., quality of house, car, neighborhood, clothing). Elderly persons are often deprived of valued statuses in both kinds of economic roles; they are retired from their work roles and, simultaneously, their fixed incomes leave them unable to maintain valued standards of consumption.

The legitimation offered for this loss of valued statuses is the idea of "retirement." Retirement is supposed to be an economic and moral vindication for growing old. It is described as a time for individualism (e.g., the freedom to move away to a retirement resort, play golf, lounge around, putter in the garden, and escape social obligations). The concept of retirement implies that the individual has earned this escape by having fulfilled life's social obligations. This individualism (if, indeed, the retired person could afford such luxuries in retirement) does epitomize what younger members consider to be freedom and a desirable reward. It cannot, however, provide meaning to life and death, a sense of belonging or self-worth, for the retired person (Kearl, 1980).

With no discernable future or possibility of immortality, this life is made even more problematic in its ending. Often biological death follows the individual's social death by many years; the individual may become physically, financially, or mentally unable to sustain interactions that the society considers "alive." Yet the person is kept biologically alive, often by extreme measures of medical intervention. It becomes difficult to die "on time." The medical supervisors of death not only treat it as meaningless, but they also often segregate dying persons from family, neighbors, or friends who could support their personal meaning system. Religion has traditionally given meaning and dignity to old age and dying. Attempts to retain these values are not supported, however, by the structure of modern society. Old age and dying are generally perceived as times to fear.

Conversion

The capabilities of religion for providing the individual with a sense of both meaning and belonging are especially evident in the process of **conversion.** Conversion means a transformation of one's *self* concurrent with a transformation of one's basic *meaning system*.[1] It changes the sense of who one is and how one

[1]Throughout this discussion we will emphasize the broad concept of *meaning system* more than the specific term *religion*. This usage is helpful because the processes described here apply to other comprehensive meaning systems as well as to specifically religious ones. The processes of conversion and commitment can apply not only to religious changes but also to psychotherapeutic and political transformation.

belongs in the social situation. Conversion transforms the way the individual perceives the rest of society and his or her personal place in it, altering one's view of the world.

This definition of conversion distinguishes simple changes in institutional affiliation from more fundamental alterations in the individual's meaning system. An Episcopalian who marries a Roman Catholic may join the Catholic church to accommodate the spouse's wishes. Such a change of affiliation is not necessarily a conversion. Similarly a Presbyterian who moves to a new town and, finding no local church of that denomination, joins a Congregational church has probably not—strictly speaking—converted. Such denomination switching is relatively common in America and is strongly correlated with socioeconomic mobility (Stark and Glock, 1968:183–203). Sometimes switching denominational affiliation symbolizes a more dramatic transformation of self and meaning system; typically, however, it is not a conversion but simply a change of affiliation from one organization to another. Yet we will see how important a new group affiliation *can* be in making the change of self and meaning system possible.

Kinds of Conversion

There is considerable diversity even among "real conversions." One distinction is the degree of transformation that takes place. How different are the new meaning system and self from the former ones?

Radical Transformation. The extreme case is a radical transformation of self and meaning system such as when a highly committed Conservative Jew converts to a fundamentalist Christian world view. Not only are such extreme conversions relatively uncommon, but they rarely occur as dramatically as popular imagery implies. The processes by which such radical transformations occur are actually similar in kind, though usually not in degree, to less extreme conversions (see Berger and Luckmann, 1966:157–163). These processes are described in greater detail in the next section.

Consolidation. Less extreme cases include conversions in which the new meaning system and self represent a consolidation of previous identities. Some young men who became ba'ale teshuvah—members of strict Orthodox Jewish yeshivot (i.e., commune-schools)—had come from non-Orthodox Jewish homes but rejected their Jewish way of life and had then tried various alternative world views (especially countercultural "trips" such as meditation, communes, and drugs). Becoming Orthodox was not a return to their former Jewishness because their new meaning system and selves were dramatically different from the old ones. Yet the way of life of the ba'ale teshuvah enabled these members to consolidate elements of both their former identities into a new, "superior" self (Glanz and Harrison, 1977). Similar identity consolidation occurs in many conversions to the Jesus People, the Meher Baba cult, and Catholic Pentecostalism (Gordon, 1974; Harrison, 1974a; McGuire, 1977; Robbins and Anthony, 1972).

Reaffirmation. Another less extreme type of conversion is an alteration of self and meaning system representing a reaffirmation of elements of one's previous identity. Many adolescent "conversions" fit this model. It is difficult to specify how much change such conversions really entail. Often they involve no change in one's religious affiliation, yet exhibit real changes in the individual's personal meaning system and sense of identity. Roman Catholics who become Pentecostal (i.e., in the Catholic Charismatic Renewal) typically undergo a conversion experience, yet remain Catholics and often become even more active in parish life. They change their personal meaning systems and selves, but they interpret these changes as consistent with their former meaning system. They view their former religiosity as a vague groping for the truth, which they now have found. This type of conversion does not necessarily entail a total rejection of the previous meaning system.

Quasi-conversions and Rhetorics. By contrast, some identity consolidating conversion experiences involve little or no change in meaning system and sense of self. Many religious groups expect young members to make a personal faith decision and to undergo a conversion experience as they approach adulthood. Such groups provide opportunities, such as retreats or revivals, in which the necessary conversion experience is more likely to occur. These experiences, while very real and meaningful to participants, are often not conversions (as defined) but rather rituals of reaffirmation of the person's existing identity and meaning system (Wimberley et al., 1975; Zetterberg, 1952). Even these quasi-conversions, however, occur by some of the same social processes as more radical transformations of self; both are forms of religious socialization and are thus comparable in many respects (cf. the conversion rituals of Esalen encounter groups, Holloman, 1974).

The main difficulty in distinguishing the degree of change that occurs in any given conversion is that the individual who converts reinterprets past experiences in relationship to the new meaning system. Therefore it becomes difficult to determine what amount of the convert's description of the changes experienced represents the objective process of conversion and how much expresses the convert's subjective reinterpretation of those events. The convert constructs the story of conversion, drawing on a socially available set of plausible explanations or "rhetoric." Several rhetorics may be used to "explain" conversion: rhetorics of choice, rhetorics of change, and rhetorics of continuity.

Rhetorics of choice emphasize how much the change resulted from personal, often agonizing decision. Our society places much value on individual decision, so these rhetorics are prominent in explanations of conversion. In a culture where personal decision was less valued or discouraged, rhetorics of choice would not be emphasized; indeed, the convert might not even experience "making a personal decision" (Tippett, 1973).

Rhetorics of change emphasize the dramatic nature of personal change in the conversion. Converts may compare the evil or unhappiness of their previous way of life with how wonderful their new way is.

Rhetorics of continuity focus on the extent to which one's new meaning system and self are the logical extension of earlier beliefs and experiences. The convert might remember important past experiences as tentative steps toward the newfound truth.

Religious groups often encourage the application of one type of rhetoric over another. Thus Catholic Pentecostals generally encourage new members to interpret their conversion as continuous with their former way of life; whereas Jesus People typically encourage new members to interpret their experience as a dramatic change. Because the main source of information about conversion is the converts themselves—and because their explanations of events surrounding their conversions are reinterpretations consistent with their new meaning systems—it is difficult to evaluate evidence about conversions. Some sociological theories of conversion have mistaken these interpretations and the rhetorics that express them for the objective events of the conversion (Beckford, 1978a; Burke, 1953; Freund, 1969).

Accounting for Conversion

A theoretical understanding of how conversion occurs is nevertheless worthwhile because it reveals much about the connection between the individual's meaning system, social relationships, and very identity. Since conversion consists in a change of the individual's meaning system and self, it has social, psychological, and ideational components. The social component consists of the interaction between the recruit and other circles of associates (e.g., parents, friends, co-workers). The psychological component refers to emotional and affective aspects of conversion as well as to changes in values and attitudes. The ideational component includes the actual ideas the convert embraces or rejects during the process. These ideas are rarely very philosophical or theological; they are simply a set of beliefs that both justify the new meaning system and negate the former one.

Factors in Conversion. An adequate theory of conversion must take all of the aspects mentioned into account without overemphasizing any single component. Some theories give too much weight to social factors by creating the image of a passive person being pushed and pulled by various social forces. Although very real social pressures are exerted on the potential convert, the person who converts is not a passive object of these pressures. Conversion entails an interaction during which the recruit constructs or negotiates a new personal identity (Beckford, 1978a; Berger, 1967; Straus, 1979). Furthermore, only some of those exposed to such social pressures do decide to convert.

Some theories of conversion overemphasize ideational components of the process. These theories are consistent with the ideological claims of the religious groups themselves. Religious groups like to believe that the truth value of their beliefs alone is sufficient to compel a person to convert. The content of the belief system *is* a factor in conversion. Some beliefs are more appealing than others to people in certain circumstances; indeed, the potential convert will likely be recruited to a group whose perspective is consistent with that person's previous outlook, even though the specific content of the group's beliefs may be unfamiliar (Greil, 1977; Harrison, 1974b). Also, we must acknowledge people's religious reasons for their religious behavior and not try to reduce every motive to some psychological function.

Nevertheless ideas alone do not persuade a person to convert. Even in the scientific community where objective facts and the truth value of interpretations are supposed to be paramount, there is considerable resistance to change from an established interpretive paradigm to a new one—even when the old paradigm is inconsistent with the "facts" (Festinger, 1957; Kuhn, 1970). How much more are religious believers, with their emphasis on supraempirical reality, likely to resist changing their ideas? Thus although the ideational component is important in the appeal of a new belief system, it is not sufficient to bring about conversion.

Other theories place too great an emphasis on psychological factors in conversion, explaining the change entirely in terms of the individual's personality, biography, and personal problems. Psychologistic explanations are attractive because they mesh with many of our individualistic cultural values. Nevertheless they are too one-sided, leaving out social situational factors and other important components. Also some of these theories tend to assume that conversion to unusual religious groups (e.g., "cults") entails "sick" behavior. Yet adherents' behavior is quite understandable and rational within their alternate meaning systems. If one believes that astrological forces influence human events, it is perfectly rational to act in accordance with those forces.

"Brainwashing." One particularly misleading psychologistic model of conversion is the "brainwashing" metaphor. This model is based on studies during the 1950s of the processes by which certain American personnel in the Orient were pressed to convert to Chinese Communism. The popular image applied to this process was "brainwashing," conveying the idea that the convert's mind was cleansed of prior beliefs, values, and commitment, then filled with a new belief system. Psychological studies of this process identified several factors producing conversion against the wills of the converts (Lifton, 1963; Sargant, 1957). Various social scientists have subsequently generalized the interpretations of this drastic type of political conversion to other forms of conversion. Some accurate parallels do exist between forcible "brainwashing" and conversion, but these characteristics apply to all forms of resocialization. Thus the training of soldiers for combat and rehabilitating juvenile delinquents also involve these processes. To say that conversion is a form of resocialization does not mean that it is therefore an extreme, involuntary form of resocialization.

The key problem with the "brainwashing" metaphor is its ideological use and potential application for abuses of civil liberties. Nonconverts often feel threatened by the conversion of someone close to them. The convert has rejected their own dearly held views and norms and has indirectly threatened the nonconvert's own meaning system. When people cannot understand why an individual would *want* to convert to an unfamiliar religious perspective, they find "brainwashing" an attractive explanation. This metaphor implies that the converting individual did not change voluntarily. The metaphor also allows people to negate the ideational component of the convert's new meaning system. A convert's parents can feel, "He doesn't believe those ideas because they are meaningful to him but because his mind has been manipulated." In its extreme form, the "brainwashing" metaphor has been recently used to justify the denial of converts' religious liberty on the ground that they do not know their own minds (Robbins, 1977; Shupe et al., 1977).

An interesting parallel with the current anticult charge of "brainwashing" is the nineteenth-century anti-Mason movement. Freemasonry is now a legitimate, middle-class form of fraternal organization, but it was severely attacked in nineteenth-century America as subversive to democracy. Other, now respectable groups that were attacked (often violently) were Roman Catholics and Mormons. The key themes of the movements against Masonry, Roman Catholicism, and Mormonism emphasized that, unlike conventional denominations that claimed only partial loyalty of their members, these groups allegedly dominated their members' lives, demanded unlimited allegiance, and conducted some activities in secrecy (Davis, 1960).

This parallel suggests that the "brainwashing" controversy is an ideological issue at another level (see Richardson, 1981; Robbins and Anthony, 1979). The society defines as "deviant" one who is *too* committed to religion, especially authoritarian religion. The resocialization processes themselves are less of an issue than the legitimacy of the group's religion itself. To illustrate this discrepancy, two researchers compared conversion and commitment processes of the Unification Church of Sun Myung Moon and similar contemporary sects with the nineteenth- and early twentieth-century practices of the now socially acceptable Tnevnoc "cult." The Tnevnoc practices were essentially comparable and seem bizarre until we discover that the authors were actually referring to life in the convent— which, spelled backwards, is Tnevnoc (Bromley and Shupe, 1979b). The chief difference between many modern "cults" and groups such as Roman Catholicism, Freemasonry, and Mormonism is that the latter groups have now achieved social legitimacy.[2]

Keeping these cautions in mind, we can examine some of the factors in conversion. By emphasizing conversion as a *process* rather than an event, we take into account the fact that the convert has both a history and a future. Although an individual may experience conversion as a discrete event, numerous other experiences lead up to and follow that event that are also parts of the conversion. The following description examines the sequence of events in the process of conversion; but let us remember that no single step in the sequence is itself sufficient to "cause" conversion (Beckford, 1978a; Heirich, 1977).

Predisposition to Conversion

Several personal and situational factors can predispose people to conversion by making them aware of the extent to which their prior meaning system seems inadequate to explain or give meaning to experiences and events. By contrast, if individuals can satisfactorily "handle" experiences and events within the framework of their meaning system, they have no desire to seek alternative meanings for their lives. Sometimes the individual who acutely feels the need for a new set of meanings becomes a *seeker*—that is, a person who actively looks for a satisfactory alternative belief system. A seeker often tries many different alternative beliefs and practices (Balch and Taylor, 1977). More often, however, the individual experiences the desire for a more satisfactory meaning system as a vague tension, a malaise.

Many converts describe a crisis that they felt was a turning point in their lives. It is very difficult to evaluate the extent to which such crises actually precipitate

[2]In order to reduce the impression that conversion and commitment processes characterize only "weird" religions, I have drawn examples from both traditional and "new" religions.

the individual's conversion. Some crises may disrupt a person's life so completely that the individual has difficulty integrating them into the previously held meaning system. Natural disasters, war, and personal tragedy are particularly acute challenges. Serious illness or unemployment may be experienced as turning points. Social events such as an economic depression or anxiety over social conditions (e.g., crime or erosion of morals) may predispose people to conversion. Nevertheless such crises do not *cause* religious conversion. Religious conversion is one among several possible resolutions of tensions and problems created by the crisis. Thus serious illness might predispose one person to convert to a new meaning system; another person with a similar illness might find great meaning and comfort in his or her existing meaning system and have that belief confirmed by the crisis experience. Diverse other responses are possible, including alcoholism, political conversion, psychotherapy, suicide, and so on. Individuals converted to religious meaning systems are typically people whom previous socialization has predisposed to a religious perspective (see Greil, 1977; Lofland, 1966, 1977).

Determining to what extent the convert's description of a crisis experience is the result of after-the-fact interpretation of events is also difficult. Some religious groups encourage their members to witness about their conversion experience by telling the group how they came to "see the light." Whether the events thus described were really critical when they occurred is therefore difficult to reconstruct. Often the new group itself promotes the recruit's experience of a crisis. Much of the initial interaction between group members and the potential convert is devoted to making the recruit dissatisfied with the prior meaning system. Similarly many groups raise the recruit's anxiety over social and personal problems. Jehovah's Witnesses, for example, often approach strangers with a message about common worries—war, inflation, crime. By "mediating" anomie, the group encourages the individual to convert. The group encourages an experiential crisis of meaning by emphasizing order-threatening conditions and magnifying the potential convert's feelings of dissatisfaction, fear, and anxiety, which the person may have previously felt only vaguely (Beckford, 1975b:174).

Initial Interaction

Most recruits are drawn to the group by friends or relatives. In addition to introducing the newcomer to the group and its beliefs, these preexisting networks of friendship account for the plausibility of the beliefs and the attractiveness of belonging. Thus a person might be impressed by a roommate's happiness in a religious group and be curious enough to "check it out." The fact that a person whom one knows and likes belongs to the group attests to the normalcy or desirability of the group's way of life (Gerlach and Hine, 1970; Lofland, 1966).

Through interaction with members of the group, the recruit is gradually resocialized into that group's way of life. This resocialization consists of the individual's reshaping of identity and world view to become consistent with those considered appropropriate by the group. Several social processes enable the individual to make this transformation. Group support is particularly important. The recruit enjoys warm, affective relationships with the new group. Members of the Unification Church, for example, shower the potential member with attention and affection (sometimes called "love bombing"). These bonds affirm the new self and meaning system. As the recruit gradually withdraws from competing social relationships, the new group's opinions become increasingly important (Berger, 1967:50–51).

At the same time, the recruit also weakens or severs those relationships that support the old self. Former attachments compete with new commitments, symbolize a world view that the recruit wishes to reject, and are based upon an identity that the recruit wishes to change. Imagine, for example, that through two good friends you are introduced to a group of American Sufis (Sufism is a mystical sect within Islam). Suppose that you learned enough about the group that you decided you would like to join them. How would your non-Sufi friends and relatives react? Your roommate might say, "Oh, come off that mysticism kick. I liked you better when you were a drinking buddy." Imagine your parents' reaction when you announce at supper that weekend, "Guess what, Mom and Dad, I've decided to join this fantastic bunch of Sufis, and I'm going out to the west coast to live in a commune with some of them!" Most converts find their former set of friends less than supportive of their newfound truth and new self. Relationships with the new group therefore become even more important to counteract opposition from others.

During this resocialization, recruits learn to redefine their social world. Relationships once valued become devalued, and patterns of behavior once undesirable become desirable. New believers may redefine their families to exclude the biological family and to include the new family of fellow believers. A Shaker hymn thus celebrates the severance of old family ties:

> Of all the relations that ever I see
> My old fleshly kindred are furthest from me
> So bad and so ugly, so hateful they feel
> To see them and hate them increases my zeal . . .
>
> My gospel relations are dearer to me
> Than all the flesh kindred that ever I see . . .
> (quoted in Kanter, 1972:90).

This process results in a whole new way of experiencing the world and oneself. The individual comes to "see" the world with an entirely different perspective; indeed, the new believer may say, "I once was blind, but now I see." This phrase is not merely metaphorical, because the new perspective actually causes the individual to *perceive* the world differently. That which was marginal to consciousness becomes central, and that which once was focal becomes peripheral. Every world view entails the selective perception and interpretation of events and objects according to its meaning system. Conversion means adopting new criteria for selecting (Jones, 1978).

Recruits also redefine their own biographies. They remember episodes that appear consistent with the newfound perspective and interpret them as "part of what led me to the truth." Events are reinterpreted in terms of new beliefs and values. Remembering how proud she was to have achieved scholastic honors in school, one young woman said, "What a fool I was back then to have put so much store on worldly achievements."

The actual interaction between the recruit and the group is especially important in bringing about this transformation of world views. The most obvious action of religious groups is **proselyting** potential converts. Proselyting means that an individual or group actively tries to persuade nonbelievers to become believers. Some religious groups (e.g., Jehovah's Witnesses) do much proselyting among nonbelievers; others (e.g., Conservative Jews) do virtually none. Although proselyting activities are relatively conspicuous to outsiders, they are important mainly as a commitment mechanism for already converted members (Beckford, 1975b; Festinger et al., 1956; Shaffir, 1978).

Mutual witnessing within existing friendships appears to be especially effective in bringing about the recruit's conversion to a new meaning system. Thus the newcomer may mention an apparent coincidence that had recently happened, and a group member may respond, "That was no coincidence. That was God trying to show concern for you so that you will change your life." Or a member might say, "I used to be just like you. I had my doubts and didn't know what to believe, but now it all fits together. Now I can see what I was missing." Through these informal interactions, the recruit may gradually "try on" the interpretations suggested by members and apply their meaning systems to personal experiences. Thus the new believer comes to share their distinctive world view.

Symbolizing the Conversion

The part of the conversion process typically identified as "the conversion" is essentially some form of *symbolizing* the transformation that has already been occurring. The convert affirms the new identity by some symbolic means considered appropriate in that group. In many Christian groups, baptism is meaningful as a symbol of conversion. Other ritual expressions of the new self include speaking in tongues (i.e., glossolalia) and witnessing. Some groups have very formal means for symbolizing transformation; others have more informal symbols that are not obvious to the nonbeliever (Gerlach and Hine, 1970; Lebra, 1972).

Although conversion is a gradual process, many recruits who have decided to convert adopt some of the symbols of conversion rather dramatically. Part of the resocialization itself is learning to act, look, and talk like other members of the group. Like recruits to the police force, the marines, or medical profession, new religious recruits often avidly imitate what they perceive to be the demeanor of full-fledged members. New "premies" in the Divine Light Mission, for example, often tried to appear "blissed out." This imitative action—which might be called "doing being converted"—is an important part of the resocialization process. It is, however, often mistaken by observers as evidence that a dramatic conversion has been accomplished.

Some groups may encourage the new member to seek a conversion experience. This special emotional and spiritual event thus symbolizes the person's full conversion. Such experiences, however, are only part of the larger conversion process but are valued ways of symbolizing the transformation in some groups. Often these conversion experiences are brought about in carefully orchestrated settings. In a revival meeting, the timing of the altar call is synchronized with music and spoken message to proclaim, in essence, "Now is the appropriate time to have that special experience you came for" (W. Johnson, 1971; Walker and Atherton, 1971).

Another symbolic expression of the new self is changing one's name. Nuns traditionally changed their names upon taking their vows. The new name both symbolized the person's new identity and helped confirm that identity every time she was addressed. Some groups also encourage converts to confess the wrongness of their previous way of life. Among the Society of Brothers (Bruderhof), such a confession event symbolizes the conversion and demonstrates how new members' views of themselves have been transformed (see Zablocki, 1971:239–285). In the confession, converts affirm their new selves by derogating the behavior of their old selves. These symbols of conversion illustrate the complexity of the larger process of resocialization (see Goffman, 1961, especially his comparison of the "mortification of self" in several different institutional settings).

Commitment

The process of conversion does not end when the recruit formally joins the group and symbolically affirms the conversion. Rather the conversion process is continued in the **commitment** process, by which the individual increasingly identifies with the group, its meaning system, and its goals. Commitment means the willingness of members to contribute in maintaining the group because the group provides what they want and need. Commitment therefore implies a reciprocal relationship. The group achieves its goals by fulfilling the needs of its members, and the members satisfy their desires by helping to maintain the group. Persons who are totally committed to a group have fully invested themselves in it and fully identify with it. Commitment is the link between the individual and the larger social group. A person cannot be coerced into commitment but decides to identify with the interests of the group because of personal values, material interests, or affective ties (Kanter, 1972:65–70).

Conversion is a resolution of the individual's problems with former meaning systems and former self, but conversion alone is not sufficient to resolve new problems. The group's commitment processes help prevent the individual's doubts and new problems from undermining the conversion. The final result of the entire conversion process is not merely creating new members but creating members who will invest themselves in what the group is believing and doing. The same process also ensures the commitment of all members, new and old, to the group's values and objectives. *Commitment processes build plausibility structures for the group's world view and way of life.*

The level of commitment that a group expects varies. Most major denominations in the United States do not expect intense commitment from their members or for that commitment to influence all aspects of their lives. Other religious groups (e.g., Pentecostal and Holiness groups, as well as many communal groups ranging from Hassidic Jews to the Bruderhof, Trappist monks, and the Unification Church) expect members to demonstrate intense religious commitment in all spheres of daily life. Commitment mechanisms in dissenting or deviant groups are especially important because of their difficulty in maintaining their world view in face of opposition both from established religious groups and the larger society. All social groups, however, need some commitment from their members in order to maintain the group and achieve their goals (see Gerlach and Hine, 1970). And all social groups (including nonreligious groups such as the army) utilize commitment measures similar to those used by religious groups.

The processes by which the group fosters commitment are similar to processes of conversion. Both processes urge members to *withdraw* from competing allegiances and alternate ways of life, and both processes encourage members to *involve* themselves more deeply in the life of the group, its values and goals. These commitment mechanisms are used to some degree by all social groups. Groups desiring more intense or total commitment of members, however, are likely to use more extreme commitment processes. Groups gain greater commitment of members by asking them to sacrifice something for the group, but the degree of required sacrifice varies widely. Most religious bodies ask their members to give up some of their money and time for the group's goals and projects; and some groups expect their members to tithe a specific, substantial percentage of their income. Still other groups ask members to give up all belongings to the group and to live communally.

Withdrawal from Competing Allegiances

Any degree of sacrifice enhances the individual's commitment because giving up something makes the goal seem more valuable. Sacrifice gives observable evidence to the group that the member is committed, and it "weeds out" members who are not sufficiently committed. Religious groups further encourage sacrifice by signifying it as a consecration, so the act of sacrifice gains sacred status. Some groups ask members to sacrifice time and energy (e.g., devoting a certain number of hours each week to proselyting new members). Some groups expect members to abstain regularly or periodically from certain foods or from alcohol, tobacco, drugs, or sexual relationships. Several Christian groups encourage or require their members to fast during Lent. Either for all members or for an elite core group, many religious groups place special value on celibacy. Other groups may expect members to do without "worldly" pursuits (e.g., dancing, going to movies, wearing make-up or stylish clothing). Such sacrifices are demanded by most contemporary religious groups, especially marginal ones. Celibacy, for example, figures in the commitment process of such diverse groups as Roman Catholic clergy, some neo-Pentecostals, the Divine Light Mission, and the Unification Church. Vegetarianism and abstinence from drugs are commonly required sacrifices among many youth culture groups (see Kanter, 1972, for examples from nineteenth-century communal groups; for contemporary examples, see Gardner, 1978).

Some sacrifices may also be interpreted as forms of **mortification**, the process of stripping the individual of vestiges of the "old self." Groups seeking to resocialize their members into a new identity consistent with the group's beliefs and values often encourage mortification. Members are asked to let go of those areas of life that compete with the new, desired self. They may have to wear prescribed dress and hairstyle, do without make-up or jewelry, and give up certain prized possessions. They are asked to sacrifice not because these things are wrong in themselves but because using them supports the "old self." Other forms of mortification include public confession, giving up control over one's time and personal space, and relinquishing personal choice in a wide range of matters (Goffman, 1961; Zablocki, 1971).

The group sometimes promotes further withdrawal of members from their former way of life by asking them to renounce competing relationships. Many sects and cults discourage members from interacting with the "outside world" and may adopt special social arrangements to insulate members from outside influences. Groups such as some Mennonites, Jesus communes, and Christian monks geographically separate themselves from the rest of society. Other groups insulate their members by operating their own schools, places of work, and social clubs. The group may also exercise control over the communication media to which members are exposed or may limit interaction with outsiders.

More important than physical withdrawal from "the world" is the creation of psychic boundaries between the group and the outside. By use of these boundaries, members come to think of the group as "we" and the rest of society as "they." Furthermore, members perceive their in-group as good or superior and the outside as evil or degraded. Thus the individual member's withdrawal from competing activities is motivated not only by controls that the group exercises but especially by the wish to identify with the in-group and to avoid the negative influences of the outside.

Withdrawal from competing relationships often entails changes in the member's relationships with parents, spouse, and close friends. Typically the individual identifies with outside relationships less and less, while simultaneously drawing closer to fellow group members. As we have seen, this disengagement from relationships that do not support the member's new identity and beliefs is partly necessary to maintain the individual's new world view. Many religious groups try to exert some control over the member's choice of a marriage partner. Marriage to someone who does not support (or who even opposes) one's world view can undermine the believer's meaning system. Also critical is competition between religious groups over the socialization of children from a "mixed" marriage.

The group frequently tries to guide or control even its members' relationships within the group. Close relationships among a small part of the group may detract from commitment to the group as a whole. The attachment of a married couple to each other or of parents to their children can compete with their involvement in the larger group. Groups that seek intense commitment from their members often have special structural arrangements to reduce this competition. The Oneida commune of the nineteenth century had a form of "open marriage" that diminished the pairing off of couples. Other groups (e.g., the Israeli kibbutzim) consider children to belong to the whole community rather than solely to the biological parents.

These processes all promote commitment to the group by encouraging individual members to withdraw themselves from those aspects of their former life that prevent them from being fully a "new self." The degree to which any given religious group asks its members to withdraw from nongroup loyalties depends largely upon the type of group. The more marginal, sectlike groups typically expect high levels of attachment. Their commitment processes are therefore more intense and extreme than those of ordinary denominations.

Attachment

At the same time that groups encourage members to withdraw from other allegiances, they also urge members to become more and more involved in the group itself, drawing them into greater oneness with the group. This sense of unity is clearly related to the concept of belonging, discussed in Chapter 2. Activities that draw the member into the fellowship and consciousness of the larger group promote both the cohesion of the group and the commitment of individual members. These commitment mechanisms make belonging to the group an emotionally satisfying experience. Commitment mechanisms for attachment are also likely to differ according to the intensity of the commitment desired by the group. Groups that expect intense commitment of members utilize stronger measures to promote attachment to the group.

The "we feeling" of group consciousness is promoted by homogeneity of membership. The more alike members feel, the easier it is for the group to gain a sense of unity. Established religious bodies typically achieve member homogeneity by self-selection. Individuals choose to join a church or synagogue with membership characteristics comparable to their own social status, racial, ethnic, or language group, and educational and religious background. Sectlike groups, by contrast, have more selective memberships, screening out or discouraging unacceptable members. Sectlike groups put greater emphasis on resocializing new members, thereby creating more homogeneity (Kanter, 1972:93, 94).

Group unity is also enhanced by the sharing of work and possessions. The extreme form of such sharing is full communal living, in which all possessions are held in common and all work is performed together. At the opposite pole are nominal forms of sharing, such as gathering Thanksgiving baskets for the needy or a painting party to decorate Sunday School rooms. Even these minimally demanding kinds of sharing promote a sense of unity in the group. Much sharing in religious groups consists of people taking care of each other. Group members may aid the family of a hospitalized member by caring for the children, preparing meals, and comforting the worried spouse. This kind of sharing promotes the commitment not only of the family receiving care but especially of those giving the care.

Regular group gatherings also bring about greater commitment of members, and such gatherings need not be for overtly religious purposes. A church supper helps increase members' feeling of belonging to the group. Communal groups meet very frequently, sometimes each day. Other sectlike groups also urge their members to meet often. Some groups hold prayer meetings three nights a week in addition to Sunday services and church socials. Not all religious groups, however, identify commitment to the congregation as critical. Some groups emphasize both family-level religiosity and supracongregational commitment as very important. Religious gatherings of the family (e.g., the family saying the prayers of the rosary together or praying special Sabbath blessings, Shabbat b'rachot) serve similar functions of commitment but not necessarily to the congregation.

The content of group gatherings can also promote the commitment of individual members. **Ritual** is one particularly important aspect of a group gathering. By ritual, the group symbolizes meanings significant to itself. Ritual gives symbolic form to group unity, and participating individuals symbolically affirm their commitment. Ritual both reflects and acts upon the group's meaning system. Too often we tend to think of ritual as being empty and a matter of "going through the motions." Even going through the motions can promote a sense of unity, but in many groups the content of ritual is highly meaningful and especially successful in creating a sense of oneness. Rituals important in many religious groups include communion and other ritual meals, healing services, symbols of deference, embraces, special prayer postures, hymns, and rituals of purification.

Mutual witnessing continues to be as important in the commitment process as in the initial socialization or conversion of the believer. Through witnessing, members show themselves and others how their daily lives can be interpreted in terms of the group's meaning system. This kind of witnessing is prominent in Pentecostal and Jesus movement prayer meetings and in the satsang of the Divine Light Mission. Witnessing is a transformative process. All events, thoughts, and experience are transformed into significant events, meaningful thoughts, and special religious experiences. Everyday and nonbelievers' interpretations of events are devalued during witnessing and replaced with religious interpretations. Witnessing can be relatively public or can occur in the setting of a small fellowship group or family. The public proselyting of Jehovah's Witnesses, Mormons, and Hare Krishnas is different from the relatively private witnessing of the evangelical Women Aglow movement or the pentecostal Full Gospel Businessmen's Association. Groups that consider themselves in opposition to the rest of "the world" are more likely to emphasize witnessing as a commitment mechanism (cf. similar functions in Alcoholics Anonymous, Weight Watchers, and psychotherapeutic groups; see Allon, 1973; Jones, 1975; on witnessing in religious groups, see Kroll-Smith, 1980; McGuire, 1975; Shaffir, 1978).

Commitment to a group can be strengthened if the group convinces the member that the group itself is extraordinary. If, for example, members become convinced that the group is in itself the exclusive path to salvation, they are more likely to remain with the group. Groups that expect the imminent end of the world typically portray themselves as the elect who will be saved. Other groups represent their rituals and practices as necessary for salvation in the next life. Many of these groups teach that fallen-away members will be even worse off than people who never knew the "right" way.

Group practices that promote a sense of awe further emphasize the significance of the group itself. These practices make the actions of the group appear more than mundane; mystery, magic, and miracles surround the group actions. When the leaders "receive directions" from God, as among Mormons and Pentecostals, the directions seem far more awesome than if members had voted on them. Social and symbolic distance also promote a sense of awe. Thus medieval churches used physical barriers (e.g., rood screens) and space to separate the body of the congregation from the central ritual performance. Even today many religious groups have certain sacred spaces in their places of worship where ordinary members cannot routinely go. These practices may not have been deliberately created to generate commitment, but the production of a sense of awe does result in enhancing members' commitment.

Summary

This analysis of the processes of religious socialization, conversion, and commitment illustrates the interrelationship of religious meaning and religious belonging. The individual's meaning system is socially acquired and supported through early socialization and interaction with other believers throughout life. If the individual changes meaning systems, it is through social interaction. And the processes that promote commitment to the meaning system and the group supporting it are fundamentally social processes.

Social factors are important in shaping the individual's religion, and examination of critical periods in the individual's life cycle suggests some of these factors. Early socialization in the context of the family, neighborhood, and ethno-religious community is particularly important in establishing not only the basic beliefs and values but also the connection between the individual's belief system and very identity. Rites of passage to new statuses are often filled with religious significance. Passage to adulthood and marriage illustrate some of the ways in which religion shapes critical moments as the individual takes on a new social identity. Middle age and old age are, however, problematic in this society, and there are no satisfactory transitions into these devalued statuses. The society's secularized conception of time may be an important cause of some of these problems. Evidence about the nature of the interrelationship between the individual's religion and social factors is, however, generally limited either to non-modern examples or to studies of narrowly defined, church-oriented religion. Thus this chapter has only suggested some of the directions that further research into the individual's religion might take.

Conversion is essentially a form of resocialization similar to nonreligious resocialization. Through interaction with believers, the recruit comes to share their world view and takes on a new self consistent with that meaning system. Conversion includes a range of changes: radical transformation of self and world view, identity consolidation, and reaffirmation. Some changes are mere transfers of organizational affiliation and not real conversions of world view and identity. The process of conversion funnels recruits from a general predisposition to conversion, through interaction with group members, to growing identification with the group and its belief system. The conversion process is generally gradual, although it may appear sudden and dramatic because of the way it is symbolized by some individuals or groups.

Commitment mechanisms promote the loyalty and attachment of all members, new converts and old members alike. Groups such as most denominations, which expect only partial commitment of members, typically use less extreme commitment mechanisms than do sectarian groups, which expect members' total commitment and immersion in the life of the group. The process of commitment involves simultaneously the individual's withdrawal from competing allegiances (e.g., by sacrifice) and greater attachment to the group (e.g., by frequent interaction with fellow members). Through these commitment processes, the group builds a firm plausibility structure for its meaning system.

Recommended Readings

Articles and Essays

Erving Goffman. "Characteristics of Total Institutions." *Asylums*. Garden City, N.Y.: Doubleday, 1961, pp. 3–74.

R. Kenneth Jones. "Paradigm Shifts and Identity Theory: Alternation as a Form of Identity Management." *Identity and Religion*, Hans Mol, ed. London: Sage Studies in International Sociology, 1978, pp. 59–82.

James Richardson, ed. *Conversion and Commitment in Contemporary Religion*; issue of *American Behavioral Scientist* 20, 6: 1977, with articles on conversion and commitment in numerous recent movements; reprinted as *Conversion Careers* (Beverly Hills: Sage, 1978).

Books

Leon Festinger, Henry W. Riecken, and Stanley Schachter. *When Prophecy Fails*. New York: Harper & Row, 1956. A fascinating account of a group that received a prophecy of the imminent end of the world.

Rosabeth Moss Kanter. *Commitment and Community*. Cambridge: Harvard University Press, 1972. Using evidence from nineteenth-century American communitarian ventures, this book presents a well-organized theoretical schema for analyzing commitment.

John Lofland. *Doomsday Cult*. Englewood Cliffs, N. J.: Prentice-Hall, 1966. An ethnography of the early stages of American development of a now-famous new religious movement. See also Lofland's article in the *American Behavioral Scientist* issue recommended above.

Benjamin Zablocki. *The Joyful Community*. Baltimore: Penguin, 1971. This study of a modern communal religious group, the Bruderhof, includes a particularly good section on conversion and commitment in the community.

CHAPTER FOUR

Official and Nonofficial Religion

*I*n the United States, the mention of "religion" or "being religious" typically evokes the image of church-oriented religion. When we think of religion, we generally think of Protestantism, Catholicism, and Judaism. When we think of being religious, we tend to locate that religiosity in the social framework of Old First Church, Saint Mary's Church, or Temple Sholom.[1] Church-oriented religion is a prominent and important social form of religion in Western societies, but there are other modes that do not conform to the "official" model of religion.

This chapter contrasts official religion and its characteristic expressions of religiosity with "nonofficial" religion and religiosity. Both of these models illustrate the capacity of religion to provide meaning and belonging. A related topic in this chapter is the difficult problem of how to measure or scientifically explore the quality of an individual respondent's religion and religiosity. The Extended Application at the end of this chapter describes the social definitions of women's roles by both official and nonofficial religions and the concurrent shaping of women's religion and religiousness.

The Official Model of Religion

The development of a specialized official religion distinguishable from popular or folk religion and other nonofficial religious elements is the result of the historical process of institutional differentiation. Earlier religion was relatively diffused throughout all aspects of social life; the practice of religion was relatively unspecialized. Modern religion, by contrast, is characterized by **institutional specialization:** standardization of the world view in a well-defined doctrine, religious roles performed by specialists, and an organization to control doctrinal and ritual conformity, promulgate group teachings, and promote organizational

[1]For sources on official religions in the United States, see the Recommended Readings at the end of this chapter; also see Glazer, 1957; Heilman, 1976; Lavender, 1977; Marty, 1970b; Moberg, 1962; Sklare, 1971; Sklare and Greenblum, 1967; Warner, 1961; Weisberger, 1958; Winter, 1961.

programs (see Luckmann, 1967:66; also Bellah, 1964). Interestingly, this same process of differentiation created the possibility of organized irreligion—the institutional expression and consolidation of beliefs and practices of hostility or indifference toward religion. Organized irreligion (e.g., the Secularist, Positivist, and Ethical movements) closely parallels official models of religion (see Campbell, 1971).

Specialized institutions for religion thus become the focus for societal attention to religion. Each institutionally specialized religion typically consolidates its beliefs, values, and practices into a coherent model. These official models typically include a prescribed doctrine, set of ethical standards, cultic expression, and institutional organization.

Doctrine

The official model of a religion is a coherent and consolidated meaning system, articulated by doctrinal experts (e.g., theologians) and typically promulgated only after official approval. Although church doctrine changes over time, a church can state its official model of religion fairly specifically at any one time: "This is what we stand for." Religions vary as to the extent of doctrinal sophistication and the importance of formal, prescribed doctrines. The Roman Catholic church has a vast, complicated doctrinal system, with some teachings having the weight of dogma (i.e., doctrines to which members are obliged to assent). By contrast, Judaism has no dogma but emphasizes the continual unfolding of religious truths through study of sacred scripture and texts; nevertheless Judaism has some fairly explicit definitions of its shared meaning system.

Ethics

Official religion also characteristically prescribes a set of norms and regulations consistent with the group's doctrine. These obligations for behavior specify what actions are necessary to be a member in good standing. They include ideals toward which members should strive. Simultaneously, official religion usually utilizes specialized religious measures for the regulation and control of conduct so that misconduct may be noted and punished. In religions containing normative prescriptions that are complex, the organization sometimes supports specialized religious courts and ethical specialists to interpret the body of regulations. Other religions, whose ethical norms may be just as strong, rely on informal social control measures.

Cultic Expression

Each religion has a set of observances and devotions by which its meaning system is ritually expressed. Official religion tends to encourage standardized cultic expressions such as a liturgy or formal order of worship. Even less central expressions (e.g., devotions) are often standardized. Such standardized forms of expressing religious beliefs and sentiments include the Roman Catholic "Way of the Cross" and the Eastern Orthodox ritual of kissing ikons. Some religions emphasize spontaneity in cultic expression; even so, however, the religion encourages certain regularized ways of being spontaneously religious. A minister might pray in his or her own words but choose words appropriate to the King James version of the Bible (e.g., "Almighty God, Thou hast showered us with Thy abundance"). Official religion also typically utilizes ritual specialists—priests, ministers, cantors, music directors, organists, choirs, and liturgical experts. Thus official models of religion consolidate and standardize the cultic expression of religion.

Institutional Organization

Official religion typically organizes itself as a specialized association. It develops organizational specialists such as a professional clergy, organizational hierarchies (both lay and clerical) and often a host of auxiliary functionaries (e.g., religious teachers, church librarians, secretaries, program directors, and building service personnel). There are often formal specifications and procedures for membership and jurisdictional boundaries (e.g., parish boundaries). There are programs to be organized—Sunday Schools, "outreach" and "mission" programs, fund raising, youth clubs, study groups, and so on.

Especially important in the institutional organization of religious groups is the form of polity adopted. Polity refers to the arrangements for exercise of legitimate authority in the organization. The three characteristic forms found in most Western religious organizations are episcopal, presbyterian, and congregational polity. Episcopal polity refers to an organizational arrangement in which authority is centralized in a hierarchy (i.e., a pyramid of channels of authority). Thus in the Roman Catholic church, local parishes are served by priests (sometimes hierarchically arranged even in the parish itself) who are responsible to bishops. The bishops place priests in the local parish, and the congregation has no official authority. Similarly the bishops are responsible to the pope, using his delegated authority in their dioceses. Other examples of the episcopal form of polity include Eastern Orthodox churches and Episcopalianism; Methodism has a modified form of episcopal polity. Presbyterian polity is a form that utilizes a representative government by both clergy and laity. The local church is run by its clergy and lay selected representatives. They, in turn, are responsible to a higher authority of elected representatives such as a presbytery, synod, or general assembly (as in Presbyterianism).

The congregational form of polity is characterized by high degrees of autonomy of the local congregation, including the power to call or dismiss clergy (see Elazar, 1976; Harrison, 1959). This form is characteristic of Jewish congregations, Baptists, and the United Church. Denominations with congregational polity are less likely to conform with a uniform doctrine and ethical or ritual standards among congregations than denominations with other kinds of polity. Similarly, as developed further in Chapter 7, individual congregations in denominations with the congregational form of polity can be highly resistant to external pressures for change, ignoring the urgings of national denomination councils and firing change-oriented clergy. For the same reason, however, congregational and presbyterian forms of polity are more receptive than episcopal polity to the initiatives or needs of local congregations.

Individual Religiosity in the Official Model

The specialized religious institution mediates the official model of religion to the individual believer. Thus, for example, being a Presbyterian might be experienced in terms of attending Presbyterian Sunday worship services and Sunday Schools in a particular building of one's congregation; receiving communion in the Presbyterian church and being a member of the committee that washes the communion cups; interacting with Presbyterian clergy; singing in the church choir; having a grandfather who is a member of the Session (i.e., elected Board of Elders); having once memorized but now forgotten the Westminster Confession of faith and answers to the catechism; and learning other Presbyterian beliefs and norms in Sunday School and adult discussion groups or from sermons. In other words, the individual member is socialized into the model of his or her church.

For this reason, individual religiosity in official religion can be described in terms of its conformity to the official model. The individual's beliefs are somehow related to church doctrine, and the individual's ethical standards are measured by conformity to the ethical teachings of the official religion. Cultic expressions of the religion are translated in terms of individual observances and devotions. The individual's relationship to the institutional organization is expressed as membership and participation in that organization (see Luckmann, 1967:74).

Thus it is possible for a sociologist studying an official religion to operationalize—to create a working definition of—individual religiosity in terms of the officially defined model. The Roman Catholic church (especially before Vatican II) used a fairly explicit official model of expected individual religiosity. Thus in his studies of Roman Catholic parishes, Fichter (1951a, 1954) was able to operationalize individual religiosity for research purposes, using criteria such as Mass attendance, reception of communion, sending children to parochial schools, participation in parish activities such as Holy Name Society, and interaction with clergy. This approach to operationalizing the concept of religiosity works, to some extent, *only* because the official model of Roman Catholic religion was precise and mediated to individual members.

Nevertheless we cannot infer that these aspects of official religion account for *why* the individual member participates in any aspect of it. We cannot infer that the nearly 40 percent of Americans who attend religious services each week do so in precise conformity with what the official model of that religion puts forth as the purpose and meaning of those services. One researcher suggests that the typical churchgoer is primarily interested in "friendliness and fellowship, the chance to meet 'good' people and associate with them" (Wood, 1970:1066). Thus although the official model of religion has implications for individual religiosity, there is little indication that all aspects of official religion hold equal importance for each individual believer.

Differences from the Official Model

Official religion, then, is a set of beliefs and practices prescribed, regulated, and socialized by organized, specifically religious groups. These groups set norms of belief and action for their members, and they establish an official model of what it means to be "one of us." Nevertheless the actual religion of the individual member may not correspond very closely to the official model. What is the *operative faith* of the individual? What norms, ritual actions, and beliefs hold priority in the individual's life?

A number of factors bring about this discrepancy between the individual's religion and the official model. One factor is how the individual has been taught and socialized into the official model. Some persons have not learned the official model of their group's religion. The official belief systems of Christian and Jewish groups, for example, generally include a set of moral norms called "the Ten Commandments." One study of Christian church members showed that individual knowledge of the content of these commandments varied widely. Overall, only 55 percent of the Protestant and 74 percent of the Roman Catholic respondents said that they knew the Ten Commandments—that is, the content, not the exact words (Stark and Glock, 1968:144). Many members may not know items of official belief such as catechisms, creeds, and confessions of faith. Furthermore, members vary in how adequately they have internalized the official model. It is one thing to know that one's group holds certain beliefs; it is another to believe them oneself.

Individual members may have incorrect knowledge as evaluated by the official definitions of the belief system. While representatives of religious organizations may decry this misinformation or lack of knowledge, it is an understandable product of socialization. In socialization, the official model is mediated (if taught at all) through other persons who are significant in the child's life: parents, friends, teachers, clergy. The child may be exposed to a relatively incoherent assortment of stories, admonitions, images, threats, and examples.

The official model is often overlaid with other religious themes, perhaps drawn from folk religion, mythology, popular culture, or the teacher's own "misinformed" view of the official model. For example, one woman said: "I was in my thirties before I realized that a lot of the stuff I learned about religion in grade school wasn't the official church teaching. I'm sure the church has some theology about sin and grace, but to this day whenever I hear those words I think of what my religion teacher in fifth grade taught us about good angels whispering in our right ears and bad angels urging us in our left ears." Although official religion is characteristically a coherent, consistent body of beliefs and practices, the individual's version of it is not necessarily coherent or consistent. Individuals vary in how much consistency they expect in their own lives, but many people appear to be comfortable with highly incoherent assortments of beliefs and practices.

Individual members may also deviate from the official model of religion in their priorities, often emphasizing aspects of belief and practice that the official model holds as relatively unimportant. Thus a religious group may emphasize norms against cheating and stealing, whereas an individual member may downplay those norms while emphasizing norms against drinking and gambling.

Sometimes individual members may disagree with the official beliefs and practices. A sizable proportion of American Roman Catholics do not agree with the official church teaching on birth control (see Greeley, 1976). In the 1950s when official national organizations of major Protestant denominations made strong statements about Christian responsibility in the issue of racism, many individual members chose to disagree with these teachings (Hadden, 1969). Similar recent disagreement has occurred in both Protestantism and Roman Catholicism over teachings on homosexuality, women's roles, abortion, war, and divorce. Even less volatile and less current teachings do not receive the full assent of members. How many Presbyterians fully believe the historically central doctrine of predestination (i.e., the belief that God knows and decides beforehand who is destined to salvation or damnation)? Likewise, though belief in a hell is part of official Roman Catholic and most Protestant teaching, only 70 percent of American Roman Catholics and 68 percent of Protestants polled believed in a hell (Alston, 1972:180).

The operative religiosity of individuals may vary considerably in degree. Some people are simply more interested and involved in religion than others. Various religious groups expect different minimal levels of individual religious expression, but even within these groups there is considerable variation. One problem in measuring religiosity is operationalizing the concept to account for all of the different ways of being religious. Just as individuals select various official beliefs and practices with which they agree, so too they vary in their chosen ways of being religious. One expression of religiosity may be church attendance; another, watching a religious TV show at home. For one individual, social activism may be an essential expression of religion; another individual might emphasize interior religiosity to the complete exclusion of social action.

It is therefore difficult to describe individuals' religions merely by the name of the official religion to which they belong. Two Roman Catholics may be as different from each other in their individual operative religions as a Roman Catholic is from a Baptist or Jew.

Measuring Religiosity

In recent years, sociologists have attempted to understand the impact of religion upon society by studying the religious attitudes and beliefs of individuals. They have asked, for example, whether highly religious persons are more or less likely than less religious persons to be prejudiced toward other ethnic, racial, and religious groups. Other studies have correlated individuals' religious attitudes with their attitudes toward work or education. Typically these studies apply the research methods of large-scale opinion surveys to understand religion.

Because we need to know more about the values, attitudes, feelings, and experiences that motivate the individual believer, this emphasis upon understanding individual religiosity is worthwhile. The methods and measures used, however, have serious shortcomings that cannot be overcome by minor refinements. One problematic issue is that most of this research has not been interested in the individual's religion per se but in generalizations about the "sum" religiosity of larger groups (e.g., denominations or ethnic groups). Thus the research does not really try to grasp the total picture of each individual's religion and commitment to it; instead it isolates certain readily measurable aspects of each individual's religion, then lumps these together into a composite picture of the larger group.

The second major problem with attempts to measure religiosity is in creating measurable operational definitions of "religion" and "religiosity." Proceeding from fairly narrow substantive definitions of religion, most measures of individual religiosity define it in terms of the official models of specific organized religions—particularly traditional Protestant Christianity. In these operating definitions, "religion" refers to the respondent's affiliation with an institutionally identifiable belief system (e.g., Greek Orthodox or Seventh Day Adventist). "Religiosity" refers to the intensity of commitment to this belief system, as expressed in institutionally identifiable attitudes or behaviors (e.g., receiving communion or agreeing with the group's moral condemnation of certain actions). As with all methodological approaches, this "way of seeing" is also a "way of not seeing" (Burke, 1935:70). The perspective of official religion focuses the concepts of religion and religiosity but simultaneously makes other modes of religion and religiosity "invisible." Let us now examine some of the most commonly used measures of religiosity.

Unidimensional Measures

Many studies have characterized the individual's religion or religiosity by a single measure. One familiar measure is religious affiliation or preference. A questionnaire may ask the respondent to indicate whether he or she is Protestant, Catholic, Jew, other, or "none." A further refinement of this is specification of the denominational affiliation (e.g., Presbyterian, Southern Baptist, Conservative Jew, Mormon, etc.). These categories then become the basis for broad comparisons of behavior (e.g., college attendance) or attitudes (e.g., approval of desegregation).

Another measure focuses somewhat more on the quality of the individual's religious participation or involvement. The survey may ask "How important is your religion to you in your everyday life?" Or it may seek some quantitative measure of commitment such as frequency of church attendance. Some studies combine several such measures into an index of religiosity; such an index may include frequency of church attendance, frequency of receiving communion, and percent of income donated to the church.

These definitions of religiosity are severely limited, and not all religious groups emphasize such expressions of religiosity as important for their members. Some groups urge their members to tithe a minimum of 10 pecent of their incomes; other groups do not consider tithing a necessary mark of a religious person. Also, individuals differ in their ways of being religious. One person might express religion by meditating regularly, another by attending church, another by reading certain literature, another by participating in a civil rights demonstration. Recognition of these variations led to the construction of multidimensional measures of religiosity.

Multidimensional Measures

Only relatively recently have research designs recognized variations in religiosity. Some studies as early as the 1950s demonstrated important differences in involvement among members of the same religious organization (Fichter, 1951a, 1954). In the 1960s, researchers began to formulate more formal distinctions of dimensions of religiosity (Fukuyama, 1961; Lenski, 1963). The most influential of these is the classification proposed by Glock (1965). He distinguishes five dimensions: experiential, ritualistic, ideological, intellectual, and consequential.

    a. The **experiential dimension** includes feelings or sensations that are considered to involve communication with "divine essence." It refers, for example, to a feeling that one has been saved or healed, a feeling of deep intimacy with the holy, or a sensation of having received a divine revelation of some sort.

    b. The **ritualistic dimension** includes religious practices such as worship, prayer, and participation in certain sacraments.

    c. The **ideological dimension** refers to the content and scope of beliefs to which members of a religious group are expected to adhere.

    d. The **intellectual dimension** encompasses the individual's knowledgeability about the basic tenets of the group's beliefs and sacred scriptures.

    e. The **consequential dimension** includes the effects of religious belief, practice, experience, and knowledge upon the individual's behavior in institutional settings that are not specifically religious (e.g., business, voting, family, and leisure time activities).

If these dimensions are discrete factors, each dimension must be translated into operational (i.e., working) terms in order to measure it. The most serious shortcoming of this process is the quantitative study of individual religiosity. No research has yet defined these dimensions in terms that are not biased toward the orthodox position of certain historic (i.e., traditional Judeo-Christian) expressions of religiosity. In their study of American church members, Stark and Glock's operational definition of these five dimensions illustrates such a bias (Stark and Glock, 1968:22–80). Thus a person who assented to a higher proportion of the following beliefs in an index of the ideological dimension was considered more religious than someone who assented to only some:

    a. unqualified certainty in the existence of God
    b. belief in a personal God
    c. belief in miracles as described in the Bible
    d. belief in life after death
    e. belief in the actual existence of the devil
    f. belief in the divinity of Jesus
    g. belief that a child is born into the world already guilty of sin (i.e., original sin)

By these measures, liberal denominations appear less religious than conservative ones, and liberal members of any denomination appear less religious than conservative members. Devout Quakers would, by these measures, typically score very low on religiosity.

Many other researchers built uncritically upon these multidimensional indices. Most of their working definitions of dimensions of religiosity result in measurements of beliefs *about* these other dimensions rather than actual behavior. Rather than tapping the meaning of ritual to the individual, such scales often ask questions like "Do you feel it is possible for an individual to develop a well-rounded religious life apart from the institutional church?" (See Faulkner and DeJong, 1966.) While answers to questions such as this are interesting in themselves, they hardly measure a person's actual ritual experience. Although statistical analyses of these five scales show them to vary independently of each other, a valid criticism has been raised: Are they perhaps only separate aspects of a single dimension, that of *ideological commitment*? Thus may the belief scales identify some of the content of the individual's ideology, while experiential, ritualistic, intellectual, and consequential scales measure expressions of strength of commitment to that ideology? (See Clayton and Gladden, 1974; Weigert and Thomas, 1969.)

Recognition of the cultural biases of some ideological items tapped in these scales has led Glock and others to formulate parallel measures for emerging religious patterns in America. In an ambitious study of nontraditional religious affiliation in a California community, Glock and his co-workers included several non-Christian options such as Eastern mysticism, astrology, Transcendental Meditation, Satanism, and Yoga (Glock and Bellah, 1976; see also Glock and Wuthnow, 1979; Wuthnow, 1976b). This research asked about religious practices other than specifically Christian ones—whether respondents meditated, for example, and what kinds of techniques they used in meditation (e.g., a mantra, drugs, breathing techniques, prayer, etc.).

Although such studies greatly expand the range of religious beliefs and practices considered, they are nonetheless limited to discrete, identifiable clusters of beliefs. It may not be possible to devise a research instrument to tap all possible religious beliefs, practices, knowledge, and experiences held by any individual in a culture as diverse as America's. Survey research is predicated upon measuring the distribution of opinions, attitudes, or attributes that can be specified in advance (i.e., in wording the questions of the survey). Such a specification is only possible by using the criteria of official religion. A number of features of religion and religiosity in contemporary societies make it problematic to assume that an individual's religion can be adequately described by measuring its correspondence to orthodox official religion (Luckmann, 1973).

Let us now consider some of the ways in which the religion of the individual may differ from official religion.

Nonofficial Religion and Religiosity

Alongside or overlaying official religion is another pattern of religious belief—**nonofficial religion.** Nonofficial religion is a set of religious and quasi-religious beliefs and practices that is not accepted, recognized, or controlled by official religious groups. While official religion is relatively organized and coherent, nonofficial religion includes an assortment of unorganized, inconsistent, heterogeneous, and changeable sets of beliefs and customs (Towler and Chamberlain, 1973). Nonofficial religion is sometimes called "common," "folk," or "popular" religion because it is the religion of ordinary people rather than the product of religious specialists in a separate organizational framework. Only in societies where religion is separated as an institution from other institutional spheres does an official model of religion emerge, leaving elements of belief and custom not accepted as "official" to be carried on outside the religious institution (Luckmann, 1967:66,67). Individuals often practice both the official and common religion simultaneously; others adhere only to official or only to common religious patterns.

"Pop" Versions of Official Religion

Common religion is no single entity, and its elements are diverse. One aspect is a popular version of official religion but completely uncontrolled by official religious organizations. A large body of inspirational literature exists that is nontheological and unrelated to the official religion of its readers, and the religion promulgated in this literature is largely quasi-magical, emphasizing religious techniques. One author of many such books, Dr. Norman Vincent Peale, urges, "Learn to pray correctly, scientifically. Employ tested and proven methods. Avoid slipshod praying" (quoted in Schneider and Dornbusch, 1957:479). A parallel and even more popular source of common religion is inspirational programming on radio and television. Some mass media preachers gain a sufficient following and build up an organization that approximates a cultlike or sectlike group (as described further in Chapter 5). Reverend Ike, for example, has built a successful organization of his media audiences, with regular glossy magazines to advertise the good fortunes of those who followed his prayer plans or used his prayer cloths. Oral Roberts, who began as a popular revivalist and faith healer, developed a large, well-financed, sectlike organization. He has more recently, however, affiliated with an official denomination, and his image has become similar to that of denominational clergy. Also, followers of established religion often simultaneously adhere to popular religion.[2]

The ideas and practices from popular culture religion are widespread. Artifacts of popular religion bear some resemblance to those of official religion: plastic Jesus on the car dashboard, gold-plated crosses on neckchains, bumper stickers proclaiming "I Found It" or "My God Is Alive; Sorry About Yours," plaques, plates, and posters with messages such as "Smile, God Loves You." One shrine of popular religion is Holyland, U.S.A.—a large sculpture garden where busloads of tourists visit various scenes depicting biblical events such as Noah's Ark and the Crucifixion (see the videotape "Welcome to Holyland"; see also Elzey, 1975). Popular religion also includes religious or quasi-religious themes from patriotism or nationalism (explored in detail in Chapter 6). National symbols such as the flag or Statue of Liberty form parts of some individuals' belief systems and are often indistinguishable from elements of official religion.

Superstition and Magic

Another overlay from common religion onto the official model consists of a variety of superstitious and magical beliefs and practices. Some superstitions pertain directly to practices of official religion. Asked why she had all of her babies christened, one woman responded, "Don't know. People have it done. It keeps

---

[2]In my own research, for example, numerous active Roman Catholic respondents also subscribed to Oral Roberts's "seed faith" plan.

them safe like wearing a St. Christopher" (quoted in Towler and Chamberlain, 1973:23). Another somewhat magical use of official religion is stichomancy—the practice of divining or getting a "message" from random opening of the Bible. Similarly quasi-magical attitudes often accompany religious actions. At the end of a healing service observed in a mainline denomination, the minister offered to bless salt and oil for home prayer for healing. With a rustling of brown paper wrappers the congregation opened the spouts of salt boxes and lids of cooking oil bottles so the blessing could "get in." This overlay suggests a difficult methodological problem: how to interpret a situation in which members participate in rituals of official religion with attitudes and motives inconsistent with the official model.

Much superstition is related to more mundane matters and represents an attempt to control or explain one's environment. One study in England found superstitious beliefs and practices to be fairly common. Thus 22 percent of the sample believed in lucky numbers and 18 percent in lucky charms, 15 percent avoided walking under ladders, almost half threw spilt salt over their shoulders, and over 75 percent touched wood for protection. Some superstitious actions were not serious, but a core of 6 to 8 percent of the sample said they became uneasy if they did not perform the appropriate actions. This study found persons who characterized themselves as religious more likely to be superstitious than those characterizing themselves as nonreligious; churchgoing "religious" persons, however, were much less superstitious than nonchurchgoing "religious." This evidence suggests that for some religious persons, official and common religious beliefs and practices become indistinguishably merged but that churchgoing may filter out nonofficial elements of belief (Abercrombie et al., 1970:98, 113; see also Jahoda, 1969, regarding the affinity between belief patterns of superstition and official religion).

The Paranormal and Occult

Other beliefs and practices concern **paranormal occurrences** (i.e., events outside the usual range of experiences). Belief in paranormal occurrences is fairly widespread. Approximately one-fourth of Americans believe they have seen a ghost or spirit of the dead (Greeley, 1975:36). Another study (McCready and Greeley, 1976:132) reported that 27 percent of respondents felt they had undergone an experience of being really in touch with someone who had died. In the same study 59 percent reported experiences of déjà vu (i.e., the sense of having already seen a place where they had never been before), 58 percent reported experiences of ESP (extrasensory perception), and 24 percent reported clairvoyance (i.e., seeing distant events as they were happening). Some persons attribute great significance to paranormal experiences; whole belief systems (e.g., Spiritualism) allocate special meaning to such experiences. Other persons who have had such out-of-the-ordinary experiences recognize them as unusual but place no special interpretation upon them.

Extrascientific explanations and techniques are also part of common religion. These are ways of interpreting and manipulating the natural and social environment that are not accepted by this culture's official religious or scientific groups. Included are beliefs in astrology, hexing, palmistry, numerology, amulets and charms, water divining, UFOs, divination (by Tarot, pendulum, rod, I Ching, entrails), and white and black witchcraft. A major focus of extrascientific practices is healing (e.g., warding off the "evil eye," divining causes of illness, conjuring, herbal cures, and enlisting the aid of the spirits for curing or causing illness). Some of these beliefs derive from the folk traditions of various ethnic groups in America (see, for example, studies reported in Crapanzano and Garrison, 1977; also Roebuck and Quan, 1976). Some evidence exists, however, that marginal medical beliefs and practices are not uncommon among middle-class, relatively well-educated persons. Marginal medicine often overlaps the official model of religion in many religious groups, as exemplified by miraculous and faith healing. Some of these beliefs and practices are organized into cultlike or sectlike groups; others are highly individualistic and are transmitted by separate practitioners or anonymous media such as magazines.

Beliefs and practices pertaining to paranormal occurrences and extrascientific explanations and techniques are part of what is generally termed the "occult." **Occultism** is a set of claims that contradict established (i.e., official) scientific or religious knowledge. This focus upon the anomalous makes the occult seem strange and mysterious (Truzzi, 1974a:246). Some observers have suggested that the 1960s and 1970s were periods of occult revival in American popular culture (Marty, 1970a; Truzzi, 1972). The esoteric and occult have long been part of countercultural currents in Western societies. Many wide-ranging innovations have begun in the "seedbed" of the esoteric, and modern medicine, chemistry, and psychology owe much to the esoteric sciences of earlier times (Tiryakian, 1974:272,273).

Although some of the recent interest in esoteric beliefs and practices may be merely countercultural experimentation or fads, many people take their belief in the occult seriously. Witchcraft exemplifies beliefs and practices followed by adherents with varying degrees of seriousness and involvement. At one end of the spectrum are people for whom witchcraft is a fad or form of entertainment. Others believe in witchcraft and therefore seek occasional spells for health, protection, and success; they might also ascribe special importance to astrological events such as solstices and eclipses. At the other end of the spectrum are people who are fully involved in the beliefs and practices of witchcraft, belong to a group (i.e., coven), and organize their lives around witchcraft as a counterofficial religion.

There is a distinction between white and black magic. White witches employ their magic for only beneficial purposes such as healing. They often emphasize the continuity of their tradition with the medieval European white witches—"wise women" and men who combined pre-Christian symbolism and lore. It is not uncommon for white witches also to belong to church groups of official religion. One interesting contemporary development of witchcraft and neopaganism has been the adoption of some of their symbols and organization for the expression of feminism. Some women are proud of the deviant heritage that the white witch represents (Culpepper, 1978). Practitioners of black magic use their powers for evil as well as good ends. They believe they have allied themselves with the forces of evil (i.e., Satan), from which they obtain power and direction. Both strains of witchcraft are practiced in organized groups but may also be practiced by single individuals (Alfred, 1976; Bainbridge, 1978; Truzzi, 1974b).

One study of a Satanist group found some interesting therapeutic consequences of the group's beliefs and practices. The rituals enabled members to modify their formerly maladaptive behavior and thus be more effective in their social lives. One young man overcame his fear and anxiety about women through group erotic rituals and "love magic"—by which he also incidentally learned good grooming and how to make himself socially presentable. A recurring theme in the magic of this Satanist group was the gaining of personal power. Satanist beliefs and rituals enabled members to overcome their sense of powerlessness, victimization, or manipulation by other individuals or uncontrollable forces. Both black and white witchcraft offer their believers a way of interpreting experiences and events, a way of coping with the ambiguities and contradictions of everyday life, and a way of organizing life experiences—all of which may indeed have the effect of giving believers a greater sense of power and control (Moody, 1971; 1974).

Covens and "churches" of witchcraft are examples of a larger category of esoteric groups, the secret societies. Secret societies have long been a part of nonofficial religion. Mystery cults, kabbalistic groups, Freemasonry, and Rosicrucianism exemplify their variety. Mystery and awe surround the esoteric knowledge protected by the secret society, and initiation rituals symbolize admission of the member to each level of secret knowledge. The protection of this secrecy promotes the solidarity of the group (Simmel, 1906; Tiryakian, 1974:266, 267). Seldom is there any clear border between secret societies that are overtly religious and those that are not specifically religious. Similarly some religious sects or cults (e.g., the Divine Light Mission) are comparable to secret societies because they are organized around a *gnosis* (i.e., special knowledge).

Another strand of esoteric culture that is a much more familiar part of common religion is **astrology**, a set of beliefs and practices predicated upon the idea that impersonal forces in the universe influence social life on earth. Believers try to read and interpret zodiacal signs (e.g., the position of the stars at the time of one's birth) in order to predict outcomes of the influence of those forces, to choose the best moment for certain actions or the best probable course of action, and to discern when humans bear responsibility or blame for certain outcomes. Under the general category of astrology fall a wide variety of beliefs and practices ranging from highly sophisticated, complex speculations to pop versions such as newspaper horoscope columns (Fischler, 1974).

Astrological beliefs and practices are widespread in America. According to one survey, 22 percent of the population believes that astrological predictions are correct. Knowledge of zodiacal signs and general interest in horoscopes is even more common (Gallup Poll, 1976a:25–27). Another estimate suggests that approximately 10 million Americans are fully committed adherents, with an additional 40 million involved at lower degrees of commitment (cited in Wuthnow, 1976a). Although some of the symbols and imagery of astrology were used by the 1960s youth culture (e.g., the song "Age of Aquarius" in the musical *Hair*), belief in astrology is spread across all age categories. One study found that although young people were somewhat more likely to know about astrology and to be interested in it, a higher percentage of older persons were actually committed to astrology (Wuthnow, 1976a:159).

The nature of belief in astrology illustrates the methodological difficulty of studying nonofficial religion. Astrological beliefs are widespread, significant parts of many people's world views. Some people hold them in combination with official religious beliefs; for others, they are substitutes for official religion. There is no "church" of astrology. Although there are some individual astrological practitioners, most adherents learn their beliefs and practices through relatively anonymous media—books, newspapers, magazines. Some evidence suggests that, like superstition, commitment to astrology is strongest among traditionally "religious" persons who are not involved in official religion (Wuthnow, 1976a:166).

Interpreting Nonofficial Religion

It would be a mistake to view nonofficial religion as a vestige of rural or folk religiosity. Although some elements of common religion (e.g., root doctors and herbalists) are kept alive by distinct rural or recently rural subcultural groups, other aspects of nonofficial religion are characteristic of urban mass society. Astrology is more prominent in an urban milieu than in a rural one (Fischler, 1974:287). Furthermore, some items of nonofficial religion have been borrowed from earlier folk religions but given new significance (e.g., white witchcraft).

One interpretation suggests that modern (especially urban) society is increasingly characterized by a new mode of religiosity, in which individuals select components of their meaning systems from a wide assortment of religious representations. But while traditional representations from official religion may be among the components selected, other elements are drawn from popular culture—newspaper advice columns, popular inspirational literature, lyrics of popular music, the Playboy philosophy, "women's magazine" versions of popular psychology, horoscopes, night school courses on meditation techniques, and so on (Luckmann, 1967:103–106). This interpretation may somewhat overstate the contrast of this eclectic religiosity with that of earlier times; it is entirely probable that earlier generations held widely varying versions of official religion, melding together combinations of folk beliefs, superstition, pagan customs, and misinformed interpretations of the official model of religion to form individual meaning systems. The sharp contrast between official and nonofficial religion is probably itself a product of relatively recent social processes by which society has come to define religion as the domain of official religious institutions, and by which religious organizations have articulated their distinctiveness from popular religion.

The complex threads woven together to comprise the individual's operative religion make it difficult to describe that religion by reference to any single model such as an official religion to which the person may belong. Thus the religion of a person who is a member and occasional attender of an Episcopalian church may simultaneously include orthodox Episcopalian beliefs and practices, popular religious items gleaned from inspirational literature and television, patriotic piety, popular psychology from *Reader's Digest*, careful attention to certain superstitious practices, pieces of astrological advice, and beliefs and techniques learned in an adult course on psychic healing. This amalgam of beliefs and practices is not at all unusual.[3] Evidence on the distribution of nonofficial religious beliefs and practices shows that many adherents are also adherents of official religion. Only a small portion of nonofficial religion is practiced in lieu of official religion.

Merely listing the elements of a person's religion does not adequately describe it. We also need to know which beliefs and practices are central and which are peripheral. Perhaps psychic beliefs are very important to one individual, but astrological beliefs are relatively unimportant. Likewise we need to know when the individual applies which beliefs and practices. The believer may turn to official religion to help socialize children but seek nonofficial religious help for healing a chronic back problem. We need more information about the effective religion of individuals in its complexity and richness.

Extended Application: Women's Religion and the Social Definition of Gender Roles

As we have seen, the individual's religion is a personally meaningful combination of beliefs, values, and practices that is usually related to the world view of a larger group into which that individual has been socialized.[4] In socialization, the individual typically receives many of these beliefs, values, and practices from representatives of the larger group such as parents and teachers. Much of this received meaning system becomes internalized—that is, made a part of the individual's own way of thinking about self and others. The meaning system received by the individual includes a number of beliefs, images, and norms about that group's definitions of maleness and femaleness. All religions have addressed the theme of human sexuality and gender roles because sexuality is a potent force in human life and because gender is, in most societies, a major factor in social stratification.

This analysis will focus first upon how women's religion influences their gender roles and identities, illustrating some of the concepts in Chapter 3 on the individual's religion. A similar application could be drawn for men as males, showing how their gender roles are linked with religion, although this application is not pursued here.

Second, this analysis will illustrate why focusing only on official religion and religiosity is sometimes misleading. As religion became a differentiated institutional sphere, many of women's religious roles and expressions were excluded from official religion and, if continued at all, were kept alive in nonofficial forms such as healing cults, popular religiosity, mediumship, witchcraft, and spiritual midwifery. We need to examine the structural bases for women's status; official religious institutions have historically epitomized the structural and ideological

[3]This example is, in fact, drawn from my own research, in which many respondents described these and more elements of belief and practices.

[4]This extended Application exemplifies concepts in both Chapters 3 and 4.

suppression of women. The religious legitimation of their gender role, then, raises some interesting questions about women's religiosity. Do they come to think of themselves as the official model of their religion portrays them? Impressive historical evidence exists that nonofficial religion is one vehicle for women's assertion of a different religious role. A related question is whether official religions are capable of changing to legitimate and express gender equality even if they were to adopt these goals.

Gender Role Definitions

The definitions of maleness and femaleness are culturally established. On the basis of these definitions, a group develops and encourages certain social differences between men and women. U.S. society expects and encourages little boys to be more active and aggressive than little girls; little girls are expected and encouraged to be more polite, passive, and nurturant. In socialization, males and females are taught their culturally assigned **gender roles**—the social group's expectations of behaviors, attitudes, and motivations "appropriate" to males or females (Davidson and Gordon, 1979:11–13). Historically religion has been one of the most significant sources of these cultural definitions of gender roles; and religion has been a potent legitimation of these distinctions.

Through socialization, the group's definitions of appropriate women's roles become part of the individual woman's self-definition. She evaluates herself in terms of these definitions: "I am a good girl/daughter/woman/mother/wife." The group's definitions of gender roles are subtly interwoven into the individual's learned "knowledge" about the social world. They are embodied in the language and imagery of the group and thus indirectly shape the members' thought patterns. The culture's use of words such as "bitch," "slut," "sweetie," "doll," "housewife," and "mother" has strong evaluative connotations. These words imply qualities that some people attribute to women and for which there are no obvious male equivalents. Numerous words (e.g., "slut") exist for promiscuous women; there are no equivalent words for promiscuous men. Similarly a man who is said to "father" a child performs a single biological act; a woman who "mothers" a child provides continuing nurturant care. The language embodies the different standards of the society for men's and women's roles (Lakoff, 1975). In learning the group's language, the individual internalizes these images and symbols. Specifically religious symbols and images also shape the individual's gender role concept.

While both men and women belong to the same official religions, the individual's religion is not necessarily a small carbon copy of the group's entire official stance. Women's versions of a certain religion are probably very different from men's versions; a woman may focus on those aspects of the group's world view that speak to her social situation. Thus an Orthodox Jewish man's personal religion might focus upon his public ritual roles (e.g., carrying the Torah and forming part of a minyan, i.e., the ten men necessary for a prayer gathering to be official). He might emphasize the intellectual development, discussion of sacred texts, and careful application of religious law expected of men in the Orthodox community. Women, by contrast, have few ritual duties (e.g., the ritual bath after menstruation, making the Sabbath loaf, and lighting Sabbath candles). Their religion is more likely to be focused upon the home, in instructing the very young, and in enabling the men of the home to participate in their public religious roles. The very meaning of being Jewish is thus probably very different for the men than for the women. Central religious activities (e.g., attending Sabbath services at the synagogue and family worship around the Sabbath candles) also probably mean something different to each sex.[5]

A woman's religious experience and what she holds religiously most important are qualitatively different from men's religious experience and focus. Women's religion is nevertheless shaped heavily by the larger religious group because it is not a separate religion. The larger group attempts to form the individual's role through its teachings, symbols, rituals, and traditions. Thus in the example of the Orthodox community, women's religion is strongly influenced by men's ideas of what a properly religious woman should do and be. Men interpret the Law and run the congregation and the religious courts. In most historic (i.e., official) religions, women have had considerably less power than men in establishing social definitions of appropriate gender roles. In the Roman Catholic church, at least since the time of the early church, men have held all significant positions of authority to set and interpret religious norms, practices, and beliefs. The beliefs, ritual expressions, norms, and organizational structure of official religion, in short, effectively subordinate women.

The religious legitimation of women's roles is very similar to the religious legitimation of other caste systems. As shown further in Chapter 7, religion is often used to explain why certain social inequalities exist. These explanations justify both the privileges of the upper classes or castes and the relative nonprivileges of the lower ones. A **caste system** is a social arrangement in which access to power and socioeconomic benefits are fixed, typically from birth, according to certain ascribed characteristics of the individual. In the Hindu caste system, an individual of the highest caste has certain permanent prerogatives, benefits, and responsibilities merely by virtue of having been born into that caste. Medieval feudalism was a similar system, in which individuals born into a given socioeconomic stratum could move up or down relative to others of that stratum but could not aspire to the power privileges of higher social strata.

Modern societies typically emphasize individual achievements as a basis of socioeconomic status more than traditional societies; however, elements of caste are still important. Race is one ascribed characteristic that still figures into socioeconomic status in most modernized countries (the situation of racial castes in the United States is developed in Dollard, 1949). A black man might aspire to become a doctor (i.e., an achieved status) and rise in status relative to other blacks, but his ascribed status (i.e., race) interferes significantly in his chances of achieving a high status relative to white doctors.

Gender is another major basis of caste in modern societies. Women are generally excluded from access to power and socioeconomic status available to men. The expectation that housework is "women's work" exemplifies women's

---

[5]There is little empirical evidence about exactly how men and women experience religious rituals and events, but some clues appear in Myerhoff, 1978:207–241. Some parallels may also be drawn from studies of how different racial castes, socioeconomic strata, and ethnic groups differently experience similar religious rituals and belief systems.

caste status. No matter how great a woman's achievement in art, business, or scholarship, the society still expects that she is the one responsible, by virtue of her gender, for the menial tasks of housecleaning. Such gender role expectations have socioeconomic implications. Employers often assume that since men who live with women are not expected to do similar amounts of work at home, women will not have as much time and energy to devote to the job; this expectation then becomes the justification for denying women opportunities for economic achievement (Glazer-Malbin, 1976). Women's status in most religious groups is also circumscribed by caste. Gender is far more important than theological or spiritual qualifications in determining whether an individual can perform certain rituals such as carrying the Torah or consecrating the communion elements.

Caste status confers necessary, but not sufficient, advantages to men's chances for recognition, power, and prestige. Not all men obtain these privileges in the social system, but maleness is virtually a prerequisite for them. Men's superior caste status does not necessarily make life comfortable and pleasurable for all individual men. Some men also suffer exploitation and discrimination—but not because of their gender. Religiously legitimated caste distinctions thus do not empower all men; they do, however, disempower all women by virtue of their gender identity (see Ruether, 1975, for an analysis of sexism as a prototype of domination in Western society).

Religious Legitimation of Caste

Symbolism and Myth. Religion contributes to, or legitimates, a caste system in a number of ways. Often religious symbolism embodies a caste-stratification system. It may depict the higher deities as male and the lower deities (or even negative spiritual forces) as female. The Hindu goddess Kali represents "female illusion," symbolizing in the story of Shiva's entanglement with her the eternal struggle that men must wage against the evils of orientation toward material existence (Daly, 1973; Hoch-Smith and Spring, 1978:4).

Similar distinctions are embodied in the language of religious literature and ritual. The language of the Bible lends itself to caste distinctions between men and women (Russell, 1976). Similarly the words of the Mass imply not only the maleness of God, but also the maleness of "his" saved; the ritual words say that Christ's blood was shed for "all men." Efforts to have the wording changed to gender-neutral terms (e.g., "all people") have recently been rejected by American Roman Catholic bishops (see *New York Times*, Dec. 16, 1979). The language of Orthodox Jewish prayer makes gender caste distinctions even more explicit. Daily morning prayer includes "Praised are you, O Lord our God, King of the Universe, who has not created me a woman." Conservative Jews have changed this wording to "Praised are you, O Lord our God, King of the Universe, for making me an Israelite"; whereas Reformed Jews do not use this blessing at all (Priesand, 1975:57–60).

Creation stories in male-dominated cultures often assign to women the responsibility for the presence of evil or the troubles of the present world. In these myths, women's presumed characteristics of sexual allure, curiosity, gullibility, and insatiable desires are often blamed for both the problems of humankind and for women's inferior role. The Hebrew myth of Lilith describes that the Lord formed both the first man and the first woman from the ground. The first woman, Lilith, was equal to Adam in all ways, and she refused what he wanted her to do (including his sexual demands). In response to Adam's complaints, the Lord then created Eve from Adam's rib, thus making her inferior and dependent. In one version of the story, Lilith persuaded Eve to eat from the Tree of Knowledge; thus both the "good" woman through her gullibility and the "bad" woman through her wiliness and willfulness brought about the expulsion of humankind from the Garden of Eden (see Daly, 1978:86; Goldenberg, 1974).

In general, Christianity, Judaism, and (to a lesser extent) Islam and official Buddhism allowed that women were, in principle, equal to men before God, even though they were socially unequal. Thus unlike other religions of their time, these religions held that women might aspire to salvation or spiritual perfection as much as men. This idea was not only revolutionary but also quite tenuous, however; eight centuries after the founding of Christianity, church authorities continued to express doubts about whether the souls of women were equal to those of men (Weber, 1963:105; see also Carmody, 1979).

Moral Norms. Religion typically creates or legitimates the **moral norms** that define what is appropriate to male and female gender roles. Thus each culture has different ideas about appropriate clothing for males and females and religious norms of modesty often give these concepts a moral connotation. Earlier Christian missionaries in Polynesia and Africa introduced different norms for clothing (especially for women) to the native peoples not merely because they thought Western customs of dress superior but especially because, according to their moral norms, the natives' state of dress or undress was sinful.

Historically, religious moral norms have been very important in defining the appropriate gender behavior of men and women. Many moral norms of religious groups are gender-specific (i.e., separate expectations for women and men). Religion shaped norms pertaining to sexual behavior (e.g., regarding premarital and extramarital sexual activity). It influenced norms of dress, physical activities, entertainments, and drink. Religion also legitimated gender distinctions in work roles, home responsibilities, childcare responsibilities, education, marriage responsibilities, political responsibilities, and legal status.

Organization. Religious organization is also a framework that supports gender caste systems. Access to positions of authority and to central ritual and symbolic roles (e.g., the priesthood) is limited or denied to women in most historic religions. Control of ritual and symbolic roles is an important source of social as well as "spiritual" power. Women's lack of power is often symbolized and communicated through their inferior ritual status (see Wallace, 1975).

Ritual Expression. Ritual and symbolic roles (e.g., the role of celebrant of the Mass or reader of the Torah) have become the focus of some women's dissatisfaction with their religion's treatment of women because these roles are important symbols of power and status. Most official religions have allotted women a ritual position in the home. Women light Sabbath candles, lead family rosary, arrange family altars, participate in family Bible readings and mealtime grace, and lead young children in their prayers. Women are typically responsible for arranging the observance of religious holidays in the home, including keeping a kosher kitchen at Passover, preparing feast and fast meals, and bringing home blessed palms and holy water for home use. These ritual activities are seen as consistent with her gender roles as mother and homemaker.

In public rituals women's traditional roles have been clearly subordinate. Men have traditionally held all important leadership and symbolic roles; women were allowed to be present (under certain circumstances) but silent. Women and children were historically segregated in the congregation, sitting in separate pews or separate parts of the room from men. Sometimes they were further hidden by screens or veils. One explanation of these arrangements is that they were intended to prevent women's presence from distracting men. Another explanation is that since women are not regarded as real *persons* in the central action, they are merely allowed to observe as unobtrusively as possible. Whatever the historical background, the segregation and veiling of women clearly communicated their inferior status (Borker, 1978). In many religious groups, women were not allowed in certain sacred places (e.g., on the altar platform or behind the screen where central ritual actions occurred). Most religious groups traditionally held that women required special purification after menstruation or childbirth before they could return to participate in group worship or key rituals (e.g., receiving communion).

Religious groups are inherently conservative because they base their beliefs and practices upon the tradition or scripture produced in an earlier era. Thus Christian groups often justify their exclusion of women from central ritual roles by reference to Saint Paul's views of the proper place of women:

> I desire then that in every place the men should pray, lifting holy hands without anger or quarreling; also that women should adorn themselves modestly and sensibly in seemly apparel, not with braided hair or gold or pearls or costly attire but by good deeds, as befits women who profess religion. Let a woman learn silence with all submissiveness. I permit no woman to teach or to have authority over men; she is to keep silent. For Adam was formed first, then Eve; and Adam was not deceived, but the woman was deceived and became a transgressor. Yet woman will be saved through bearing children, if she continues in faith and love and holiness, with modesty (1 Tim. 2:8–15, RSV).

Similar texts exist in other historic religious traditions. Although the Buddha's approach to women's roles was revolutionary relative to Hindu tradition (e.g., he allowed women to become monks and considered them capable of aspiring to spiritual perfection), he prescribed a greatly inferior role for them. When his favorite disciple Ānanda asked him why women should not be given the same rank and rights as men in public life, the Buddha replied, "Women, Ānanda, are hot-tempered; women, Ānanda, are jealous; women, Ānanda, are envious; women, Ānanda, are stupid" (cited in Schweitzer, 1936: 95).

Changing Religious Roles for Women. Acceptance of changes in religious roles for women frequently hinges upon whether a group accepts religious traditions as literal truths and divinely ordained. Groups that emphasize orthodoxy to literally interpreted religious traditions are resistant to any kind of change. Thus Orthodox Judaism, Eastern Orthodoxy, some strains of Roman Catholicism, orthodox Islam, and fundamentalist Protestantism generally oppose changing the ritual and symbolic roles of women. Other religious groups interpret their traditions or scriptures differently. Thus some groups believe that Saint Paul's restrictions, as previously quoted, are merely the product of his culture's gender role distinctions rather than part of the central message of the Christian tradition. Generally those religious groups that are least open to change in women's roles are also more conservative toward other social changes as well. A group's approach to defining women's roles merely reflects its general attitude about the relationship of its tradition to the conditions of modern society. (We will further describe these diverse stances in Chapter 5.)

Thus the religious heritage of a group does not determine its arrangements. Many contemporary religious groups have integrated women more into the central ritual actions; most Protestant and Reformed Jewish congregations allow laywomen the same privileges as laymen. Roman Catholic and Conservative Jewish congregations are more divided in their treatment of laywomen. There is some resistance in Roman Catholic churches to allowing laywomen to serve as lectors, altar servers, and Eucharistic ministers (who distribute communion, especially to homebound and hospitalized parishioners). Similar controversy exists in Conservative Jewish congregations over whether to allow girls to have the full equivalent of the boys' bar mitzvah (i.e., admitting women to central lay ritual roles).

The issue of the ordination of women is the most controversial because of its great symbolic importance and because the role of the clergy is more powerful than lay roles. The significance of the ordination of women is that it presents an alternative image of women and an alternative definition of gender roles. Thus the ordination of women has an impact upon lay people as well as clergy. Nevertheless the experience of women who have been ordained so far (e.g., in the Presbyterian and United Methodist churches and in Reformed Judaism) is far from equality. Women are underemployed, paid lower salaries, and are less likely to be considered for the better positions. A church may employ a woman as "assistant minister" with special responsibility for youth programs. Although she may occasionally lead worship services, she is not seen as having an important leadership or decision-making role; being in charge of youth activities is consistent with traditional roles of women (Verdesi, 1976).

Power and Sexuality

Evidence from relatively simple societies suggests that religious distinctions between males and females accompanies social distinctions between them, especially in the division of labor. An interplay of power is involved in establishing social inequalities. Religion and human sexuality are both important sources of power, partly because of the mystery, awe, and intensity of the experiences they engender. Those who possess religious power in a social group frequently attempt to control the use of sexual power because they view it as a threat to their power base. On the individual level likewise, many religions view the use of sexual power as diminishing or distracting from spiritual or religious power. The regimen of the 3HO movement (Happy-Healthy-Holy —an American version of Sikh/Hindu religion) severely restricts the frequency of sexual intercourse of members, not because members believe there is anything intrinsically wrong with intercourse but because sexual activity is believed to drain the individual's spiritual energy (Gardner, 1978:120–133; Tobey, 1976).

Female sexuality has historically been perceived as a source of dangerous power to be feared, purified, controlled, and occasionally destroyed by men. General ideas of carnal female sexuality have existed for centuries. Some Western cultural forms of these ideas include images of the enchantress, the evil seductress, the movie queen, and the prostitute. Other cultural images of dangerous female power include the witch, the nagging wife, and the overpowering mother (Hoch-Smith and Spring, 1978:3).

There are several plausible hypotheses for such emphasis on the powers of female sexuality. Douglas (1966) suggests that female sexuality is perceived by males as dangerous and impure because it symbolically represents females' power to counteract the dominance of men. Societies in which there is ambiguity about the legitimate sources of male dominance over females are more likely to develop beliefs in sexual pollution by females than are societies in which women's position is unambiguous; that is, if formal and informal social power is unambiguous (whether or not a society has established a subordinate position for women), men are less likely to fear sexual pollution. Fear of female sexuality is particularly characteristic of societies in which male dominance over females is a primary feature of social organization. The Pygmies, for example, have a division of labor and power structure in which gender is relatively unimportant and have little concern over sexual pollution (Friedl, 1975; Sacks, 1974).

Douglas (1966) cites the contrasting example of the Lele tribe of Zaire. The men of this tribe use women as something of a currency of power, by which they claim and settle disputes. They fight over women and use their dominance over women as a symbol of their status relative to other men. Women of the tribe challenge total male dominance by playing off one man against another and by manipulating men. The men of the Lele have considerable fear of pollution concerning sex and menstrual blood. Women are considered dangerous to male activities and contact or intercourse with a menstruating woman is believed to be contaminating. Fear of the power of female sexuality is related to the disruptive role that women sometimes play, upsetting the order of a male-dominated system of rewards and privileges, in the society. Female sexuality is therefore symbolized as chaotic, disordering, and evil.

Sexuality and Religious Images of Women

The theme of sexual pollution is prevalent in more developed, historic religions as well. The dominant religious images of women in Western societies are built upon a dualistic image of female sexuality: The evil side is the temptress/seducer/polluter, and the approved side is the virgin/chaste bride/mother. Religiously approved roles for women are rather narrowly limited to expressions of these images and are defined and legitimated by reference to Scripture, tradition, and role models (e.g., biblical women or saints). Approved roles emulate the motherhood of a biblical Sarah or Mary, the wifely faithfulness of a Rebekah or Saint Elizabeth of Hungary, or the virginal chastity of Mary or Saint Agatha (souces of female images in the Judeo-Christian heritage are explored in essays in Ruether, 1974; see also Clark and Richardson, 1977; Hyman, 1973).

The narrowly sexual base of these dominant symbols of femaleness contrasts dramatically with representations of men in ritual and imagery. Whether a man is a virgin matters little in his religious status or participation in ritual. Women are represented as one-dimensional characters in ritual and imagery; their images are based almost exclusively on sexual function (Hoch-Smith and Spring, 1978:2–7). The Roman Catholic church honors a number of both female and male saints by dedicating the Masses of certain days to their memory and commemoration of their particular virtues. Men are remembered as martyrs, popes, bishops, doctors of the church (i.e., recognized scholars and teachers), kings, abbots, and confessors of the faith (i.e., typically missionaries). Women are remembered as virgins, virgin martyrs, martyrs, holy women, and queens. Saint Agatha is one woman so commemorated because she was tortured and killed for resisting the sexual advances of the Roman governor. The prayer said on a virgin martyr's feast day reads: "O God, one of the marvelous examples of your power was granting the victory of martyrdom even to delicate womanhood" (Maryknoll Fathers, 1957:807; recent changes have altered the significance of these commemorations but not the relative treatment of men and women). Even women renowned for their organizational skills, intellectual ability, literary accomplishments, and spirituality (e.g., Saint Theresa of Avila, a famous mystic who also brought about the reform of her order and administered its convents) are venerated as "virgins."

Women's Religious Identity
Sense of Self-worth. Such imagery serves to reinforce the distinctions of the caste system. On the one hand, it places some value on "good" women's roles. Such symbolism can enhance the individual's sense of self-worth by showing her existence as part or imitative of some larger reality. She may think, "Although my position is lowly, it is part of something bigger"—a larger cosmic picture. One Christian writer advised women to hold themselves in more esteem. She suggested: "So as you go about your daily schedule, try reminding yourself about the Lord's point of view: 'Here is the beloved of the Lord playing with her children,' or 'Here is the beloved of the Lord sitting down at the desk' " (Morgan, 1976:11). Religion often explicitly links spiritual rewards with the fulfilling of caste obligations. A Hindu woman learns that she will be rewarded in the next life with a higher status (perhaps as a man) if she obediently fulfills the role requirements of a woman in this life. Similarly Christian women are urged by New Testament authors to be submissive to their husbands, thus fulfilling the proper order (in an analogy of the relationship between the body and the head).

On the other hand, while the religious legitimation of women's roles gives meaning to their subordinate position, it does not necessarily make them happy or give them a positive identity. In the Sinhalese religion in Sri Lanka, for example, both the Buddhist doctrine and the folk religious imagery describe women as vehicles for impermanence and sorrow. The law of karma holds that all actions and thoughts have results in the future, including future rebirths of the individual. The desire for life and the illusions of the world perpetuate rebirths and thus sufferings. Suffering refers not only to pain but also to the imperma-nence, emptiness, and insubstantiality of this existence. Buddha taught that escape from this suffering is possible only by detachment from desire, especially for life in this world.

The Buddhist imagery of women portrays them as particularly caught in this web of rebirth. Because women represent birth, they are themselves a symbol of the force of karma that maintains suffering in the world. They are also seen as the source of men's karma because they are among the things that men most desire. Yet women's desirability (i.e., sex appeal) is as impermanent and illusory as the rest of this world. Thus women are especially entangled in the web of karma and have greater difficulty detaching themselves (AmaraSingham, 1978). In Bud-dhism, as in Western religions, women are used to symbolize to men and women alike the undesirable qualities of human existence. Women represent suffering and evil.

We know very little about the actual impact of these perspectives upon women's identities. Such imagery and symbolism surely influence how a woman feels about herself. Does she, by participating in such a religion and culture, come to perceive herself as inferior and impure, more prone to sin, and a cause of males' sin and suffering? If participation in such rituals and symbols does not lower a woman's self-image, it must be because she is able to separate herself from them or experience this part of religion in some unofficial way.

At the same time, however, religion has traditionally provided women with positive roles and images (albeit severely limited ones), which bring reward and recognition in their fulfillment. For a woman to aspire to achievements in men's arenas would be deviant and punished by the social group. But she may aspire to achievements in women's spheres with no competition from men and be re-warded. These values, too, are internalized. The woman who is successful in fulfilling the mother role comes to perceive herself positively in those terms. She feels good about herself because she has achieved a desired status or has per-formed valued roles.

In Victorian society, the cultural and religious legitimations of motherhood and women's role in the home achieved a new synthesis. The Victorian ideal of womanhood, as reflected in women's magazines and public statements in the nineteenth century, was one of "piety, purity, submissiveness, and domesticity" (Welter, 1966, part I).[6] The emerging capitalist-industrial society of the nineteenth century made both the home and religion increasingly marginal to the arenas of power and production. Ideological responses of many religious organizations and revivalists to this privatization struck a responsive chord among middle-class women who were enmeshed in the privatization of the home. An "evangelical domesticity" resulted that emphasized the home and women as the primary vehicles of redemption. The rhetoric of preaching and the themes of gospel

---

[6]The instance of Victorian gender roles illustrates the fact that men's roles too are often limiting and burdensome. In this case, men were given the full burden of providing for the family by work away from the "comforts of home." The moral expectations of the husband/father as sole provider for a family are relatively recent in Western history.

hymns of this period portrayed the home as the bastion of tranquillity in a turbulent world. Woman's image was that of the keeper of this refuge who, through her piety and purity, was the foremost vehicle of redemption, in opposition to the aggressiveness and competition of the public sphere (Sizer, 1979). Thus the religious ideology of evangelical domesticity celebrated the privatization of the home and women's roles, further reinforcing the caste distinctions between men and women. At the same time, it enhanced this narrow role in women's eyes by claiming redemptive significance for it.

Sanctions for Deviance. The religious definition of gender roles is supported by religious sanctions (i.e., punishments) for deviance from them. Men as well as women are subject to negative sanctions for failure to fulfill gender role expectations, though conformity to the broader, more powerful male social role is less onerous than complying with the restrictive, less powerful female role. Religion, as we shall see in Chapter 7, is a powerful force for social control. One of the most effective sources of such social control is the individual's own conscience. The person who has been socialized into a certain way of thinking about gender roles feels guilty if he or she fails to fulfill these expectations. One young woman who had learned that "women naturally and instinctively feel great affection for their children" felt guilty that her initial reaction to her newborn child was not a great outpouring of maternal love.

Those who control religious power (especially in official religion) frequently use specifically religious sanctions to enforce gender roles. Recent history provides the examples of a Mormon woman excommunicated for her active support of the Equal Rights Amendment to the Constitution; and a Roman Catholic priest silenced by Vatican and Jesuit officials for his challenges to the church's treatment of women (among other issues). In Iran, the political power of fundamentalist Islam has resulted in strong restrictions of women's public roles and appearances, as symbolized by the mandate of returning to the *chador* (i.e., veil).

Historically the intertwined power of religious organizations with other social institutions gave religion more influence in the control of deviance than in modern society. The persecution of witches in the Middle Ages (and until as recently as the end of the seventeenth century) was focused primarily upon women, who were presumed weaker and therefore more vulnerable to the influences of the devil. As illustrated further in Chapter 8, authorities typically singled out women who deviated from religiously established norms for females— wise women, healers, midwives. Suspected women (e.g., widows and "spinsters") were disproportionately likely to be relatively independent of men. Witchhunts such as the massive medieval persecutions were primarily concerned with purification. Women in particular were considered threats to social purity because of cultural assumptions about their sexuality and because anomalous (i.e., independent) women were perceived as dangerous and disruptive. A substantial number of women were put to death or tortured as witches; scholarly estimates suggest that several hundred thousand witches were killed during the Inquisition.[7] There has

[7]Figures vary greatly from 30,000 to 9 million (sources cited in Daly, 1978:183). See especially Daly's essay on European witchhunts, as well as Szasz, *The Manufacture of Madness* (1970); and Anderson and Gordon, "Witchcraft and the Status of Women—the Case of England" (1978:2). Daly

been no parallel persecution of men *as men*, although men were persecuted as members of other minorities (e.g., Jews).

Alternative Definitions of Women's Status and Roles

Women's Religious Groups. One of the most effective social controls of women has been the limitation and prevention of separate, autonomous women's religious groups. Religion has historically had the potential for promoting social change among colonial peoples and subordinated racial and ethnic groups because, in organizing around a religious focus, such groups have often mobilized to press their social and economic concerns. Unlike racial and ethnic minorities, however, women have not generally formed separate religious groups in Western societies. Male-dominated religious organizations have been understandably threatened by the possible power of autonomous women's groups.

Medieval sisterhoods (including religious orders, lay orders, and numerous unofficial bands of religious women) offered socially approved roles for women who could not or would not fit the primary gender roles of woman as wife and mother. Socially anomalous women (again, typically widows and unmarried women) found in these sisterhoods both security and opportunities for achievement not available to other women in society. Medieval abbesses, for example, were often relatively powerful leaders of large organizations. Church officials, however, kept these groups under relatively tight control (e.g., by regulations restricting sisters' freedom to come and go in "the world"). Like other dissenting, change-oriented groups (e.g., early Franciscans), women's groups that asserted alternative roles were often coopted and controlled.

Feminism had a specific role in the development of sisterhoods in the Anglican church during the nineteenth century (M. Hill, 1973a). The Victorian image of women, as we have seen, emphasized domesticity. Furthermore, the middle- and upper-class Victorian "lady" was educated to be an ornament in the home; her enforced leisure was evidence of her husband's social status. Women such as Florence Nightingale who asserted any other role for themselves were severely criticized. The Anglican church had dissolved monasteries and convents in its initial break with the Roman church in the sixteenth century, and in the nineteenth century strong voices were raised against reestablishing brotherhoods or sisterhoods in the church. Nevertheless nascent feminism, combined with a considerable demographic surplus of women, exerted pressures to create acceptable social roles for women who would work in "unladylike" jobs such as nursing, running settlement houses, teaching the poor, and running hospices for derelicts. The creation of acceptable deviant roles for women was perceived as an attack on the Victorian home and women's proper duties. One bishop stated:

> The rules which I have myself laid down as most necessary in my dealing with
> such communities [the sisterhood] have been the following:—To point out that

---

notes the widespread religious legitimation of violence against women. The Indian *suttee*—burning of widows—and African clitoral circumcisions are among the ritual "gynocides" examined in her provocative book. She notes that male-dominated scholarship has not shown as much concern over such historical events as the European witchcraze and institution of the *suttee* as over comparable genocides such as the Nazi Holocaust, observing that scholars have glossed over gynocide such as the *suttee* by calling it a "custom." Daly doubts that they would refer to comparable atrocities in the Holocaust as "Nazi customs."

the first of all duties are those which we owe to our family. Family ties are imposed direct by God. If family duties are overlooked, God's blessing can never be expected on any efforts which we make for His Church. Every community, therefore, of Sisters or Deaconesses ought to consist of persons who have fully satisfied all family obligations (cited in M. Hill, 1973a:277).

Even among those who approved of the idea of women's religious groups, there was disagreement about the degree of autonomy to allow them. Religious sisterhoods were much more problematic than brotherhoods to church authorities because sisterhoods allowed the possibility of women directing their own work and running their own organizations. The less radical alternative of the office of deaconess (in which women workers would be under the direct supervision of male clergy) was proposed because "women need more support than men" (cited in M. Hill, 1973a:276). Women were gradually allowed into "unladylike" areas of work, partly through the transitional institution of the sisterhood. The potential for feminist protest was, however, somewhat coopted, especially as women's groups were brought under greater control by authorities and their work was gradually redefined as "women's work." Nursing, for example, was consistent with the serving and nurturant image of women as dependent upon doctors (male) for decision making. As women's professions became more respectable, women's religious groups became less important as vehicles for feminist aspirations.

Specifically women's religious groups still remain potentially expressive of women's social and religious interests. Within Roman Catholicism, much of the pressure for the ordination of women comes from the ranks of women's religious orders. Some women's groups have creatively used their greater education and structural independence. But the main arena for the expression of feminist concerns has become public sphere organizations. The privatization of religion means that religious achievements are similar to domestic accomplishments: Neither really "count" as symbols of achievement in the larger society. Conflicts within religious collectivities over appropriate roles for women primarily result from religion's tendency to continue legitimating traditional roles for women in *both* public and private spheres.

New Religious Movements. New religious movements are often a vehicle for the assertion of alternative religious roles for women. Religious movements of nonprivileged classes have typically allotted equality to women, at least in their formative years (Weber, 1963:104–105). Many of the medieval millenarian movements initially allowed women virtual equality. The Protestant Reformation's principle of the "priesthood of all believers" was initially interpreted as opening important roles to both laywomen and laymen. Many religious movements of the eighteenth century, and later the Great Awakening, granted equality to women. The Shakers believed that their founder, Mother Ann Lee, was the Second Coming of Christ, thus completing the manifestations of Christ (male and female). The late Victorian period was one of nascent feminism, and alternative women's roles were an important part of the beliefs and practices of Pentecostal and Holiness religion, Salvation Army, Seventh Day Adventists, Christian Science, Theosophy, and New Thought (Robertson, 1970:188,189).

New religious movements are more amenable to alternative gender roles because they are based upon an alternative source of authority. Traditional ways of doing things are protected by the established religious collectivity, but new religious movements are often based upon charismatic authority (see Chapter 7), which is not bound by tradition. The charismatic leader says, in effect, "You have heard it said that . . . , but I say to you. . . ." This new source of authority allows a break from tradition. Weber (1963:104) points out that as the emphasis upon charisma fades and the movement becomes established, these movements tend to react against keeping women in roles of authority, typically redefining women's claims to charismatic or other authority as inappropriate or dishonorable behavior. This process is illustrated in the contemporary Pentecostal movement among Roman Catholics. These groups believe that the Holy Spirit speaks and works directly through human vehicles, men or women. Initially women were generally equal to men in the movement, but as the movement became larger and more organized, much pressure was exerted for women to become subordinate to men. The "gifts of the Spirit" that men claimed to have received began to be different and more powerful than women's. Some (male) leaders of the movement borrowed from their conservative Protestant counterparts a theology of "headship" to legitimate the developing subordinate role of women (Fichter, 1975; McGuire, 1981).

The role of women in developing religious movements is thus a result of alternative sources of authority and power. Many of these movements are understandably appealing to women who are excluded from status and privilege in the dominant religions. Weber (1963:104) accounts for some of the appeal of Christianity and Buddhism by noting that relative to the religious competitors of their times and regions, their subordination of women was less extreme. Similarly the religious movements of the late Victorian era appealed to women because of their alternate definitions of women's roles. Recent new religious movements also focus upon gender roles but generally reassert traditional rather than new ones. Thus the Jesus People, neo-Pentecostal movements, evangelicalism, Hare Krishna (Krsṅa Consciousness), and the Unification Church (of Reverend Moon) define women's roles very conservatively. The availability of nonreligious modes of asserting new gender roles may have eclipsed the religious modes of dissent. Even for religious feminists, religious organizations are not "where the action is." The reassertion of traditional gender roles in new religious movements may be seen as a reaction against these nonreligious feminist movements.

Can official religion create or encompass new or changing roles for women? Sociological analysis suggests the answer is a qualified yes. On the one hand, religious images and symbols are elastic; they can be changed and reinterpreted. On the other hand, traditional images and symbols of women are generally negative and resistant to change. Since much of the power of symbols and ritual is in their reference to tradition, they are essentially conservative. While religious movements are able to express women's dissent and create new social roles, religious movements have historically returned to traditional or bureaucratic forms of authority as they become settled—and in so doing have reverted to less innovative roles for women. Women's religious groups have the potential of focusing and asserting their social concerns; yet they have been historically controlled and coopted by (male) authorities of the dominant religion.

Nonofficial Religion. While the dominant religious groups have allocated women few if any important ritual roles, women have often found important symbolic roles outside the approved religious structure. Women have been prominent as healers, mediums, and midwives. These roles, as further illustrated in Chapter 8, often paralleled approved religious or medical roles and functions. Just as men have been prominent in official religion as it became a differentiated institution, women have been important in "common" or nonofficial religion. Nonofficial religion has provided women with a *chance to express their own specific concerns for meaning and belonging.* Midwifery, for example, has traditionally been a highly spiritual role (see Dougherty, 1978; Paul, 1978). In nonofficial religion, women have opportunities for leadership and power, as exemplified by the status of women mediums, faith healers, and astrologers. Some nonofficial religion is organized as specifically feminist dissent (e.g., some contemporary witchcraft covens). Much of the nonofficial religion discussed in this chapter may be understood as a way in which individuals assert alternative definitions of reality. Women throughout the ages have asserted alternative roles for themselves through religious expression.

Conclusion
Religious groups' treatment of women's roles and women's sexuality is essentially an issue of *power.* If women obtained greater power than they have traditionally had, they could redefine themselves religiously and socially. On the other hand, religious legitimations and organizations presently work against their obtainment of that power.

This Extended Application, while focusing on women's roles, illustrates more broadly how religion comes to embody and further legitimate caste stratification and power. Our analysis suggests that nonofficial religion sometimes represents one form of counterassertion (albeit often incoherent and fragmented) of power and self-worth by those excluded from power in official religion. If this is true, we need to pay more serious attention to nonofficial religion and its complex relationship with official religion.

Summary

This chapter has contrasted official religion and its characteristic forms of individual religiosity with nonofficial religion and religiosity. Official religion is a set of beliefs and practices that are prescribed, regulated, and socialized by organized, specifically religious groups. Nonofficial religion, by contrast, is a set of religious and quasi-religious beliefs and practices that are not accepted, recognized, or controlled by official religious groups. Official religion is relatively coherent and organized, but nonofficial religion includes an assortment of unorganized, inconsistent, and heterogeneous beliefs and practices.

The official model of religion is clearly identifiable. Its elements—doctrine, cultic expression, ethics, and organization—are mediated by religious institutions. These institutions consolidate and control the religion's definitions of what it stands for. The relative specificity of these official models of religion enable researchers to develop measurable criteria of religiosity. Such measures are, however, bound to the orthodox official models of religion, making them of limited use in understanding religious change and nonofficial religion. Nonofficial religion is more widespread than generally recognized, and it overlaps official religion in both content and adherents.

The Extended Application demonstrates how religion influences women's gender roles and identities. Religious organizational structure, myths, and symbols embody and legitimate subordinate caste status for females—a point of conflict in many religious groups today. As the Extended Application suggests, some aspects of nonofficial religion involve ways by which persons who are unrecognized or even disempowered by official religion have asserted themselves. Thus nonofficial religion and religiosity are both serious and relevant to our understanding of religion as a whole.

Recommended Readings

Articles

The following articles tap some of the methodological issues discussed in this chapter:

J. E. Faulkner and Gordon DeJong. "Religiosity in 5-D: An Empirical Analysis." *Social Forces* 45, 1966:246–254.

Charles Glock. "On the Study of Religious Commitment." Research Supplement to *Religious Education* 57 (4), 1962; reprinted in Glock and Stark, *Religion and Society in Tension* (Rand McNally: Chicago, 1965).

Joseph Ryan. "Ethnoscience and Problems of Method in the Social Scientific Study of Religion." *Sociological Analysis* 39 (3), 1978:241–249.

Books

Michael H. Ducey. *Sunday Morning: Aspects of Urban Ritual.* New York: Free Press, 1977. An analysis of the ritual of Sunday morning worship services of four churches (Evangelical United Brethren, United Church of Christ, Roman Catholic, and Missouri Synod Lutheran); especially useful for appreciating the implication of ritual action, patterns of authority, power relations, and tension with the dominant society.

Andrew Greeley. *The American Catholic: A Social Portrait.* New York: Basic Books, 1977. Based on NORC surveys, this series of capsule descriptions portrays post-Vatican II American Catholicism, emphasizing communal bases of identification.

Bernard Martin, ed. *Movement and Issues in American Judaism: An Analysis and Sourcebook of Developments Since 1945.* Westport, Conn.: Greenwood, 1978. A collection of essays on contemporary Judaism in America and Canada, including such topics as Jewish religious movements, demography, education, and intergroup relationships.

Martin Marty. *A Nation of Behavers.* Chicago: University of Chicago Press, 1976. A church historian's interpretation of current styles of religious behavior, many of which cut across denominational lines. Patterns of religious behavior include descriptions of mainline religion, Evangelicalism and Fundamentalism, Pentecostal-charismatic religion, new religions, ethnic religion, and civil religion.

CHAPTER FIVE

The Dynamics of Religious Collectivities

Religious groups have a variety of organizational forms. Some have loose boundaries and relaxed authority structures; others have clear-cut boundaries and rigid authority structures. Some groups are large and relatively anonymous, others are small and face-to-face. Many collectivities expect their members to organize their day-to-day life around their religious commitment, while many others expect only partial and segmental commitment. The task of classifying organizational patterns is not an end in itself, but understanding the varieties of religious collectivities, as they change in time, helps us analyze the internal dynamics of a religious group and its relationship with the larger society.

Types of Religious Organization

Weber (1963:65) first introduced the sociological concept of sect, referring to an association that accepts only religiously qualified persons. Weber was especially interested in how different kinds of religious collectivities were related to social change. The religious community of Jesus and his followers, for example, was qualitatively different from the religious community within the established Jewish religion of his time. Weber noted that while charismatic leadership frequently stimulated social change, the process of trying to maintain and defend innovation typically resulted in routinization. **Routinization of charisma** is the process by which the dynamism of charismatic leadership is translated into the stability of traditional or bureaucratic organization. The very organization of a community of followers is thus part of this process of routinization (Weber, 1963:60,61; see also Weber's essay "Sect, Church and Democracy," 1968:1204).

Weber's distinction between church and sect was amplified by his contemporary, Ernst Troeltsch, a theologian and church historian. Troeltsch was interested in tracing the social impact of certain ideas or "teachings" of Christian churches in

Europe. He thought that three types of religious organization were implicit in Christian teachings, and a given group developed along one of these three lines depending upon its relationship to its social environment (Steeman, 1975:202–203). Troeltsch's three types were: church, sect, and mysticism. His application, however, focused mainly upon church and sect as a dichotomy. The residual concept of mysticism reflected important insights but is not properly a separate type of organization because mysticism exists within all other types of collectivity.

The Development of the Church-Sect Dichotomy

Troeltsch characterized the **church** as a type of organization that is essentially conservative of the social order and is accommodated to the secular world. Its membership is not exclusive but incorporates the masses. The **sect**, by contrast, is exclusive, aspiring to personal perfection and direct fellowship among members. The church is characteristically an integral part of the social order, while the sect stands apart from society in indifference or hostility. Thus there is a tendency for the church to be associated with the interests of dominant classes, whereas the sect is connected with subordinate classes. The church has an objective institutional character. One is born into it, and it mediates the divine to its members. By contrast, the sect is a voluntary community of fellowship and service; relationships with fellow members and the divine are more direct. According to Troeltsch, both types are logical results of Christian beliefs.

The church type, exemplified by the Roman Catholic church of the thirteenth century, is of diminishing significance. The medieval synthesis of church and society was undermined, partly because of the challenges of the sects. Later church-type organizations like Calvinism in Geneva or the free churches (e.g., Congregationalism) in England and America achieved considerable synthesis with their societies, but the synthesis was based upon a general Protestant consensus rather than upon a monopoly of legitimacy (Steeman, 1975:194).

Troeltsch (1960:381) forecast that modern society would be increasingly characterized by his third type of religious association: "idealistic mysticism" or "spiritual religion" (see Garrett, 1975). This is essentially a radical religious individualism. It lays no emphasis upon the relations between believers; any association among them is based upon a "parallelism of spontaneous religious personalities." Such groups are indifferent to sacraments, dogmas, ethical norms, and organization. Mysticism tends to resist control by authorities and is thus a threat to organized religious forms. Nevertheless, because it tends to be uninterested in changing the church or the world, it does not have the social impact of sect-type groups. While Troeltsch developed the category of "idealistic mysticism" to describe a particular historical phenomenon—eighteenth- and nineteenth-century German Lutheran mysticism—he suggested that it also described the religion of contemporary educated classes. He viewed this trend with pessimism because he considered some organizational and historical continuity necessary to the continued existence of religion (Campbell, 1978; Troeltsch, 1960:798,799).

Troeltsch's categorization was intended primarily for comparing and contrasting concrete historical developments rather than for creating a classification scheme. Later formulations, built uncritically upon Troeltsch's, inherited the historical limitations of his focus. Thus in Troeltsch's scheme, the church-type and sect-type are polarized extremes, reflecting the historical situation of late medieval Christendom, in which class structure was generally polarized and religious institutions were relatively undifferentiated from economic and political ones. Similarly this lack of differentiation made it possible for religious dissent to be simultaneously politico-economic dissent. Any attempt to apply this dichotomy to modern societies stumbles because the modern situation is vastly more complex (Robertson, 1970:117).

The Development of Other Types

This difficulty of applying the church-sect dichotomy to the American situation prompted Niebuhr (1929:25) to add the type **denomination,** which was characterized by accommodation to society comparable to that of the church but lacking the ability or intention to dominate society. Niebuhr's main interest was the process by which sects were transformed into other organizational forms. To him, the initial enthusiasm of the sect appeared limited to the first generation (i.e., to those who consciously chose to belong). After the initial fervor, the sect must either compromise with the "world" or be organizationally weakened. A sect that compromises moves toward a denominational stance—organized religion accommodated to society. Niebuhr's typology was less neutral than Troeltsch's. As a theologian, Niebuhr used the schema to criticize some religious groups for their accommodation to the stratification system—a symptom of secularization and divisiveness, in his view (Martin's 1962 clarification of the concept of denomination eliminates much of the value-laden quality of this schema).

Further clarifications were added by Becker (1932) who developed the category **cult.** The cult is characterized by a loose association of persons with a private, eclectic religiosity (subsuming Troeltsch's category of idealistic mysticism). Yinger (1970:266–273) delineated another type, the **established sect,** which retains its sectarian dissent while becoming relatively organized and lasting beyond the first generation. This category recognized groups such as Jehovah's Witnesses and Seventh Day Adventists, which remained sectarian despite their longevity and complex organization.

Other distinctions have led to further subtypes. Yinger's version in 1946 had four types; in 1957, six types with three subdivisions of "sect"; and in 1970, six types with the additional subdivision of two kinds of "universal church." Yinger wanted a model of religious organization applicable in all cultures, so he had to refine the typology to include non-Western religious collectivities. It is debatable whether or not church-sect typologizing can be applied to other cultures. Some sociologists argue that the basic theme of the category (i.e., religious group versus the "world") is specific to the development of Christian churches. The theology of the Incarnation (i.e., God-as-human) illustrates this tension. Thus Christianity is more likely to develop a wide range of religious collectivities (e.g., church, sect, cult, denomination) than other religions such as Hinduism, which does not have the same tension with the "world" (Berger, 1967:123; Martin, 1965:9, 10, 22). If, on the other hand, a typology is applicable *in principle* to a certain range of social phenomena, the fact of which types are *not* found in certain contexts is significant (Robertson, 1970:121). For example, if "denomination" is defined in a way that could in principle be applied to all societies, the fact that denominations do not exist in, say, Iranian Islam is worth discussing.

Similarly it is sociologically interesting if a type appears significant in one period of history and not in another. Although the Buddha preached nonengagement in sociopolitical activities, Theravada Buddhism (one major strain of Buddhism) became closely linked with most Southeast Asian monarchies (i.e., Siam, Burma, Laos, Sri Lanka, Ceylon, Cambodia, etc.) from about 1000 to the mid-1800s. Its churchly hegemony was interrupted not by sectarian strife but by European colonialism. The impact of colonialism was to put Buddhism—still the majority religion—into a position of marginality relative to the dominant colonial society. Buddhism became more sectlike relative to society and thus a vehicle for nationalist dissent. Recently, however, Southeast Asian societies have experienced a differentiation of religious institutions from economic and political spheres because of both capitalistic and socialistic influences so that religious collectivities do not have their former potency as vehicles for dissent (Houtart, 1977). These examples suggest that typologies of religious organizations can be extended beyond the Christian context if cautions are taken to base categories on sociological rather than on doctrinal characteristics.

The church-sect categorization of religious groups has been heavily criticized, and some sociologists suggest doing away with it (Goode, 1967). Some critics note the historical and cultural limitations of the model, even with its later refinements. Others criticize the parsimony and lack of precision in the contruction of types. The typology is not clear-cut, so it has limited empirical usefulness. Criticism is especially directed at the static uses of the concepts. Rather than viewing religious collectivities as dynamic and changing, some sociologists have applied the concepts as a rigid taxonomy (see especially critiques by Johnson, 1963, and Robertson, 1970:116 ff.). Nevertheless the church-sect categorization has formed the basis for some of the most important work done in the sociology of religion. Sociologists have investigated sects and other organizational forms as vehicles for social dissent and change. They have studied why people join sects, how socioeconomic status of members is related to the type of collectivity, and the dynamics of sects and other organizational forms in relationship to their social environment. Thus this categorization, while analytically imperfect, has been a productive and stimulating basis of inquiry.

Refining the Typology

The church-sect line of typologizing appears to have considerable analytic value, so we will now consider some necessary clarification.

First, we can distinguish between forms of organization of a religious collectivity and modes of orientation of individual members. The concepts "church," "sect," "denomination," and "cult" have been used variously to describe both of these aspects. This usage leads to confusion because members of one type of religious group (e.g., a denomination) may very well have several different modes of religious orientation; some may be sectarian, others denominational, in orientation. For this reason, we will separate discussion of organizational forms and member orientations.

Second, categories should be based upon *sociologically* important characteristics. Two criteria used by sociologists appear especially useful: the relationship between religious group and the dominant society (Johnson, 1963); and the extent to which the religious group considers itself to be uniquely legitimate (Robertson, 1970:120–128). The relationship between religious collectivity and its social environment has been a key theme since Troeltsch and Weber. Furthermore, it reflects a basic tension between values derived from religious sources of authority and other values in the society. No organization could neutralize this tension, though each type responds differently to it. The tension derives in part from the peculiar nature of religious sources of authority, but the general typology also applies to nonreligious organizations (see Figure 5.1). We will note in Chapter 8 the church-type characteristics of the dominant medical system, in contrast to sect-type organizations of alternative systems. Similarly political splinter groups often display sect-type characteristics relative to churchly or denominational dominant organizations (Jones, 1975; Lipset, 1959; O'Toole,1976).

Basically the church-sect typology is a general developmental model for any organization defining itself as uniquely legitimate and existing in a state of positive (i.e., church) or negative (i.e., sect) tension with society (Mayrl, 1976:28). The additional categories of denomination and cult present a general model of similar positive (i.e., denomination) and negative (i.e., cult) tension, but in this case either the organization does not claim unique legitimacy or the society prevents it. This model is depicted in Figure 5.1.[1]

Self-conceived legitimacy	Group/society tension	
	Positive	Negative
Unique	CHURCH	SECT
Pluralistic	DENOMINATION	CULT

Figure 5.1   Organizational "Moments" of Religious Collectivities

[1]This schema is similar to that of Swatos (1975, 1979). His model refers to monopolistic or pluralistic *societies*, whereas this model refers to pluralistic or monopolistic *claims to legitimacy*. Part of the tension with the dominant society depends upon the extent to which the collectivity attempts and succeeds in getting its claims to legitimacy recognized.

Church. The church considers itself uniquely legitimate and in a relatively positive relationship with society. The church does not recognize the legitimacy of claims of any other religious group. Its message is *"Extra ecclesiam nulla salus"* (Outside the church there is no salvation). Its response to competing claims may be to ignore, suppress, or coopt the competing group. The church is basically accepting of society but—to the extent that religion is differentiated from other institutions—it exists in tension with other institutions. Thus, for example, the church might use its status to attempt to change the political or economic arrangements of society. Overall, however, church-type organizations tend to support the societal status quo.

At the same time, the model emphasizes the extent to which society also accepts the church. Membership in a church-type organization is not considered deviant or unusual. The church type is exemplified by the Roman Catholic organization of thirteenth-century Europe and the Theravada Buddhism of feudal Southeast Asia. In both instances, the church-type organization claimed an effective monopoly of legitimacy (although Buddhism was less aggressive toward minority religions), and there was positive tension between the church and society. The church type legitimated political power and the economic system, accepted the goals and values of society, and, in turn, was approved and protected by society.

Sect. The sect is a religious organization that considers itself uniquely legitimate and is in a relatively negative relationship with the dominant society. The sect does not accept the legitimacy claims of the church or of competing sects; like the church, it proclaims itself the only way. The sect, too, may adopt any number of strategies to deal with competing groups: withdrawal from their influence, aggressively attacking, or trying to convert and absorb them. By contrast, however, the sect is also in conflict with society. This relatively negative tension between the sect and its social environment is both a threat to the continued existence of the sect and a potential basis for social change. Essentially the sect is a form of social dissent, exemplified by the Anabaptists of Reformation times, and Shakers, Mormons, Rappites, Quakers, and Christadelphians in eighteenth- and nineteenth-century America. Contemporary sectlike groups in American society include the Amish, Mormons, the Jewish Hassidim, Jehovah's Witnesses, Seventh Day Adventists, and Pentecostal and Holiness groups. Some new religious groups such as the Children of God, Unification Church, Synanon, and People's Temple are also sectlike (see Barker, 1977; Bromley and Shupe, 1979a; Hall, 1979; Richardson, 1979b; Richardson et al., 1978).

Denomination. The denomination is in a positive relationship with society and accepts the legitimacy claims of other religious collectivities. It is perhaps even more generally accepting of society than the church because, with its pluralistic power base, it is less able to control society. Also in tension with the "world," the denomination acts upon and reacts to society, but usually from the sense that the "world" is "okay" (see Berger, 1961). Examples of denominations include most major American religious groups—Presbyterians, Congregationalists, American Baptists, Methodists, Lutherans, Episcopalians, Roman and Eastern Catholics, Reformed and Conservative Jews. Similarly, in Japan, religious groups such as the Pure Land and Zen divisions of Buddhism exemplify denominational pluralism (cf. Morioka and Newell, 1968).

Cult. The cult accepts the legitimacy claims of other groups and is in a negative relationship with society.[2] Like the denomination, the cult does not claim to have *the* truth, and is tolerant of other groups' claims. At the same time, the cult is critical of society. Like the sect, the cult is a form of social dissent; however, its dissent is likely to be less extreme because of its pluralistic stance. Historical examples were medieval healing cults and nineteenth-century Spiritualism. In contemporary American society there are numerous cults, including Arica, Vedanta, astrology, flying saucer groups, Silva Mind Control, 3HO, Rosicrucianism, and American Zen. Other movements such as Divine Light Mission, Scientology, and Transcendental Meditation were cults in some stages of their development or at some but not all organizational levels (see Downton, 1979; Ellwood, 1979; Jackson and Jobling, 1968).

A Dialectical Process. Finally, our model illustrates the constant tension and dynamism in the process by which a group tries to effect its religious convictions. There is an ongoing dialectical process between the religious collectivity and its social environment. The religious group responds to changes in its social situation; it can also effect changes in that situation. The types delineated in Figure 5.1 are not fixed categories but are *moments* in a dialectical process.[3]

Because the model is based upon fluid processes, in order to categorize a collectivity it is necessary to specify (1) societal context, (2) level of analysis (e.g., national, regional, or local), and (3) time period. Thus we can classify the Roman Catholic organization as a church relative to French society of the thirteenth century. Relative to American society of 1840, however, the Roman Catholic organization was more of a sect, because it neither accepted nor was fully accepted by society. Later in America, especially after Vatican II, the Roman Catholic organization appears to have become increasingly a denomination, because it is more accepting of and accepted by society and is more tolerant of other groups' claims to legitimacy.

It is necessary to specify the level of analysis because the relationship to society of a national group may be different from that of a local group affiliate. In some isolated rural areas, small local churches, while affiliated with a national sect, are churchlike organizations relative to their subcultural setting. These groups are often the only church serving their community. Many members do not

[2]The cult type is included to cover the diversity of religious collectivities, but it is distinctive from the other three types in its acceptance of members' partial allegiance. Some observers would suggest that the cult type is sufficiently different from the other three types that it should be excluded from the typology. The cult type, retained here for analytic purposes since it best describes a wide range of contemporary religious collectivities, may nevertheless not be strictly comparable with the other types in this model.

[3]Recent changes in Western societies have reduced the impact of religion on society (see Chapter 8), but the model offered in Figure 5.1 covers societies and historical periods in which religion's impact is more evident. This model of religious processes can be compared with the Marxian theory of *praxis*—the ideological context of the relationship between theory and practice in social movements. Mayrl (1976:28) notes the irony that Marxism as a social movement has also experienced a parallel (i.e., sect-to-church) shift from critical praxis to adaptation to the social situation.

even know about religious alternatives, and the groups are able to enforce their monolithic status. They are fully at home with the culture of that locale, often the only one that its members know. Although such groups may be nationally part of a sect, at the local level they may operate very much as a church. Another example is the People's Temple of Jim Jones, affiliated at the national level with a denomination (Disciples of Christ); but in California and later Guyana, it increasingly became a sect.

Variables Related to Organization Type

Some typologies of religious collectivities have included criteria that we will present as variables rather than as definitive. One such variable is the *degree of organizational differentiation, specialization, and complexity*. Churches and denominations have generally tended to be larger, more complex organizations than sects and cults. The development of specialized ministry, bureaucracy, and formal organizational structure seems to accompany churchlike and denominationlike forms. It is unwise to include this feature as definitive, however, because it would detract from recognizing the real dissent of some highly organized groups. Both Jehovah's Witnesses and Scientology are highly differentiated and complexly organized, yet both have retained their negative tension with society. To allow for this variable, the terms **established sect** (Yinger, 1970:266–273) and **established cult** (or "centralized cult"; Nelson, 1969:233) may be used for highly organized groups that retain their sectarian or cultic stance. There are no terms in use for the parallel types—relatively simple, loosely organized churches and denominations such as Unitarian Universalists and some Baptist groups.

Another variable, treated as definitive by some theorists, is the *degree of elitism* of a collectivity (see Robertson, 1970; Wilson, 1970; Yinger, 1970). This variable is a common characteristic of sectarianism as a mode of religious orientation, but it is probably a by-product of the two definitive variables in the model; that is, groups viewing themselves as uniquely legitimate are more likely to consider themselves superior to "nonlegitimate" groups. Troeltsch (1960) observed that the church tended to have unrestrictive membership requirements and that members were often "born into" it rather than joining it, as in a sect. This depiction, however, underplays the extent to which the church, too, could be exclusionary when that suited its purposes. In the height of its power, the Roman Catholic church in Europe excommunicated dissidents, labelled heretics and witches, and controlled who could become members. The early part of the Inquisition in Spain (mid-fifteenth to mid-sixteenth centuries) was directed largely at ferreting out *Conversos* (i.e., converts, principally from Judaism) who were not "good Christians." These "converts" were suspect because they had joined the church to escape death at the hands of Christian mobs (in the years preceding the Inquisition, 50,000 Jews had been killed and an estimated 2 million had "converted"; Longhurst, 1962:39).

Whether a group is inclusive or exclusive depends largely upon its relationship with its social environment at any given time. At some times, it suited the needs of churches to be exclusive, just as at times it was useful for sects to be inclusive. A number of early American sects accepted whole families as converts during phases of group expansion. Similarly the Mormons, during their highly sectarian early years, promoted emigration from Europe to their American frontier communities; their appeal was not only to religious conversion but also to socioeconomic needs (Taylor, 1966:26,27).

Other typological variables such as clergy-lay distinctions, forms of organizational polity, degrees of centralization, patterns of authority, and attitudes toward authority are all important for sociological exploration. These characteristics have not been included in the model. One variable treated by some authors as almost causal is the socioeconomic status of members. Troeltsch and Niebuhr had observed that sects were generally composed of lower-class members, whereas church and denomination membership was characteristically middle- and upper-class. In the period described by Troeltsch (1960), religious dissent (i.e.,sectarianism) was a viable form of socioeconomic and political dissent because the church was so completely connected with the social, political, and economic arrangements of society. The social class character of sects in contemporary society is much less clear. Political dissatisfaction (of the right or left) is expressed in religious sectarianism, but the poor and dispriviledged are not the only (or even the main) constituencies of sectarian dissent. Wealthy, relatively powerful persons are also attracted to contemporary sects, especially those expressing dissent of the political right.

Another variable is whether the religious group functions to integrate its members into society or whether it results in disintegrative functions (Robbins et al., 1975). As the last part of this chapter will show, the same religious movement may serve integrative and disintegrative functions simultaneously. Thus some Jesus movement groups socialized their counterculture youth members into values of the dominant culture—hard work, deferred gratification, marriage, and obedience to authority. At the same time, however, the sect-type structure of the groups removed members from the larger society, biological family, and former friends. Integrative and disintegrative functions of religious groups are important, but they are not sufficiently clear-cut to use in defining typologies.

Modes of Religious Orientation

It is helpful to distinguish sectarian, cultic, denominational, and churchly orientations from sect, cult, denomination, and church as organizational types, because several different orientations can occur within the same collectivity. The model of religious orientation types shown in Figure 5.2 is derived from the previous typology of religious collectivities. It is based upon the characteristic commitment patterns of members belonging to the types of religious collectivities discussed. Although each type in Figure 5.2 corresponds to a type of group, members of a group often display several different orientations.

Types of Religious Orientation
The two key characteristics for defining "typical" orientations of individual members are (1) the extent to which the member's role as a religious person is segmented into a separate role or is expected to be diffused throughout every aspect of the person's life; and (2) the extent to which the individual judges self

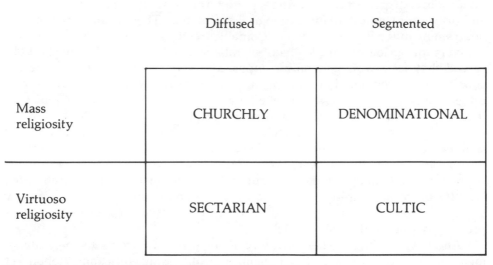

Religious emphasis · Religious "role"

	Diffused	Segmented
Mass religiosity	CHURCHLY	DENOMINATIONAL
Virtuoso religiosity	SECTARIAN	CULTIC

Figure 5.2   Modes of Individual Religious Orientations

and others according to standards of "mass" or "virtuoso" religiosity. These qualities are present in varying degrees, so we can speak of relatively "mild" or "strong" sectarian, cultic, denominational, or churchly orientations.

Figure 5.2 ties together a number of theoretical and empirical observations about sectarianism. Some theorists (Parsons et al., 1961:251) have suggested that one of the main characteristics of sectarianism is much less differentiation of members' religious role from other social roles (e.g., work or family). The sectarian orientation means that the religious role is the master role, pervading and subordinating all other aspects of the person's life. By contrast, a denominational orientation is more segmented and the religious role is separate from other aspects of life; this does not mean that the religious role is not important, but it has less influence in the total picture of daily life.

The second variable refers to a related normative aspect: the extent to which one judges oneself and others by standards of "virtuoso" religiosity. **Religious virtuosi** are those who strive for religious perfection (however defined) and are not satisfied by the normal levels of religiosity of the masses (Weber, 1963:163–165). The person may define religious perfection in terms of some moral , ascetic, or mystical ideal. Individual orientations are therefore guided by whether the religious role applies to all spheres of life and by whether it is judged by the norm of perfection.

Sectarian. The sectarian orientation is characterized by normative virtuosity and diffusion of the religious role (cf. Knudsen et al., 1978). The sectarian orientation toward perfection is part of the reason for the sect's negative tension with the "world." Sectarian dissent is a form of judgment of the imperfection of the rest of society. The sectarian orientation insists upon the pervasiveness of the religious role, which is, ideally, the organizing principle of work, family, leisure activities, political stance, and personal life. This commitment to perfection and the diffuseness of the religious role explain why sectarianism is frequently characterized by total commitment (Wilson, 1967:1–45; 1970; cf. nonreligious institutions described in Coser, 1974).

Denominational. The key features of a denominational orientation are an acceptance of ordinary levels of religiosity and a religious role segmented from other aspects of life. This orientation is satisfactory for most members of a denomination because their beliefs and practices are less at odds with society than are those of the sect. Because denominations consider their world view as pluralistically legitimate, commitment tends to be more individualistic. Members feel free to select not only a "church of their choice" but also which elements of that religious view they wish to accept. The social acceptability of denominational membership, together with this individualism, make the characteristic orientation of denominationalism somewhat resemble commitment to other voluntary organizations such as Kiwanis, Junior League, Elks, or League of Women Voters. This does not mean that the religious content of denominationalism is not important, but commitment is much less intense or urgent than in sectarianism. One study found that denomination members were less intensely involved in their religious group than sect members. Members of denominations were much less likely than sect members to consider church membership very important, to restrict their friendships to fellow members of the congregation, or to restrict their membership to religious community organizations (Stark and Glock, 1968:101, 166, 172).

Cultic. The cultic orientation is also prevalent in contemporary religion, either by itself or in combination with denominational modes. It is characterized by separation of religious roles from other aspects of life, as in denominationalism. By contrast, however, a cultic orientation also involves seeking a higher level of spirituality, comparable to sectarian "perfection" except that the definition of perfection is less specific and more eclectic. Members' commitment is that of the seeker, permanently searching for particles of truth from a wide variety of sources. Cults do not assert unique legitimacy, and members with a cultic orientation often draw upon several different groups, either simultaneously or serially. A person deeply involved in Spiritualism may be simultaneously "into" Silva Mind Control and also be an active Methodist.

This individualism is a distinctive feature of cultic adherence because it contributes to the precariousness of cults as organizations. Cultic individualism means that no clear locus of authority exists beyond the individual member, and there is thus no way to handle "heresy" and therefore no clear boundaries between members and nonmembers. In the cultic mode, as in the sectarian, the individual finds some mutual support from fellow believers, but this group contact is less strong because of the characteristic pluralism and individualism (Campbell, 1977; Martin, 1965; Wallis, 1974; 1977).

Churchly. The major characteristics of the churchly orientation are acceptance of a "mass" standard of religiosity and a religious role diffused throughout everyday life. Religious commitment is very general, sustained by the whole fabric of society, and does not simply comprise the religious group itself. Religious activity may be considerable or negligible, but rarely does the individual consciously choose to be religious. Although church-type religious organizations do not exist in American society, individual churchly orientation is possible in certain subcultural settings (e.g., a Hispanic subcultural enclave).

The differentiation between types of religious collectivity and characteristic modes of individual orientation helps explain the diversity of orientations within a given group. Churches and denominations in particular, but also sects and cults, often have members with very heterogeneous orientations. This diversity is important in understanding the dynamics of religious groups. The interaction of these members often leads to important transformations in the collectivity itself. Such diversity, however, complicates the task of analyzing religious collectivities.

In one study, considerable diversity was found within the same denomination, with some members having highly sectarian patterns of involvement. Sectarian members of one denomination also resembled sectarian members of other denominations in several important ways—especially socioeconomic status. Table 5.1 illustrates some of these findings. These figures suggest that sectarian

Table 5.1   Sectlike Religiosity and Individual Status among Congregationalists, Presbyterians, Disciples of Christ, and Baptists

Religiosity High on Sectlike Involvement	Individual Status				Denomination
	Upper	Middle	Working	Low	
%	22	27	32	37	Congregationalists
Number	1386	1145	572	102	
%	33	41	51	52	Presbyterians
Number	711	674	471	129	
%	36	45	43	56	Disciples of
Number	387	396	284	52	Christ
%	42	48	50	56	Baptists
Number	171	233	218	75	

Source: Adapted from N. J. Demerath, III. *Social Class in American Protestantism*, Rand-McNally, Chicago, 1965: p. 119; used by permission.

orientations exist even in denominations that are not sects or sectlike (e.g., Congregationalism). Regardless of denomination, furthermore, sectarian orientation varies according to socioeconomic status. The percentage of members with strong sectarian involvement increases as social status decreases (Demerath, 1965; see also Dynes, 1955). The sectarian pattern of involvement may, however, be a product of an intervening variable, localism (discussed in Chapter 3). Persons of higher socioeconomic status may be generally less sectarian because their social mobility and educational levels promote a cosmopolitan orientation. Thus the relationship between sectarian orientations and socioeconomic status may be, at most, indirect. As noted in Chapter 3, sectarianism is a cognitive minority's strategy for maintaining the plausibility of its belief system. The sectarian orientation would, therefore, serve believers of any socioeconomic status.

The denomination must cope with the conflict produced by these differing orientations; but if it can balance the opposing impulses of sectarianism and denominationalism, the organization may emerge stronger. A parallel is the strength gained by medieval Roman Catholicism when it incorporated the sectarian impulse in the form of monasticism. Conflicting modes of orientation often exist in developing religious movements, too. Thus in the early years of the Catholic Pentecostal movement (now called the Catholic Charismatic Renewal), sectarian and cultic orientations were both prevalent. Sectarian adherents tended to be highly involved in the prayer group and likely to view Pentecostalism as the only way to be "really" a Christian. They were more likely than cultic adherents to consider their religious role as the master role in their lives. Cultic adherents, by contrast, were more likely to have segmental commitment to their prayer group and were less likely to view the movement as having the exclusive truth (Harrison, 1975; McGuire, 1981). These two orientations have produced considerable tension within the movement, with the cultic adherents decrying the others' elitism and authoritarianism, and the sectarian adherents denouncing the lack of commitment and the independence of those with a more cultic orientation. The resolution of conflicts such as this is a significant part of the transformation of religious collectivities.

Conflicting Orientations: Dissent Within

The coexistence of conflicting religious orientations within the same collectivity is described by Wach (1944:173–186) in his concept of **ecclesiolae in ecclesia** (i.e., little churches within the church). These groups consist of members of the church (or denomination) who are dissatisfied with the spiritual or moral tenor prevailing in the church and advocate a different kind of religiosity, often aiming at eventual conversion of the entire church. Essentially these groups embody sectarian or cultic dissent *within* the larger collectivity (i.e., church or denomination). Their members press for a different tension between the collectivity and the "world" and are dissatisfied with the imperfection of the church. Wach distinguished three general kinds of *ecclesiolae*.

Collegium Pietatis. The simplest form is only a step beyond individual protest: the **collegium pietatis** (i.e., an association of religious colleagues), which is essentially a cultic orientation within the larger collectivity. According to Wach's description, these collegia do not see their beliefs and practices as uniquely legitimate. They are loosely organized, stressing individual attitudes and seeking greater personal perfection. Historic examples of collegia include German pietism in the early part of the reformation, early years of the Society of Friends (i.e., Quakers), and the Oxford Group Movement in nineteenth-century Anglicanism. Similarly Karaism (eighth and ninth century), Kabbalism (especially sixteenth and seventeenth century), and neo-Kabbalism (twentieth century) among Jews spawned groups like the collegia. Contemporary examples of collegia include loosely organized prayer or fellowship groups within larger religious organizations. Societies related to some special method of spirituality or specific religious practice (e.g., rosary society, a healing cult, or adherents of a shrine) could also be collegia.

Fraternitas. Although common religious ideals and experiences are sufficient to draw people together as in collegia, many groups seek a closer association—a sense of community. The establishment of groups with some measure of communal life marks the **fraternitas** (i.e., brotherhood). Their communality, however, is integrated more by "spirit" than formal organization; thus they are often in conflict with the larger collectivity. Such groups often have egalitarian concepts of fellowship. The fraternitas also represents a somewhat cultic orientation within the larger collectivity. Examples include the Brethren of the Common Life (fourteenth century), early Moravians (eighteenth century), Methodist fellowship groups (especially nineteenth century), and the earliest years of the Bruderhof and kibbutzim (twentieth century). The "underground church" movement in American Roman Catholicism (especially in the 1960s) and the havurah movement in Judaism (1970s) are contemporary *fraternitates.*

The Order. Wach's third type of internal dissent is the **order,** characterized by greater stratification and specialization of functions and a more rigid conception of community. The order is essentially the organization of sectarian dissent *within the church (or denomination)*. It expects the individual's total commitment. Members are bound in their adherence to the religious community and in their renunciation of competing ties. Monasticism is the most obvious and universal example of the order. Through the institution of monasticism, the church absorbs and segregates sectarian protest. At the same time, the order may occasion reform in the larger collectivity, such as the reforms in medieval Roman Catholicism brought about by Cistercians (twelfth century). Monasticism is a feature not only of Christianity but also of Islam, Buddhism, Jainism, and Taoism; but in different cultures it has different meanings because the characteristic tension between church and social environment is different. There is often much tension between the order and the larger collectivity of which it forms a part. Even though the order may compromise its dissent, it represents a considerable source of independent authority within the collectivity.

Contemporary examples of orders include modern descendants of medieval Roman Catholic monastic orders and nineteenth-century Anglican orders. Other order-type collectivities include "covenant communities" among Catholic Pentecostals and the Ecumenical Institute, Iona, and Taize, which are ecumenical Protestant communal groups in the United States, Britain, and France, respectively. The order is an expression of the sectarian elite within a larger collectivity and is the ultimate social organization of virtuoso religiosity. The collegium and fraternitas likewise express vituoso religiosity, but in much less organized and homogeneous form.

Members of all these "ecclesiolae in ecclesia" tend to be religious virtuosi, as are members of sects and cults. Part of the nature of their negative tension with "the world" is their dissatisfaction with ordinary religiosity. Even where religious virtuosi have not banded together in "little churches within the church," there is a marked sectarian impulse among a religious elite (Berger, 1958; Fichter, 1951a, 1954). The main difference between orientations of the order and the sect is the order's willingness to accept a dual standard of religiosity—one standard for the elite and one for the masses. Sectarians, by contrast, do not tolerate this distinction and see their standard as the only way (M. Hill, 1973a). Protestantism has historically tended to spawn sects rather than to incorporate dissent into orders because it is more likely to reject the dual standard (Martin, 1965:191–193).

The pressure to change brought by religious virtuosi is analytically different from the impetus to change in the challenge of a charismatic leader and followers. The charismatic leader proclaims a new message and new basis of authority. Religious virtuosi, by contrast, generally call for a return to the "true" tradition; authority is legitimated by reference to tradition. While this latter pressure for change is less threatening to the larger collectivity, it still has considerable potential for stimulating dramatic changes through something of a "revolution by tradition" (M. Hill, 1973a:3). Thus dynamic processes within religious organizations themselves sometimes bring about major changes in the collectivity; and the existence of conflicting orientations within the same groups helps account for some of these transformations.

Dynamics of Religious Collectivities

An interesting subject in itself is how a religious group comes into being. What brings people together? What attracts them to the group? What repels them from other alternatives? What holds them together? What shapes their organization and collective direction? Even more important, however, is the relationship between the formation of the group and larger social processes. What social factors contribute to the formation of a new religious group? What factors promote or inhibit its success, and how does the developing religious group interact with its larger social environment? Developing religious groups have often had impact both on society and on the collectivities against which they were dissenting, so the dynamics of religious collectivities are linked with the process of social change. At the same time, social change has historically been an impetus for religious change, so religious dynamics indirectly reflect larger social processes.

The Formation of Sects and Cults

Social factors, as well as theological ones, appear to be very important in the formation of new religious groups. The formation of religious movements and new religious collectivities has generally been explained by three social factors: socioeconomic or other deprivation, social dislocation, and socioeconomic change.

Deprivation. The fact that sect membership is disproportionately drawn from the lower classes has been noted by several authors (see Aberle, 1962; Lanternari, 1963). Sects are a vehicle for dissent from society as well as from the church, so persons who are relatively comfortable with society are unlikely to participate. On the other hand, the most destitute stratum, partly because of its characteristic fatalism and sheer lack of resources, is rarely involved. Furthermore, economic deprivation is not sufficient to explain such movements because middle- and upper-class persons are also drawn to sects. Thus contemporary sects such as Hare Krishna (Krsña Consciousness), Children of God, and the Unification Church have had wide appeal among comfortable middle-class youth. If deprivation is a factor in the formation of sects, the concept needs clarification to fit these diverse empirical situations.

Toward such clarification, Glock (1973:210) proposed the notion of **relative deprivation,** which refers to "any and all of the ways that an individual or group may be, or feel disadvantaged in comparison either to other individuals or groups or to an internalized set of standards." People's subjective assessment of their circumstances, rather than objective circumstances themselves, is the key criterion. Glock also notes that economic deprivation is only one of several ways that a person can feel deprived; a person can also feel social (i.e., status), organismic (i.e., physical), ethical (i.e., philosophical), or psychic deprivation. These two latter types are somewhat ambiguous. Ethical deprivation refers to the experience of value conflicts, especially those of intellectuals trying to reconcile their philosophical standards with the realities of the larger society. Psychic deprivation refers to lack of a meaningful value system by which to interpret and evaluate one's life.

Glock suggests that the type of deprivation felt influences whether a movement will survive and what kind of organization it develops. Another factor is the external environment; that is, whether societal sources of deprivation persist as, for example, an economic depression (Glock, 1973:210–213). By distinguishing noneconomic sources of deprivation, this model allows for middle- and upper-class adherents to religious movements. Glock suggests that while economic deprivation is likely to be expressed in the sect, psychic and organismic deprivation are more likely to produce cultic responses. Thus lower-class persons are more likely to predominate in a Holiness sect than in Spiritualism.

The existence of relative deprivation does not *cause* a movement of dissent, but it does create a pool of dissatisfied persons who, if mobilized, would express dissent through a political or religious movement; the actual mobilization of dissatisfied persons will be discussed later in this chapter as movement organization. The deprivation model is helpful in conceptualizing the relationship between sources of dissatisfaction and a movement's social base. It does not, however, adequately explain why dissatisfied persons should choose a particular movement. Furthermore, in applying the model empirically, there is a tendency to reason from after-the-fact evidence. Some interpretations suggested that because a movement provided X, that provision constitutes evidence that recruits were deprived of X. Nevertheless the deprivation model is useful in understanding not only sect formation but also subsequent transformations in the organization of the collectivity.

Social Dislocation. Another interpretation suggests that sects and cults arise to express and respond to the problems of social dislocation of some people. The Holiness movement spread rapidly in the 1930s among rural people who had recently migrated to urban environments. One study of this process interpreted the movement as a result of "culture shock" produced by rapid transition from the stable rural environment to the city (Holt, 1940). Sects and cults allow members to protest against their new environment while simultaneously overcoming some of the difficulties of dislocation by finding a new community among group members. Movements responding to social dislocation would thus be organized as small, close-knit communities.

This interpretation holds that sects and cults offer members a surrogate community or family in the face of the impersonality, isolation, or confusion experienced in society. This explanation has been applied to the appeal of Pentecostalism among Puerto Ricans in New York City (O'Dea and Poblete, 1970), Italian immigrants (Parsons, 1965), West Indian immigrants in England (Calley, 1965), and storefront urban churches among blacks (Frazier, 1974; Washington, 1964). It has also been applied to some new religious movements such as the Jesus People (Petersen and Mauss, 1973) and the Unification Church (Kim, 1977). Like deprivation theories, the social dislocation model is useful in describing why an available pool of potential recruits may find a religious movement attractive. It also illustrates how a movement can express dissent and simultaneously resolve some of its members' problems. On the other hand, this model does not account for many religious movements. Relatively few members of neo-Pentecostal movements among Roman Catholics, Presbyterians, Episcopalians, and Lutherans have experienced serious social dislocations such as migration, unemployment, or family disruption. Similarly members of some groups (e.g., TM and est) may rely little upon fellow members as family or community surrogates. Thus although the dislocation model is useful, it is not sufficient to explain these sects and cults.

Socioeconomic Change. A third approach to understanding the impact of the larger society upon the formation of sects and cults is the emphasis upon socioeconomic change. One study of historical millenarian movements suggested that the key factor was the ambiguity surrounding a disaster (natural or social) that produced the impetus for such movements (Barkun, 1974). Another study examined a period of prolific movement development, the early nineteenth century in upper New York State. Evidence about the revivals, experimentation, and development of new movements in this time suggested that they were correlated with dramatic economic fluctuation, which had produced alternating rising expectations and disappointments (Cross, 1965). Another interpretation suggests that religious and political movements arise in response to major changes in the world economic order. The type of movement that develops depends, according to this theory, upon whether its adherents are central or peripheral to emerging sources of economic power (Wuthnow, 1978; cf. Anthony and Robbins, 1978).

All available evidence suggests that a strong relationship exists between social conditions and the development of sects and cults. None of the existing models alone is adequate to explain this relationship, though they are not necessarily wrong. What is needed is a sufficiently complex model that incorporates varied causes. Focusing on socioeconomic concomitants of religious movements, however, may lead to ignoring or downplaying the reasons given by members for the group's formation. Religious aspirations themselves are important sources of religious movements. Religious virtuosi seeking to perfect their spiritual lives, cultic seekers looking for new techniques for spiritual experience, persons dissatisfied with the level of religiosity available to them in other collectivities—for these people, *religious* aspirations are foremost among their reasons for joining a developing religious movement. Indeed, parent organizations such as a church often give impetus to such movements by raising members' aspirations. Vatican II and changes within the Roman Catholic church in years immediately following the Vatican Council may have raised religious expectations of church members to such a degree that they subsequently sought developing movements either within the church (e.g., Cursillo, Underground church movement, and Charismatic Renewal) or outside it.

Movement Organizations

Just as our typology of religious collectivities can be viewed as a general typology of organizations in tension with their social environment, so too can the processes by which religious groups change be understood as general. Some useful insights into these processes come from the theory of movement organizations (see Beckford, 1975a). This approach explores how social movements organize themselves toward achieving their goals, how they recruit, consolidate, and deploy members, how they maintain their organization and arrange leadership. This approach has been fruitfully applied to a study of the Young Men's Christian Association (YMCA) (Zald, 1970), a Jesus movement commune (Richardson et al., 1978), Jehovah's Witnesses (Beckford, 1975b), Pentecostalism (Gerlach and Hine, 1970), and Catholic Pentecostalism (Harrison, 1974a, 1974b, 1975).

The factors of deprivation, social dislocation, and massive social change may provide the impetus for a religious movement, but aspects of the movement organization itself determine whether or not the movement will develop and spread. One study of the spread of Pentecostalism identified several movement organizational factors including (1) the relationship among local groups of the movement—flexibly linked networks of local groups promoted the movement's spread; (2) recruitment along the lines of preexisting class social relationships—family and friends; (3) emphasis on a clearly defined commitment act or experience; (4) an ideology offering a simple, easily communicated interpretive order, a sense of sharing in the control and rewards forthcoming, and a feeling of personal worth and power; and (5), emphasis on the perception of real or imagined opposition (Gerlach and Hine, 1968). The researchers found that this model applied not only to expressly religious groups but also to other dissenting movement organizations such as the Black Power movement (Gerlach and Hine, 1970).

Not all of these contributing factors are present or significant for all movements. Jehovah's Witnesses, a rapidly spreading movement, recruit very little among preexisting networks of social relationships (Beckford, 1975b). Some cults recruit almost totally anonymous persons. In 1975, Bo and Peep, who preached salvation through the aid of extraterrestrial beings with flying saucers, recruited over one hundred members (who gave up jobs, family ties, and material possessions) in four brief meetings, usually after less than six hours contact with any member of the group (Balch and Taylor, 1977). Nevertheless the approach is helpful for analyzing some of the ways in which the internal organization of a movement influences its outcome. It also suggests some of the ways (e.g., increasing the perception of opposition) that the group itself influences the tension between itself and its social environment.

Organizational Transformations

Considering the dynamic forces built into our model of religious organization types (i.e., church, sect, denomination, cult), it is not surprising that groups change from one type to another. Forces for change exist within the organization itself (as demonstrated by the "ecclesiolae in ecclesia") and in the relationship of the group to its social environment. The processes by which a religious group changes from one type of organization to another are sociologically important because they reflect both the impact of the group on society and the influence of society upon the group.

Institutionalization: O'Dea. A movement cannot have any lasting impact upon society without some measure of **institutionalization**—that is, the creation of some objective structure by which it tries to realize its values and goals. O'Dea (1961) delineates five inherent dilemmas that institutionalization poses for any social movement.[4] On the one hand, institutionalization enables the emerging movement to express and spread its perspective; on the other hand, it contains built-in tendencies toward stagnation and disorganization, separating members from the initial shared experiences of beliefs that hold them together. Religious reform or revival movements are prototypes of this process, but other movements such as civil rights, environmentalism, communes, and political reform movements also wrestle with the dilemmas of institutionalization.

One such dilemma is the organizational contradiction of **mixed motivation**. According to O'Dea, the earliest stages of a movement are characterized by a singlemindedness of followers; either the cause or the charismatic leader unites members' motivations. As the movement stabilizes, other motives come to the fore: desire for prestige, expression of leadership and teaching abilities, drive for power, search for security, respectability, economic advantages, and so on. The institutionalized movement is stronger precisely because it is able to mobilize the self-interested as well as the disinterested, but members' pursuit of vested interests often conflicts with some of the movement's original ideals. A movement that relies totally upon members with "pure," disinterested motives has little chance for survival, especially after the departure of the charismatic leader who initially united the members. On the other hand, mixed motives frequently lead to compromise and corruption of the movement's ideals.

A second dilemma involves the movement's **symbol system**—its language, ceremonies, and physical symbols of central meanings. In the earliest stages of a movement, members develop symbols by which they attempt to share significant experiences. These special words, ceremonies, and objects express (however incompletely) what it means to be a part of the movement and its distinctive way of life. Without this objectification (i.e., transforming subjective experiences into concrete, shared images), there would be little basis of commonality among

---

[4]The following synopsis of five dilemmas from O'Dea (1961) is used with permission.

movement members. Shared symbols hold the members together and become part of the message they carry to prospective recruits. At the same time, however, there is an inherent tendency in the process of institutionalization for these symbols to become remote from the experiences and meanings that shaped them. They are cut off from the subjective experience of members who use the symbolic objects, group language, or ceremonies; they become ends in themselves or "things" to be manipulated for achieving ends. For example, the "kiss of peace" was an early Christian symbol of communal love, forgiveness, and unity. In many settings now, however, the "kiss" is merely a ritualistic handshake "performed" at a designated part of the worship service. Without symbolization, the central meanings of the movement cannot be transmitted or shared, but symbolization (i.e., objectification) contains the inherent risk that symbols will become alienated from the subjective life of the members.

Movements also face the third dilemma of **organizational elaboration of structures versus movement effectiveness.** As Weber (1947:358ff.) pointed out, the long-term impact of a movement hinges upon transformation of bases of authority and leadership from a charismatic mode to either traditional or legal-rational structures. When a movement becomes established, there is a strong tendency for the organization to calcify around the memory of the early dynamism; its own tradition becomes the rationalization for why things should be done a certain way.

Early stages of movement organization involve simple structures such as the charismatic leader and followers or leader, core followers, and other followers. The transition to legal-rational structures is typically accompanied by the elaboration and standardization of procedures, the emergence of specialized statuses and roles, and the formalizing of communication among members. The early years of the Divine Light Mission in the United States were characterized by rapidly growing, loosely affiliated local ashrams (i.e., groups of devotees, usually living communally), united mainly by devotion to the ambiguous charismatic figure of Guru Maharaj Ji. As the DLM became increasingly structured and centralized, leadership and power focused in the movement's Denver headquarters. The guru's desire to consolidate his power and authority over the American movement resulted in greater formalization: rules and regulations for ashram living, standards for recruited "candidates," and pressure toward certifying movement teachers (Pilarzyk, 1978:33–37). While such division of labor and formalization of structures make the growing movement more efficient, the process may also make it less effective in the long run. The bureaucratic impersonalism and complexity may obstruct some of the movement's original goals. Members come to feel more peripheral to the movement, and their motivation becomes problematic.

A fourth internal dilemma is the **need for concrete definition versus legalism.** On the one hand, the movement's message must be translated into concrete terms in order to apply to people's everyday lives. On the other hand, the concretization that occurs as the movement becomes institutionalized promotes a legalistic approach to those very terms. The ethical insights of a religious movement might be translated into concrete moral rules (e.g., a norm against consuming alcohol); then, if a legalistic approach to this rule arises, members are reproached for breaking the "letter of the law" (e.g., using vanilla extract, which contains alcohol, in baking). Legalism reduces the insight of the ethical message to petty conformity.

The fifth dilemma of institutionalization is that of **power.** The developing movement needs to structure itself so that its message and meaning remain firm. It needs to protect itself, both from threats within and without its boundaries. A certain amount of internal power gives the nascent movement strength against threats that would dissolve it. On the other hand, that same power may be asserted against deviant and dissenting members. Members' compliance may be assured by external pressures or coercion rather than by inner conviction and commitment. Similarly desire for power and influence may motivate movement leaders to assert themselves in other institutional spheres, diverting the movement from its original message and goals. The direction taken by the leadership of the People's Temple illustrates one (albeit extreme) resolution of this dilemma. A number of its practices (e.g., the move to Guyana and the requirement that members give up personal property) can be understood as efforts to overcome the inherent precariousness of charismatic leadership. They were strategies to consolidate power, similar in kind to strategies adopted by leaders of other nascent charismatic movements (see Johnson, 1979).

O'Dea (1961) describes these five contradictions as dilemmas to emphasize the extent to which neither direction (institutionalized or noninstitutionalized) is completely satisfactory. The very processes that would enable a social movement to realize its ideals contain inherent contradictions, which simultaneously prevent the movement from accomplishing these goals. The concept of dilemmas, however, is somewhat misleading, because rarely does a social movement make conscious choices to institutionalize. Nevertheless O'Dea's analysis is useful for showing that frequently criticized features of institutionalized religion (or any other institutionalized social movement) are actually results of the ways in which that movement has organized itself for effectiveness and social impact.

All religious organizations, from the small, informally organized sect to the largest bureaucratically organized church, can be analyzed for how they acquire and use the resources of ideas, people, and materials. Organizations can also be compared for how they socialize, recruit, and control their members. And they can be examined for their structural qualities: specialization, centralization, formalization, and authority relationships (Beckford, 1975a:34–92). Transformations in religious groups frequently involve changes in some of these organizational aspects. Thus sects developing into denominations frequently become more bureaucratically organized. These organizational qualities are not definitive (e.g., not all sects that become bureaucratically organized are transformed into denominations) but rather reflect the inherent tension between the religious group and its social environment. Thus examination of how change occurs in different types of religious organization focuses on the two key characteristics defining our model of organizational types. Transformations in religious groups can be analyzed in terms of two questions: (1) How does the group's sense of its monopolistic or pluralistic legitimacy change, and (2) what are some of the forces affecting the group's tension (negative or positive) with its social environment?

Sect Transformations. The dynamism of sectarian dissent makes the sect a potential force for social change. Yet successful sects seem to accommodate to society with great regularity, eventually becoming indistinguishable from denominations (Niebuhr, 1929). The transformation of sect-type groups into denomination-type groups is more prevalent in American society than other possible transformations such as sect-to-cult or sect-to-church. These latter directions are also theoretically possible, however. Sects can become churches, both by accommodating to the larger society and by consolidating their position to achieve a monopoly of legitimacy. Christianity began as a minority sect within Judaism, and in its spread to other cultural settings it gradually consolidated its position, achieving an effective monopoly of legitimacy under Constantine.

Similarly sects can change into cults. Since this transformation involves giving up claim to unique legitimacy, the process is often the result of authority dissolution within the group. If a charismatic leader has successfully organized the group around his or her personal authority to present "the truth," the death or downfall of that leader might delegitimate that "truth." If the group comes to view those teachings as pluralistically legitimate, it is likely to become a cult (if it survives the leadership crisis at all).

A good example of this dissolution is the development of one flying saucer cult (Festinger et al., 1956). The group initially began as a cult, one of several groups from which members drew their inspiration, but gradually became a sect, especially as its role in the prophesied imminent end of the world was made clear by the increasingly authoritative pronouncements of group leaders. The failure of the prophecy undermined the authority of key leaders and eliminated a major basis for the group's distinctiveness—its position as the "elect" to be saved by flying saucers. Although failure of the prophecy did not destroy the group altogether, it gradually became more cultlike again, receding into the general cultic milieu.

Sects and cults are organizationally more precarious than denominations and churches because dissent and deviance are difficult to maintain in the face of opposition from other religious groups and the larger society. Sects, in particular, are likely to clash with the church and society because of their claim to unique legitimacy. On the other hand, history provides several examples of groups that sustained their sectarian dissent and never developed denominational patterns. The Old Order Amish have for many generations preserved their distinctive beliefs and way of life, largely by withdrawing into their own communities.

Such groups may be considered *established* sects (Yinger, 1970:266–273), groups engaged in sectarian dissent that have organized their internal and external social arrangements toward the perpetuation of their distinctiveness. Some of the internal arrangements that promote the success of social movements—the quality of leadership, commitment and recruitment processes, social control, and ideology—enable sects to become more stable. Arrangements for the relationship of the group to society also promote the establishment of sects; the group may withdraw physically from the rest of society, like the Amish. Or it may migrate to a more favorable environment, like the Hutterites and Bruderhof (Peters, 1971; Zablocki, 1971). Or it may insulate itself by regulating members' contact with nonmembers and the rest of society, like the Hassidim (Poll, 1969; Shaffir, 1974), censoring or forbidding exposure to mass media, limiting occasions of visiting with nonmembers, or absorbing members so totally that outside influences cannot affect them. Such insulation may intensify the group's sectarianism, as in the case of the Exclusive Brethren (Wilson, 1967:287). Established sects have effectively developed boundaries—physical, ideological, or symbolic—between themselves and the threatening "world." Interestingly, pluralistic societies make it difficult for sects to establish these boundaries because such societies are more likely to be tolerant of the sect and not intensify its sense of opposition. In a totalistic society, by contrast, social opposition can fortify the sect's boundaries, indirectly promoting its survival.

At the same time, however, established sects appear to be somewhat more accommodated in some aspects than new sects. They may be less strident in their claims of uniquely legitimate authority, or they may develop a slightly more positive tension with "the world," perhaps relaxing part of their stand. Their relationship with society depends partly upon how society relates to them. The dominant social or religious group may become more tolerant, allowing the sect greater freedom to maintain its distinctive ways. The development of Mormonism into an established sect resulted partly from internal organization and partly from gradual tolerance by society.

Sects become denominations by giving up their claim to exclusive legitimacy and by reducing their dissent, accommodating to society. Certain kinds of sects tend more to such changes than others. Sects that express their dissent by withdrawing from society are less vulnerable to accommodation pressures than are sects that aim to convert society (Wilson, 1967:26–27). Similarly sects that dissent against the evils of society are more resistant to transformation than sects emphasizing individual sin or anxiety (Yinger, 1970:272).

The process of accommodation is not necessarily all on the part of the sect; the dominant religion or social group can change as well (B. Johnson, 1971). As the society or established church changes, the sect's tension with that larger group also changes, and the sect may be thrust toward greater or less negative tension with society.

The transformation of sect to denomination is not always in one direction. A group may move toward denominationalism, then have an internal "reform" and move back toward sectarianism. In the 1880s, the Society of Friends (i.e., Quakers) underwent a crisis, in which some members criticized the group's growing compromise with "the world." There were both sectarian and denominational orientations within the group, which had gradually became prosperous and denominationlike. During the crisis, members returned to their historical roots and decided to eliminate a number of their more denominationlike practices (e.g., having ministers and birthright membership) (Isichei, 1967:181). Our model of types of religious collectivities consists of dynamic forces on two continua. Thus we can imagine groups moving in either direction on either continuum: becoming more or less pluralistic, and having more or less negative tension with society.

The prosperity of the Quakers illustrates another factor in sect transformation. Does the very success of a group make it difficult or impossible to retain original ideals and dissent? It is easier for group members to reject the things of "the world" if they are too poor to afford them. As the sect members become established and increasingly respectable in the community, there is pressure to relax restrictions and become more like their neighbors.

These changes are further promoted by the fact that children of the generation that founded the sect have not had the distinctive experiences of their parents. The second generation's commitment to the group may be serious, but certain issues that were very important to their elders may not hold much significance for them. The "sabras" (i.e., subsequent generation) of the Israeli kibbutzim did not have the intense group experience of hardship and fellowship of the initial Zionist pioneers who settled on the land in the newly created Jewish homeland. The pioneers had forged a group vision of an ascetic communal existence, but subsequent generations of members do not have that unique experience as the basis of their commitment (Spiro, 1970:38–59).

A number of studies have suggested that the values and social interaction of some sects, while dissonant from those of the larger society, have the unintended effect of making members more prosperous and acceptable by the standards of society. Certain fundamentalist Christian sects encourage their members to work hard and reliably, to respect authority, and to refrain from drinking, smoking, gambling, and entertainments. Thus sect values increase the likelihood of members' earning steady wages while not spending that money—except on religious activities. The overall effect is that members are socialized into acceptable roles in society and are able to enjoy material comforts (Johnson, 1961); their sectarian dissent inadvertently brings dissidents "back" into the dominant society. This process does not occur in all groups, however. Sects that live communally withdrawn from society are better able to control the socialization of their members and to disperse material comforts over the entire religious community. Some sects, in fact, socialize their members into roles that are extremely dysfunctional in the larger society, making exit from the sect very difficult (Beckford, 1978b). Nevertheless material success is a built-in threat to some sects, because it is more difficult to dissent from a society in which one has a stake and is enjoying some benefits.

Similarly organizational success is a threat to sect stability. If a sect is successful in attracting many members and expanding into new geographical areas, it may grow more denominationlike. The group may become bureaucratized and rely upon religious specialists—ministers, fundraisers, religious teachers, and so on. Some established sects (e.g., Jehovah's Witnesses) demonstrate the possibility of retaining the dissenting stance under a complex organization. Nevertheless organizational success brings structures that make it difficult to retain the initial sectarian enthusiasm and small-group intensity.

Cult Transformations. Cults are highly precarious organizational forms. Their characteristic pluralism together with their members' general individualistic mode of adherence make them more unstable than other types of religious collectivity. The typical cult transformation is from cult to sect, but some cults are able to stabilize their groups as established cults. Spiritualism, now nearly 135 years old as a movement, has retained its cultic form. It is loosely organized around independent Spiritualist "mediums," some of whom are affiliated in a network of contacts but with little organizational control or authority (Nelson, 1969).

By contrast, a large number of groups that began with a cultic phase have transformed into sects. The Jesus People (Richardson, 1979a), Christian Science (Wallis, 1973), the Bruderhof (Zablocki, 1971), Scientology (Wallis, 1977), and the Unification Church (Lofland, 1966) all began as cult-type groups. The fragility of cults as social organizations results from their indistinct and pluralistic doctrine, their problem of authority, and the individualistic, segmental mode of commitment characteristic of cultic adherents. In the transformation from cult to sect, the key feature is the arrogation of authority; certain members successfully claim strong authority, thereby enabling them to clarify the boundaries of the group belief system and membership. The successful claim to strong authority gives leaders a basis for exercising social control in the group and for excluding persons who do not accept the newly consolidated belief system. Movement toward sectarianism may be a deliberate strategy of cult leaders or simply the by-product of other organizational decisions (Wallis, 1974, 1977).

Other factors promoting this cult-to-sect transformation, in addition to internal group factors, include factors relating to individual members and to the social environment. Interaction between the cult and other elements of society sometimes promotes the transformation. Largely because of the material and moral encouragement of branches of certain established sects and denominations, the Jesus movement's initial cultic independence was transformed. It became increasingly sectlike, consolidating its belief system along the lines of these outside groups (Richardson, 1979a). One element of this belief system was a greater emphasis upon authority in the religious community and in families.

Other cult transformations (to denomination or church) are theoretically possible but uncommon. It is unlikely that a group with cultlike organizational characteristics would have any propensity toward becoming a church. On the other hand, the cult's characteristic pluralism would seem to have strong affinity with the pluralistic tolerance of denominations; yet there are few if any documented instances of a cult transforming directly into a denomination. Instead, cults apparently first undergo internal organization changes, often becoming more sectlike, and later edge toward being more denominationlike. Christian Science began as a cult but experienced the early consolidation of authority of Mary Baker Eddy. Its organizational form was somewhat sectlike for most of its history, though its middle-class members were often more cultic in their style of adherence. With increasing social acceptability, the group now appears to be moving toward the denomination end of the typology.

Denomination Transformations. The denomination is the predominant organizational form of religious groups in America today. Widespread religious pluralism is, however, a relatively recent phenomenon, so there is little historical evidence concerning denominational changes. History provides several examples of groups arising as denominations and becoming established as denominations. The Reform movement among Jews was from its outset more tolerant and positively oriented toward society than its Orthodox predecessor (see Steinberg, 1965). The movement required organizational stability and popular acceptance before it could become an established denomination. Similarly Congregationalism and Methodism were born as denominations rather than sects (Martin, 1965:4). Some of the mainline black denominations (e.g., the African

Methodist Episcopal church) also began as denominations. Theirs was never a theological protest against the parent group but mainly a reorganization to allow blacks to achieve leadership and other important roles in their church (Washington, 1972).

A group that begins as a denomination but moves away from its stance of pluralism is likely to develop a more sectlike organizational form. The Salvation Army, for example, became a sect after its more pluralistic beginnings (Robertson, 1967). Just as sectarianization is a strategy for consolidating control in cults, so too are denominations susceptible to sectarianization. But societal pluralism in America makes it highly unlikely that a denomination could achieve a sufficient monopoly of legitimacy to become a church.

Changes in society appear to be influencing some denominations toward a more sectlike status. To the extent that society does not support or accept key beliefs of groups, they may develop a sectlike organization to protect those beliefs and practices. Societal changes are creating more negative tension between many established religious groups and society, thus encouraging sectlike responses (see Roof, 1978:215–227). For example, increasing sexual "permissiveness" in society presses denominations that do not accept this attitude to retreat toward a more defensive, negative posture.

Church Transformations. Similarly changes in social setting create changes in modes of organization in church-type collectivities. If a group is unable to maintain its monolithic status, it cannot continue as a church-type collectivity. Churches that retain their claims to unique legitimacy are likely to take on sectlike characteristics. The Roman Catholic church of early twentieth-century immigrants in America maintained a highly sectarian stance to protect its members from the beliefs and practices of the predominantly Protestant culture. More recently its greater tolerance of other religions has moved American Roman Catholicism toward a denominational form. In England, the transformation of the Church of England (i.e., Episcopalian) from its churchlike form to a denominational form was primarily the result of increasing society-wide pluralism (Swatos, 1979). Church-to-sect and church-to-denomination are the two main historical transformations of church-type collectivities.

Implications of Organizational Transformations
The types of religious collectivity characteristic of various periods or societies vary. Changes in religious collectivities often reflect responses to society. Religion may be undergoing some significant changes in its social form and location (as Chapter 8 will describe in more detail). An examination of transformations in religious collectivities can help us grasp some emerging patterns.

Sectarianism in Contemporary Society. Whether as a deliberate strategy or simple adaptation, increasing sectarianism may well be necessary for certain religious groups in contemporary society. The primary, close-knit, face-to-face relationship is an important part of the sectarian orientation because it supports the believer in the face of real or perceived opposition. The group helps maintain the believer's assurance of being part of the "one way" despite a hostile or unbelieving "world." The close-knit group provides support for a **cognitive minority**—a group of people whose world view differs from that of the dominant society. Primary group relationships provide a structure within which the believers' distinctive world view is plausible, whereas outside the group that world view is disconfirmed (Berger, 1967:163).

To the extent that *any* religious group attempts to maintain its distinctiveness and applicability to all aspects of life, it runs counter to developments in society—especially the compartmentalizing of religion into the private sphere. Even established religious groups take on some qualities of the traditional sect as they organize to protect their beliefs, practices, and values in the face of society's lack of support. The group must provide its own social support for its beliefs and way of life. Members become a cognitive minority and therefore structure their interactions with each other and the "outside" to protect their world view (Berger, 1967:163ff.). This change toward sectarianism is, however, primarily a *reaction* to changes in society. Any group, regardless of how extreme or mainstream its beliefs, that seeks a different role for religion in society is thrust into a minority position.

Privatized Religiosity in Contemporary Society Other types of religious collectivity are well suited to privatized religiosity. Denominations that focus upon religiosity in the private sphere (i.e., family, community, parish)—and cults, with their characteristic individualism and eclectic approach to beliefs and practices—fit very well into their privatized slot. Neither claims exclusive legitimacy, and neither expects its beliefs and practices to govern behavior in all aspects of social life. A member of an Eastern cult or a Human Potential group may find in them greater interior peace and joy, relief from stress and tensions in everyday life, and more satisfying ways of relating to others. At the same time, the person may be an effective corporate manager whose religious beliefs and practices do not challenge or guide behavior in the business world. The cult can perform an adaptive role, providing meaning and a sense of belonging without conflicting with members' roles in a highly differentiated society (Robbins et al., 1975).

In this context, we can examine the significance of emerging religious movements in contemporary Western society. The last two decades have witnessed the emergence of several new religious movements and the rebirth and transformation of some old ones. Although most of these movements are clearly still religious minorities, they have attracted significant numbers of people. In 1976 the Gallup Poll found that about 12 percent of those polled were engaged in one or more of these recent movements (i.e., mysticism, Oriental religions, yoga, Transcendental Meditation, and the charismatic renewal). Cultic movements, TM and yoga, accounted for 4 percent and 3 percent of the response, respectively. Mysticism (which could be practiced in combination with most other religious perspectives, including traditional religions) accounted for 2 percent, as did the charismatic renewal, which includes members of many traditional religions such as Episcopalianism, Lutheranism, and Roman Catholicism. A further 1 percent were involved in an Eastern religion. Projecting from this sample, these figures suggest that approximately 19 million Americans are involved in these diverse religious movements (Gallup Poll, 1976a).

The sheer number and diversity of new religious movements makes it difficult to generalize about these developments. Some groups (e.g., Zen Buddhism) are based upon elements borrowed directly from traditional Oriental religions. Others (e.g., Sokka Gakkai and the Unification Church) are syncretic religions that emerged in the Orient and took on further dimensions in their American translation. Some emerging religions such as the Jesus People, the charismatic renewal, and neo-Evangelicalism are adaptations of older Christian movements. Other movements such as Arica took their inspiration, as well as some of their language, from the Human Potential movement—an amalgam of religious and psychotherapeutic beliefs and practices.

The following Extended Application suggests a sociological interpretation of these emerging religious movements.

Extended Application: Emerging Religious Movements

The image of the new religious movements that have caught the attention of the press, public, and social scientists is of a diverse, colorful, strange, or exotic assortment of religious groups. The picture includes saffron-robed, head-shaven youths on street corners singing "Hare Krishna." It includes troups of hippielike young people "praising the Lord" in rural communes. It includes Eastern gurus, flashy evangelists, door-to-door witnessing, religious gatherings in football stadiums, flower distribution in airports, vegetarian restaurants, incense manufacture, records and tape cassettes with new hymns or religious messages by group leaders. It also includes the more somber image of several hundred adherents who committed mass suicide in a remote jungle. Getting beyond the sensationalistic treatment that such movements have received in newspaper and television coverage is difficult. The preceding discussion of the types and transformations of religious collectivities is useful in providing a framework for interpreting the bewildering variety of new religious movements.

Analyzing sects, cults, denominations, and churches is more than a mere exercise in typologizing. The foremost purpose of categorizing religious collectivities is to conceptualize a situation and then to ask: Of what larger phenomenon is this an example? The types of collectivities characteristic of emerging religious movements are related to their cultural setting. For this reason, two movements by the same name have very different significances in different societies. An upswing of interest in Pentecostalism has occurred in both the United States and Colombia, but the social location and social organization of these movements suggest that Pentecostalism has a totally different social significance in Colombia than in the United States (Flora, 1976).

In Chapter 2, these movements were interpreted as a response to a perceived lack of normative order or moral unity. There are many other possible responses to such situations, but religion has historically been one important form of response. *The particular social forms taken by a religious response to moral ambiguity are themselves directly related to the nature of the society.* By examining emerging religious movements, we gain some insight into the nature of contemporary society.

The Variety of Emerging Religious Movements

Writing around the turn of the century, Durkheim (1965:475) made some predictions about the future of religion that ring surprisingly true today:

> If we find a little difficulty today in imagining what these feasts and ceremonies of the future could consist in, it is because we are going through a stage of transition and moral mediocrity. The great things of the past which filled our fathers with enthusiasm do not excite the same ardour in us, either because they have come into common usage to such an extent that we are unconscious of them or else because they no longer answer to our actual aspirations; but as yet there is nothing to replace them. . . . In a word, the old gods are growing old or already dead, and others are not yet born. . . . it is life itself, and not a dead past which can produce a living cult.

The new religious movements appear anomalous because they have emerged precisely at a time when religion, as this society has traditionally known it, seems weakest. While theologians were exploring the meaning of the "death of God" and church administrators were trying to cope with membership slippages and general drops in attendance—and while social scientists were debating the thesis of "secularization" (see Chapter 8)—new religious movements emerged, and many of them flourished. Some of these movements are particularly interesting because they appealed to societal sectors that seemed least likely to be attracted to conventional religious movements—young, educated, cosmopolitan, comfortably middle-class persons.

The apparent newness and uniqueness of these developments are, however, misleading. New religious movements have been emerging throughout America's history, in part the result of American religious and cultural pluralism. The diversity of sects that characterized America's early religious pluralism brought one Puritan minister to call the sect-filled commonwealth of Rhode Island "the sewer of New England." Later periods of great religious fervor were the Great Awakening (1730s) and the Second Great Awakening (1790s onward). The latter continued for some years and stimulated pioneer revivalism in the Western expansion well into the nineteenth century. The early nineteenth century saw many religious and communal experiments such as Ralph Waldo Emerson's Transcendental Fellowship (which spawned the Brook Farm commune) and John Humphrey Noyes's Perfectionists (out of which the Oneida commune was born). Millenarian groups such as Seventh Day Adventists and, later, Jehovah's Witnesses were founded and became especially active as the turn of the century approached. A related movement, Fundamentalism, arose within Protestantism and caused considerable controversy. The Holiness movement, out of which Pentecostalism emerged, also brought about conflict in some churches. A very different, late Victorian development was the rise of Spiritualism and related cults such as "animal magnetism" (i.e., hypnosis) and various healing groups, including New Thought and Christian Science. A number of nonofficial religions flourished, though the actual size of their followings is unknown; many of these groups drew upon occult traditions of Europe such as Gnosticism, kabbalism, astrology, Rosicrucianism, and so on (Ahlstrom, 1972, 1978).

Recent new religious movements are, from this perspective, simply the latest in a long history of eruptions of religious fervor. Even the more exotic new religions emerged from a preexisting social base. The two main sources of new religious movements are the Judeo-Christian heritage and the more amorphous nonofficial religious area or "cultic milieu" (Ellwood, 1978). The Judeo-Christian strain is a fertile source of new religions because of its built-in tendency for cycles of renewal, reform, and schism. In recent times, there is an inherent potential for religious retrenchment to organize itself in sectarian forms, especially as the dominant culture in Western societies becomes less consistent with conservative Jewish/Christian ideologies.

Another segment of new religious movements emerged from the already present but unorganized stratum of nonofficial religion. Most ideas and many ritual practices of numerous new religions were already present in the cultic milieu, but the new movements shaped the ideas and adherents into an organized form. Some new religious movements claim to be totally new; others emphasize that they are older even than historical religions such as Christianity. Nevertheless as a social phenomenon, even the more exotic new religions have their roots in identifiable clusters of prior beliefs and practices.

Nonofficial religion tends to spawn cults (as defined earlier in this chapter), though some of these are eventually transformed into sects through changes in the authority pattern. One main reason for this tendency is that nonofficial religion itself is seldom a coherent, authoritative, organized belief system; adherents are often loosely affiliated, drawn together only by vaguely similar perspectives or parallel beliefs. Cults emerge from the amorphous background of nonofficial religion; they organize around a teacher or a technique and are inherently fragile because cultic adherence is highly individualistic and eclectic. Thus they typically dissolve back into the diffuse milieu from which they came, and members find other focuses for their beliefs and practices within the larger nonofficial religious setting. From the perspective of official religion, then, with its emphasis upon organizational permanence and numbers of adherents, cultic religious movements are insignificant. This view, however, overlooks the considerable staying power of general cultic ideas and of the numerous adherents who subscribe simultaneously to official and nonofficial religion (Ellwood, 1978).

For all their apparent diversity, new religious movements generally share four central themes. The first is an emphasis upon *religious experience*. In contrast to the more rational ways of knowing prevalent in society, these groups encourage direct experiencing through mysticism, meditation, or secret knowledge.

A second central theme is *power*, to which new religious movements offer their adherents access. Some groups describe this power as purely spiritual; others suggest that the power obtained can affect other spheres—moral, political, economic, physical, and mental. Although the ways in which various new religious movements conceptualize and use their power are quite diverse, the empowerment of adherents is a desired goal.

A third key theme is *order*. Some groups emphasize a sense of order that implies authority, firm moral norms, and judgment. Others conceptualize order in terms of harmony and tranquillity.

The fourth theme, that of *unity*, is common in new religious movements. Some groups emphasize unity through communalism or religious redefinition of family. Others focus on psychic or physical unity, exemplified by their emphasis upon holistic healing.

An examination of two contemporary American religious movements exemplifies some of the diversity and similarities among the new religions. The Catholic Charismatic Renewal (or Catholic Pentecostalism) is a movement arising directly from the Judeo-Christian heritage and parallels a similar neo-Pentecostal movement among Protestants. Silva Mind Control exemplifies the more cultlike movements arising from the context of the cultic milieu, scientism, and therapeutic group movements. The beliefs, rituals, and organizational structure of the Catholic Charismatic Renewal (CCR) contrast strongly with those of Silva Mind Control (SMC), but both movements emphasize the four themes just described.[5]

Catholic Charismatic Renewal

The CCR began in 1967, growing out of a prayer and fellowship group of faculty and graduate students at Duquesne University. By 1980, the movement had approximately 750,000 members. Never a "youth culture" movement, though its appeal has extended to college campuses, the CCR has a membership that is predominantly middle-aged. Its members are also generally well educated and middle-class (belying the notion that such movements flourish only among the disadvantaged). The movement attracts active Roman Catholics, many of whom have previously participated in church-approved religious activities or movements such as Christian Family Movement, Marriage Encounter, and Cursillo. These other movements serve both as a funnel of potential recruits to CCR and as a source of the encounter language and experience orientation of CCR.

The broader background of the CCR movement includes the events of Vatican II (in the early 1960s), which provided impetus for much rethinking and rearranging in all aspects of the Roman Catholic church. Vatican II made "renewal" an acceptable goal. The beliefs and practices of Catholic Pentecostalism are directly related to earlier movements, including a wave of Protestant neo-Pentecostalism in the early 1960s, the Protestant Pentecostal movement of the early twentieth century, and religious millenarianism of the late nineteenth century. Reformist movements have arisen many times within Roman Catholicism; some split off as sects, some were incorporated within the church as orders and similar organizations, and many others simply disintegrated. Thus the Pentecostal reformist movement within Roman Catholicism in the twentieth century is not a totally new religious movement; the CCR emerged from a long history of comparable ones.

The CCR is prototypical of recent reform movements within traditional Western religions. It proclaims that religion is relevant to all spheres of members' lives, and it seeks to renew that relevance by reference to an earlier tradition or Christian way of life. Pentecostalism especially emphasizes the life of the early church (as described in the biblical book of Acts, for example) as a basis for Christian life. In particular, Pentecostal movements expect their members to experience the "gifts of the Spirit," such as those received by the early church at Pentecost. Most

---

[5]This information is based upon my own research, fully reported in *Control of Charisma*, 1981; descriptions of SMC are drawn from Westley, 1978a, 1978b.

contemporary reform movements, especially in Christian groups, attempt to recover the purity and orthodoxy of an earlier religious way of life; they are thus relatively conservative. Because they attempt to apply this religious orthodoxy to all spheres of everyday life, they also tend to be sectarian (as explained earlier in this chapter) in their organizations and characteristic orientations to the group and society.

The CCR emphasizes themes comparable to most other new religious movements: experience, power, order, and unity. Their interpretation of these themes are similar to those of some other new movements in Christian settings but differ in certain important ways from the new religious movements of Eastern, psychotherapeutic, or cultic inspiration. In the CCR, religious experience is framed in terms of the "gifts of the Spirit." Members seek a "baptism of the Holy Spirit," which produces inner experiences (e.g., a sense of peace or joy), and is often manifested by the special "gifts." Emphasis upon these gifts ("charisms") accounts for the movement's self-designation as "charismatic" (this should not be confused with the sociological term *charisma*, which is not necessarily a religious quality). The most frequent charism is the "gift of tongues" (i.e., glossolalia), by which members pray in verbalizations that are not recognizable languages. Less spectacular gifts such as wisdom, faith, and love are also believed to be received in this baptism. Charismatic prayer groups expect to receive other gifts as they mature "in the Spirit." These include, among others, gifts of healing, discernment of spirits, knowledge, prophecy, and interpretation of prophecy.

These groups emphasize knowing God through experience, rather than just knowing about God. Personal experience (e.g., praying in tongues) and group experiences (e.g., hearing a prophecy—believed to be God speaking directly to the group through one of its members) are of primary importance in the CCR. These experiences are closely related to the movement's emphasis upon power. The belief system holds that the Holy Spirit is powerful and that this power is available to the individual through the charisms. Accordingly the Holy Spirit empowers the individual for better prayer, personal transformation, fighting evil, and personal healing. Similarly the group is empowered in its battle with evil and in its prayer, praise, and healing. Thus religious experience is seen as both validating the group's belief system and empowering its members in their personal lives and relationships with others.

These beliefs and practices are also related to the movement's emphasis upon order. One expression of this emphasis is the movement's reaffirmation of a strong moral order—a sense of right versus wrong. Sin, repentance, confession, forgiveness, and salvation are important themes in its teachings. This focus on moral order accompanies the movement's dualistic stance. Members use the image of "warring" against Satan, a war conceptualized as a battle of powers, explaining that the experience of God's power makes members more aware of the power of the "Evil One" (i.e., Satan). Many "gifts of the Spirit" are used in this war; the gift of discernment, for example, enables members to distinguish God's inspirations from those of the devil. Prayer meetings and healing rituals typically include prayers to exorcise the devil and prevent "his" influence on the group. Dualism, the belief in the opposition of cosmic forces of Good and Evil (as discussed in Chapter 2), is a response to moral ambiguity, an assertion of order.

Another expression of the CCR's emphasis upon order is its internal structure. Although the prayer meetings characteristically appear to be loosely organized and spontaneous outpourings of religious feeling and praise, the local prayer group and the larger movement organization are usually highly structured. Movement leadership teaches that the authority structure of the group is related to Spirit-given gifts. The hierarchical organization is legitimated by a belief in "headship and submission." A member may have headship over certain others, who are expected to submit to that person's guidance; simultaneously a husband or father is considered to have headship over his wife and children, who are expected to submit to his authority, and so on. The movement is highly critical of the lack of moral order in the rest of the church and society.

The theme of unity is also prominent in the CCR. Full union of the individual with other believers and with God is held as the ideal. As suggested in Chapter 6, moral order and group cohesion are closely intertwined. The prayer group is one expression of this theme of unity. Prayer group members pray together frequently, help each other in times of need, counsel each other, share material goods when needed, and express feelings of unity with each other. In this sense, the prayer group is an expansion of the family or neighborhood, fulfilling in a religious context some of the functions no longer assumed by most contemporary families or neighborhoods. A further extension of the unity theme is the development of communalism within the movement. Some members have formed intensive communities in which they share housing, finances, childcare, meals, and housework, in addition to their prayer life together. At the same time, this unity of the small, close-knit group of fellow believers serves to protect prayer group members from "the world," shoring up members' defenses against those aspects of modern society that the movement decries.

Silva Mind Control

SMC was founded by José Silva in the late 1960s and is representative of many of the new religious or quasi-religious movements that have derived from the Human Potential movement—an amalgam of partly religious, partly psychologistic, partly cultic themes, termed the "encounter culture" by some observers. Like CCR, SMC has considerable appeal to middle-aged, middle-class, generally better educated persons. In recent years, it has become even further "normalized" in the form of adult school classes. The movement offers (for a fee) to develop its adherents into "active psychics." Members are taught techniques for becoming clairvoyant, telepathic, and psychic healers. The belief system includes explanations for why people cannot use their perceptions adequately before "training"; bad idea habits and "negative thinking" prevent full realization of human potential for perception and mental control.

The ideas and practices of this movement seem strange and unfamiliar in comparison to traditional Christian notions such as expressed by the CCR. SMC is, however, only one of the latest eruptions of these ideas and practices. Practices of telepathy, clairvoyance, and psychic powers have long been part of the cultic milieu and were particularly emphasized in many nineteenth-century cults; the use of psychic powers for healing was important in many movements (e.g., New Thought). These earlier movements were combined with some elements of Christianity in Mary Baker Eddy's teachings, which eventually developed into Christian Science (early twentieth century). Another strand of the Human Potential movement is a development of human consciousness through special kinds of interpersonal encounter. Although the philosophy of the "encounter culture" is often explained in terms drawn from psychology, it has its precedent in other earlier religious movements such as Pietism (Oden, 1972). The most obvious, early nineteenth-century parallel was Noyes's Perfectionism. The Perfectionist commune Oneida practiced consciousness raising, complex marriage, mutual criticism, and "women's lib" on a scale far more dramatic (relative to its time) than most contemporary Human Potential groups. Thus the recent emergence of themes of Human Potential and psychic powers is not a unique development. New religious movements such as SMC are simply the latest in a well-established stream of alternative religious practices.

SMC is a good example of the cult-type new religious movements. It poses an alternative belief system, emphasizing aspects of belief and practice not accepted in the rest of society, yet it is generally tolerant of other belief systems. Adherents are seldom committed solely to SMC and often simultaneously or serially participate in other religious groups as they seek further techniques, experiences, and particles of truth. The organization and structure of SMC groups is typical of certain kinds of cult-type groups. There is a national administrative center, local chapters organized by individual instructors, and students. Members respect José Silva as a "developed" man with psychic talents worth emulating, but they do not elevate him to ultimate authority or treat him as superhuman. Likewise instructors have little authority over the lives of students; their relationship is generally limited to class time and class subjects—learning of the appropriate beliefs and techniques.

SMC also emphasizes the central themes of experience, power, order, and unity. Unlike CCR, however, it defines the experience in terms of the individual's self rather than some transcendent Other (e.g., the Holy Spirit). SMC teaches that individuals' inner essences are different from their everyday personalities. The desired experience or knowledge pertains to that inner essence, through which control and extraordinary powers may be exercised. Although these teachings are accompanied by considerable scientific-sounding explanation, adherents do not seek to "understand" the results of techniques, only to experience them.

Power and control are major themes in SMC, as the very name implies. SMC teaches that the source of power is in the individual, requiring only knowledge and practice to tap. Sometimes instructors use the image of an internal laboratory with controls that the individual can manipulate after learning how to enter the internal lab and use them. The climax of initial training sessions is a healing ritual, in which newly trained adherents are asked to try to heal, at a distance, the illness of a person whom the healer has never met. Tapping newly acquired psychic abilities, the adherent is supposed to develop a description of the person and illness, then diagnose the illness and heal the person. This healing ritual emphasizes the psychic powers of new adherents.

Emphasis on order is also important in SMC though there is little concern for traditional moral formulations. Instead, disorder is interpreted as the confusion of everyday reality. SMC teaches that a major obstacle to achievement of psychic power and control is the cluttered, disordered state of people's minds. Meditation techniques are devices to "clear" the mind of "beta-waves," negative thinking, and other bad idea habits. In contrast to CCR, the sources of disorder are believed to be purely internal, not a transcendent Other (e.g., Satan). This difference means that the two kinds of groups have very different conceptions of individual responsibility for one's condition.

The theme of unity is expressed by SMC in its emphasis upon psychic and physical unity—the wholeness of the individual. Unlike the CCR, there is little concern for unity among adherents, though some camaraderie does develop among students in a training class. Instead, SMC encourages an individualistic approach, with each person seeking to improve his or her own powers. This individualistic mode of adherence is characteristic of cults; fellow believers may be helpful but are rarely considered essential to the individual's own success in achieving the group's ideal.

One interpretation of the upswing of interest in cult-type religions such as Human Potential groups is that they are possibly fulfilling Durkheim's prophecies about the shape of religion in modern pluralistic society: the "cult of man." Durkheim (1969:26) stated:

> As societies become more voluminous and spread over vaster territories, their traditions and practices   . are compelled to maintain a state of plasticity and instability which no longer offers adequate resistance to individual variations. These latter, being less well contained, develop more freely and multiply in number; that is, everyone increasingly follows his own path.

Elsewhere Durkheim (1951:336) predicted that in complex societies, religion would focus on the enhancement of the human personality because this would be all that members of such diverse societies would have in common. Traditional religions locate the sacred outside the individual, reflecting (according to Durkheim) the self-consciousness of the whole social group. Although the "cult of man" would express and dramatize social relations, sacred power in such religion would be located within each individual (Westley, 1978a:139). The idealization of individual humanity lends itself to cult organization, with its characteristic pluralism and individualism.

Implications of New Religious Movements

The emergence of numerous, diverse religious movements at this point in history may have come as a surprise to many observers, especially those predicting the demise of religion. New religious movements have emerged, as we have seen, from a broad background and long history of similar movements. Nevertheless in interpreting this latest eruption of religious movements, we need to ask why they are emerging now and why these particular types of movements are finding such wide appeal.

One approach suggests that new religions develop in response to crises in world economic order and that the type of religious movement varies according to the location of adherents relative to the bases of economic power (Wuthnow, 1978). Another possible interpretation views new movements (in modern Western societies, at least) as responses to the disintegrating old bases of moral or political order. This interpretation explains dualistic movements such as the CCR and Jesus movement as protests against the moral relativism and permissiveness of American culture; other new movements (e.g., Human Potential and imported Oriental religions) turn the moral relativism into a virtue (Robbins et al., 1978).

Another approach suggests that these movements represent two kinds of responses to the demands of modern societies on individuals. Cultlike groups offer the ability to control and change one's social "face"—to manipulate one's social identities—while at the same time reaffirming a hidden-core self (Bird, 1978, 1979). Sectlike groups address the same problem of self by consolidating all social identities into a single, central, religiously defined self and by strengthening the institutions (e.g., religious group and family) that control and support that self.

Although all of the new religious movements assert alternate meaning systems and practices, their opposition to the dominant culture and religiosity is limited. Neither sectlike nor cultlike movements are generally involved in social activism, though some of the conservative sectlike groups have overlapping membership with other socially or politically conservative groups. Cult-type groups, with their characteristic pluralism, are particularly accepting of many dominant culture values. They propose an alternative world view and practices that emphasize neglected aspects of reality, but this alternative conveniently enhances adherents' chances for success or, at least, happiness in the context of the dominant society (Bird, 1978:181).

Sectlike groups, while encouraging members to see a gap between their way and the "ways of the world," are often similarly accommodated to the values of the dominant culture. Members of CCR prayer groups frequently witnessed that God had blessed them with success on the job or with material goods, as evidence of God's power. The tension of contemporary religious movements with the rest of church and society appears to be segmented or privatized, and the apparent impotence of such protest may be related to wider issues of secularization, as discussed in Chapter 8 (see Bellah, 1976; Wallis, 1978; Wilson, 1976).

This tension of new sects and cults with the society raises the issue of their long-term impact. Religious movements are potential sources of social transformation (explicated further in Chapter 7). Are the new religious movements transformative? Or do they serve merely to integrate their adherents into the dominant society (see Hargrove, 1978; Robbins et al., 1975)? Many of the movements themselves explain their privatistic situation as a positive feature. They assert that real social change will emerge through their movement by the transformation of individuals. They are not typically critical of the social structure but focus their criticism of society upon the private sphere: the individual, family, and community.

Nevertheless social movements such as these have in the past often influenced the society indirectly. Their ideas filter into the mainstream culture, and they serve as experimental models for the rest of society. The idea of holistic health and treatment of illness has filtered (in a watered-down form) from religious movements to mainstream medical schools. Whether such influences are ultimately transformative cannot yet be known. Are the new religious movements bringing about a "new age" or ushering in the millennium? Or are they ways of smoothing such unpleasant aspects of modern life as loss of freedom and control in the public sphere and doubts about self and interpersonal relations in the private sphere? These implications suggest why an understanding of new religious movements and their impact is important for gaining an understanding of the society as a whole.

Summary

Religious collectivities and their variety have been the subject of much analysis and typologizing. The dynamic model presented in this chapter emphasizes the ever-changing form of religious collectivities. The church-sect typology is a general developmental model for any organization defining itself as uniquely legitimate and existing in a state of positive (i.e., church) or negative (i.e., sect) tension with society. By contrast, cults and denominations do not claim unique legitimacy.

This model distinguishes between types of religious collectivity and types of religious orientation of members. The two main criteria for defining typical orientations are (1) the extent to which the person's religious role is diffused throughout all aspects of life, and (2) the extent to which the person adopts standards of virtuoso religiosity for judging self and others. Diverse orientations can exist within the same collectivity. The tension between two or more different religious orientations sometimes produces change within the organization or stimulates formation of a new group.

Religious collectivities typically change as they interact with their social environments, organize themselves toward achieving their goals, recruit, consolidate, and deploy members, and arrange their organization and leadership. As a new movement becomes institutionalized, it faces several dilemmas. The very processes that would enable the movement to realize its goals simultaneously change the movement and reduce its chances of attaining those goals.

Emerging religious movements illustrate this model of religious collectivities and orientations. Despite apparent diversity, new religious movements generally emphasize four common themes: religious experience, power, order, and unity. Interpretations of these movements focus on the issue of whether they are ultimately transformative of society or serve only to better integrate their members into their social niches.

Recommended Readings

Essays and Essay Collections

James Beckford. *Religious Organization: Current Sociology* 21 (2), 1975. An extensive essay and annotated bibliography applying a movement organization approach to religious collectivities.

Jacob Needleman and George Baker, eds. *Understanding the New Religions.* New York: Seabury, 1978.

Thomas Robbins, Dick Anthony, and James Richardson. "Theory and Research on Today's 'New Religions.'" *Sociological Analysis* 39 (2), 1978:95–122. An excellent review of the literature and bibliography on new religious movements. (This issue also contains several other useful articles on religious movements.)

Bryan R. Wilson, ed. *Patterns of Sectarianism: Organization and Ideology in Social and Religious Movements*. London: Heinemann, 1967.

Irving Zaretsky and Mark Leone, eds. *Religious Movements in Contemporary America*. Princeton, N.J.: Princeton University Press, 1974.

Case Studies

James Beckford. *The Trumpet of Prophecy: A Sociological Study of the Jehovah's Witnesses*. New York: Halsted-Wiley, 1975. A fascinating account of the development and organization of one of the fastest growing religious sects.

James Richardson, Mary Harder, and Robert B. Simmonds. *Organized Miracles: A Sociological Study of a Jesus Movement Organization*. New Brunswick, N.J.: Transaction, 1978. Using several different social scientific approaches, this study analyzes a Jesus movement organization as it developed over several years.

William Swatos, Jr. *Into Denominationalism: The Anglican Metamorphosis*. Society for the Scientific Study of Religion, Monograph Series 2, 1979. This study examines the history of Anglicanism (i.e., Episcopalianism) in England and colonial America for the organizational changes by which it developed from church to denomination.

Roy Wallis. *The Road to Total Freedom: A Sociological Analysis of Scientology*. New York: Columbia University Press, 1977. A highly controversial movement is examined especially for its organizational transformations.

CHAPTER SIX

Religion, Social Cohesion, and Conflict

R eligion contributes to both social conflict and cohesion. Some people find it surprising or objectionable that religion should be a force for conflict as well as cohesion. In many respects, however, the aspect of conflict is merely the obverse of social cohesion; some conflict is an integral part of what holds groups together. Religion's significance as an expression of a group's unity also makes it significant as an expression of that group's conflict with another group.

We must keep a neutral conception of conflict and cohesion. A tendency exists in our society to think of conflict, in the abstract, as "bad"; cohesion, in the abstract, seems "good." Yet when we examine some concrete instances of cohesion and conflict, we see that we evaluate the *content*, not the process, as good or bad. Was Moses's confrontation of the pharoah necessarily bad because it was conflict?

In this chapter we will first examine the ways in which religion reflects or contributes to the cohesion of a social group. Particularly problematic is the issue of whether religion contributes to the integration of complex societies such as the United States, and we will explore this issue by examining the civil religion thesis. Then we will analyze the relationship between religion and social conflict, focusing on those aspects of religion and society in general that contribute to or reflect social cleavages. Finally we will apply these understandings to the case of "the troubles" in Northern Ireland, where religion is an important factor in civil strife.

Religion and Social Cohesion

> Blest be the tie that binds
> Our hearts in Christian love.
> The fellowship of kindred minds
> Is like to that above.
> (Hymn, John Fawcett, 1782)

147

The theme of social cohesion is central to sociology. What makes society possible? What integrates separate members into a larger whole, the identifiable entity we call "society"? Society is more than an aggregate of people who happen to share a certain time and space. While made up of individuals, society is not reducible to individual beliefs, values, and behavior. Social norms and traditions existed before the individual and have a force that is external to the individual. In a society with a norm against cannibalism, for example, persons known to violate the norm will be punished regardless of whether or not they agree with the norm. Another evidence of the external quality of society is the process of socialization, in which the child is confronted with the given expectations, language, and knowledge of that society.

What, then, is the nature of the unity of society that gives it this powerful quality? How is the individual linked to the larger society? How does the society gain the commitment and cooperation of its members? According to integration theories, societal cohesion and stability are assured by the functioning of institutions (e.g., religion, education, and the family) that represent the larger social reality to the individual and enable the individual to accept personally that definition of reality.

Religion as Necessary to Societal Integration: A Functionalist Approach

There are two main approaches to the significance of religion in social cohesion. The first holds that religion is *necessary* for the cohesion of society because *it integrates the society's members through common values and goals*. This perspective is premised upon an image of society as a relatively stable structure of functionally integrated elements; that is, every element contributes to the maintenance of the system's equilibrium. Furthermore, it assumes that every functioning social structure is based on the value consensus of its members. The following statement typifies this approach:

> The reason why religion is necessary is apparently to be found in the fact that human society achieves its unity primarily through the possession by its members of certain ultimate values and ends in common. Although these values and ends are subjective, they influence behavior, and their integration enables this society to operate as a system (Davis and Moore, 1945:244).

This interpretation assumes that society requires integration and that religion is necessary to provide this integration.

These assertions are challenged by some theories suggesting that modern societies do not require integration at the level of culture (e.g., values, norms, consensus) but are adequately organized by formal ties (e.g., laws and contracts) and rewards (e.g., patterns of consumption). This second approach leads to the conclusion that although religion does contribute to the cultural integration of a modern society, such integration is unnecessary to the overall cohesion of the society. These interpretations are discussed further in Chapter 8 and are related to the thesis of a civil religion, discussed later in this chapter.

Religion is one important contributing factor in societal integration. Religious symbols can represent the unity of the social group and religious rituals can enact that unity, allowing the individual to participate symbolically in the larger unity they represent. The Christian ritual of communion is not only a commemoration of a historical event in the life of Jesus but is also a representation of participation in the unity ("communion") of believers. Also, to the extent that a religion imparts important values and norms to its members, it contributes to their consensus on moral issues. Especially significant is religion's ability to motivate believers' commitment and even sacrifice to the group's purposes. By referring to a sphere that transcends everyday life, religion encourages individuals to seek the good of the group rather than their own interests. This consensus and commitment of members is largely a positive effect, but religion also wields powerful negative sanctions for noncooperation. Again, by reference to a transcendent realm, religious sanctions are more potent than earthly punishments.

Integration theories of society stress the equilibrium and harmony of the group. They show the ways that religion helps to maintain equilibrium whenever events threaten it. For example, funeral rituals help a group regain its social balance and morale after the death of a member (Malinowski, 1948:18–24). Religious healing is often a way of reintegrating the deviant member into the group (several essays in Kiev, 1964, illustrate this). The balance of political and economic power is often ritually expressed and confirmed (see Benedict, 1934; Lewis, 1971). Changes of social status (e.g., marriage, adulthood, or adoption) are integrated into existing status arrangements through religious symbols and rituals (Van Gennep, 1960).

Most examples of religion contributing unambiguously to social cohesion are from relatively simple, homogeneous societies. If religion is coextensive with society, its contribution to social cohesion is generally clear. Many societies, however, are not coextensive with a single religion, and its contribution to societal cohesion is less clear in these situations. What is the basis of cohesion in a society such as the United States, in which many competing religions exist and a relatively large number of persons participate in no religious group? What is the function of religion for cohesion where conflicting societies presumably share the same religion (e.g., two warring Christian nations)? How can integration theories explain situations in which a religion arises in a society to conflict with the established ways of that society? Although religion does contribute to social cohesion in complex, heterogeneous societies, its role is not very clear-cut. In such societies, the basis of society-wide integration is problematic.

Religion as an Expression of Social Cohesion: Durkheim
The second approach to social cohesion and religion holds that religion is the *expression* of social forces and social ideals. This perspective emphasizes that *wherever there is social cohesion, it is expressed religiously*. The classical statement of this theoretical approach is Durkheim's, and his insights are sufficiently important to explore in some detail. Throughout Durkheim's works—on the division of labor and on deviance, education, and religion—the theme of social cohesion is central (Bellah, 1973). The relationship of the individual to the larger society was relatively unproblematic for Durkheim because he identified the larger social group as the source of individuation. His theory of religion illustrates this resolution.

Durkheim based his discussion of religion on anthropological evidence about the beliefs and practices of Australian aborigines because he believed that their religion would illustrate the most elementary form. Although some of the material he used has been discounted by later anthropological investigations, Durkheim's general theory of religion is still useful for understanding some aspects of religion, particularly in relatively homogeneous societies. As noted in Chapter 1, Durkheim's definition of religion rests upon a distinction between the "sacred" and the "profane." Religious beliefs express the nature of sacred things and human relationships with them; religious rites establish the proper conduct in the presence of sacred things.

According to Durkheim (1965:22), religion is in its very essence *social*. Religious rites are collective behavior, relating the individual to the larger social group. And religious beliefs are **collective representations**—group-held meanings expressing something important about the group itself. Durkheim may have overstated the social aspect of religion, as Malinowski (1948:65) later pointed out, since subjective and even purely individual religious experiences figure importantly in virtually all religions. The experiences sought by the Christian mystic or a participant in a Sioux initiation rite, for example, are highly individualistic, though their meaning is derived from group-held beliefs and imagery. Furthermore, Malinowski noted, not all times of collective effervescence are religious, nor are all religious gatherings necessarily unifying (see Geertz, 1957). Bringing people together for a periodic religious ritual creates the potential for friction, especially in times of stress or hunger. Nevertheless Malinowski agreed with Durkheim that religion provides a necessary basis of moral cohesion to the social group.

Durkheim observed that a sense of *force* was central to primitive religions. The totemic principle that represented abstract force to the Australian tribes was comparable with other primitive religions' awe of a force (e.g., "mana," "orenda," and "wakan" in Polynesian and North American tribes). Durkheim emphasized that religious force was not an illusion. Although the symbols for expressing this force are imperfect, the force that people experience is real—*it is society*. Durkheim described religion as a system of shared meanings by which individuals represent to themselves their society and their relations to that society. Thus religious meanings are metaphorical representations of the social group, and participation in religious ritual is experience of the transcendent force of society itself (1965:257).

Thus Durkheim resolved the individual-to-society relationship by presenting individuals as transcending themselves in communion with the greater reality— society itself. But Durkheim added that this force is not entirely outside the individual; it must also become an integral part of the individual's being because society cannot exist except through individual consciousness. By this twofold relationship, religion assures the commitment of society's members and empowers them to act accordingly. Thus religious beliefs are idealizations by which society represents itself to its members. Religious rites renew these representations by rekindling the group's consciousness of its unity. At the same time, they strengthen individuals' commitment to the group's expectations and goals (Durkheim, 1965:especially Book 3, Chapter 4).

How do collective representations and collective rituals link the individual to the larger social group? Durkheim's emphasis on language and ritual suggests two ways of understanding this individual-to-society link. First, language and other symbol systems (e.g., religious symbols) depend upon shared meanings, and meaning requires a shared reality. By exploring how language and other symbol systems articulate a group's reality, sociologists may come to a better understanding of how people subjectively share that reality (see Fabian, 1974:249–272). Second, studies of ritual can point to how the individual is related to the larger society. Participation in certain religious rituals appears to reduce the sense of boundaries between participants, producing an experience of unity (see Douglas, 1966, 1970; Turner, 1969, 1974a, 1974b). Both language and ritual articulate the unity of the group and serve to separate that group from others.

Durkheim's emphasis upon the significance of ritual for both the individual and the collectivity points to some interesting problems of describing religion in modern society. Moving from primitive religions to world and civil religions, Durkheim (1965:474, 475) asserted that all societies need regular events to reaffirm their shared meanings and central ideas. He saw no basic difference between specifically religious commemorations, such as Passover or Christmas, and civil rituals, such as Independence Day or Thanksgiving. Thus Durkheim implies that in modern nations (e.g., his own country, France) religious representations and rituals may comprise the civic religion of the national collectivity. This hypothesis has been applied to American society too, as the following discussion shows.

The Civil Religion Thesis

The civil religion thesis is important because it proposes that a religious basis exists in the unity of even highly differentiated, heterogeneous societies. **Civil religion** is "any set of beliefs and rituals, related to the past, present, and/or future of a people ('nation') which are understood in some transcendental fashion" (Hammond, 1976.171). Civil religion is the expression of the cohesion of the nation. It transcends denominational, ethnic, and regional boundaries. The civil religion has its own collective representations, by which the nation represents an ideal of itself to its members. It has its own rituals, by which members commemorate significant national events and renew their commitment to their society. Despite many debates over definitions of civil religion, the thesis appears useful for describing a number of social phenomena.

Many American civil ceremonies have a marked religious quality. Memorial Day, Fourth of July, presidential inaugurations, all celebrate national values and national unity (Bellah, 1967; Cherry, 1969; Lerner, 1937; Warner, 1953). There are national shrines such as the memorials in Washington, D.C., the Capitol itself, the birthplaces of key presidents, war memorials, and other "special" places. It is not their age or even historical significance but their ability to symbolize the transcendence of the nation as a "people" that inspires awe and reverence. A visitor to Independence Hall said, "Just standing here sends chills down my spine." National shrines are "sacred," in Durkheim's sense of the word. Likewise there are sacred objects of the civil religion—especially the flag. Interestingly the Bible is probably also a sacred object in civil religion, not because of its content but because it signifies an appeal to God as the ultimate arbiter of truth and justice. The extent to which these ceremonies, shrines, and objects are set apart as sacred can be seen in the intensity of outrage at inappropriate behavior or "desecration." Some people were arrested during the 1960s for wearing or displaying a copy of the American flag improperly (e.g., on the seat of their pants).

American civil religion also has its myths and saints. Lincoln is a historical figure who particularly symbolizes the civil religion. His actions and speeches contributed to the articulation of that religion in a time of crisis, and his life from his humble birth to his martyrdom typifies values of the civil religion. Other "saints" include key presidents (Washington, Jefferson, Wilson, Franklin D. Roosevelt, Kennedy), folk heroes (Davy Crockett, Charles A. Lindberg), and military heroes (MacArthur, Eisenhower, Theodore Roosevelt). Similarly there are stories that exemplify valued traits (e.g., the Horatio Alger rags-to-riches genre) and images (the frontier). Socially important myths include the American Dream—the land of plenty—unlimited social mobility, economic consumption, and achievement. While these shrines, saints, and ceremonies are not religious in the same sense as, for example, Greek Orthodox shrines, saints, and ceremonies, they are still set apart as special and not to be profaned. They are an important element of nonofficial religion (as described in Chapter 4) and exist alongside— separate, yet related to—official church religion.

If civil religion is the expression of the integration of a society, we might expect its especially powerful articulation at the resolution of a conflict. Just as tribal rituals "heal" internal strife and celebrate the unity of the tribe, so too does the rhetoric of inaugural speeches and court pronouncements represent the resolution of conflict and appeal to the overarching integration of the group (Hammond, 1974). The symbolism of civil religion is also very evident when the nation is believed to be threatened by an enemy. During wartime, members' commitments and sacrifices are given special significance. Even one's vegetable garden becomes a symbol of patriotic effort—a "victory garden."

American Civil Religion: Bellah. The visibility of these rituals, shrines, and symbols enables us to specify them more easily than the belief content of civil religion. What values and idealizations does American civil religion represent? Robert Bellah (1967) characterizes American civil religion as the articulation of the country's relation to God. According to Bellah, civil religion has a seriousness and integrity that go beyond mere political rhetoric and religion-in-general. Bellah examined presidential inaugural addresses, finding references to God in all but one (i.e., Washington's second inaugural, which was extremely brief). In these contexts, the deity was referred to as the ultimate grounding of America's mission and responsibility. Thus civil religion transcends the will of the people and its concrete expressions. Characterizing American civil religion as *idealization*, Bellah emphasized that the critical factor is the people's commitment to these idealizations (i.e., a "covenant"), not their success or failure in fulfilling them. As idealization, the civil religion provides criteria for judgment and change. This transcendent point of reference is the basis of a prophetic and revolutionary image of America. For example, Kennedy's inaugural address concluded:

> Now the trumpet summons us again—not as a call to bear arms, though arms we need—not as a call to battle, though embattled we are—but a call to bear the burden of a long twilight struggle, year in and year out, "rejoicing in hope, patient

in tribulation"—a struggle against the common enemies of man: tyranny, poverty, disease and war itself. . . . Finally, whether you are citizens of America or of the world, ask of us the same high standards of strength and sacrifice that we shall ask of you. With a good conscience our only sure reward, with history the final judge of our deeds, let us go forth to lead the land we love, asking His blessing and His help, but knowing that here on earth God's work must truly be our own (quoted in Bellah, 1967:1).

According to Bellah, American civil religion is related to biblical religion, yet is distinctively American. Biblical symbolism (e.g., chosen people, promised land, new Jerusalem, death and rebirth) are prominent themes. On the other hand, the civil religion is genuinely American and parallels the biblical religions, not replacing them. Civil religion and Christianity, accordingly, are clearly divided in function: Civil religion is appropriate to actions in the official public sphere, and Christianity (and other religions) are granted full liberty in the sphere of personal piety and voluntary social action. This division of spheres of relevance is particularly important for countries such as America, where religious pluralism is both a valued feature of sociopolitical life and a barrier to achieving a unified perspective for decision making. By having a civil religion for the public sphere and a diversity of particular religions in the private sphere, the social structure has cohesion with the sense of individual freedom of choice. The success of this division is, however, problematic in American society.

Bellah (1975:139–163) argued that this civil religion has gone through times of trial in which the national cohesion and will of the people to be true to their ultimate ideals were uncertain. He identified the Revolutionary War and especially the Civil War as such trials—crucibles in which the civil religion was refined and strengthened. America is now going through a third time of trial, according to Bellah, because the covenant between the people and the God of their civil religion has been betrayed by the people and their leaders. Proclaiming the American civil religion "an empty and broken shell," Bellah was clearly using the idealization in its prophetic sense. The problem, he said of the Nixon era, was not merely that the leaders were a band of wicked people but that they failed to understand America's principle, because of the general corruption of the entire society.

What emerges from sociological descriptions of American civil religion is a picture of diverse—even conflicting—values associated with what is central to the American people. Bellah's version implies a single, clear-cut, yet ever-developing ideological stance. But is the American civil religion a unified entity? And if not, does it have the capacity to be unifying? Is the civil religion to which Kennedy's inaugural address appealed the same as that to which Nixon's second inaugural speech appealed? Nixon said:

Above all else, the time has come for us to renew our faith in ourselves and in America.

In recent years, that faith has been challenged.

Our children have been taught to be ashamed of their country, ashamed of their parents, ashamed of America's record at home and its role in the world. . . .

Let us be proud that our system has produced and provided more freedom and more abundance, more widely shared, than any other in the history of man.

Let us be proud that in each of the four wars in which we have been engaged in this century, including the one we are now bringing to an end, we have fought not for selfish advantage, but to help others resist aggression.

Let us be proud that by our bold, new initiatives, and by our steadfastness for peace with honor, we have made a breakthrough toward creating in the world what the world has not known before—a structure of peace that can last, not merely for our time, but for generations to come.

We are embarking here today on an era that presents challenges as great as those of any nation, or any generation, has ever faced.

We shall answer to God, to history, and to our conscience for the way in which we use these years (quoted in Bellah, 1974; this essay includes Bellah's reappraisal of his thesis in light of Nixon's version of civil religion).

The triumphalism of the Nixon version of civil religion is in marked contrast with the critical, prophetic version reflected in Kennedy's speech.

Priestly and Prophetic Modes. One explanation of the disparity is the distinction between "priestly" and "prophetic" versions of civil religion (Marty, 1974). The **priestly version** of American civil religion celebrates the greatness of the nation, its achievements and superiority. The **prophetic version** calls the nation's attention to its offenses against the idealizations for which it stands. Both versions are very much a part of American thought and rhetoric, but they are clearly in conflict. During the 1960s and 1970s these versions were used to justify opposing stances on America's engagement in Viet Nam. One set of bumper stickers during that period proclaimed, "America—Love it or leave it!" Another set of bumper stickers retorted, "America—Change it or lose it!" Are these expressions of the *same* civil religion?

While Bellah's characterization of American civil religion strongly emphasizes a prophetic strand, nationalistic sentiments and beliefs of the priestly version also have a religious quality. Bellah emphasized that civil religion involved subordination of the nation to principles that transcended it. The priestly version of civil religion, by contrast, frequently devolves to worship of the nation itself or to indentification of God's will with the aims of "our kind of people." This version of American civil religion has historically been used to legitimate intolerance, as illustrated by the entire history of anti-Oriental agitation since 1850, culminating in the internment of American Japanese during World War II (H. Hill,1973).

Even the most vulgar forms of American civil religion have considerable appeal and motivating power, exemplified in the prosecutor's speech to the jury at the trial of some Communist labor organizers in 1929:

Do you believe in the flag of your country, floating in the breeze, kissing the sunlight, singing the song of freedom? Do you believe in North Carolina? Do you believe in good roads, the good roads of North Carolina on which the heaven-bannered hosts could walk as far as San Francisco? . . . Gastonia—into which the union organizers came, fiends incarnate, stripped of their hoofs and horns, bearing guns instead of pitchforks. . . . They came into peaceful, contented Gastonia, with its flowers, birds, and churches . . . sweeping like a cyclone and tornado to sink damnable fangs into the heart and lifeblood of my community. . . . They [the people of Gastonia] stood it till the great God looked down from the very battlements of heaven and broke the chains and traces of their patience and caused them to call the officers to the lot and stop the infernal scenes that came sweeping down from the wild plains of Soviet Russia into the peaceful community of Gastonia, bringing bloodshed and death, creeping like the hellish serpent into the Garden of Eden (quoted in Pope, 1942:303-304).

There is a religious quality to these images of the nation, representing people's sense of their unity and capable of motivating them to action for the group. The legitimating capacity of these ideas and sentiments, whether in their most noble or most vulgar expression, suggests that a broad concept of "civil religion" is useful.

Statements of leaders are helpful because they evoke images they count on to motivate their followers to commitment and action. Nevertheless we need a more refined and neutral conception of civil religion and much more evidence about the *operative* civil faith of the American people.

Some Empirical Evidence. The limited attempts to verify the concept of civil religion empirically have produced mixed results. One study analyzed the Honor America Day of July 4, 1970 (Streiker and Strober, 1972). This event, chaired by Billy Graham and Bob Hope, illustrated the themes and appeal of priestly versions of civil religion, and the study is particularly interesting for showing the interface between official church religion and civil religion. Another study of the same July 4 celebration examined the editorials of one hundred U.S. newspapers for civil religious themes (Thomas and Flippen, 1972). Few of the themes that Bellah characterized as central to civil religion were mentioned in these editorials. Themes such as "life, liberty, and the pursuit of happiness" were frequently mentioned but they were not linked with God, the key figure of transcendence in Bellah's thesis.

Another set of studies operationally defined civil religion somewhat differently (Wimberley, 1976, 1979; Wimberley et al., 1976). Respondents were asked their opinions of such statements as: "We should respect a President's authority since his authority is from God," "God can be known through the historical experiences of the American people," and "If the American government does not support religion, the government cannot upold morality." These studies discovered a distinctive civil religious dimension of belief, separate from both church religiosity and political commitment. Nevertheless this civil religiosity, as operationally defined, tapped more of the priestly than the prophetic version of civil religion. This separate civil religious dimension generally correlated with conservative theological and political views, across boundaries of religious or political affiliation.

One study identified highly conservative civil religious themes in the appeals of Rev. Moon and his Unification Church (Robbins et al., 1976). Moon's comment on the Watergate crisis included:

This nation is God's nation. The office of the President of the United States is, therefore, sacred. God inspired a man and confirms him as President through the will of the people. He lays his hand on the Word of God and is sworn into office. At this time in history God has chosen Richard Nixon to be President of the United States of America. Therefore, God alone has the power and authority to dismiss him (quoted in Robbins et al., 1976:120).

As Moon's theology illustrates, civil religion has inherent potential for dualism—good versus evil, us versus them, God's people versus the godless or anti-Christ, and so on . Another study (Jolicoeur and Knowles, 1978) found civil religious themes prominent in the literature of American Scottish Rite Masons.

The problem with measuring the concept of civil religion may be similar to that of measuring other forms of religiosity. Bellah's definition refers to an orthodoxy, ·the "original" tradition of the nation, in which the meaning of the transcendent point of reference (i.e., God) was taken for granted, a common denominator. If we wish to discover the operative civil faith of the American nation, attempting to measure it in terms of that orthodoxy may be a methodological mistake; just as it may be a mistake to assume that we can measure Christian religiosity by counting the respondents who agree that "Jesus was the divine son of God." Studies such as those cited, which use the orthodox tradition of American civil religion as a starting point, may be missing an entire strand of civil religion in which the transcendental referent is not the God of the orthodox tradition. If the idea of God is no longer taken for granted as a common assumption, important versions of civil religious thought and sentiment may exist that do not refer to God but still represent the citizen's tie with the nation in a transcendental fashion.

Further research is needed to discover the extent of typical American participation in a more broadly defined civil religion. How effective are the rites and symbols of civil religion in evoking strong sentiments of unity and commitment among society's members? What do idealizations of America mean at the level of the average citizen? To what extent does this civil religion give meaning and contribute to the identity of ordinary citizens? What is the capacity of the civil religion to motivate the commitment and sacrifice of members to the nation's goals? What kinds of events and situations bring about change in the civil religion, and how does it handle internal conflict? The concept of civil religion seems useful in explaining many American phenomena, but its usefulness would be greatly enhanced by a broader, less ideological application of the term and by much more evidence concerning its varieties.

Religion and Nationalism. Thus far we have focused primarily on American civil religion. Is the concept of civil religion useful for describing similar phenomena in other societies?

Essentially, civil religion may be a very general form of nationalism. A useful distinction at this point is between state building and nation building. **State building** refers to developing an authoritative, utilitarian organization for expediently conducting a country's internal and external business. **Nation building** refers to developing a country's sense of solidarity and identity as a people. An example of this analytical distinction is the Spanish peoples. Most Spaniards both participate in the Spanish state and identify with the Spanish nation, but the Catalonian minority do not feel part of the Spanish national identity or solidarity, even though they are subject to the authority of the Spanish state (see essays in Eisenstadt and Rokkan, 1973). Although nationalism has been a continuing political force in history, civil religion may be the response of modern and modernizing peoples to their peculiar problems of nation building.

Civil religion is clearly an element in nation building. It can give national solidarity and identity a religious quality, enabling peoples of diverse tribal, regional, ethnic, and religious groups to come together in a central, unifying cultural experience. It does not always successfully accomplish this task of unification, but successful nation building often entails civil religious solidarity. This nation-building potential can be seen in the attempt to develop an Arab civil religion in the Middle East. Lacking an Islamic tradition of effective political participation, some Arabs are consciously trying to develop Islam into a national (i.e., civil) religion. They present Muhammed as an Arab hero whose convictions inspired him to initiate a new civilization, create an Arab culture, and unify the Arab peoples. The deity of Islam is portrayed as mandating an Arab destiny (Hermassi, 1978). This kind of Arab civil religion stands in a similar relationship to its Islamic roots as American civil religion does to Protestantism. Like American civil religion, Arab religious nationalism has its potential for prophetic criticism. Both Arab and American civil religions contribute to the process of nation building in the face of internal divisions.

Forms of Civil Religion. Some sociologists have applied the civil religion concept to other countries than the United States (McGuire, 1975; Moodie, 1975; Robertson, 1978; Shils and Young, 1953). More analyses of this kind will clarify the extent to which American civil religion differs from other national versions. American civil religion appears to be one of four different forms of religious link between the citizen and the nation. In America, the civil religion is differentiated from both the state and church (i.e., as particular religions). The civil religion, as Bellah (1967) pointed out, is appropriate to the public sphere, and particular religions apply to the private sphere. A second form of linkage is an ostensibly secular version of nationalism exemplified by the U.S.S.R., where civil religion and state are linked but differentiated from particular religions (which are totally privatized). In the two other forms, church (i.e., particular religion) and state are not differentiated. The church is sponsor of the state in one form; and in the other, the state is sponsor of the church (Coleman, 1970; Geertz, 1963). These latter two types are less obvious cases of civil religion because they are so closely linked with particular religions. The first two types are better suited to religiously heterogeneous nations because the civil religion is differentiated from particular religions. This very differentiation, however, may itself cause certain problems of integration.

Robertson (1978:175) suggests that the idea of a civil religion arises in response to a sense of imbalance between the individual and the state or society. He describes this gap as an imbalance between *identity* and *authority*, stating that civil religion expresses "the nature of the personal identity/society authority connection, when individual (at least sub-national) 'identity work' is perceived to make societal functioning ineffective and/or inefficacious." Differentiation between the spheres of life in which this "identity work" occurs (e.g., family, neighborhood, particular religions, ethnic community) and the spheres of public life (e.g., work, law, politics) is very great in modern societies. Civil religion may be so prominent in America because American society is the prototype of such a highly differentiated society. Another observer (J. F. Wilson, 1979:174) suggests that civil religion is a political-religious revitalization movement in a new system of global order.

The civil religion thesis is an important sociological concept. It explains certain aspects of American religiosity that are not related to particular religions. It provides a hypothesis for understanding expressions of national unity in a heterogeneous, highly differentiated society. American civil religion, as described by Bellah and Robertson, is related to the apparent weakness of particular religious institutions in the public sphere. This suggests that the development of a separate civil religion may be related to processes of modernization and secularization.

Finally the civil religion thesis proposes a basis for the relationship of the individual to the larger modern society. It allows, in theory, the societal needs of cohesion and commitment of members and the individual needs of identity and belonging to be met by the same social processes. To what extent American civil religion really accomplishes this linkage remains unclear. We need to know to what extent people identify their interests and sense of belonging with the nation as a whole. Or, by contrast, to what extent do they locate their interests and community in particular segments of the society that are in conflict with other segments? The relationship of the individual to society is a critical issue in understanding modern societies. If a civil religion can effect a special kind of individual-to-society connection, it forms an important clue to that understanding (Bellah, 1978; Robertson, 1978). And if a civil religion is unable to achieve that connection, the reasons for this inability are also useful for our understanding of modern society.

Religion and Social Conflict

> *Mine eyes have seen the glory of the coming*
> *of the Lord.*
> *He hath trampled out the vintage where the*
> *Grapes of Wrath are stored.*
> *He hath ruled the fateful lightning*
> *of His terrible swift sword.*
> *His truth is marching on.*
> *Glory, Glory, Hallelujah . . .*
> *His truth is marching on.*
> ("Battle Hymn of the Republic,"
>   Julia Ward Howe, 1861)

This hymn, which has as its context both particular (Protestant) religions and American civil religion, illustrates the capacity of religion to inspire and reflect social conflict. In this section, we shall consider factors that make religion a powerful basis or reflection of social cleavages.

Conflict as the Obverse of Cohesion

We must keep in mind that cleavage and conflict are, in many respects, merely the "other side of the coin" of cohesion and consensus. We tend to think of conflict as a breach in sociation, but as Simmel (1955:18) reminds us, conflict is one form of sociation. Simmel emphasized that "a certain amount of discord, inner divergence, and outer controversy, is organically tied up with the very elements that ultimately hold the group together."

Thus our discussion of religious expression of social cohesion is necessarily related to a consideration of conflict as well. For example, the Doukhobors are a religious sect in Canada and the United States whose values and way of life often conflict greatly with those of the dominant society; members sometimes clash with educational, social welfare, and police authorities (Hawthorne, 1955). Their strong cohesion as a group sets them off from non-Doukhobors. At the same time, their experience of opposition from the rest of society increases their group's cohesion and commitment. So cohesion at one level of association can produce conflict on another level; and conflict from the outside can contribute to internal cohesion.

Religion has been historically related to conflict at several levels. Perhaps the most obvious has been conflict *between* religious groups, especially when religious boundaries are coextensive with political boundaries. Religion played an important part in the reconquest of Spain by "the Christian monarchs" (end of the fifteenth century). This event was accompanied by powerful "us-against-them" sentiments, resulting both in expulsion of the Moors (i.e., Moslems) and suppression of indigenous Jews. Conflict between religious groups within modern nations tends to be more subtle (e.g., much of the anti-Semitism in America); but when religious boundaries are coextensive with other boundaries (e.g., social class, race, or ethnicity), open conflict can erupt.

Another level of conflict arises *within* a religious group. Conflicts during the early part of the Protestant Reformation exemplify this type, as protesting groups were defined as splinter groups within the Roman Catholic church. Similarly most established denominations and sects began as internal conflicts in parent groups.

Sectarian religious groups also exemplify another level of conflict—between a religious group and the *larger society*. Sometimes the conflict results in reprisals by the larger society, as when courts override family or educational arrangements of the Mormons, Amish, and Doukhobors and jail Quaker conscientious objectors. And sometimes sectarians express conflict only by condemning and withdrawing from the "ways of the world."

Social Sources of Conflict

Social Cleavages. Some religious cleavages have their sources in the organization of society. As noted in Chapter 2, religious belonging is one basis of self-identification. A strong sense of belonging (e.g., to a national, religious, kinship, or ethnic group) entails a sense of barrier between members of that group and those outside it. Because religion is one important basis for group identification in society, it is a potential line of cleavage (Coleman, 1956:44, 45). A closer look at religious conflict, however, suggests that the situation is more complex. Often religious boundaries overlap with other lines of cleavage such as social class, race or ethnicity, political or national allegiance, and so on. What appears to be a religious struggle may be also an ethnic or social class conflict.

When religious divisions are coextensive with other lines of cleavage, it is difficult to distinguish the exact role of religion in conflict. In 1844, Protestants and Roman Catholics in Philadelphia engaged in armed combat. Protestants were angered that the Catholic bishop had persuaded the school board to excuse Catholic children from religious instruction, which was then a standard part of the public school curriculum. Mass meetings were held to attack the change, and a Protestant crowd marched into a Catholic neighborhood. Street fighting and general rioting resulted, and Protestant mobs set fire to several houses and Catholic churches. As violence mounted, the governor sent the militia, against which the Protestant mob fought with its own cannon and muskets. Thousands of Catholics fled the city (Shannon, 1963:44).

On the surface, this historical event appears to be a simple case of religious conflict, but the divisions between Roman Catholic and Protestant were also cleavage lines of ethnicity, economic interest, politics, and neighborhood. Catholics involved were almost all Irish, and many were recent immigrants. Protestants were largely part of a rising political stream of anti-immigrant fervor, later culminating in the "Know-Nothing" Party (1854). Economic factors included the competition of immigrants with WASP "natives" for jobs. While the extent of anti-Catholic prejudice at that time should not be understated, it is nevertheless difficult to distinguish elements of religious conflict from other sources of divisiveness.

Because religion is often coextensive with other lines of cleavage, it is frequently used as a way of expressing other divisions. A South African can use loyalty to the Dutch Reformed church to express many other loyalties: racial (white, as opposed to black), ethnic (Afrikaner/Dutch, as opposed to English), language (Afrikaans and rabidly anti-English), and political (Afrikaner Nationalist Party; see Moodie, 1978). Overlap of cleavage lines also means, however, that sometimes religious conflict masks other, perhaps more fundamental cleavages. Religion has often been a legitimation for political and economic conflict.

Both the rhetoric and inspiration of religious conflict can cover aspirations for political power or economic gain. Right-wing radio evangelists of the 1930s, Protestant minister Gerald L. K. Smith and Roman Catholic priest Charles E. Coughlin, organized a politico-religious campaign. Virulent anti-Communism, anti-Semitism, and nativism were central to their message. Coughlin attracted a radio audience of approximately 10 million weekly listeners, who contributed so much mail and money that he needed 145 clerks. Together Smith and Coughlin organized the Union Party for the 1936 presidential elections. After the defeat of their presidential candidate, Coughlin emphasized anti-Semitism even more, primarily as a symbol of his attack on the country's economic and money system. Although Coughlin received some active church opposition and very little official Roman Catholic support, this right-wing coalition had special appeal to discontented urban Catholics, the elderly, and rural poor (largely Protestant). The political ambitions of the coalition were served by the anti-Semitic and anti-"subversive" messages proclaimed with religious teachings over the radio (see Bennett, 1969; Lipset, 1963). In this example, a religious cleavage between Christians and Jews was exploited to further political ends.

The Marxian Perspective. Marxian interpretations hold that religious conflict is merely the expression of fundamental economic relationships. Accordingly the dominant class attempts to impose ideas (including religious ideas) that legitimate its interests. Or it may exploit existing religious divisions among subordinate peoples to prevent them from realizing their true class interests. As we will note in Chapter 7, religion can contribute to legitimation of the existing social system and also express real conflicts in that system (Turner, 1977b).

According to Marxian theory, religious dissent is often an expression of economic dissatisfaction, but its religious nature prevents dissenters from fully realizing their economic class interests. Religious conflicts have often divided members of the working class when their true interests, according to Marx, would be best served by uniting against the common enemy, the ruling class.

Part of the reason why Marx's predictions of increasing class conflict have not eventuated in many modern societies is that their members are subject to many **cross-pressures** other than social class interest, thus making religion a less volatile source of conflict too. Cross-pressures refer to the conflicting loyalties that individuals feel when they identify with several different roles and reference groups (Coleman, 1956:46). An example of cross-pressures is the conflicting loyalties felt by a black woman who manages the local branch of a bank, lives in an integrated, middle-class suburb with pleasant Jewish and Irish Catholic neighbors, and belongs to a local Baptist church. When an issue arises in which different attachments conflict (e.g., whether tax monies should be used to fund abortions for poor women), she may acutely feel the cross-pressures. Her loyalties to poor blacks or to women may urge her to support funding the abortions; her identification with her religion or the privileged classes may press for the opposite stance.

In many societies, this kind of cross-pressure is absent or minimal because all major meaningful kinds of personal identification coincide. If the dominant class is of a totally different race, religion, and cultural background from the subordinate class (as in many colonial societies), the potential for social conflict is great because there are few conflicting loyalties within the person. In America, lines of cleavage—religious, ethnic, racial, economic, residential, regional, political—are seldom coextensive. Although real status inequalities exist (e.g., whites and Protestants are considerably overrepresented among the political and economic elites), geographical mobility, relative economic mobility, and mass communications have contributed to blurring the lines of cleavage. The existence of these cross-pressures within individuals means that the likelihood of concerted conflict along any *one* line of cleavage (e.g., social class or religion) is reduced (Coleman, 1956:47).

Because religious cleavage sometimes masks other cleavages does not mean, however, that there are not real religious interests involved. Protection of religious interests frequently results in conflict. The struggle for *religious liberty*—the freedom to hold and practice the religion of one's choice—has been a recurrent cause of political conflict. Violent suppression of the Huguenots (i.e., French Protestants) resulted in continued conflict from their inception in the early 1500s until 1789. The Huguenots persisted in asserting their right to practice their religion, and the conflict included civil wars, mass emigration, massacres, and torture. To many people today, religious intolerance seems impolite and, at worst, unjust. We find it difficult to understand why religion would be the basis of such strong antagonism.

Conflict over Bases of Authority. One of the key reasons why religion can result in such extreme conflict is that it not only reflects lines of cleavage in society, but it can also challenge the bases of legitimacy by which authority is exercised. The French rulers believed (probably accurately) that the Protestant world view constituted a challenge to the basis of their authority because that authority was justified largely by the Roman Catholic world view. Religious ideas and interests have historically been significant forces in establishing authority.

Authority, in contrast with power relations, requires that subjects consider it legitimate. **Legitimacy** means the social recognition of an authority's claims to be taken seriously, and it implies negative social sanctions for failure to comply with authoritative commands. Conflict is implicit in authority relationships because they involve dominance and subordination. Yet they are based on more than pure power. Other considerations (e.g., scientific or religious knowledge) may also be sources of legitimacy of authority. There is constant potential for conflict between authorities who base their claims on different sources of legitimacy. When religion is related to civil disobedience (e.g., the actions of the Berrigan brothers in the 1960s and 1970s), religion is largely the basis of challenging the civil authority's source of legitimacy. This kind of civil disobedience is saying, in effect, "Your rules and practices may be right according to your authority, but our actions appeal to a higher basis of authority."

The place of religion in societal authority relationships is complex because religion is both a *basis* of legitimacy and, often, the *content* of authoritative pronouncements; thus the pope pronounces religious messages and bases his claim to speak authoritatively on religious tradition. Religion has historically been an important source of conflict because it offered both a basis for legitimacy of authority and a set of ideas around which conflict centered. The apparent decrease in religion's role as a source of authority in modern society is due partly to its loss of legitimacy—its capacity to compel people to take its claims seriously.

Sources in the Nature of Religion

The nature of religion and religious groups also contributes to social conflict. In many respects, this capacity for promoting conflict is simply the obverse of religion's ability to engender social cohesion. Religion is one way of expressing the unity of the "in-group"—"our people." This in-versus-out dichotomy, however, applies both to conflict outside and within the group.

Conflict with Outsiders: Boundaries. This distinction between in-group and out-group implies distancing oneself from outsiders. Just as religious rituals celebrate the identity and unity of the group, they simultaneously maintain the boundary between that group and outsiders. Not only do religious groups protect their external boundaries, but they are also concerned with internal purification—another potential source of conflict (Douglas, 1966, 1970). The we-they dichotomy is both a structural and cognitive framework that includes how people think about themselves and others. This cognitive boundary is based upon the fact that "we" have shared central experiences that "they" have not. In-group language embodies these shared experiences and further distinguishes "us" from "them." "Born-again" Christians consider their religious experience an important distinction between themselves and others, and their ways of witnessing to their special experience of being "born again" symbolize this difference.

Religion figures importantly in the socialization of children in most societies and thus becomes part of the "we-they" cognitive framework from an early age. Developing a sense of religious belonging, children come to think of themselves as part of the in-group and share their group's way of perceiving the rest of society. This cognitive framework may also include the perception of others as enemies or inferior to members of one's in-group. The values and attitudes learned in one religious group often vary considerably from those taught children in another group. Thus religion's significance in socialization enhances its potential for divisiveness (Coleman, 1956:54, 55; Gorsuch and Aleshire, 1974; Wach, 1944:36).

Conflict with Outsiders: Particularism. Certain religious perspectives appear to promote conflict. Particularist world views encourage intolerance and prejudice toward the out-group. Religious **particularism** is the viewing of one's own religious group as the only legitimate religion (Glock and Stark, 1966:20). The clash of world views in a complex society is resolved in a number of possible stances: "Our way is totally right, theirs is totally wrong"; "Their way is good, our way is better"; "Our ways are both right but appropriate for different people"; "Their way and ours are essentially the same, and apparent differences are only incidental matters." The belief systems of some religions include particularist judgment of nonbelievers.

Indeed, religious particularism seems to require a sense of opposition; one's own religion is seen as triumphant over some other. The in-group needs an out-group against which it can compare itself (Glock and Stark, 1966:29; Raab, 1964).[1] Religious world views that involve a particularistic stance toward the rest of humankind hold greater likelihood for promoting conflict than less triumphalistic world views.

Groups with particularistic world views are often able to mobilize the efforts of their members precisely because of this sense of opposition. Particularism enhances militance for one's beliefs. The strong element of religious particularism in Islam promoted its early missionary expansion throughout the Middle East, west to North Africa and Spain, east toward India and Southeast Asia, and north toward Eurasia. This particularism, combined with religiously legitimated militance, was also embodied in the *jihad* (i.e., holy war)—a recurrent feature of Islamic conflict. Contemporary conflicts in Lebanon, Iran, and Indonesia have been viewed as jihads (see Utrecht, 1978). The idea of missionary expansion is foreign to most non-Western religions because relatively few religions combine

[1]For example, a few years ago I was talking with a boy of about twelve who had recently been confirmed in his church. Responding to my query about what that meant to him, he said, "It means being willing to fight and even die for Christ." I asked whom he thought he had to fight, and he replied, "I don't know—I guess the Jews." Nascent anti-Semitism perhaps, but probably only a reflection of the boy's sense that his Christianity had to triumph over some other group. The Jews may have been the only non-Christian group he had ever heard of.

the particularism of having "the truth" with the mandate to convert the entire out-group. Interesting parallels with Christianity and Islam, however, are the world views of contemporary totalistic movements such as nazism and communism. Communism is particularly comparable to traditional Christianity in its particularism and sense of opposition, militance, and missionary activism (see Coser, 1973; Zeldin, 1969).

Internal Conflict in the Religious Group: Deviance and Control. This same in-group versus out-group dichotomy applies to the relationship of the group toward its own members who are defined as deviant or heretical. Again, conflict is the obverse of cohesion. The way in which a group treats a deviant member involves some form of conflict by which the group exerts its control. **Deviance** is behavior that is contrary to norms of conduct or expectations of a social group. Because it is the group that sets norms and identifies individual instances of deviant behavior, analysis of deviance describes the group as much as the deviant member (Becker, 1963). If a group sets a norm (e.g., against gambling) and labels a member as deviating from this norm, the group is both punishing the gambler deviant and proclaiming its own identity as a nongambling people.

Especially in small, closely knit societies or religious groups, the group's social control over deviant members can be powerful. Mennonites sometimes "shun" deviant members. Family and neighbors refuse any social interaction, sometimes for years, until the deviant repents of a "sin" or recants a "heresy." Because religion is often a source of the social group's norms and values, it is frequently important in the social response to deviance. The actions of the deviant member are seen as not only hurtful to the group but a violation of things that the group holds sacred.

Durkheim (1965:Book 3) emphasized that "piacular rites" (e.g., expiation for wrongdoings and cleansing of impurities) are just as expressive of the group's core unity and force as "positive rites" (e.g., communion). By ritually reincorporating deviant members who repent, both individual and group are strengthened in their solidarity around the norm. Threat of deviance from within is potentially more disruptive than opposition from outsiders because insiders "ought to know better"; outsiders can be dismissed as uninformed and ignorant of the "truth." Insiders must be taken more seriously as "one of us." A fellow member who goes against an important group norm becomes an affront to the essential unity of the entire group.

Deviance may contribute to group solidarity even when the deviant member is not repentant. In uniting against the deviant member, the group is strengthened. Even more than external opposition, internal conflict with the deviant member sharpens the group's sense of its boundaries and norms (see Durkheim, 1938:65–75; Mead,1918). Collective rejection of the person accused of adultery reminds the entire group how much it should abhor adultery. Sometimes norms may be unclear or changing, and collective treatment of the deviant member may actually articulate the norm. In recent years, for example, numerous community or religious groups have attempted to proscribe or punish homosexual practices. These actions are not merely a reflection of antagonism toward homosexuals; more importantly, they are groups' attempts to assert their norms in a situation where societal norms are unclear or changing. By uniting against what they define as deviance, they are confirming their own norms for themselves.

Religious groups with particularistic world views appear especially intolerant of deviance. Their certainty of their own total rightness increases their condemnation of the wrongness they perceive of any other beliefs and practices. Particularistic religious groups give deviant members more reason to fear group sanctions. If you have been socialized in a religion that you believe is uniquely true—the only path to salvation—you are not likely to consider leaving the group. You are likely to try very hard to follow its rules for behavior, accept its punishments for infringement, and hope never to be forced to leave. If you accept the group's claims to be the only true religion, expulsion (i.e., excommunication) is the worst possible punishment. In uniting against the deviant, members of particularistic religious groups gain both a sense of solidarity and a sense of their own moral rightness; they are triumphant over external and internal opposition. The core of righteous members of such groups often develops purist and elitist characteristics, which further promote the likelihood of conflict.

Internal Conflict: Issues of Authority and Heresy. Internal strife in religious groups can develop over nonreligious interests too, including socioeconomic issues, leadership and power, and other social cleavages within the group. Nevertheless conflict over religious ideas and practices frequently centers upon the issue of **authority,** which implies control both of the organization (however small) and over the articulation of central beliefs and practices. The separation of Eastern ("Orthodox") and Roman Catholicism was fundamentally a conflict over authority. Ostensibly the schism was over theological issues such as whether Christ was "of the same substance" as God the Father or was "similar" to the Father. Behind these theological issues, however, were deeper sources of conflict: Greek philosophy and polity versus Roman philosophy and law. In particular, the split represented the Eastern patriarchs' dissatisfaction with the consolidation of church power and authority in the hands of the single Western patriarch (i.e., the pope in Rome). The specific theological issues, important as they were to conflicting parties, did not cause the split; the issue of authority in the church was the central source of conflict (Niebuhr, 1929:111-117; "Orthodox Eastern Church" 1943, 16:938–939).

Other sources of conflict over authority are religious revelations. Because religious experience and ways of knowing are so intensely private, there is always the potential for believers to receive revelations or come to interpretations that differ from official ones. Revelations, prophecies, insights, and new interpretations of scripture and tradition have all been significant sources of intragroup conflict in most major religions.

When members assert a belief or practice that differs in some important way from those authoritatively established, it is often defined as not mere deviance but **heresy.** This kind of dissent implicitly challenges the existing authority structure of the group. It suggests that the entire group should consider a different basis for its core beliefs and practices. The labeling and condemnation of heresy is the official leadership's assertion of its authority in the face of the challenge. The vigor with which labeled heresies have historically been prosecuted illustrates the seriousness of their challenge to established religious authority.

Conflict over authority is exemplified by the issue raised in the Roman Catholic church of "Americanism," which Pope Leo XIII condemned as heretical in 1899. Americanism generally referred to the idea that religion should be adapted to the individual cultures in which it is practiced; specifically it meant that the American culture required a different brand of Catholicism than European cultures. The origin of this perspective is attributed to missionaries to the Americans in the mid-1800s. They sought to adapt their missionary appeals to the peculiar characteristics of American culture, especially its democratic and pluralistic organization. Latent in the papal condemnation of Americanism, however, was the assertion of one particular system of church authority (Rome/pope/curia-centered) over another system (national/bishops/collegia-centered). The possibility that any national church authorities might develop separate strains of teaching authority was perceived as a direct challenge to the existing system of authority (Cross, 1958; McAvoy, 1957; Mirbt and Anon., 1943).

The label of "Americanism" continued to suppress much internal dissent in the American Roman Catholic church in the first half of the twentieth century. These same issues of authority were central in the deliberations of the First and Second Vatican Councils (1869 and 1962). The Roman Catholic church provides clear-cut examples of the definition of heresy because it has developed specific measures for defining and dealing with it. But Protestant history also involves numerous instances of heresy, schism, and clash over authority. While the particularist world view of many Christian groups promotes this kind of internal conflict, non-Christian religions (e.g., Hinduism, Islam, and Shinto) have also known many schisms and internal divisions.

Internal conflict over heresy is a dynamic process. It can mobilize members of the group for action against the heresy and indirectly promote internal changes. Or the group can absorb the alternative beliefs and practices, changing in the direction of alternative authority. Even in the suppression of heresy, the group impels adherents of the heresy to form an alternative social movement. The history of Christian sects illustrates this dynamism.

Religion is thus an important factor in social conflict, both within the group and with outsiders. This potential for conflict results both from qualities of religion and religious groups themselves and from the nature of the society as a whole. Nevertheless the aspect of conflict is basically the obverse of social cohesion; a certain amount of conflict is part of the very structure that holds groups together. And because religion is one important way by which groups express their unity, it is also a significant factor in conflict. This dual relationship is illustrated in the Extended Application section of this chapter: an examination of recent conflict in Northern Ireland.

Extended Application: The Conflict in Northern Ireland

Recent civil strife in Northern Ireland illustrates religion's capacity to promote both cohesion and conflict. The history of divisions in Northern Ireland is long, complex, and confusing to outsiders. This brief essay focuses on the religious dimension of this struggle, recognizing that other important historical, political, economic, and social factors are also involved.

Religious Conflict?

One receives the impression from television and newspaper coverage that the strife in Northern Ireland is purely religious, with two antagonistic camps— Roman Catholic and Protestant—pitted against each other in senseless, deadly violence. The image is puzzling to most Americans, who see the antagonists as so similar to each other. Unlike our national experience with conflict over segregation and discrimination, the opposing sides in Northern Ireland appear to share the same racial stock, language, and social class. These apparent similarities are, however, based upon only a casual glance. Participants themselves apply finer distinctions; they are quick to identify someone as "one of us" or "one of them" on the basis of simple items of information—name, address, or school attended.

Nevertheless the only differences apparent at a superficial level of analysis center around religion. Many Americans find it difficult to believe that religion is so important to anyone as to be worth fighting over. Others note the relative ease with which both Catholic and Protestant Irish immigrants adjusted to the heterogeneous and pluralistic religious scene in America (MacEoin, 1974b:1, 2). To participants in the Northern Irish conflict, however, the salience of religion as a genuine source of antagonism is unquestionable. In 1970, a British Broadcasting Corporation (BBC) interviewer asked a Belfast Protestant, "What do you have against the Roman Catholics?"—to which the response was, "Are you daft? Why, their religion of course" (cited in Rose, 1971:247). Americans and other outsiders ask: Is the conflict in Northern Ireland indeed a religious one?

This analysis will suggest that the answer is yes, but with qualifications. The conflict is not over theology or doctrine. It does not center on Protestantism or Catholicism, as most adherents of these religions in America or elsewhere in Europe know them. The conflict in Northern Ireland could perhaps best be understood as the outcome of two mutually exclusive *civil religions*: one "Protestant" (or, more accurately, "Orangeism") and the other "Catholic" (strongly identified with "Republicanism"). Although the concept of civil religion is controversial, it appears useful in explaining the Northern Irish situation of religiously focused political strife.

Conflicting Civil Religions

As suggested earlier in this chapter, American civil religion appears to be one of several forms of religious tie between citizens and the nation. In America, civil religion is separate from both state and church (i.e., particular religions). American separation of church and state makes possible (and, some sociologists would argue, necessary) a civil religion that *transcends* particular religions. Northern Ireland, by contrast, represents a situation in which religion (Protestant) is not separated from the state. Religion is a significant consideration in political decision making, in applying social policy, in the actions of police and other officials, in the curriculum of national schools, and in the content of mass media. Relatively few persons in the country doubt that religion should be linked with the state;

there is, however, profound dissension over *which* religion should shape the nation.

The nation-building potential of civil religion is evident in the intense conflict between these opposing views. Both Protestant and Catholic civil religions in Northern Ireland entail visions of nationhood. Whatever their political thrust, both national visions are also intensely religious in both content and style. Each group builds its own version of national identity imbued with religious significance, and each group engenders a strong sense of "us" against "them."

While particular religions (i.e., Roman Catholic and various Protestant groups) contributed to the creation of these opposing civil religions, they cannot control them. The civil religions are *separate religions*, with dynamics of their own. Thus religious leaders in both camps who attempt to quell the violence typically have little power over the strong sentiments set into motion in the name of religion. Similarly the distinctiveness of Northern Irish civil religions from particular religions helps to explain why adherents are sometimes strongly critical of church leaders who are interested in ecumenism (i.e., interfaith tolerance and activities). Rather than follow their church leaders into interfaith activities, many believers use the civil religion as a basis for denouncing them.

The opposing civil religions of Northern Ireland illustrate that social cohesion is often the obverse of social conflict. Each group is held together largely by its sense of opposition to the other group. Both groups—especially the Protestants—are thrust into enclaves of tribal togetherness out of fear of the other. Reformation and Counter Reformation symbols and myths that are several hundred years old shape these fears and lock believers into nationalistic ideologies that cannot accommodate full religious pluralism.

The Social Context

Northern Ireland was created in the 1920s after rebellion against Britain, when twenty-six counties of Ireland became a self-governing dominion (eventually recognized as an independent republic). The other six counties, an area of 5,200 square miles in the northeast corner of the island, continued their union with Britain—that is, the United Kingdom (MacEoin, 1974b:8–10). The part of the island retained by Britain included most of the industry and was economically and strategically important. Partition of the island in the 1920s encompassed as much area as possible in the British-held part without upsetting Protestant electoral dominance.

Roman Catholicism is the largest single denomination in Northern Ireland, accounting for 35 percent of the population in 1961. The other two-thirds of the populace is Protestant, mainly Presbyterian (29 percent) and Church of Ireland (i.e., Episcopalian, 24 percent). The Republic of Ireland, by contrast, is predominantly Catholic, so that on the island as a whole Catholics outnumber Protestants approximately three to one (MacEoin, 1974b:11, 12).

Irish Protestants and Catholics tend to be more fundamentalist and theologically conservative than their counterparts in America and England. Both groups exemplify religious particularism, the belief that one's group is the only legitimate religion. The self-righteousness and sense of opposition characteristic of particularistic world views make both groups strong sources of intolerance. Religious polarization in Northern Ireland has produced a social and psychological split in which there are no neutrals; even unbelievers are identified as Protestant or Catholic unbelievers. One of the most important products of this religious polarization is that the public does not believe (indeed, cannot conceive of) groups that claim to be nonsectarian (Beach, 1977).

All aspects of life in Northern Ireland are divided by these religious poles. There are separate Protestant and Catholic neighborhoods, playgrounds, schools, social clubs, charitable organizations, political parties, youth activities, sports, newspapers, and cultural events. As suggested earlier in this chapter, religion is especially likely to be a source of conflict between groups when it is coextensive with other important sources of identity. In Northern Ireland, religion is coextensive with almost all other significant social divisions.

Much of the social segregation results from systematic discrimination against Catholics, especially since the 1920s partition. To protect their power and economic advantages, Protestants severely discriminated against Catholics in employment, housing, civil service, public board appointments, electoral districting, and representation. By restricting housing for Catholics to certain neighborhoods and then gerrymandering the boundaries of voting districts, Protestants were able to maintain strong majorities in the councils of communities where they were numerically the minority. But not all segregation of Catholics was imposed by Protestants. Segregated Catholic schools are supported by the Catholic church hierarchy, partly in order to retain greater control over the socialization of Catholic youths and to protest the (Protestant) religious content of national school instruction (see Menendez, 1973).

The net effect of such total segregation is that few of the cross-pressures that could reduce prejudice and conflict operate in Northern Irish social life. Polarization makes it difficult, if not impossible, to socialize with persons outside one's enclave. "They" are not real persons; "they" are described only by group myths, not by personal contact. Indeed, polarization has produced strong social controls. In-groups punish members who overstep boundaries and are too friendly to the out-group. Members of both enclaves have been beaten, tarred and feathered, and even killed for crossing the social boundaries. Sometimes religious sanctions are brought to bear on people who do not stay in their religious enclave. One Catholic bishop refused to confirm children who were not sent to Catholic schools. Some Protestant ministers use their pulpits to denounce fellow Protestants who accept ecumenism.

These current polarizations are the result of a long history, which figures significantly in the myths, symbols, and legends of the two civil religions. This history, however briefly presented here, is critical for understanding of contemporary sentiments.

Some Historical Background

Although the history of England's involvement in Ireland may be traced to the twelfth-century Norman conquest, events of the seventeenth century were especially critical in shaping contemporary problems. In the sixteenth and seventeenth centuries, the chief objective of England's Irish policy was to prevent Ireland from becoming a center for English rebels or a stepping stone for continental enemies.

Thus under the Tudor monarchs, the English began a system of plantations in Ireland, substituting loyal English settlers for potentially disloyal Irish or Old English landholders. The plantation system was particularly important in shaping the religious composition of Northern Ireland (Beckett, 1966:38–63).

Plantation and Insurrection. In the seventeenth century, the policy of plantation was extended with vigor and increasingly religious overtones. The English wished to disempower the native Irish and Old English landholders (predominantly Roman Catholic) and substitute new English and Scottish settlers (Protestant). The most extensive and successful plantation was in the province of Ulster (northern Ireland). Large areas of Ulster (i.e., counties Armagh, Cavan, Derry, Donegal, Fermanagh, and Tyrone) were confiscated and given to immigrant English and Scottish landholders. Since the seventeenth century, there has been a major social class distinction between the English (generally Church of England, called "Protestant") settlers and the Scottish (Presbyterians, Covenanters, etc., called "Dissenters"). Some Scottish-Irish later identified with the native Irish because of their own previous experience of discrimination from the English. In today's Northern Ireland, however, both Anglicans and Dissenters generally view their Protestantism as "common ground" against Catholicism. Some of these seventeenth-century settlers removed the Irish tenants from their land and replaced them with British tenants, while many kept their Irish tenants. Only about 2,000 British families lived on these Ulster plantations by 1628. Thus the large-scale removal of native Irish that the government intended did not occur (Beckett, 1966:64–74; Clarke, 1967).

Discontent of the native Irish festered, and in 1641 insurrection broke out, especially throughout the north of Ireland. Ulster natives (mostly Catholics) attacked the Protestant colonists and seized many towns and fortifications. The Ulster insurrection had special significance to the English, who were then involved in a civil war between Royalists (largely Catholics and Anglicans) and Parliamentarians (mostly Puritans and Dissenters). Exaggerated tales of the 1641 massacres served as fuel for the English reconquest of Ireland. In 1649, Oliver Cromwell (a Puritan) landed in Ireland with a force of 12,000 soldiers and began a campaign so ruthless that 330 years later he is still identified as perhaps the most hated symbol of English oppression. Cromwell saw his mission as not only to quell a royalist uprising but also to bring divine revenge for the 1641 massacres. Reporting on his conquest of Drogheda, after which some 2,000 townspeople were put to the sword, Cromwell wrote, "I am persuaded that this is a righteous judgment of God upon those barbarous wretches, who have imbrued their hands in so much innocent blood" (cited in Beckett, 1966:79, 80).

The settlement following this reconquest solidified English dominance. The settlement forced all "disloyal" landlords to forfeit their lands, and new "loyal" settlers took their places. Catholics were particularly affected by this policy because the English parliament felt that they were, by definition, disloyal to English interests. In 1641, the majority of Irish landlords had been Catholic; after the Cromwellian settlement, the majority were Protestant (Beckett, 1966:74–81). Catholics lost virtually all political power, since representation in parliament was based on landholding.

A subsequent revolution in England further polarized the Irish situation. The English monarch James II (a Catholic) was supplanted by a Dutch (Protestant) ruler, William of Orange (after whom the Orange Order of Northern Ireland is named). Irish Catholics sided with James II, and he brought his army to Ireland, hoping to reconquer England from that base. The Protestant colonists of Ireland had sided with William of Orange, who then brought an expeditionary force to Ireland. James took Dublin and laid seige to Londonderry (i.e., Derry), the main source of Orange resistance, but the city held out for fifteen weeks until reinforcements came. In 1690, the two armies met in a decisive battle at the River Boyne, and James was beaten on July 12. William's victory not only secured his position as king of England but also established Protestant supremacy in Ireland (Beckett, 1966:90–95; Simms, 1967).

These events, which occurred over three hundred years ago, are still enshrined in the civil religions of Protestants and Catholics in Northern Ireland. The Catholic civil religion celebrates the heroes of the revolutionary uprising, and the Protestant civil religion commemorates the Orange defenders. In contemporary Derry, an annual (and sometimes violent) Protestant celebration parades the walls of the old city and proclaims to the Catholics living below the walls the seventeenth-century slogan "No Surrender" (see vivid descriptions in MacEoin, 1974b:87, 227, 232). In Belfast, July 12 is a major Protestant holiday with bonfires, parades, speeches, and a mock battle to commemorate William's victory at the Boyne. The defeat is remembered in the Catholic civil religion as merely one of a long string of Protestant and English acts of oppression and injustice (the myths and images of this civil religion figure significantly in Irish literature, especially of the era immediately preceding the 1916 uprising; see Thompson, 1967). Thus the history of "our nation" is remembered differently by the two groups. Events centuries past are the basis for two completely opposed sets of myths, legends, and heroes.

The Deepening Split. Events following 1690 further deepened the rift between Protestants and Catholics. Catholics were effectively excluded from Parliament, and a number of "penal laws" excluded Catholics (the great population majority of the island) from Parliament, army and militia, positions in municipal corporations, all civil service, and the legal profession. Laws of inheritance and land tenure were changed so that it was virtually impossible for Catholic landholders to leave land to a Catholic heir. The laws forbade Catholics from sending their children abroad for education, and Catholics were forced to pay tithes to the (Protestant) Church of Ireland. These laws, in effect for over one hundred years, had the desired result of suppressing Catholic political and economic power. The first widespread nationalist movement, arising in the first half of the nineteenth century, focused on the issue of "Catholic emancipation," especially from strictures on political representation and voting. This history laid the basis for the distinctively Roman Catholic character of modern Irish nationalism (Beckett, 1966: 96–144).

Meanwhile the economy and political situation in Ulster (the north) developed further apart from the rest of Ireland. Ulster included the only developed industrial sector in the country, and Ulster business owners and industrialists feared nationalist separation from Britain—their primary source of markets and supplies. Ulster was also the locus of the only large Protestant enclave, which felt threatened by the prospect of a Catholic nationalist movement in power. Some English politicians deliberately manipulated these fears in their fight against Irish home rule (i.e., allowing an independent Irish parliament). They "played the *Orange card*"—that is, encouraged religious fears and sectarian strife, advising violent resistance if the British Parliament should pass a home-rule bill. Lord Randolph Churchill visited Belfast in 1886 to encourage Protestant fears of home rule and left the slogans "Home Rule Is Rome Rule" and "Ulster Will Fight; Ulster Will Be Right"—mottos kept alive in contemporary Protestant civil religion in Northern Ireland (Beckett, 1966:146–157).

In the nineteenth century, both Protestant and Catholic national visions grew. Sometimes they were embodied in organizations and movements, but more generally they developed as an attitude or part of a world view of the respective communities. The development of these nationalisms illustrates the distinction between *particular* religions (i.e., Roman Catholic, Presbyterian, and Church of Ireland) and Catholic and Protestant *civil* religions. The Roman Catholic hierarchy frequently opposed the nascent Irish nationalism, even though the movement was heavily Catholic. As the twentieth century approached, church leaders found their interests more closely allied to those of the establishment. They were particularly unhappy with the socialist strain of the pro-independence labor movement. Thus while the Catholic hierarchy encouraged a general antagonism toward Protestants, it discouraged the growing Catholic nationalism. Similarly, especially in the North, the Orange Order and related Protestant groups developed their power and beliefs independent of particular Protestant churches, yet with their approval. Both Protestant and Catholic religious leaders generally encouraged distrust toward each other, but Protestant and Catholic civil religions developed independently of the churches.

The nature of the Irish Revolution (1916–1921) itself laid the grounds for the present conflict. The fighting was primarily between two relatively small, irresponsible armed forces, neither of which was controlled by its government. The British government was unable to exercise control over its special force, the "Black and Tans," and the Irish Republican Army (I.R.A.) was not responsible to the Dail (the newly established Irish independent parliament). Never actually militarily "won," the revolutionary war did prepare both sides for a compromise: the division of the island into a politically independent part and a unionist part (see Beckett, 1966:157–166). The significance of irresponsible paramilitary forces in that conflict laid the groundwork for contemporary paramilitary violence in Northern Ireland; and the I.R.A. (Republican nationalist) and Ulster Volunteer Force (Orangeist) are offspring of the armed forces of the Irish Revolution.

Since Partition. The 1921 treaty that followed the Irish Revolution established partition of the country. Northern Ireland consisted of six counties, which together had a Protestant majority of approximately 65 percent, but the Catholic minority was large and dominant in several localities. These six counties had a parliament in Belfast and remained in "union" with England—thus the political tag "Unionist," retained even today. The other twenty-six counties (overwhelmingly Catholic) were given an independent dominion parliament in Dublin that eventually proclaimed the country a republic. The border was arranged to keep as much economically advantageous area for Northern Ireland as possible while retaining Protestant political dominance. Slogans of Unionists during border disputes (1922–1925) figure in their contemporary religion: "Not an inch" and "What we have we hold" (McCracken, 1967).

The fears of Protestant Unionists in Northern Ireland erupted in violence during the treaty years. Armed mobs in Belfast viciously attacked Catholic neighborhoods, forcing Catholics to depend upon the I.R.A. (i.e., the branch of the revolutionary army that is now an illegal paramilitary secret society) to protect them. Often Protestant fears were deliberately exploited by (Protestant) employers to prevent Protestant and Catholic workers from uniting in labor disputes. With unemployment at 30 percent during the 1930s depression in Belfast, Catholic and Protestant workers organized a bipartisan demonstration. In response, Orange Order leaders stepped up their appeals to religious sectarianism, suggesting that the dearth of employment was all the more reason to discriminate against Catholics. The grand master of the Belfast Orange Lodge (and subsequent member of the Northern Ireland Senate) said in 1933:

> It is time Protestant employers of Northern Ireland realized that whenever a Roman Catholic is brought into their employment it means one Protestant vote less. It is our duty to pass the word along from this great demonstration, and I suggest the slogan should be: "Protestants, employ Protestants!" (quoted in MacEoin, 1974b:66).

The social and political pattern that emerged from increasing sectarianization severely discriminated against the Catholic minority in housing, jobs, law enforcement, and elections. Proportional representation in Northern Ireland's Parliament was an early casualty of the Protestant struggle to retain power. Abolition of proportional representation guaranteed that minority parties could not coalesce to counterbalance the Unionist party. The Northern Ireland government also approved a systematic gerrymandering of electoral districts so that Catholic voters were isolated and underrepresented (see McCracken, 1967). Immediately prior to the present strife in Northern Ireland, gerrymandering resulted in Derry's 20,000 Catholic voters being able to elect only 8 councillors, compared to 12 councillors elected by only 10,000 Protestants. Similarly in Omagh, Catholics comprised 61 percent of the population but elected only 9 of the town's 21 councillors; in Dungannon, Armagh, Enniskillen, and other large towns, Catholics were systematically deprived of a fair proportion of power in county and town government (London Sunday Times Insight Team, 1972:34, 35; MacEoin, 1974b: 58–59).

Catholics were also discriminated against in housing. This feature was politically significant because until 1969—when the British government forced the Northern Irish govenment to change its electoral practices—only householders and their wives could vote. Thus policies that prevented Catholics from becoming householders also kept down their voting strength. City and county councils have controlled the allocation of much housing, apartments and single-family dwellings alike. These councils gave strong preference to Protestants in public housing, and they further restricted Catholics by reducing the number of new houses built in their neighborhoods. In predominantly Catholic Derry, the Protestant-controlled city council built only 136 houses between 1958 and 1966 and none after 1966. Partly as a result, over a thousand single-family housing units in the city were occupied by more than one family and sometimes by seven or eight. Over 1,500 families (almost all Catholic) were on the waiting list for housing, with an average of ten years waiting time (London Sunday Times Insight Team, 1972:35–37; MacEoin, 1974b:59).

Widespread job discrimination was the result of preferential treatment of Protestants in both private and public employment. Belfast's largest employer, the shipyards, had in 1971 only 400 Catholic employees out of 10,000 (London Sunday Times Insight Team, 1972:36). Northern Irish public officials systematically granted more and superior jobs to Protestants. In 1961, Catholics accounted for only 13 of 209 officers in professional and technical grades of Northern Irish civil service, and there was only 1 Catholic out of 53 people at the top administrative grade of civil service. Catholics were also greatly underrepresented on the twenty-two public boards in charge of such services as housing, tourism, hospitals, and electricity. Disproportions created since partition have not been substantially altered by recent "reforms." In 1973, Protestants retained 95 percent of the 477 top civil service positions (MacEoin, 1974b:67–69).

The religious segregation of entire occupations and industries also meant that Protestants had an effective stranglehold on large areas of vital services. When in 1974 the British got several government groups to agree to share some political power with Catholics, the plan was destroyed by a brief strike of Protestant workers. These workers controlled entire occupations so strategic that their strike paralyzed the country. Despite the widespread discrimination, however, the Protestants are not generally much better off economically than Catholics. Since both groups are largely working class, the conflict is not class conflict; Protestants of all classes unite against Catholics of all classes (cf. O'Brien, 1974; Rose, 1971). The economic discrimination has direct political implications, however. There is higher unemployment among the Catholic working class than among the Protestant working class, thus encouraging workers to emigrate (usually to England) to find jobs. The higher emigration rate of Catholics counterbalances their higher birth rate, preventing them from becoming the population majority (see London Sunday Times Insight Team, 1972:29–31).

Protestants also controlled "law and order." Before the British intervention, the two main police forces in Northern Ireland were the RUC (Royal Ulster Constabulary) and the B-Specials (Ulster Special Constabulary). The RUC was established at partition and was supposed to be bipartisan. Catholics, however, were never proportionately represented on the force and, when recent strife broke out in the 1960s, were less than 10 percent. The B-Specials was a militia, almost exclusively Protestant. Indeed, the prime minister of Northern Ireland boasted in 1922 that "it is also from the ranks of the Loyal Orange Institution that our splendid B-Specials have come" (quoted in MacEoin, 1974b:62). Catholics had a reasonable basis for their suspicions that police forces used their power against the interests of the Catholic community. There is evidence that in some conflicts, the B-Specials openly joined Protestant mobs against Catholic civilians (see London Sunday Times Insight Team, 1972:132–142).

In addition to possessing an arsenal (e.g., armored cars and automatic weapons), both of these forces were allowed discretionary powers by the Special Powers Act (introduced as a "temporary" measure in 1922 and eventually made permanent). This act, a source of considerable embarrassment to the British government, abridged civil freedoms by allowing any police officer to search, arrest, and imprison suspects without warrant, charge, or trial. A 1935 British inquiry concluded that "the Northern Ireland government has used Special Powers toward securing the domination of one particular political faction and at the same time toward curtailing the lawful activities of its opponents" (cited in MacEoin, 1974b:61–62).

Grave dissatisfaction with these features of Northern Irish life led to the 1964 formation of the Northern Ireland Civil Rights Association (NICRA), patterned after the American civil rights movement. Its demands were modest. They were: (1) "one-man-one-vote" in local elections, (2) removal of gerrymandered boundaries, (3) laws against discrimination by local government and provision of machinery to deal with complaints, (4) allocation of public housing on a points system, (5) repeal of the Special Powers Act, and (6) disbanding of the B-Specials (London Sunday Times Insight Team, 1972:49). The confrontations that resulted from the generally nonviolent demonstrations of NICRA occurred largely because the Northern Ireland government refused to recognize the legitimacy of the movement's grievances and equated it with Republicanism—the movement for national independence from Britain. Protestant enclaves similarly saw the civil rights demonstrations as "them" organized against "us." The stage was set for a long period of sectarian violence: Protestants versus Catholics and both Protestants and Catholics versus the British.

This capsule history of strife in Northern Ireland illustrates how two groups, defined by their religions, became so utterly segregated in their associations that cross-pressures that could have prevented polarization never developed. The combination of this segregation with the religious particularism of each group makes the situation especially volatile. Systematic political and economic suppression of a large religious minority of natives by a colonial power made the resulting conflict reflect nationalistic as well as religious sentiments.

Now let us examine some of the chief characteristics of the opposing civil religions of Catholics and Protestants.

Catholic Civil Religion

The national vision identified as Catholic in Northern Ireland is one of a united republic, encompassing all counties of the island. Thus it is necessary to view the conflict in the context of the religious and political situation of the Republic of Ireland, as well. Although some Catholics in Northern Ireland do not favor union with the Republic of Ireland because of its lower standard of living (especially its social welfare benefits), they are nonetheless likely to identify themselves as Irish and feel a strong tie to the Irish cultural heritage (Beckett, 1966:175). A more militant version of this civil religion draws upon the centuries-old Irish revolutionary myth; this version envisions the (Catholic) natives rising up to overthrow the oppressive (Protestant) colonial power. This militant nationalism does not accept the validity of the settlement that partitioned Ireland. A 1968 survey showed that 33 percent of the Catholics in Northern Ireland approved "on balance" the constitution of Northern Ireland, a proportion probably reduced by subsequent polarization. The study concluded that Northern Ireland is a state that is governed without consent (Rose, 1971:189). Refusal to accept the Northern Ireland government's right to rule further feeds Protestant citizens' notions that Catholics are disloyal or traitorous.

An important factor in the Catholic civil religion of Northern Ireland is its readiness to accept the church-state relations of the Republic of Ireland as normative. Thus Protestant fears are fed by what they see as the effects of the Catholic church on political and social policies in the neighboring Republic of Ireland. Although the influence of the Catholic church in the Republic is indirect, it is still potent (see MacEoin, 1974a, 1974b; O'Brien, 1974; Schmitt, 1973; Sheehy, 1969; Whyte, 1971). The Roman Catholic Church is the established church in the Republic of Ireland (Eire), including in its membership 95 percent of the Republic's population. The 1937 constitution of Ireland declared, until it was abridged in 1972, "a special position of the Holy Catholic Apostolic and Roman Church as the guardian of the Faith professed by the great majority of the Citizens" (Article 44 quoted in Whyte, 1971:24–61). Although the Protestant minority in the Republic is seldom discriminated against, the Catholic church has influenced legislation and social policy with which Protestants are unhappy. The Catholic church's considerable influence in national (i.e., public) schools affects Protestants, especially in areas where they are not numerous enough to support alternative schools. Church-influenced legislation in areas of "private" morality (e.g., divorce, contraception, and censorship) is likewise seen as unfairly restrictive by many Protestants. Thus even though Northern Ireland is politically distinct from the Republic of Ireland, both its Protestant and Catholic nationalisms refer directly to beliefs and practices of the Republic.

The salient imagery and ritual in the Northern Irish Catholic civil religion are symbols of independent Ireland: the flag ("tricolor"), the Irish language, national anthem and ballads of independence, celebration of heroes, and events of revolution. These symbols are always near the surface of interactions with the opposing group. Even nonsectarian events (e.g., civil rights demonstrations) are often the occasion for invoking the symbols of this civil religion; despite organizers' plans, demonstrators sometimes break into singing nationalistic ballads and hymns or unfurl a tricolor flag. These are natural expressions: Catholic militance on behalf of their rights has long been equated with nationalism. Catholic civil religion in Northern Ireland likewise often celebrates—with even more vigor than in the Republic—the heroes and events of Irish revolution: Emmet, Pearse, Connolly, Tone, Father Murphy, the Easter Insurrection, the Fenian Rebellion, Catholic Emancipation, Land League, Gaelic League, United Irishmen. All of these elements mesh together in a national vision.

This nationalism is both anti-British and anticolonial (i.e., against Protestant "settlers"). The British "peace-keeping" forces in Northern Ireland have been embattled from both sides and are intensely disliked by both Protestants and Catholics; both groups believe the troops to be siding with their opposition. Even moves by the British government to pressure the Protestant powers in Northern Ireland to recognize some Catholic rights are distrusted by the Catholic community. Britain has a long history of political maneuvers resulting in detriment to the Irish.

The Catholic civil religion in Northern Ireland is generally more tolerant of Protestants than the Protestant version is of Catholics. This acceptance is largely because Protestants, too, were prominent in the revolutionary heritage of Ireland. Protestants such as Wolfe Tone and Robert Emmet, inspired by the ideals of the French Revolution, led Irish revolts and are celebrated as martyrs in the civil religion of Catholic nationalists.

Protestant Civil Religion

The Protestant civil religion of Northern Ireland is, by contrast, virulently anti-Catholic. A 1968 survey found Northern Irish Protestant antipathy to Catholicism to be considerably greater than Catholic antipathy toward Protestantism (Rose, 1971:256). The religious form of Protestantism as a civil religion in Northern Ireland is particularly evident in the power and influence of the Orange Order. Orangeism is essentially the state religion of Northern Ireland. The Unionist party, which has dominated the government since its inception, has close, overt links with the Orange Order and is almost exclusively Protestant. Lord Craigavon, prime minister of Northern Ireland from 1921 to 1940, proclaimed, "I am an Orangeman first and a politician and a member of this parliament afterwards. . . . All I boast is that we are a Protestant parliament and a Protestant state" (cited in MacEoin, 1974b:53). More explicit about the link between the controlling party (i.e., Unionist) and Orangeism is the opinion of Brian Faulkner, prime minister of Northern Ireland before Britain stepped in to rule the province directly in 1972. Faulkner stated:

> There is no alternative to the invincible combination of the Orange Order and the Unionist Party. . . . The Unionist Party relies upon the Orange Order and likewise we in the Order trust the party. That vital faith must never be jeopardized by either partner (cited in MacEoin, 1974b:243).

The Orange Order, founded in 1795, has been especially strong in Northern Ireland in this century. The grand master of the Belfast Orange Lodge (the largest of the several lodges in the country) described the Order as "basically religious and only coincidentally political, a fellowship of all who embrace the Reformed faith, founded to safeguard the interests of the Protestant people against the aggressions of the church of Rome which historically claims to have power over princes" (cited in MacEoin, 1974b:31). The salvation theology of Orangeism requires a sense of opposition: It fights for salvation not only from sin but also from Catholicism. The grand master further stated, "We have to fight the pretensions of the church of Rome. . . . I am convinced that it has never stopped its efforts to obscure the gospel, and I believe we must contend for the way of salvation through Christ."

The Orange Order maintains monolithic control over Protestant opinion. It includes in its membership one-third of Protestant men in Northern Ireland. It includes all social classes, Church of Ireland and Dissenters alike, and its strength is estimated at 100,000. Together with active women's and youth auxiliaries, it involves more than 90 percent of the Protestant community in some places (MacEoin, 1974b:62). Not all Protestants believe in Orangeism, but Orange ties are essential to gaining many jobs, political offices, appointments to legal and medical positions, and housing.

The anti-Catholic stance of Orangeism is directly relevant to the Protestant national vision in Northern Ireland; a fundamental premise of that vision is that Catholics must not be allowed power. When some Catholics attempted to work within the Northern Irish political system in the 1960s, Unionist leaders tried to prevent their participation on grounds of their religion. One of the foremost Unionist leaders stated:

> I would draw your attention to the words "civil and religious liberty." The liberty we know is the liberty of the Protestant religion. . . . it is difficult to see how a Roman Catholic, with the vast difference in our religious outlook, could be either acceptable within the Unionist party as a member, or bring himself unconditionally to support its ideals. Furthermore to this, an Orangeman is pledged to resist by all lawful means the Ascendancy of the Church of Rome (cited by London Sunday Times Insight Team, 1972:37).

According to Northern Irish Protestant civil religion, Catholicism is incompatible with the Protestant conception of democracy, and the Protestant nationalist vision is, by definition, opposed to Catholic power. William Craig, Northern Irish Minister of Home Affairs in 1968, said, "When you have a Roman Catholic majority, you have a lesser standard of democracy"—or, as the London Sunday Times Insight Team (1972:46) translated his stand, rule by the people is not a great idea if they are the wrong people. This anti-Catholic stance is celebrated in the fiery speeches of Orange parades and commemoration of their history, Protestant heroes, and legends. One popular Protestant tune, called "Croppies (i.e., Catholics) Lie Down," goes:

> *Poor Croppies, ye know that your sentence was come,*
> *When you heard the dread sound of the Protestant drum.*
> *In memory of William we hoist his flag,*
> *And soon the bright Orange put down the Green rag.*

Although this national vision is inimical to the prospect of union with the Republic of Ireland, it also includes strong anti-British sentiment. Northern Irish Protestants are keenly aware of their inferior status in the British class structure and resent being treated as colonials. The militant version of the Protestant civil religion holds that loyalty to the British Crown is contingent upon the British enforcing the Protestant ascendancy of the seventeenth-century "Revolution settlement" (MacEoin, 1974b:40, 285).

Nationalism without Nation Building

The Protestant and Catholic national visions of Northern Ireland appear to fit our model of civil religion, albeit in a different form from that of civil religion in America. Both Protestant and Catholic versions are mutually exclusive images of the nation. Both entail extensive myths, legends, rituals, and symbols of a long history of growing separation of peoples. Both civil religions entail imagery of the "chosen people." The Protestant version defines themselves as God's chosen people struggling to maintain the truth in a land of paganism and idolatry, while the Catholic version describes the Gaelic peoples as the chosen children of God, oppressed by the Protestants. Commenting on this Old Testament imagery, one astute observer remarked, "One could say that Ireland was inhabited, not really by Protestants and Catholics, but by two sets of imaginary Jews" (O'Brien, 1974:288).

The efforts of nonsectarian political groups, concerned clergy on either side, and various ecumenical peace groups to defuse the religious antagonisms in Northern Ireland are typically thwarted because the conflict is less between particular religions than between two civil religions. The differences in belief and practice between the particular religions—Protestant and Catholic— are important but are only a small part of this conflict. The division is essentially over national identity and vision, which are strongly shaped by a long history of experiences and cultural differences between the two groups.

As suggested earlier in this chapter, civil religion in many countries has considerable potential for modern nation building, forging unity from diverse peoples of a state and bridging barriers of language, particular religion, tribalism, and regionalism. In the case of Northern Ireland, however, neither civil religion has this potential. The state governs without consensus, and the people operate from opposing senses of national identity. Another model of civil religion or of church-state relations would serve the interests of nation building better, but the issue of what nation to build is still a political issue.

Summary

Religion is a source of both social cohesion and social conflict. It contributes to the cohesion of a group and, at the same time, expresses its unity. Durkheim suggests that the moral unity of the group itself is the source of the sense of religious force or power experienced by participants. Thus religious rituals incorporate members into the group by reminding them of the meanings and obligations of being "one of us." The civil religion thesis is an attempt to understand the expressions of moral unity of modern societies. It suggests that the nation may have a religious expression distinct from the particular religions of the people.

Religion contributes to social conflict because it is one basis of social cleavage. In societies where other loyalties cut across religious ties, religion is less likely to be a focus of serious conflict. Nevertheless religion's capability for defining the boundaries of "us" against "them" makes it an inherently potential source of conflict. Particularist world views especially tend to intolerance and conflict. Religious groups are also subject to internal conflict over issues of deviance and control, authority and heresy.

The aspects of religion that promote both conflict and cohesion are illustrated by the strife in Northern Ireland. While particular Protestant and Roman Catholic religions have historically contributed to the active bigotry and intolerance there, a broader religious division—that between opposing civil religions with national visions, one Catholic and one Protestant—may also exist.

Recommended Readings

Articles

Robert N. Bellah. "Religion and Legitimation in the American Republic." *Society* 15 (4), 1978:16–23.

"Civil Religion in America." *Daedalus* 96, 1967:1–21; reprinted in Faulkner (1972), Newman (1974), and McNamara (1974) readers and in Richey and Jones collection, listed below.

James S. Coleman. "Social Cleavage and Religious Conflict." *Journal of Social Issues* 12, 1956:44–56; also Bobbs-Merrill reprints S-47.

Phillip Hammond. "Religious Pluralism and Durkheim's Integration Thesis." In *Changing Perspectives in the Scientific Study of Religion*, Allen Eister, ed. New York: Wiley, 1974, pp. 115–142.

Rodney Stark and Charles Glock. "Prejudice and the Churches." In *Prejudice, U.S.A.*, Charles Glock and Ellen Siegelman, eds. New York: Praeger, 1969; reprinted in Glock (1973) and abridged in McNamara (1974).

Books

Emile Durkheim. *Elementary Forms of the Religious Life*. New York: Free Press, 1965. Especially the introduction; Book 1, Chapter 1; Book 2, Chapters 6, 7; Book 3; and conclusion. Durkheim's classical study uses illustrations from the religion of the Arunta of Australia to explicate his theory of the social foundations of religious beliefs and practices.

Andrew Greeley. *The Denominational Society*. Glenview, Ill.: Scott, Foresman, 1972. This book is a readable, almost journalistic synthesis of data and interpretations of American religion. Particularly useful are his capsule descriptions of Protestant, Roman Catholic, and Jewish experiences in American history and his treatment of religion as an ethnic phenomenon.

Will Herberg. *Protestant-Catholic-Jew*. Garden City, N.Y.: Doubleday, 1960. Herberg's description of the "American way of life" as a quasi-religious belief system and his descriptions of Protestant, Catholic, and Jewish history in America are especially useful. While somewhat dated, this essay on religion in American life during the 1950s is still provocative.

Robert Lee and Martin Marty, eds. *Religion and Social Conflict*. New York: Oxford University Press, 1964. Many essays in this collection, though somewhat dated, are good analyses of the role of religion in social conflict in the United States.

Russell Richey and Donald Jones, eds. *American Civil Religion*. New York: Harper & Row, 1974. This collection includes reprints of key essays by Bellah, Mead, and Warner. New material, originally presented in a conference on this theme, is uneven, but essays by Wilson, Marty, Bellah, and the editors are useful.

CHAPTER SEVEN

The Impact of Religion on Social Change

*T*he process of social change highlights the relationship between religion and other aspects of the social system, especially the economic and political spheres. This chapter examines some of the key ideas about the interrelationship between religion and social change. Because the issue of religion and social change is so complex, its division in this chapter is largely for analytical purposes. We shall first examine the ways in which religion supports the status quo and inhibits change, then follow by examining how religion promotes social change. The concluding analysis poses the questions: Under what conditions does religion have the greatest impact on society, and under what conditions is religion's influence likely to inhibit or promote change? Discussion of these questions is followed by an Extended Application to the case of black religion in America.

Factors in Social Change

The processes involved in social change are complex. It is difficult to isolate a single aspect such as religion in a chain of events that result in social change. For analytical purposes, we can speak of aspects of religion that promote or inhibit social change, but in most cases both are occurring simultaneously. As the example of millenarianism (discussed in Chapter 2) shows, a religious movement that arises in response to social change may itself help bring about social change.[1] A further complexity is the meaning of religion. Do we mean religious ideas, religious personages, religious movements, or religious organizations? All of

[1] In framing the topic as an interrelationship, we are rejecting theories that treat religion as *nothing but* an epiphenomenon to other social processes, though we will discuss some of these theories later in this chapter. Any effort to present this complex relationship in the brief space of a chapter necessarily entails great simplification. Suggested sources at the end of the chapter and in footnotes can direct interested readers to further examination of this important theme.

these aspects of religion need to be considered; yet, in any given situation, the relationships are often very complex.

We need to remember that change itself is neither necessarily good or bad. **Social change** refers to any alteration in the social arrangements of a group or society. Of particular sociological interest is change that results in basic structural rearrangements (e.g., a new basis for social stratification or a change in a group's fundamental mode of decision making). Although the process of change itself is neutral, we often evaluate specific changes and potential changes by culturally established criteria. For example, we might consider the development of modern technology to be good or bad, but the criteria by which we make this judgment are not inherent in the process of change itself.

The effect of religion on a social development is not necessarily intentional. A religious idea or movement may become transformed into something very different from what its originators intended, and the influence of religion is often indirect. The Society of Friends (i.e., Quakers) became one of the foremost reformist sects in Christianity, even though their initial thrust was millenarian and somewhat mystical. As the movement developed, the Quakers' values of hard work and rejection of "worldly" amusements contributed to the wealth of numerous families in the sect. Their other values (e.g., a strong personal conscience on social and political issues) stimulated their active participation in political and social reforms. They were prominent in abolitionism and the underground railroad, established self-help projects during and after the famine in Ireland, and were active in campaigns for prison and legal reform. Thus the ascetic, inward ideals of the original movement were transformed—first into monetary philanthropy and later into social activism (Isichei, 1967; Wilson, 1970: 178–181). The impetus for its monetary philanthropy was the *unintentional* economic change produced by religious values, and the resulting social activism exemplified an *intentional* change orientation, or deliberate stance of opposition to the dominant society (Westhues, 1976).

Religion Supports the Status Quo

There is an inherently conservative aspect to religion. Religion can evoke a sense of the sacred precisely because of believers' respect for tradition and continuity. Religious symbols link the believers' present experience with meanings derived from the group's tradition, and religious beliefs that are taken-for-granted truths build a strong force against new ways of thinking. Practices handed down through tradition as the god-approved ways are highly resistant to change. Although other aspects of religion promote social change, important elements in religion maintain the status quo.

A central theme in the sociology of religion is the relationship between religious ideas and the nature of the social groups that hold them. Social stratification, in particular, appears closely correlated with religious belief. **Stratification** refers to the differential distribution of prestige and privilege in a society according to criteria such as social class, age, political power, gender, or race. Religion has a different significance to various strata in a society, and different religious ideas will probably appeal to different groups in the society's stratification system. In America, Episcopalians and Congregationalists (i.e., United Church) draw members disproportionately from the upper classes, while Holiness and Pentecostal groups draw relatively large proportions of members from the lower classes (Demerath, 1965). Similarly, religious ideas of a social group often reflect social caste, as illustrated by black religion later in this chapter.

Interest Theories: Marx and Engels

The connection between stratification and religious ideas has often been explained by interest theories such as Marx and Engels's explanation of religion as ideology. **Ideology** is a system of ideas that explains and legitimates the actions and interests of a specific sector (i.e., class) of society. The classical Marxian approach applies the concept of ideology only to ideas that embody the vested interests of the dominant classes; thus the term has come to have a negative evaluative connotation. The concept of ideology applies more broadly to religion, however, if it is used neutrally. In this usage, ideology also refers to belief systems defending the interests of a socially subordinate group, thus justifying reform or revolution (Geertz, 1964; Lewy, 1974).

According to the dominant strain of Marxian analysis, the fundamental basis of social action is **material interests,** referring to considerations that give economic benefits and power to a person or group. Religious and philosophical ideas are seen as mere epiphenomena, after-the-fact explanations that justify or mask real motivations for behavior.[2] Another school of Marxian thought has, especially in recent years, emphasized the relative autonomy of religion. This school strives to study religious belief systems in themselves, locating them in a larger social-historical context. These theorists retain the insights of Marx and especially Engels but focus on the complex *reciprocal* influences between religion and social structure. By treating the relationship as complex, this latter Marxian approach identifies both the passive and active, conservative and revolutionary elements in religion (this strain of Marxian thought developed from the interpretations of Gramsci, Lukacs, and the Frankfurt school, among others; see Maduro, 1977, and Mayrl, 1976).

Another concept explaining the change-inhibiting aspects of religion is the idea of **alienation,** which is central to the Marxian definition of religion, as noted in Chapter 1. Marx used this concept to analyze the false consciousness that he believed religion engendered. Marx (1963:122) asserted:

> All these consequences follow from the fact that the worker is related to the *product of his labor* as to an *alien* object. For it is clear on this presupposition that the more the worker expends himself in work the more powerful becomes the world of objects which he creates in face of himself, the poorer he becomes in his inner life, and the less he belongs to himself. It is just the same as in religion. The more of himself man attributes to God the less he has left in himself.

---

[2]This dominant strain—"dialectical materialism"—is represented by the interpretations of Plekhanov, Bernstein, Kautsky, and later Stalin. Marx himself did not develop a careful, unified theory of religion; the writings of Engels and Kautsky were more fruitful for further development of Marxian theory of religion. For a lucid and critical examination of these early theorists, see McKown, 1975.

Religion, according to Marx, is the projection of human needs and desires into the realm of the fantastic. Religious alienation is thus the understandable reflection of the false consciousness inherent in this social system. Marx's insight into the change-inhibiting aspects of religious consciousness centers upon the sense of domination by an alien force. Religion obscures real sources of conflict of class interests. Only a society that destroys such illusions can establish itself on the "truth of this world."

In this context, Marx stated that religion is the "opium of the people." He considered the distress that people expressed in their religion to be real but religion itself as an illusion preventing people from doing anything effective to remedy their condition. Religion soothed their distress, but any relief was illusory (Marx, 1963:43, 44). Often religion draws off dissent and zeal that might otherwise promote revolution. Thus a Marxian reading of the history of the English working class suggests that the development of Methodism precluded revolution by harnessing nineteenth-century workers' dissent and fervor in a religious movement. (This thesis was first approvingly suggested in 1906 by British historian Elie Halévy; it was reexplored as a Marxian critique of English class relations by Hobsbawm, 1959, and Thompson, 1968.)

Although some evidence supports Marx's contention, studies of the correlation between religion and sociopolitical action generally suggest that the relationship is more complex, varied, and unpredictable (see D'Antonio and Pike, eds., 1964; Gerlach, 1974; L'Alive D'Epinay, 1969; McGuire, 1974; Marx, 1967). Religion does relieve the tension of economic deprivation by substituting the value of religious achievement for economic achievement, and this substitution may indeed have an opiate effect because pressure for change is defused. At the same time, however, religion offers greater self-esteem by informing believers that they are superior, according to these alternative values. Such sense of superiority has transformative power, as exemplified by the zeal of the Puritans (Coleman, 1956:52).

Interest Theories: Weber
Weber, too, noted the extent to which religious ideas served to legitimate existing social arrangements, especially the stratification system. Religion has historically explained and justified why the powerful and privileged should have their power and privilege. The wealthy might justify their privilege as a sign of God's approval of their hard work and moral uprightness. Weber observed that most religions provide **theodicies** both of privilege and of disprivilege.

Theodicies are religious explanations that provide meaning for problematic experiences—in this case, the discrepancies of stratification. For example, the Hindu doctrine of rebirth simultaneously justifies the privilege of the upper classes and gives meaning and some hope for the conditions of the lower classes. This belief explains that one's present condition is the result of behavior in one's former life. A favored situation (e.g., being born a man rather than a woman) is justified as the result of appropriate behavior in a former incarnation. Prescribed action for both the privileged and disprivileged is therefore to behave appropriately in one's present social situation in order to obtain a more favorable situation in the next life. This theodicy justifies and explains the social status of both privileged and disprivileged and deters the disprivileged from trying to change the existing arrangement—in this life, at least (Weber, 1946: 253ff.; 1963).

Religious Legitimation

Religious legitimation of the status quo is sometimes the result of direct collusion between the dominant classes and the dominant religious organizations. Religious organizations and their personnel frequently have vested interests, which they protect by alliance with dominant groups in political and economic spheres. At the same time, dominant groups often try to manipulate religion to serve their purposes. Machiavelli recognized the legitimating power of religion and recommended that lawgivers resort to divine authority for their laws. He proposed:

> It is therefore the duty of princes and heads of republics to uphold the foundations of the religion of their countries, for then it is easy to keep their people religious, and consequently well conducted and united (*Discourses*, Book I, Chapter 12, as quoted in Lewy, 1974).

Through religious legitimation, wars have been justified as "holy wars," obligations have been justified as "sacred duty," and domination has been explained as "divine kingship." The theory of the "divine right" of kings (a Western political theory legitimating monarchies and reaching its apex in the seventeenth century) explained that the monarch's right to rule is God-given and that the monarch's ultimate responsibility for conduct of the state is to God. This theory interpreted the process of monarchical succession and the coronation/anointment of kings as the working-out or expression of that God-given right. By implication, then, a ruler who gained dominance by other means (e.g., by revolution, usurping the throne, or popular choice) was not legitimate in the eyes of God. The monarch had both a civil and sacred role. Divine right made the king priest-mediator of God's will to the state. Belief in the divine right of kings both legitimated the rule of monarchs and suppressed dissent.

In the United States, the constitutionally mandated separation of church and state reduced the direct religious legitimation of political power, but religion has been a significant source of persuasion in political and socioeconomic spheres. Religion has been used to legitimate slavery and racial segregation, industrialization and antiunionism, warfare and international policy—all of which generally served the interests of the dominant sociopolitical groups. The historical processes by which religion was drawn into legitimation of these interests is, however, complex (see sociological studies of specific historical situations such as Yinger's 1946 analysis of church responses to America's participation in World War II; Pope's 1942 classic study of religion's role in quelling a major mill strike; and Hadden's 1969 study of tensions over clergy activism, especially civil rights).

Similarly religion has been used to legitimate changes favoring a dominant group (e.g., the wealthy or politically powerful). Imperialism and crusades have generally been supported by religious or quasi-religious belief systems. President McKinley explained the decision to wage the expansionist war against Spain that acquired Cuba and the Philippines as follows:

> I am not ashamed to tell you, gentlemen, that I went down on my knees and
> prayed Almighty God for light and guidance more than one night. And one night
> late it came to me this way. . . . There was nothing left for us to do but to take
> them all and to educate the Filipinos and uplift and civilize and Christianize them
> and by God's grace do the very best we could by them, as our fellow men for
> whom Christ also died (quoted in Ahlstrom, 1972:879).

Religious legitimations and institutional support have also been historically
used to promote new economic arrangements such as industrialization. A South
Carolina minister, supporting the industrialization of his region, said in 1927:

> To those who can read history it is unthinkable that any one fail to see in it all the
> hand of God bringing the many thousands from the bondage imposed upon us by
> social and economic forces which of ourselves we were powerless to con-
> trol. . . . It is imperative that we think of Southern industry as a spiritual move-
> ment and of ourselves as instruments in a Divine plan. Southern industry is the
> largest single opportunity the world has ever had to build a democracy upon the
> ethics of Christianity. . . . Southern industry is to measure the power of Protes-
> tantism, unmolested. . . . Southern industry was pioneered by men possessing
> the statesmanship of the prophets of God. . . . I personally believe it was God's
> way for the development of a forsaken people (quoted in Pope, 1942:25).

Religious Socialization

Religion legitimates not only the social system but also specific roles and
personal qualities appropriate to existing structures. By promoting certain character types (e.g., the "hard-working individualist" or the "fatalistic happy-go-
lucky" type) that are appropriate to a socioeconomic system, religion further
legitimates that system. In socialization the individual internalizes these roles (as
discussed in Chapter 3), which then come to exert an influence often greater than
external social controls. Religious socialization often indirectly supports the socioeconomic status quo by teaching attitudes and values that adapt to that system.

By observing the moral norms encouraged by a religious group, the individual will come to "fit" better into the existing social arrangement. This effect of
religion for suppressing dissent was clearly recognized by a mill official who said:
"Belonging to a church, and attending it, makes a man a better worker. It makes
him more complacent—no, that's not the word. It makes him more resigned—
that's not the word either, but you get the general idea" (quoted in Pope, 1942:30,
31). A recent restudy of this community found these attitudes prevalent today.
Mill managers still think that the most valued service of local congregations is
developing traits in workers of punctuality, hard work, sobriety, and obedience
(Earle et al., 1976:26).

Many sectarian religious groups opposed to "the ways of the world" also
teach their members values and behaviors that make them more successful in "the
world." Holiness groups, for example, resocialize their members into the values
of sobriety, hard work, and forgoing of present pleasures for future rewards
(Johnson, 1961; cf. Tyler, 1966). Similarly some new religious movements help
their counterculture members "get straight" according to the values of the dominant society (Robbins and Anthony, 1972). By legitimating "appropriate" roles
and personal norms, religion helps provide motivation for individuals to participate in the existing social and economic system (Robertson, 1977).

Social Control

Religion is a potent force for social control. Although social control can be exercised for social change, it is typically change inhibiting. External forms of religious social control are most evident. Within a religious group, sanctions for deviance from group norms are all the more potent because of their reference to the sacred. The idea of being judged not only by other humans but also by the gods is a powerful deterrent from deviance. Salvation religions such as Christianity exercise control in urging that believers conform to norms in order to assure their future salvation.

The forms of social control exercised by religious groups include informal sanctions such as ostracizing, shaming, or shunning the offender. Other measures include confession and exclusion or excommunication (Turner, 1977b). Some religious groups have highly formal controls such as laws and religious courts. The social control exercised by religious organizations varies according to their power in the society. Society-wide religious controls (e.g., the Inquisition and witch hunts) are less likely in a pluralistic society. Nevertheless America's modern equivalent of witch hunts, McCarthyism and related right-wing extremism, was supported largely by members of religious groups that did not (then) favor pluralism—Roman Catholics and fundamentalist Protestants (Lipset, 1963). Even in relatively pluralistic societies such as America, religion forms a significant basis of the laws and formal order, as well as of informal social control.

Another, relatively informal aspect of religious social control is the power of group loyalty to ensure conformity. The same loyalty can also be utilized for change-promoting action. When the group supports the status quo, however, religious loyalty ensures that the individual does nothing that would upset the group or work counter to its interests. The greater the accommodation of the religious group to the larger society, the more does members' loyalty to "our kind of people" inhibit change.

Internal religious controls are especially important. A person who is socialized into a religious perspective internalizes religious controls. Although socialization is never "perfect," most people internalize much of the normative content of their upbringing. Socialization has a built-in conservative thrust. When a person does something in order to have a "good conscience" or refrains from certain behavior to avoid a "guilty conscience," the belief system is exercising its control. Internal social controls are likely to impede change-oriented behavior because the individual feels guilty in breaking away from the learned norms.

Religion Promotes Social Change

While certain aspects of religion inhibit social change, other aspects challenge the status quo and encourage change. In some circumstances, religion is a profoundly revolutionary force, holding out a vision of how things might or ought to be. Historically religion has been one of the most important motivations for change because of its particular effectiveness in uniting people's beliefs with their actions, their ideas with their social lives. Religious movements such as the Great Awakening (i.e., several waves of revivals in America beginning in the latter part of the eighteenth century) have had tremendous impact upon society, though the outcome may not have been part of the religious goals of the movement itself. These revivals were important sources of the abolitionist movement as well as of later temperance and prohibition movements. They also had an impact on the democratization of the American polity, making way for popular participation in what was largely an oligarchy of economically prosperous citizens (Ahlstrom, 1972:349, 350; Hammond, 1979; Jamison, 1961).

In order to understand recent developments in modern societies, sociologists have reexamined their classical foundations.[3] Social change issues were central in the works of Marx, Simmel, and especially Weber. These classical theorists have provided explanations for current developments and have inspired contemporary sociologists to new understandings. One product of this new thinking has been a more profound understanding of Weber's analysis of religion and modernization, going considerably beyond the relatively superficial "Protestant ethic" studies of the 1950s. We will discuss this new approach to Weber in more detail later in this chapter.

Religion and Social Dynamics: A Neo-Marxian Approach

Another product of new perspectives to the classics has been a rethinking of the Marxian approach to religion and social change. A number of neo-Marxian sociologists insist that an appropriately complex empirical approach to the scientific study of religion cannot be substituted for, or anticipated by, theoretical constructs. Marxian theory is thus used as a perspective from which study can be conducted rather than as a static assumption (Maduro, 1977:366).

This new Marxian approach to religion results in a more complex conclusion than classical Marxian interpretations about the relationship of religion to social change. Starting from some of Engels's later ideas, these sociologists view religion as being relatively autonomous from the economic substructure. These theorists come to a more rich, complex understanding of religion by focusing on its functions as a partially independent variable in social change. In contrast to classical Marxism, neo-Marxian approaches suggest that:

> (1) Religion is not a mere passive effect of the social relations of production; it is an active element of social dynamics, both conditioning and conditioned by social processes. (2) Religion is not always a subordinate element within social processes; it may often play an important part in the birth and consolidation of a particular social structure. (3) Religion is not necessarily a functional, reproductive or conservative factor in society; it often is one of the main (and sometimes the only) available channel to bring about a social revolution (Maduro, 1977:366).

These various new approaches to classical sociological interpretations of religion press toward a more complex understanding of religion and social

[3]Among sociologists of religion, this recent revitalization of classical issues is best represented by Berger, Luckmann, Fenn, Martin, and Robertson. Robertson's 1977 and 1979 analyses are particularly incisive statements of key themes. Neo-Marxian thinking on religion has been especially lively in parts of Eastern Europe, Latin America, Germany, France, and Italy; see Birnbaum, 1973; Desroche, 1962, 1969; Kersevan, 1975; Maduro, 1975; Varga, 1975. The Frankfurt school (Germany) has developed interesting syntheses of themes from Marx and Weber; see Habermas, 1971, 1975; other contemporary works on these broader themes include Bell, 1976; Gellner, 1974; Gouldner, 1976; Touraine, 1977.

change. The question is no longer "Does religion promote social change?" but rather "In what ways and under what conditions does it promote rather than inhibit change?"

We will consider the change-promoting aspects of religion under three headings: religious ideas, religious leadership, and religious groups. In practice, of course, these frequently overlap (e.g., when a religious leader proclaims a new religious idea to a group of followers).

Religious Ideas and Meanings

Ideas themselves do not directly effect change. Ideas indirectly influence society through people whose interests (i.e., all those things that could benefit them) lie in pursuing those ideas and applying them to social action. Religious ideas therefore affect social action in two ways: They may form the *content* of what a group of people try to do; and they may shape people's *perception* of what their interests are. The movement to abolish slavery in the United States, for example, had important religious impetus. Religious ideas explained the evils of slavery; religious movements created a pool of adherents receptive to abolitionist ideas; and religious interests (e.g., desire for salvation) motivated them to put the ideas into action. For such reasons, it is appropriate for sociologists to examine the emergence of new religious ideas in history.

Religious Breakthrough: Weber. By "ideas," we mean a broad concept of meanings, such as described in Chapter 2, rather than merely the formal ideas of doctrine or theology. Weber used the yet broader notion of **ethic**, referring to the total perspective and values of a religious way of thinking. Weber (1951, 1952, 1958b) examined several world religions for those aspects of their orientations to their god and their social worlds that inhibited or promoted certain socioeconomic changes, especially the process of "modernization." In these studies, Weber examined the social location of religious ideas and innovation in each society. He sought the sources of motivation for individual action, the relationship of the individual to the larger society, and the religious ideas that shaped how individual actors in that society perceived their social world. Weber was especially interested in locating historical points of **breakthrough.** These were periods in the development of a society when circumstances pushed the social group either toward a new way of action or toward reaffirmation of the old way. The movement toward innovation in the social system constituted a breakthrough. Weber noted that religion has been historically prominent in these breakthrough developments.

Like Marx, Weber held that people's vested interests, considered in the context of certain structural conditions, explained their actions. By contrast, he felt that these interests need not be purely economic ones; people could be motivated, for example, to protect their religious standing. While religious ideas do not determine social action, according to Weber, they are significant in shaping actors' perceptions and interpretations of their material and ideal interests. Weber (1946:280) stated:

> Not ideas, but material and ideal interests, directly govern men's conduct. Yet
> very frequently the "world images" that have been created by "ideas" have, like

switchmen, determined the tracks along which action has been pushed by the dynamic of interest. "From what" and "for what" one wished to be redeemed and, let us not forget, "could be" redeemed, depended upon one's image of the world.

Weber considered religion one of the foremost sources of these ideas that shaped the direction of social action and were "switchmen" in the course of history.

In *The Protestant Ethic and the Spirit of Capitalism* (1958a), Weber analyzed one particularly important breakthrough—the development of the capitalistic mode of socioeconomic organization. He hypothesized a link between the rise of the Protestant world view and the subsequent emergence of capitalism in Western society. To Weber, capitalism was a significant factor in modernization, a process he viewed with almost prophetic misgivings. The key characteristic of modernization is its *means-end* (i.e., functional) *rationality*. Weber emphasized that capitalism is not mere greed or acquisitiveness but the rational, systematic investment of time and resources toward the expectation of future chances of profit. Furthermore, the expansion of this perspective to a society-wide economic system required socially available roles for performing these tasks: specifically, the role of the entrepreneur (Weber, 1958a:17–27; excellent brief treatments of Weber's thesis include Eisenstadt, 1969, and Robertson, 1977).

Ideas and Individualism: Weber. Weber argued that creation of a pool of individuals with the necessary values and characteristics to perform as entrepreneurs was essential to the emergence of capitalism. This development was made possible by a new form of individualism, an unintentional by-product of the main variant of Protestantism at that critical moment in history. Weber reasoned that the social role of the entrepreneur called for someone who valued hard work and considered deferred gratification as almost a virtue in itself. Early Protestantism, especially Lutheranism, contributed to this ethic by its interpretation of work as a vocation. The work of the layperson was thus viewed as a virtue, fulfilling a special call from God.

Capitalism further required persons willing to deny themselves rationally and systematically for the sake of achieving a future goal. The dominant strain of Protestantism (e.g., Calvinism, Puritanism, Pietism, Anabaptism) produced such qualities because of its **inner-worldly ascetism,** encouraging members to be active "in the world"—indeed, to prove their salvation by their socioeconomic actions. At the same time, these forms of Protestantism expected their members to forgo the pleasures "of the world"—not to spend their money on luxuries, drink, gambling, or entertainments. The "Protestant ethic" therefore became one of hard work, sobriety, financial care, and deferred gratification. Even though capitalistic gain was far from the goal of these Protestant values, according to Weber, the initial development of capitalism was made possible by the available pool of persons who shared these qualities.

Simultaneously Protestantism resulted in a powerful new source of motivation for such economic action as capitalism. Protestant beliefs produced a new form of individualism—that is, a new mode of individual-to-society relationship. Under Roman Catholicism, the individual had experienced something of a "blanket" approval. The individual's standing before God and fellow believers was certified by belonging to the church and receiving its sacraments; thus belonging to the *group* legitimated the individual member. Protestantism, especially its Calvinist varieties, offered no such security. Weber argued that the Protestant ethic made it necessary for individuals to legitimate themselves. This need for self-legitimation, combined with inner-worldly asceticism, produced a strong motivation for the kind of socioeconomic action that capitalism entailed.

Weber linked these values and motivations produced by the Protestant ethic with the emergence of capitalism, especially the critical role of the entrepreneur. Once established, however, capitalism no longer needed the Protestant ethic; mature capitalism, according to Weber, can be self-sustaining. Some sociologists, failing to recognize this point, have applied Weber's terms to current attitudinal differences between Roman Catholics and Protestants in developed countries. These studies have produced conflicting results, but there is little consistent evidence of important differences between Protestants and Roman Catholics in attitudes toward work and consumption.[4] More relevant to Weber's thesis are studies of the impact of other-worldly or inner-worldly religious attitudes in developing nations (see Eisenstadt, 1968; Waardenburg, 1978).

Numerous scholars since Weber have contested his Protestant ethic hypothesis. Some have argued that the constellation of attitudes and ideas that Weber called the Protestant ethic (if such a mind-set existed) coincided with more important socioeconomic changes such as technological developments, the availability of potential laborers, and the influx of new capital resources (e.g., from colonial holdings). They suggest that these latter factors, among others, were more significant than the Protestant ethic in the development of capitalism. Probably Weber himself would have modified his thesis had he finished his projected sociology of Protestantism before his death. *The Protestant Ethic* was among his earliest writings in the sociology of religion, and his later essays emphasized the change-promoting potential of religious sects as organizations more than the Protestant ethic per se (Berger, 1971; Weber, 1946:302–322).

Religious Imagery. Another aspect that contributes to social change is the capacity of religious meanings to serve as symbols for change. Religious symbols frequently present an *image* of future change. They create a vision of what could be and suggest to believers their role in bringing about that change. Change-oriented symbolism is often directed toward the social realm, as exemplified by the ideas of the "heavenly city," the "new Jerusalem," and the "chosen people." Religion provides symbols of tradition and continuity, but religious idealization also gives symbols to a group's desire for change. These symbols enable people to conceptualize their situation and to manipulate change-promoting elements of their social world. Sometimes the specific symbols evoked are not very effective. The future sought by a group may be impossible to realize; but genuine social structural changes are unlikely to occur unless people have new ways of thinking about

---

[4]See Greeley, 1964; see Bouma, 1973, for a detailed critique of specific empirical investigations purporting to test Weber's Protestant ethic hypothesis; the best-known study exemplifying these misunderstandings is Lenski, 1963; see counterarguments in Greeley, 1963, and Schumann, 1971; a somewhat different application is made by McClelland, 1961, with counterarguments in Robertson, 1978. Systematic critiques of the Weber thesis include Green, 1959; Samuelsson, 1964; and Tawney, 1926.

their social world—a set of symbols that evoke images of change (see Maduro, 1977:366).

Religious Leadership

Social change often requires an effective leader who can express desired change, motivate followers to action, and direct their actions into some larger movement for change. Religion has historically been a major source of such leaders, largely because religious claims form a potent basis of authority. The prototype of the change-oriented religious leader is the **prophet**, whose social role is especially significant.[5]

A prophet is someone who confronts the powers that be and the established ways of doing things, claiming to be taken seriously on religious authority. There are two types of prophetic roles. One is the **exemplary prophet**, whose challenge to the status quo consists of living a kind of life that exemplifies a dramatically different set of meanings and values. The Buddha is a good example of this kind of prophet, whose very way of life is his message. The other type is the **emissary prophet**, who confronts the established powers as one who is sent by God to proclaim a message. Most of the Old Testament prophets were of this type. The emissary prophet has historically been an important source of change because the message proclaimed offered a new religious idea (i.e., ethic) and a different basis of authority. The prophetic message was often one of judgment and criticism. Whether the message called the people back to a previous way of life or directed them to some new way, it nevertheless called for *change*.

The role of the prophet is the opposite of the priestly role. A **priest** is any religious functionary whose role is to administer the established religion—to celebrate the traditional rituals, practices, and beliefs. Most clergy and church officials in American society perform priestly roles. The basis of priestly authority is priests' location in the religious organization as representatives of that establishment, and their actions mediate between its traditions and the people. The prophet, by contrast, challenges the established way of doing things, not only by messages of criticism but also by claiming an authority outside the established authority. Thus the role of the prophet is essentially a force for change in society.

Weber proposed that **charisma** was the authority basis of leaders such as prophets. Charisma refers to "a certain quality of an individual personality by virtue of which he is set apart from ordinary men and treated as endowed with . . . specifically exceptional powers or qualities . . . [which] are not accessible to the ordinary person" (Weber, 1947:358, 359). The authority of the charismatic leader rests upon the acceptance of his or her claim by a group of followers; and upon the followers' sense of duty to carry out the normative pattern or order proclaimed by the leader. Thus the charismatic leader is a source both of new ideas and new obligations.

The charismatic leader says, in effect, "It is written . . . , but I say unto you. . . . " By word or deed, the charismatic leader challenges the existing normative pattern, conveying to the followers a sense of crisis, then offering a solution to the crisis—a new normative order. Charismatic leaders may arise

[5] This discussion of prophets and charismatic authority follows Weber's theories (1946, 1947: 358ff.; 1963).

either outside or within the institutional framework. Charismatic authority is *extra-ordinary*. It breaks away from everyday bases of authority such as that of officials or hereditary rulers. Thus in certain periods and social settings, charismatic authority is highly revolutionary.

Pure charismatic authority is, however, unstable. It exists only in *originating* the normative pattern and the group that follows it. By the process of **routinization**, charismatic authority is transformed into a routine or everyday form of authority based on tradition or official capacity, and the new religious group comes to serve the "interests" of its members. Although this routinization usually compromises the ideals of the original message, it is a necessary process for the translation of the ideal into practice. Routinization frequently dilutes the "pure" ideals and sometimes results in a comparatively static organizational form; however, it is also the process by which charisma comes to have its actual impact on history (see M. Hill, 1973b; Weber, 1963:60,61).

The history of the Christian churches is a series of charismatic innovations, routinization, and stable organization, followed by new appearances of charisma. Saint Francis of Assisi was a charismatic leader, an exemplary prophet whose message was also one of judgment—that Christian life must return to its pristine ideals of poverty, community, and simplicity. The early stages of the Franciscan movement were a serious threat to the established church and the sociopolitical order with which the church was intertwined. There was little to distinguish Franciscanism from other threats of the day—Albigenses, Waldenses, and various other pietistic movements, each with its own charismatic leaders. The other movements were eradicated, often militarily by the sheer might of the established powers. The Franciscan movement, by contrast, was encapsulated as a religious order, and its subsequent routinization made it no longer a serious threat to the church. Nevertheless the Franciscan ideals had great impact and were periodically raised as a critical standard against the complacency of the church and the order itself.

Similar cycles of charismatic innovation and routinization into organizational stability have occurred in other religious groups (and, indeed, in nonreligious institutions, such as political groups). The Mormons moved from a highly charismatic form of authority under Joseph Smith and Brigham Young to a stable, routinized form under church officials called "bishops" (many of whom are laymen). Similarly, Black Muslims have undergone several phases of charisma and routinization, each time altering the group's ideology, tactics, and form of organization.

Since it is the followers who impute charismatic authority to their leader and who put the charismatic ideal into practice, any analysis of the impact of religion on social change must examine the role of the religious group or community in that change.

The Religious Group

Whether the religious group is a small band following a charismatic leader, a growing religious movement, or a staid and established religious organization, it is a potential force for social change. This potential exists because religion— especially the religious community—is a source of power, which is a fundamental category in the sociology of religion. The same power can be and usually is, however, used to support the status quo. Religion is not only an experience of power but often also results in the sense of being empowered. Thus the followers of the charismatic leader may experience a sense of power in their relationship with the leader and with fellow believers that enables them to apply the new order to their social world.

This sense of power, especially when identified with the leadership of a charismatic figure, can give a developing religious movement great dynamism. In 1525, for example, Thomas Muntzer issued this call to battle in the German Peasants' War:

> Do not despair, be not hesitant, and stop truckling to the godless villains. Begin to fight the battle for the Lord! Now is the time! Encourage your brethren not to offend God's testimony because, if they do, they will ruin everything. Everywhere in Germany, France, and neighboring foreign lands there is a great awakening; the Lord wants to start the game, and for the godless the time is up. . . . Even if there were only three of you, you would be able to fight one hundred thousand if you seek honor in God and his name. Therefore, strike, strike, strike! This is the moment. These villains cower like dogs. . . . Have no concern for their misery; they will beg you, they will whine and cry like children. Do not show them any mercy. . . . Strike, strike, while the fire is hot. . . . Have no fear, God is on your side! (quoted in Lewy, 1974:115).

Another potential is the religious group's capacity to unite previously disparate segments of a society. Religious sentiment can bridge barriers of tribe, family, nationality, and race. Enthusiastic religious movements (e.g., the Jesus People or Pentecostals) often experience intense egalitarianism in their early stages. Similarly in some developing nations, religious groups are sometimes the only forces capable of uniting people steeped in a tradition of tribalism. The followers of Simon Kimbangu in Zaire and Jehovah's Witnesses in Kenya and Zambia exemplify this unifying dynamism. The religious community can produce a sense of group consciousness that focuses a group's awareness of its needs and interests and strengthens its efforts to achieve its goals (Lewy, 1974:217–220).

Certain forms of religious collectivity typically have greater change-oriented potential. Sects and cults are, by definition, in greater negative tension with society than denominations or churches (see Chapter 5). Sects are particularly likely to mobilize efforts for change because of their characteristic collective orientation and insistence that religion be applied to all spheres of members' lives (see Yinger, 1963). Churches and denominations, by contrast, generally have more substantial social bases for action but are less likely to challenge the status quo. As Chapter 5 demonstrates, different kinds of religious collectivities have different potential for change-oriented action. Furthermore, these collectivities experience organizational transformations that reduce or promote their dissent.

Factors Shaping the Interrelationship of Religion and Social Change

The earlier parts of this chapter explored those aspects of religion that are change inhibiting, change promoting, or both. A more complex question now arises: Under what conditions is religion likely to be change inhibiting or change promoting? The circumstances surrounding a change-oriented effort often determine the degree to which the effort is effective. Thus we also need to ask: Under what conditions is religion most likely to be an effective source of social change? And what are the social factors that maximize or minimize religion's influence in a society?

Qualities of Beliefs and Practices

Certain qualities of some religions' beliefs and practices make them more likely to effect change than other religions. A sociologist would seek to learn some of these qualities by asking the following questions.

Does the belief system contain a critical standard against which the established social system and existing patterns of interaction can be measured? Those religions that emphasize a critical standard (e.g., a prophetic tradition or a revolutionary myth) pose the potential of internal challenge to the existing social arrangements. The prophetic tradition of the Israelites was a basis for subsequent religious challenges to the established way of doing things (Weber, 1952, 1963). Similarly nations such as America, France, or the Republic of Ireland, where the civil religion embodies a revolutionary myth, have a built-in point of reference for internal criticism (Stauffer, 1974). This prophetic aspect of American civil religion was central to the appeal of the civil rights movement. Kennedy's inaugural address was likewise built upon prophetic aspects of American civil symbols.

Ethical standards also provide a basis for internal challenge to existing social arrangements. The social critic can say, in effect, "This is what we say is the right way to act, but look how far our group's actions are from these standards!" Many Americans judged their nation's conduct of the war in Vietnam as immoral. The emphasis of ethical standards within certain religions provides a regular ground for social action and change (Nelson, 1949; Weber, 1963). Furthermore, the content of norms and ethical standards influences the kinds of resulting social action. Some religious groups emphasize personal or private moral norms such as strictures against smoking, drinking, gambling, premarital and extramarital sexual activities, divorce, homosexuality, abortion, and contraception. Other religious groups put greater emphasis on public morality, focusing on issues such as social justice, poverty, corporate responsibility, ethics of public policy, and war. Both approaches may result in efforts for social change. The temperance movement of the 1920s and the antiabortion movement of recent years both exemplify movements based on personal moral norms, and the civil rights and underground church movements (as exemplified by the involvement of the Berrigan brothers) were efforts to apply moral judgments to the public sphere (McGuire, 1972; some good examples of the distinction between private and public morality are given in Pope, 1942).

How does the belief system define the social situation? Individuals' perceptions of the social situation are shaped largely by how their belief system defines that reality. If a religion informs believers that their misfortune is part of God's plan to test their faith, they are not likely to challenge that misfortune. Believers are unlikely to try changing a situation that the belief system has defined as one that humans are powerless to change. Belief systems that embody this kind of fatalism are not conducive to social activism. The belief systems of many black sects de-emphasize social action by their focus on divine Providence. One sect member said, "I don't believe in participating in politics. My church don't vote—they just depends on the plans of God" (quoted in Marx, 1967:67).

Similarly belief systems that are voluntaristic are unlikely to result in concerted efforts for change because they define problems in the social situation as the sum of all the individual shortcomings. Accordingly social ills can be overcome only by converting all individuals to the right way of life. Certain religious definitions of the situation (e.g., fatalism and voluntarism) are less likely than other religious definitions to result in concerted efforts for structural social change.

How does the belief system define the relationship of the individual to the social world? This question is a generalization of the Weberian theme described earlier in this chapter. Weber pointed out that certain belief systems encouraged different kinds of individualisms; and that this individual-to-society relationship is critical to social action. Weber also distinguished between religions that promote a "this-worldly" as compared with an "other-worldly" outlook. Buddhism's interpretation of the material world and aspirations as illusion discourages this-worldly action. By contrast, many strains of Protestantism emphasize one's "working out" of salvation in this world and one's "stewardship" (i.e., responsible use) of God-given worldly resources. These aspects of the belief system determine the likelihood and direction of action for social change.

The Cognitive Framework of the Culture

Relevant to any discussion of religion's role in social change is the cognitive mode of the culture. What are the main ways that people in a culture think about themselves and their actions? While these qualities of the culture may be related to specific items of religious belief, they are more general. Discovering the cultural aspects that shape the influence of religion on social change would include the following factors.

Is the religious mode of action central to the cognitive framework of the culture? And are other modes of action (e.g., political) foreign to the way people think? Religious modes of action may be the *only* channel people have for affecting their world; other modes of action may be not only foreign but literally inconceivable. In much of Latin America, most people's world view is saturated by religion, and religion has the potential to be a viable and vital mode of social action. Economic dissatisfaction and political dissent may be expressed in religious terms and resolved in religious modes of action (Maduro, 1977; Worsley, 1968).

In cultures where the religious mode of action is pervasive, people are unlikely to conceive of other ways of organizing for change. If another mode of action is introduced, people are likely to be highly suspicious because the idea of a group with no religious identity is impossible to them; they cannot conceive of a group for whom religion is irrelevant to mutual activities. The People's Democracy, a radical independent political movement arising in Northern Ireland during the late 1960s strife, was utterly anomalous because, in that society, a nonsectarian social group was inconceivable to most persons (Beach, 1977). In the United States, by contrast, nonreligious modes of action are both common and conceivable, partly because of the ideological separation of church and state, but also because of the high degree of institutional differentiation in modern society. Religious institutions are separated from other institutional spheres such as economic and political ones. The difference between these two cultural settings is not only in the social structure but also in the characteristic ways the people think about themselves and their actions.

Are religious roles and identification significant modes of individual action in the culture? Does it make sense in the culture for an individual to claim a religious identity or a special religious role? And are religious roles understandable forms of leadership? For Joan of Arc to make religious claims for her leadership made sense to the people of her culture, whereas similar claims in contemporary American society would probably result in derision or labeling as symptomatic of mental illness. In cultures where religion is important in determining how one thinks of oneself or how others identify one, religion is probably a more significant vehicle for change than in cultures where religious roles are less acceptable.

These aspects of religion suggest that not merely the belief content of religion determines its influence on social change but also the underlying cognitive framework of people in that culture. Sociological analysis of the change-promoting and change-inhibiting characteristics of religion must take into account these cognitive modes, which shape people's ways of thinking about themselves and their world.

The Social Location of Religion

Most sociological analyses of religion's impact on social change have focused upon the social location of religion in various societies. They refer to the structural relationship between religion and other parts of society (i.e., where does religion "fit" into the total pattern of how things are done?). Also the internal structure of religious groups is related to their larger social location. The following criteria suggest some of the structural aspects of religion in relation to society that are relevant for understanding the extent of its impact on social change.

Is religion relatively undifferentiated from other important elements of the society? In most simple societies, religion is diffuse. It permeates all activities, social settings, group norms, and events. Religion, not a separate institution, is undifferentiated even in people's ways of thinking. The person who plants seed with a ritual blessing does not think of the blessing as a separate religious action; it is simply part of the right way to plant seed. One of the definitive characteristics of modernization is *differentiation* of various spheres of social life. Relatively complex modern societies are characterized by structural (and often spatial) segregation of different parts of social life into identifiable separate institutions. This structural aspect is related to the process of secularization, as detailed in Chapter 8.

We can envision societies as falling somewhere on a continuum between these two polar types:

$$\longleftarrow \qquad\qquad\qquad\qquad\qquad\qquad\qquad\qquad \longrightarrow$$

highly undifferentiated   highly differentiated

(religion diffuse)   (religion segregated)

In societies where religion is relatively undifferentiated, any change-oriented action is also likely to be religious action. Some of the millenarian movements described in Chapter 2 exemplify religious actions that are also sociopolitical. In relatively undifferentiated societies, religious dissent is often a way of expressing political and economic dissatisfactions. By contrast, although religious action *can* express other dissatisfactions in relatively differentiated societies such as the United States, members of such societies typically think of each institutional sphere as separate and of religious action as irrelevant to the political or economic sphere.

If religion is relatively differentiated from other institutional spheres, do strong ties exist between religious institutions and other structures—especially political and economic ones? The more linkages that exist between religion and other institutional spheres, the more likely that religious movements for change are expressions of dissatisfaction with other spheres as well. Historically dissatisfaction with political and economic spheres has been prominent, but dissatisfaction with other differentiated institutions is also possible. For example, a number of contemporary religious movements show strong currents of dissatisfaction with the dominant medical system in American society.

Even in highly differentiated social structures, linkages often exist between institutional spheres. Such linkages range from formal ties (e.g., the state church in England) to highly informal connections (e.g., the "coincidence" of closely overlapping membership between a congregation and other social and political associations in a community). Earlier in this chapter we saw how religion is often used to legitimate the status quo and serve the interests of the dominant group. Religious organizations themselves often have vested interests such as lands, wealth, and power to protect. These kinds of linkages with political structures and the stratification system are precisely why religion is often used as a vehicle of dissent *against* the political or stratification system.

In societies where religion is closely linked by formal or informal ties with the state, religious movements are especially likely to have political (though not *only* political) significance. The Protestant Reformation was a highly political movement, but religious ideas were also very important. In America, where the official linkages between religion and the state are minimized, there is still a considerable informal religiosity (e.g., Congressional prayer breakfasts) and an entire set of beliefs and practices related to civil religion (as discussed in Chapter 6). The strong connection between religion and America-love-it-or-leave-it in the 1960s made plausible a specifically religious mode of political reaction. Precisely because the dominant political system was supported by mainstream religiosity, religion was a significant force for political dissent.

Similarly in situations where religion is closely linked with the stratification system, religious movements are likely to be expressions of socioeconomic dissatisfaction. Development of the array of black denominations and sects in America was partly in protest against the parent groups' complicity in a white-dominated caste system of economic rewards, status, and power. The close ties between dominant religious groups and the existing stratification system—in which the black caste was treated as categorically inferior—meant that religious protest could be a simultaneous expression of dissatisfaction with the stratification system.

Many theories about the development of religious movements focus on economic or status deprivation (as discussed in Chapter 5). Some of these theories hold the assumption that movements of religious innovation and dissent arise primarily among the poor and powerless, persons at the bottom rung of the stratification ladder; or suggest that religious movements are attempts to create other sources of status and satisfaction for people deprived of status and economic goods. Other theories propose that religious movements are a deprived people's projections of their real needs into the realm of the fantastic.

There is clearly a relationship between religious discontent and disprivilege, but it is not so simple or direct as some of these theories imply. The utterly poor and powerless rarely form change-oriented movements because of their fatalism, lack of resources, and the sheer struggle for basic subsistence. At the other end of the socioeconomic ladder, the powerful and privileged rarely form such movements because the established ways of doing things in the society serve their interests well. The broad spectrum of persons between these two poles, however, are difficult to characterize in their likelihood of forming movements for change. Nevertheless it is possible to generalize that where religion is structurally linked with socioeconomic privilege, religious dissent and movement for change are likely to express dissatisfaction with the existing distribution of privilege and power. Where such dissatisfactions are not adequately handled by the existing religious groups, fertile ground exists for new change-oriented religious movements.

Do other modes effectively compete with religion for the expression of human needs, the development of leadership, and organization of effort toward social changes? In some societies, religious groups may be the most effective vehicle for social change because they are better situated to mobilize change-oriented action. In others, other modes of action such as political or legal action may be better developed and more effective. Thus in some Latin American countries, the Roman Catholic church has been an effective vehicle for protest against repressive political regimes because it was the only dissenting group with an established network of grass-roots organization and sympathy (see Levine, 1979). Although religious groups in the United States have similar resources that could be mobilized for change-oriented action, other modes of action (e.g., political interest groups, unions, legal action) are viable alternatives.

What is the social location of religious leaders? The potential of charismatic or traditional religious leaders to effect change largely depends upon their social location: ties with a pool of potential followers, links with resources that can be mobilized in a movement, and connections with networks of related movements or leaders. Leaders of any movement require these kinds of ties. Recognizing the importance of these linkages, social organizations threatened by dissent often isolate potential leaders in a social location where they are cut off from the people and resources necessary to establish a change-oriented movement. Church officials, for example, might assign a potential "troublemaker" to a remote and tiny parish. Or they might encourage (especially left-leaning) leaders to work in college campus ministries, where they can express dissent but are unlikely to affect the general membership of the organization (see Hammond and Mitchell, 1965). Although charismatic leaders are less restricted by such official pressures than other leaders, their social location also influences the likelihood of their gaining a sufficient base of support. Whether or not religious leaders or movements succeed in their efforts for social change depends upon their location relative to social resources, organizational resources, and a pool of potential followers.

One important factor in the relative influence of religious leaders is the impact of pluralism and institutional differentiation on the salience of religious authority. In a pluralistic religious situation, competing world views each have their own spokespersons who can exercise influence that is not necessarily recognized, however, outside their immediate group. A Mormon bishop's pronouncement on a social issue may be printed in national newspapers and read with interest by non-Mormons, but it is not likely to be considered authoritative by persons outside the Mormon fold.

Similarly institutional differentiation has often led to the idea that religious leaders should speak out only on "spiritual" matters. One survey in the late 1960s found that 82 percent of the laity agreed that "clergymen have a responsibility to speak out as the moral conscience of this nation." Nevertheless 49 percent felt that "clergy should stick to religion and not concern themselves with social, economic, and political questions" (reported in Hadden, 1969:148,149). This opinion reflects the sense that religious leadership is not relevant to other institutional spheres and that "moral conscience" is generally a matter of private-sphere activities (e.g., marriage and family). Pluralism and institutional differentiation, important features of some modern societies like the United States, considerably diminish the impact of religious leadership and religious movements.

The Internal Structure of Religious Organizations and Movements
In societies where religion is relatively differentiated with distinctive religious organizations, members' access to religious power is an important variable in whether that religious group can be change promoting. A centralized priestly hierarchy that controls religious "goods" (e.g., salvation) is in a strong position of power to shape the direction and force of that group's efforts. The American Roman Catholic church was able to racially integrate its congregations and schools long before most Protestant denominations or public schools because it used an authority that superseded local authorities and opinion (see Campbell and Pettigrew, 1959, for a study of the tension between local opinion and organizational security in ministers' involvement in civil rights activism).

Centralized religious organizations typically support the societal status quo because they also have vested interests in the economic and political arrangements of that society. In some cases, however, a religious organization identifies with those out of power and privilege (e.g., when it is the religion of a colonial people). In either situation, the access to religious power can be the source of social power, whether for change or stability. Similarly religions that incorporate a more democratized sense of religious power (e.g., Pentecostalism and other forms of experiential religiosity) have the potential to convert that sense of power to social action. Typically these groups do not organize themselves for action, however, because other elements of their belief systems do not encourage social action. While the potential for change-oriented action is present in such groups, the loose internal structure of their organizations would lead to a very different form of action than that of a centralized organization.

Another feature of a religious organization that sometimes strengthens its effectiveness in social change is the degree to which a group has larger organizational support outside its immediate situation. Roman Catholic clergy in parts of Latin America are more able to challenge the politico-economic powers of their countries because it is part of an organization with a supranational base. If their religious organization had only a local base of power and authority, the clergy would more likely be suppressed or coopted by the established national politico-economic powers (Westhues, 1973). The national centralized denomination served a similar role in supporting ministers speaking out against child labor and other working conditions in mills (Pope, 1942:195–198). A study of twenty-eight American religious groups found that the ability of church leaders to carry through controversial policies (such as racial integration) is dependent on the degree of authority given them by a central formal authority. Ministers were in especially weak positions in groups with congregational polity, where their congregations had power to dismiss them without reference to a higher authority (Wood, 1970). At the same time, however, the larger organization can stifle or suppress local initiatives for change, as illustrated by the tension between the (local) Latin American bishops and the pope at the 1978 Puebla Conference in Mexico.

Extended Application: Black Religion in America

As the preceding section suggests, analysis of whether or not religion promotes change in a specific situation must take into account a complex array of variables. Sociological interpretation of black religion is necessarily complicated and results in ambiguous conclusions about the extent to which black religion has influenced social change. This section examines some developments in American black religion that illustrate its change-promoting and change-inhibiting aspects.

There is no single entity that is black religion but a number of expressions, mostly Christian, which have a common heritage in the experiences of slavery and racism. The distinctiveness of this common background makes it possible to speak of "black religion" even when describing groups with very different belief systems. While the African Methodist Episcopal church is greatly different from the Lost-Found Nation of Islam (i.e., Black Muslims), both are outgrowths of the situation of blacks in America.

In this analysis, we will examine the main organizational forms of black religion in America: denominations, sects, and cults. These forms must be considered separately, because (as described in Chapter 5) denominations characteristically express a more positive tension with the larger society than sects. Thus we would expect that black sects would be more likely than denominations to express dissent. This is not altogether true, however, as the following analysis suggests.

Black Denominations

Independent black denominations (e.g., African Methodist Episcopal and National Baptist) are the prominent religious organizations in the black community. Five major groups of Methodists and Baptists account for roughly 90 percent of all religiously affiliated blacks in America today (Lincoln, 1974:10). The historical split of these groups from their white-dominated parent denominations was neither theological nor caused by dissent over doctrinal or moral purity; it was essentially a split along lines of social caste.

Historical Roots. The religious enthusiasm aroused by the Second Great Awakening among whites was extended to blacks, especially by Methodist and Baptist preachers. Much of the emotional style of expression often associated with black religiosity was borrowed from the white revivalism of this period. This religious fervor was also intensely egalitarian. Not only did the belief systems of evangelical groups promote brotherhood, but the shared religious experience itself produced a strong sense of equality. In the period after the Revolutionary War, Methodists and Baptists directly attacked slavery and welcomed blacks into their fellowships (Washington, 1972:36–46). This new form of black religiosity was, however, typically limited to free blacks (some of them freed because of the antislavery influence of the Second Great Awakening on slaveholders). It was not extended to the masses of blacks until slavery was ended.[6]

From these beginnings grew the major black denominations. After the initial egalitarian euphoria waned, black Christians found themselves given only limited leadership roles and segregated participation in their churches. Black religious leaders and their free black followers challenged these arrangements. When Richard Allen and Absalom Jones protested segregated seating by leading a band of black Methodists out of Philadelphia's Saint George's Methodist Episcopal Church in 1787, it was the beginning of separate black denominations in America. Allen later formed the African Methodist Episcopal church, a prototype of black independent churches (Washington, 1972).

Unlike most other religious splinter groups, these churches did not differ significantly from their parent organizations in their belief systems or patterns of worship. Their dissent was based solely on the treatment of black members by predominantly white parent denominations. As a result, their organizations were essentially denominational from the start. They did not exhibit sectarian characteristics, as many new religious groups do. These independent denominations were active in abolitionism and the underground railroad, and they organized numerous educational and social service projects to help escaped blacks arriving in northern cities. After the Civil War, they were able to extend their leadership and organization to recently freed slaves.

Black Denominations in a Caste System. Black denominations and sects have a distinctive relationship to each other and to the larger society because they are exclusively the expressions of a minority community. Black religious organizations do not, on the surface, appear to fit into the standard sociological categories of church, denomination, and sect (as described in Chapter 5). This is because not even the most "established" traditional black denomination is fully integrated into the dominant society (several authors have grappled with this discrepancy,

---

[6]Genovese, 1974; Simpson, 1978; Washington, 1972; Wilmore, 1972. Caribbean blacks developed some syncretic cults, borrowing elements from African and Christian religions, but their influence upon blacks in the United States was apparently minimal; cf. Barrett, 1974; Deren, 1970; Gonzalez-Wippler, 1975; Simpson, 1965.

especially Frazier, 1974; Lincoln, 1974; Washington, 1972; Wilmore, 1972). The apparent discrepancy is clarified, however, by recognizing the extent to which *all* black institutions in the United States are part of a caste system in which they parallel white institutions without participating fully in the dominant society. Whether or not recent efforts at "affirmative action" and other programs of status integration will break down the caste elements of this system remains to be seen. Nevertheless for an understanding of the development of black religion—at least up to the mid-1960s—the **caste system** model is useful.

Envision a system of rewards, privileges, and power as a ladder. Individuals higher on the ladder enjoy more privileges and material rewards; individuals toward the bottom of the ladder receive less. All of the individuals on the ladder are competing with each other for rewards, gaining or losing relative to others on the ladder. A caste system is like two or more separate (and unequal) ladders of stratification. Individuals on the lesser ladders have the opportunity to move up relative to others on their ladder, but they are excluded from effectively competing for the greatest power and privilege in the larger society. Historically, ethnic background has been related to caste status in America, but the two most enduring caste distinctions have been race and gender.

The caste model suggests that individual blacks can achieve relatively high status within the black community and its own institutions. Black denominations and sects are stratified in a way that parallels the social class bases of white churches and sects. There are relatively prosperous, staid, and genteel black denominations, supporting professional clergy and a wide variety of community programs; there are numerous middle-class and lower-middle-class congregations of established black denominations; and there are vast numbers of religious groups—especially sects—appealing to lower-class blacks (Wilmore, 1972:195–197). The sects are often critical of both the established denominations and of the larger society—as are many white sects.

The black denominations, however, are also able to be critical of the larger society because of their location in the subordinate caste. Nevertheless neither black denominations nor most black sects *have* been particularly critical of the dominant society, largely because black people have generally accepted the American "way of life"—the dominant values and criteria for success. Although they are conscious of racial grievances, they have not typically questioned the rest of the established social order (Wilmore, 1972:213–214).

Social Factors in Black Activism and Quietism. The social activism or quietism of black denominations is related to other social factors. Their initial dynamism was not only characteristic of a vigorous new movement but was also a product of the movement's social location. Early leaders and members of independent black denominations were free and well placed to speak up for their people; they were relatively well educated, occupationally skilled, and articulate before receptive audiences of proabolitionist northern whites. Given their limited financial resources, the ability of early black churches to organize political and social welfare activism was remarkable. Some of this dynamism continued through the reconstruction period following the Civil War. The independent black denominations extended their membership to vast numbers of newly freed people and provided leadership during the brief period when southern blacks were assured political access and representation.

Despite their increased membership, black denominations underwent a dramatic retrenchment from the end of the nineteenth century to the late 1950s. The specific experiences leading to this quietist phase varied from region to region but can be generalized as two major factors: *economic struggle* and *sociopolitical discrimination and repression*. In the South, newly freed blacks struggled to make a livelihood in a shattered economy. The Compromise of 1877 led to the withdrawal of Federal troops from the South and abandonment of Federal guarantees of blacks' civil and political liberties. The last two decades of the nineteenth century were marked by considerable violence toward blacks in the South, and several thousand were victims of lynch mobs (Wilmore, 1972:192). "Jim Crow" statutes created and gave legal force to segregation in every sphere of social life. These local and state laws racially segregated schools, work places, building entrances, waiting rooms, drinking fountains, toilets, and seating in public transportation. Statutes enforced the exclusion of blacks from theaters, restaurants, parks, and residential areas. Poll taxes and discriminatory "literacy" tests effectively excluded most blacks from voting in many southern states. In 1940, only approximately 2 percent of voting-age blacks in twelve southern states "qualified" to vote (Woodward, 1957). Discrimination in northern regions at the turn of the century was less overt. There was a sizable black middle class in many northern communities, but the vast majority of blacks were unskilled and suffered considerable discrimination in competing for jobs with waves of European immigrants.

The retrenchment of black churches in the face of such massive difficulties is understandable. Individual church leaders (e.g., Bishop Henry Turner) protested the situation, but black denominations generally retreated into the segregated black community, where they became the dominant institution, providing alternatives to services and facilities from which their members were otherwise excluded. It was not so much a matter of social activism as of simply meeting their members' needs that inspired black churches to provide recreation and social clubs, social services, insurance, and a "decent" burial.

The massive, twentieth-century rural-to-urban migrations of blacks created new disruptions. Before World War I, only 28 percent of the black population lived in cities; fifty years later, 70 percent were urban dwellers (Report of the National Commission on Civil Disorders, 1968). Rural churches were crippled by losses of members and material support. Urban churches were overwhelmed by the needs of the huge influx of rural blacks, many of whom were uneducated, unskilled, and unprepared for the difficulties of the urban ghetto (see Nelsen and Nelsen, 1975:36–47). This period marked the beginning of the greatest increase in black sects, discussed in more detail later in this chapter. The city represented a double threat to many rural immigrants: It represented their first experiences with a general nonreligious world view and with a social situation where the norms and values of a small, tightly knit community did not hold. One commentator concluded: "With a basically rural orientation, most Black churches retreated into enclaves of moralistic, revivalistic Christianity which tried to fend off the encroaching secular gloom and the social pathology of the ghetto. . . . The socially involved, 'institutional' church was the exception rather than the rule" (Wilmore,

1972:221). From the end of reconstruction to the mid-twentieth century, black churches retreated from social and political activism. The churches became the focal point of black community life, but the spiritual message was largely other-worldly and moralistic. We must keep in mind, however, the external social, legal, and economic barriers, which—even more than the churches' belief systems—may have been responsible for this retreat to quietism.

Internal Organization. Black churches and sects have particular potential for social change because of their special place in the black community. Black religion is very much a symbolic expression of community (see Williams, 1974) and is a potentially unifying force, though this potential has seldom been realized. Part of the problem of unity is the internal structure of black religious organization. Black denominations tend to be highly localized and therefore difficult to organize above the congregational level. And black denominations at the national level have generally been conspicuously absent from civil rights activism. A 1962 split that created a new black denomination—Progressive Baptist Alliance—was not over doctrines or rituals but over the growing activism of progressive members.

In several localities, however, black churches of various denominations have banded together to promote change. In 1958, 400 black ministers in Philadelphia launched a "selective patronage" campaign (i.e., boycott) against industries that depended heavily on black patronage but discriminated against blacks in hiring. They used the pulpit for announcing target employers and succeeded in stopping some of the blatant job discrimination. The segregation in churches may have aided this effort, since none of the "opposition " was in the audience (Lincoln, 1974:9). Similar organizational efforts by the churches were important in the Montgomery bus boycott, sit-ins, and freedom rides (see McCoy, 1964). Black denominations, especially with their broadened national bases, have the potential for promoting nationwide programs for change. Many groups, however, have been involved with the problems of maintaining their organizations, and activism seems threatening to their stability and acceptability.

The Role of the Preacher. The example of the "Philadelphia 400" suggests another feature of black religion that is effective in promoting change: the role of the preacher. Religious leaders have greater influence in the black community than is characteristic in most white communities. Just as the black church was often the primary institution in the community, so too the preacher was the leader (Hamilton, 1972). Although this role is declining in recent years, many blacks still look to their preachers for leadership on social and political issues. Studies have shown that blacks are more likely than whites to approve of political activism from their preachers and of using the pulpit to discuss political issues (Nelsen and Nelsen, 1975).

The black clergy activists of the 1960s civil rights movement used their influence as religious leaders, and their style of leadership and exhortation was characteristic of the preacher. Clergy such as Martin Luther King, Jr., Leon H. Sullivan, Fred Shuttlesworth, Wyatt Walker, and Ralph Abernathy did not distinguish between their roles as religious leaders and civil activists. In the civil rights movement, as in some other 1960s protest movements, dissent itself had a religious quality. The importance of the civil rights movement was not only its specific achievements in gaining voting rights, desegregating educational opportunity, and eliminating discriminatory legislation but also in making blacks conscious of their power to effect change.

King's effectiveness resulted, in large part, from his ability to combine a mode of sociopolitical dissent (modeled after Gandhi—another exemplar of religious social action) with the folk religion of his people and the revival technique to which they enthusiastically responded (Wilmore, 1972:242). The interweaving of religious with political images and symbols and the utilization of religious modes of expression (e.g., hymns and "shouts") were part of the appeal that enabled religious leaders to mobilize the black community for action. King's political speeches were essentially sermons in their structure and imagery:

> We cannot walk alone . . . We cannot turn back . . . We cannot be satisfied as long as the Negro is the victim of unspeakable horrors of police brutality. We can never be satisfied as long as our bodies, heavy with the fatigue of travel, cannot gain lodging in the motels of the highways and the hotels of the cities. We cannot be satisfied as long as a Negro in Mississippi cannot vote and a Negro in New York believes that he has nothing for which to vote. We cannot be satisfied as long as the Negro's basic mobility is from a smaller ghetto to a larger one. No, no, we are not satisfied, and we will not be satisfied until "justice rolls down like water and righteousness like a mighty stream" (quoted in Spillers, 1971:24).

The leadership style of the preacher "made sense" in the black community, enabling clergy activists to move the people to action.

The same religious tradition was, interestingly, utilized by non-Christian black leaders. Malcolm X, a spokesperson for Black Muslims, was very much a "prophet" in the black religious style. Since most Black Muslims came from Christian backgrounds, their relationship to their religious leaders was probably styled after black American folk religion rather than any Islamic pattern. Although the influence of Black Muslims appears to be dwindling, they are probably one of the most important American religious movements in this century. The message of the Lost-Found Nation of Islam, especially as articulated by Malcolm X, is clearly an example of the revolutionary potential of religious movements (see Lincoln, 1973). The slogan of "Black Power," initially used by a faction of King's organization, was taken over by militant groups that preferred a nonreligious (sometimes antireligious) orientation. Many of these groups were, however, still quasi-religious in their style—only the symbols they evoked were different.

Black Sects and Cults

Sects. Black urban communities display a fascinating variety of religious groups. In addition to representative churches of black denominations, there are many sectarian groups. By far the most numerous of these are Pentecostal or Holiness congregations, which may be described as "established sects" (see Chapter 5). These sects originated at the turn of the century in a series of southern revivals (initially among whites and later among blacks). They are characterized by their literal interpretation of New Testament practices, especially manifestations of the Holy Ghost (i.e., Holy Spirit) such as speaking in tongues, divine healing, visions, prophecies, and testimony. Another vigorous sect among blacks is Jehovah's Witnesses, whose members are expected to spend several hours each week in proselyting and witnessing to the coming millennium. Most black sects are more loosely federated than black denominations. Often the local congregation exists only because a leader has gathered a group.

There are also numerous unaffiliated religious groups in black communities. These sects are frequently very similar to affiliated sects but depend upon local leadership to establish their beliefs and practices. Some of these idiosyncratic sects have grown to national importance in size and impact. Father Divine's Peace Mission (begun about 1932) ministered to several thousand black and white people. Members practiced communalism and extremely strict moral norms. The Mission was active in social welfare (e.g., feeding, clothing, and housing people, opening cooperatives and small business enterprises). It was also politically active, opposing Jim Crow and lynching (see Burnham, 1978; Fauset, 1944). The controversial People's Temple of Jim Jones was a sect that, like Peace Mission, attracted both blacks and whites and had substantial social and political programs (see Hall, 1979; Richardson, 1979b).

Some black sects are not specifically Christian, but all draw on Christian themes (at least in their initial appeal) because their potential recruits are from Christian backgrounds. Black Muslims and Black Jews exemplify this type. We can accurately call them sects both because of their internal structure and their oppositional stance toward the dominant society and its religious organizations. One particularly good example of the deliberate appeal to Christian themes is the Shrine of the Black Madonna in Detroit. This group retains much of the faith and practice of traditional black denominations, but it asserts that key biblical figures—especially the Messiah—were black. The leader stated that "the Black Muslims demand too much of a break with the past for blacks, most of whom have grown up in a Christian church of some sort. We don't demand a break in faith, or customs" (Cleage, 1967:208). Many groups such as Black Muslims, Black Jews, and the Shrine of the Black Madonna offer members racial pride and new self-images through their world views. For example, Black Muslims and Black Jews take new names to represent their new identities and to shed their negative selves (see Brotz, 1964; Lincoln, 1973; Shapiro, 1974).

Cults. The religious mosaic of the black community includes a number of cults, some of which are only superficially religious. As explained in Chapter 5, cults are somewhat like denominations in their pluralistic stance toward other religious groups, but they are dissonant from the larger society and lack the respectability of the denomination. They differ from sects in not expecting total allegiance of members; frequently members adhere to several such groups simultaneously. Black cults are diverse, ranging from a faith healer's storefront to a group gathered around a "reader." Some cult leaders are flamboyant and manipulative, such as Prophet Jones, a healer and fortuneteller, whose Detroit church "Universal Triumph, the Dominion of God, Incorporated" is remembered less for its teaching than for the wealth it generated for its leader (Robinson, 1974). Black cults, like their white counterparts, offer adherents segmented bits of meaning rather than a total package of belief and practice. A believer might seek out a reader's spiritually received advice in a marital problem, go to a healer for rheumatism, send for Reverend Ike's prayer cloth to help get a job, and also go to the local church on Sunday. Although the cults preach a world view, it is seldom a total world view like that of the sects. Adherents may be fervent, but they do not typically belong exclusively to that single religious group. Therefore cults rarely have the stability or influence of sects and denominations. For this reason, the following discussion of change-promoting and change-inhibiting influences focuses primarily upon sects. In content and organizational form, sects are more significant than cults in the black community.

The Dynamism of Black Sects. Black sects are among the most dynamic forces in that community. Their members commit much time, energy, and money to their religious groups. Sects are able to motivate their members to apply religious norms to everyday life, and many of them enforce strict moral codes. Their creativity in forms of worship and sheer enthusiasm are important expressions of the religious group's sense of community. This dynamism has strong potential for promoting change because conversion to a sectarian world view can *redefine* social reality for members. Converts to the Black Muslims, for example, gain a new way of interpreting themselves and the world around them. The belief systems of sects typically contain a negative judgment of the "ways of the world" and a millenarian vision of a future perfect society. These beliefs are potentially change promoting; but only rarely, historically, have American black sects produced fundamental social change (by contrast, African sects have been more directly responsible for bringing about social change; see Barrett, 1968; Jules-Rosette, 1979).

Quietist Attitudes. The reasons for this general quietism of black sects appear to lie in the emphases of their belief systems and the social situations in which they must operate. Many sects' world views are even more other-worldly than those of black denominations. Although members may eagerly await the millennium, few black sects actively promote its arrival (Jehovah's Witnesses are the major apparent exception, though their time-demanding activities may serve primarily as commitment mechanisms; cf. Cooper, 1974). The emphasis of many sectarian groups upon divine Providence reduces members' consciousness of human agency. Another emphasis of most sects that inhibits members from social and political activism is their emphasis on private moral norms. Many groups are strict about members' behavior. They proscribe the use of tobacco, alcohol, and drugs; insist on hard work, honesty, sexual fidelity, and modesty; and forbid entertainments such as gambling, movies, or dancing. Sometimes religious norms directly discourage activism. One woman said, "In my religion we do not approve of anything except living like it says in the Bible; demonstrations mean calling attention to you and it's sinful" (quoted in Marx, 1967:67). These strict personal moral codes often have the indirect consequence of enabling members to fit more effectively into the dominant society.

One study of black attitudes on civil rights issues found members of sects and cults to have the least militant attitudes. Members of black independent denominations (e.g., Methodist and Baptist) were substantially more militant than sect and cult members; but most militant were black members of predominantly white denominations such as Episcopalian, Presbyterian, United Church of Christ, and Roman Catholic (Marx, 1967). Some exceptional sectarian groups are seriously involved in social activism. In Chicago, a black Pentecostal preacher organized the Woodlawn Organization, a neighborhood association that operated successful tenants' rights and consumer protection programs (Brazier, 1969). Nevertheless the other-worldliness and emphasis on Providence and private (rather than public) morality make black sects generally unlikely to be involved in social and political activism.

The social location of a religious group may be an important factor in the extent to which it emphasizes activism. Direct social and political action may be a luxury that the absolutely poor have neither the material nor personal resources to consider. Many black sects have emphasized comforting and taking care of their members. One early Pentecostal leader said, "The members of my church are troubled and need something to make them happy. My preaching is not about sad things, but always about being saved. The singing in my church has 'swing' to it, because I want my people to swing out of themselves all the mis'ry and troubles that is heavy on their hearts" (quoted in Washington, 1972:67).

These groups provide a small, close-knit community of mutual care and concern, often in the center of an otherwise harsh and anonymous urban environment. Black sects may have withdrawn from action in society both from opposition to the "ways of the world" and as a response to the threatening atmosphere of their social situation. A small, close-knit group of fellow believers serves as protection against the influences of "the world," but it also narrows members' lives to a "safe" enclave. These aspects of the social situation surrounding black sects and cults, as much as the content of their belief systems, help explain their general nonactivist orientation.

Changing Factors in the Effectiveness of Black Religion in Social Activism

This Extended Application has examined the factors contributing to change-promoting or change-inhibiting qualities of black religion in America. We have considered aspects of the belief systems, the cultural framework, the social and historical situation, and the internal structure of black religious groups that bear upon their orientation toward social and political change. These aspects suggest that black religion is a highly appropriate vehicle for change-oriented actions, though it has not always been used to promote change. In particular, within the cognitive framework of many (perhaps most) American blacks, it "makes sense" to pursue goals through religious groups and under religious leadership. Indeed, until recently religious organizations may have been the only viable indigenous vehicle for black social action.

The same line of analysis, however, suggests that black religion may have a considerably diminished role in future social change because of at least three factors. The one most obvious factor to religious leaders themselves is *members' complacency* (Wilmore, 1972:195–197). If there is a growing disparity between middle-class and lower-class blacks, those who are relatively comfortable in their socioeconomic condition may be less likely to utilize their increased resources for dramatic change (the nature of social class and racial ties among blacks is controversial; see Wilson, 1978).

A second factor is the *changing structure of American society*. The very successes of the civil rights movement meant that nonreligious modes of action (e.g., political and legal) became increasingly accessible to blacks. As black groups master these modes, religious modes of social action will have less importance and will stand to lose even more significance as people come to think in terms of alternatives. Increasingly, nonreligious modes of action are accessible and "make sense" to American blacks.

The third factor in the diminished role of black religion in promoting change is that the *general forces of secularization* appear to be making inroads into the black community, much as among whites in the last several decades. The forced segregation of the black community has protected the religious world view of its members, even as immigrant Italian, Irish, and Jewish communities protected their religious world views in the first half of this century. "Making it," however, means participating in a generally secularized public sphere; religion is treated as irrelevant in the world of work, politics, education, and law. Although people can also enjoy the private sphere (e.g., community, family, religion, leisure, etc.), the meanings and values of the private sphere are increasingly irrelevant to the public sphere. The more that blacks (and other minority groups) are relatively successful in society, the more they are exposed to secularizing forces in the larger society.

Summary

Certain qualities of religion tend to support the existing socioeconomic arrangements; at the same time, however, religion also promotes social change and has considerable potential for change-promoting action in certain social situations. Interest theories explain that religion frequently supports the vested interests of the dominant social classes, legitimating their dominance, socializing believers to comply with it, and utilizing religious social controls for deviance from it. Religious elements can be potent forces for social change; religious groups, leadership, ideas, and images can promote change-oriented action.

Since the relationship between religion and social change is complex, we have focused on the conditions under which religion is likely to be change inhibiting or change promoting. Social-structural aspects of religion are important variables that influence the impact of religion on social change in any given situation. The social location of religion, the relationship of religious institutions to other institutions in society, and the internal structure of religious organizations are all criteria in determining whether religion is change promoting or change inhibiting and its degree of effectiveness in social action.

Some people in recent years have been extremely critical of black denominations and sects, claiming that they have hindered the cause of black rights. By applying some of the sociological criteria suggested in the earlier parts of this chapter, we can see that the situation is much more complex. Certain aspects of black religion do indeed inhibit efforts for socioeconomic change; other aspects, however, are highly change oriented. In some social situations, black religion has been an ineffective social force; in others, it has not only been highly effective but has possibly been the only effective vehicle for desired changes.

Recommended Readings

Articles

S. N. Eisenstadt. "The Protestant Ethic Thesis." In *Sociology of Religion*, Roland Robertson, ed. Baltimore: Penguin, 1969, pp. 297–317.

Clifford Geertz. "Ideology as a Cultural System." In *Ideology and Discontent*, D. Apter, ed. New York: Free Press, 1964, pp. 47–76.

Gary Marx. "Religion: Opiate or Inspiration of Civil Rights Militancy among Negroes." *American Sociological Review* 32 (1), 1967:64–72. Also *Protest and Prejudice*. New York: Harper & Row, 1969.

Roland Robertson. "Individualism, Societalism, Worldliness, Universalism: Thematizing Theoretical Sociology of Religion." *Sociological Analysis* 38 (4), 1977: 281–308.

Books

Guenther Lewy. *Religion and Revolution*. New York: Oxford University Press, 1974. Seventeen case studies of the role of religion in revolutionary change, including medieval millenarianism, Indian, Burmese, and African nationalism, and the Roman Catholic left in Latin America. Theoretical synthesis is thoughtful but not very thorough.

Liston Pope. *Millhands and Preachers*. New Haven: Yale University Press, 1942. A classic sociohistorical analysis of the role of religion in a famous mill strike.

Max Weber. *The Protestant Ethic and the Spirit of Capitalism*. New York: Scribner, 1958. The most readable of Weber's classical studies of religion; should be read in conjunction with Eisenstadt, listed above.

Peter Worsley. *The Trumpet Shall Sound*. New York: Schocken, 1968. A Marxian analysis of Melanesian cargo cults. Worsley's critique of Weber's social change theories is the weakest part of this highly readable, well-documented study of religion's change-promoting impact in a concrete historical setting.

CHAPTER EIGHT

Secularization

O ne process identified with social change is **secularization.** Theories of secularization propose that major changes have occurred in the social location and significance of religion in Western society over the last several centuries. There is considerable disagreement, however, over the direction and meaning of these changes. The secularization thesis is perhaps the single most important theoretical paradigm in contemporary sociology of religion. It is also the most debatable. This chapter distills some various interpretations of social change and the place of religion in modern society.

The Concept of Secularization

The secularization thesis is an interpretive paradigm in sociology, an explanation that tries to "make sense" of historical processes. The concept of secularization has been used in widely varying, often confusing ways. Major sociological traditions contained interpretations of history that were essentially theories of secularization. Classical thinkers such as Hegel, Marx, Saint-Simon, Durkheim, Comte, and Weber developed theories of social change, all of which involved interpretations of the changing significance of religion in society. Nevertheless the notion of secularization is not a purely rational construct that is amenable to proof or disproof. It is more like a mythological account—a socially important story out of which people live. Comparing the secularization thesis with myth does not mean that it is worthless as a concept but that the thesis is empirically impossible to disconfirm. Essentially the secularization thesis is an attempt to *explain the emergence of the modern world,* since many thinkers feel that modern society differs absolutely from what came before it (Luckmann, 1977:16,17). For this reason, the secularization debate is closely linked with theories of modernization—another controversial topic.

The concept of secularization has also lent itself to ideological uses (Martin, 1969:9ff.). Secularization is viewed as either a wholly desirable or undesirable process. Comte proposed that society evolved in three stages: the primitive theological state (religion), the transient metaphysical state (philosophy), and the final positive state (science). Accordingly humankind would gradually free itself of vestiges of the more primitive states (i.e., traditional religion and philosophy) and enter a state in which scientific rationality would be the paramount mode of thought. Comte envisioned sociology as the positive science to provide rational guidelines for the determination of society. In this final positive state, vestiges of traditional revealed religion would have disappeared; explanation and decision making would be guided by positivistic science, and affective unity would be achieved by a rationally acceptable "religion of humankind" (Aron, 1968:73–143). Comte's "Law of Three States" illustrates how theories of secularization are *evaluative*; that is, the place of religion in society is viewed as desirable or undesirable.

Much of the debate over secularization hinges upon definitions of religion. In general, sociologists using **substantive definitions** of religion (i.e., definitions specifying what religion *is*, usually in terms of the object of religious attention) conclude that religion in modern society is declining in significance. By contrast, sociologists using **functional definitions** of religion (i.e., definitions in terms of what religion *does*) tend to agree that the location and manifestation of religion have changed in contemporary society but that this reflects a transformation, not a decline, in religion. We will examine these conflicting interpretations more closely in a later section of this chapter.

Although much disagreement over secularization can be explained by differing definitions, the secularization controversy is also a debate about society and sociology. Implicit in the controversy are such issues as: What should society be? What should sociologists be? What are the limits of sociological observation? Is sociology directly or indirectly contributing to an undesirable social result? Weber's sociology of religion reflects both a personal commitment to scientific understanding of society and a fascinated abhorrence of what he projected as a possible end product of the systematic rational approach to social interaction— "the iron cage" of instrumentality (Weber, 1958a). One observer suggests that the secularization debate is the site of an identity crisis of contemporary sociology (Robertson, 1974:44). The secularization thesis presses sociologists to examine certain directions of society and the sociological enterprise and to make some choices or which there are no neat, scientific answers.

First we will examine the thesis of religious decline and the counterthesis of religious change. Then we will describe some of these broader implications of secularization theory, focusing on changes in the larger society and the individual's relationship to it. These change processes will suggest important implications about the nature of modern society, the situation of the individual member, and the relationship between the individual and society.

Secularization as Religious Decline

One meaning applied to the concept of secularization is the decline of religion. The image behind this thesis is that once people were highly religious and that religion informed all aspects of society. Accordingly society is becoming less and less religious, and individual lives are decreasingly influenced by religion. This hypothesis often includes the projection of virtually irreversible trends toward total secularity: Religion will disappear. This interpretation of secularization particularly lends itself to ideological uses. Secularization, as thus defined, is either utterly condemned or welcomed. Representatives of religious organizations and interests are understandably against the decline. Proponents of counterideologies such as positivism, Marxism, and Freudianism typically welcome the decline.

The exact nature of the "decline" of religion, however, is difficult to specify. Generally there are two areas of imputed decline: the religiosity of individuals, and the scope and power of religious institutions. As previously noted, the decline hypothesis hinges upon substantive definitions of religion that usually equate religion with its historical institutional expression (i.e., the churches).

Examining the Evidence
There is no clear-cut empirical evidence to show that religion is declining. The data are methodologically weak, and the results are conflicting. Proponents of the secularization-as-decline thesis point to drops in church membership and attendance, decreased belief in traditional religious concepts, and decreased power and pervasiveness of religious institutions. Empirical evidence to date does not, however, fully demonstrate these changes. Although church-oriented religion has apparently lost ground by these criteria, little conclusive proof exists that religion itself is declining. The following examples illustrate the conflicting evidence on religious decline.

Religious Belief. Most Americans express belief in the primary traditional (i.e., Christian) religious ideas. Of Americans polled in 1975, 94 percent indicated a belief in God (Gallup Poll, 1976b:13). Other traditional beliefs (e.g., in life after death, the power of prayer, and that the Bible is divinely inspired) are similarly widespread. Gauged by beliefs that people express to interviewers, traditional religious beliefs (including specifically Christian beliefs) have not dramatically disappeared. Furthermore, these traditional beliefs are still held by most youth in the United States. Among persons under thirty, 97 percent believe in God, 84 percent believe in heaven, and 71 percent believe in life after death (Gallup Poll, 1975:v).

Although the United States is one of the most industrialized countries in the world, there is evidence that in other industrialized countries—in Europe, at least—traditional religious belief is less widespread than in America. Between 1948 and 1968, belief in life after death actually increased from 68 to 73 percent in the United States, whereas it decreased dramatically in France (58 to 35 percent), Britain (49 to 38 percent), and other industrialized European countries. Similarly while the 1968 survey showed that 98 percent of American respondents believed in God, only 60 percent of Swedish, 73 percent of French, and 77 percent of British respondents indicated belief in God (Gallup Poll/Social Surveys, Ltd., 1968).

In order to evaluate the hypothesis of decline, we must obtain a perspective on changes in belief over time. Unfortunately no opinion pollsters or sociologists existed to interview a cross section of European peasants in the 1380s or Americans in the 1780s. Probably even in periods of great religious fervor, there was considerable variation in people's religious beliefs. The lack of long-term comparative data makes it difficult to document decline (especially beginning as long ago as the various theories date it—the Renaissance, the Protestant Reformation, the Industrial Revolution). In this century, evidence for the United States shows fluctuations but no overall massive trend toward decline (see Greeley, 1972b; Hertel and Nelsen, 1974; Swanson, 1968).

Other evidence, however, suggests that data generated by the opinion polls are simplistic and fail to reflect qualitative variations in belief. The percentage of respondents expressing some belief in God does not tell much, for example, about the *meaning* of that belief in their lives, nor does it show what respondents mean by the concept of God. Table 8.1 shows the variation of strength of belief and images of God held by a sample of Christian church members.

Table 8.1 Belief in God (Church Member Sample): "Which of the Following

	Congregational	Methodist	Episcopalian	Disciples of Christ	Presbyterian	American Lutheran[a]
Number:	(151)	(415)	(416)	(50)	(495)	(208)
I know God really exists and I have no doubts about it.						
	41%	60%	63%	76%	75%	73%
While I have doubts, I feel that I do believe in God.						
	34	22	19	20	16	19
I find myself believing in God some of the time, but not at other times.						
	4	4	2	0	1	2
I don't believe in a personal God, but I do believe in a higher power of some kind.						
	16	11	12	0	7	6
I don't know whether there is a God, and I don't believe there is any way to find out.						
	2	2	2	0	1	*
I don't believe in God.						
	1	*	*	0	0	0
No answer	2	*	1	4	*	*
TOTAL[c]	100%	99%	99%	100%	100%	100%

*Less than half of 1%.

[a]American Lutherans are a combination of members of The Lutheran Church in America and the American Lutheran Church. Members of these two denominations were sufficiently alike in their responses to warrant considering them together rather than independently.

As these figures show, unconditional belief in a personal God is predominant among some denominations (e.g., Southern Baptists and various sects); whereas in other denominations (e.g., Congregationalists, Methodists, and Episcopalians), members are more likely to express doubts or to qualify the image of the God in which they believe. Similar variation was reported on other traditional Christian beliefs. Only 36 percent of Congregationalists and 49 percent of Methodists firmly believed in a life after death, compared with 97 percent of Southern Baptists and 75 percent of Roman Catholics. Firm belief in the actual existence of the devil ranged from only 6 percent (Congregationalists) to 92 percent (Southern Baptists). Disbelief in the devil was expressed by 43 percent of all Protestants and 14 percent of all Roman Catholics (Stark and Glock, 1968:36,37).

These data suggest the complexities of measuring decline. The persons inter-

Statements Comes Closest to What You Believe about God?"

American Baptist	Missouri Lutheran	Southern Baptist	Sects[b]	TOTAL Protestant	Roman Catholic
(141)	(116)	(79)	(255)	(2,326)	(545)
78%	81%	99%	96%	71%	81%
18	17	1	2	17	13
0	0	0	0	2	1
2	1	0	1	7	3
0	1	0	0	1	1
0	0	0	0	*	0
2	0	0	1	1	1
100%	100%	100%	100%	99%	100%

[b]Included are The Assemblies of God, The Church of God, The Church of Christ, The Church of the Nazarene, The Foursquare Gospel Church, and one independent tabernacle.

[c]Some columns fail to sum to 100% due to rounding error.

Source: Rodney Stark and Charles Glock, *American Piety: The Nature of Religious Commitment* (Berkeley: Univ. of California Press), 1968:28–29; used by permission.

viewed were church members; but if one defines religion as supernaturalism, then many church members do not believe in religion. The authors of the study conclude that although adequate historical evidence for comparison is lacking, mainline Protestant denominations have apparently become relatively secularized, in the sense of not believing strongly in the supernatural (Stark and Glock, 1968:204–224).

Church Membership and Attendance. Two other indicators used to evaluate the hypothesis of religious decline are church membership and attendance figures, but these data are similarly difficult to interpret. Data about church membership are notoriously uneven and misleading because some groups are not precise in counting members and groups vary markedly in how they define membership. In 1977, Roman Catholic national membership figures showed a substantial decrease, reflecting in part a huge drop of 400,000 members for the Detroit diocese alone. This loss was only on paper, however, because previous Detroit membership figures were inaccurate estimates based upon a percentage of the local city population, and the new figure was based upon the diocese's actual census of members (Vecsey, 1979). If these kinds of inaccuracies are multiplied by all of the other religious organizations reporting membership, the figures could be grossly misleading. With this in mind, Table 8.2 gives the proportion of church members in the American population since 1930. While the data show a modest downward trend since a peak of 64.4 percent in 1964, recent membership figures are substantially higher than in earlier periods of this century.

Table 8.2   Church Membership in the United States as a Proportion of Population

1850*	16%
1860*	23%
1870*	18%
1880*	20%
1890*	22%
1900*	36%
1910*	43%
1920*	43%
1930	47%
1940	49%
1950	57%
1960	63.6%
1970	62.4%
1977	60.8%

*Figures for 1850–1920 are based on different method of calculation than those for 1930 and later.

Source: Adapted from data in the *Yearbook of American and Canadian Churches, 1915–1979* (editor, title, and imprint varies. Current: Constant H. Jacquet, Jr., ed. Nashville: Abingdon, 1976, printed for the National Council of Churches in Christ).

Worship attendance figures may be somewhat more indicative of church-oriented religious commitment because attendance requires more effort than

merely belonging to a religious organization. Empirical evidence is again conflicting. One survey reports an overall steady decline in church attendance from 49
percent in 1958 to 40 percent in 1971. These data are based upon self-reported
weekly attendance as a proportion of the population. This drop seems more
dramatic than it really is; most of it is attributable to post-Vatican II changes in
Roman Catholic attendance. Between 1966 and 1972, Roman Catholic attendance
dropped from 55 to 45 percent among adults under 30; 71 to 56 percent among
persons 30–49; and 76 to 69 percent among those 50 and over. Comparable figures
for Protestant attendance were 31 to 29 percent among adults under 30; 38 to 37
percent among those 30–49; and 41 to 39 percent among those 50 and over. More
recent attendance figures suggest that the rates may have stabilized near their
1972 level or even risen somewhat (Gallup Poll data, summarized in Jacquet,
1976:256,257).

Another survey shows a general upswing between 1952 and 1965 in church
attendance by church members. Interestingly, however, this latter study also
shows a corresponding decrease in the belief that religion is important in the
respondent's life. This apparent discrepancy may result from other functions such
as a sense of community that church attendance provides (reported in Marty et al.,
1968). Thus attendance data are conflicting and do not overwhelmingly support
the thesis that religion is drastically declining (see Hoge and Roozen, 1979, for
several essays on the decline thesis).

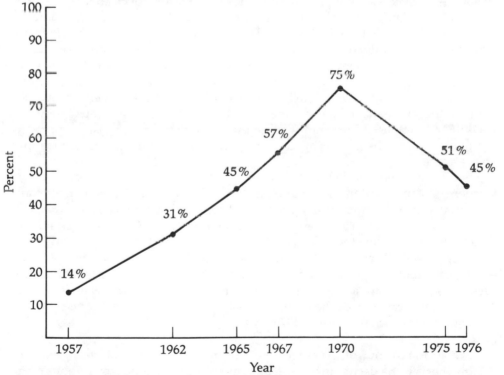

Figure 8.1 Proportion of Adult Americans Who Consider Religion to Be Losing Its Influence on American Life. Source: Data from the Gallup Poll, 1978:19. Used by
permission.

Popular Perception of Religious Decline. Another way of exploring the thesis of religious decline is by analyzing evidence for popular perception of that decline. Since 1957, the Gallup Poll has been asking the question, "At the present time, do you think religion as a whole is increasing its influence on American life, or losing its influence?" (See Figure 8.1.) In 1957, only 14 percent of the respondents felt that religion was losing influence. This figure rose dramatically to 75 percent in 1970. These data, interpreted in 1970, might have pointed to an unabated religious decline, but recent figures show a reversal in the 1970s (Gallup Poll, 1978a:19); the data reflect only the *perception* of decline, whether on the part of active churchgoers or persons disaffected from religious organizations.

Personal Salience. The data quoted on beliefs, membership, and attendance give some indication of the importance of religion in individuals' lives. While little decline has occurred, by these measures, in the proportion of Americans holding certain traditional beliefs, there has been substantial decline in the proportion who affirm that religion plays a key role in their lives. In 1952, 75 percent of survey respondents considered religion to be "very important" in their lives. Comparable figures were 70 percent in 1965 and only 53 percent in 1978 (Gallup Poll and Princeton Religion Research Center, 1978:9). Such measures are rather crude because they do not indicate what respondents meant by "religion," nor do they provide a clear picture of whether other beliefs, activities, or associations have supplanted religion as central. Although these figures are not clear evidence that religion is less important for individuals, they do suggest a pattern of decline.

Especially problematic is the lack of long-term data that would enable us to determine whether fluctuations were part of a real trend. A more serious criticism of these pieces of evidence, however, is the narrowness of their definition of religion; they almost exclusively measure church-oriented religiosity. We know little about people's nonchurch religious beliefs and practices. It is entirely possible that church members and nonmembers alike are being "religious" in other ways. For example, a Lutheran who is also a member of a charismatic prayer group may attend the parish church only sporadically but attend prayer meeting once a week.

Similarly we have little firm data about nonchurch religious practices such as frequency of meditation. The noticeable upswing of participation in unconventional religious groups in recent years also appears to belie the decline hypothesis. These emerging religious movements recruit from those stratas of society that the decline theories say should be among the most secularized (e.g., the young, well-educated, and middle classes). On the other hand, some observers suggest that contemporary cults and new religious movements (at least in Western societies) are actually further evidence of decline. They are viewed as individualist escapes from the necessary tasks of "real" religion—especially the reintegration of society (Wilson, 1976:103).

Institutional Control. Another aspect of modern society that bears on the decline thesis is the decreasing power and relevance of religious institutions over important areas of social life. Arguments from this perspective usually begin with the Middle Ages, in which the church presumably had great power and influence or controlled political, educational, legal, and charitable functions. Or it begins with the founding of America when religious organizations were important parts of every community, providing education, recreation, medical care, counseling, arbitration in personal disputes, political and legal influence, and charitable services. Evidence of decline is accordingly the loss of political power and diminished control over these other institutional spheres of life. In America, the state and a wide range of nonreligious voluntary organizations have taken over many functions previously performed by religious organizations. This usage of the idea of secularization is consistent with the origins of the term: *Secularization* meant the removal of church property from church control. The separation of church and state in America and the application of this principle in judicial decisions (e.g., the elimination of prayer in public schools) have promoted the decline of religious organizational influence.

Evidence supporting this part of the decline hypothesis would include data about the proportion of church-controlled schools and colleges, the proportion of charitable organizations run by religious groups, the proportion of persons utilizing nonreligious medical and counseling services, and so on. While specifically religious organizations apparently control substantially fewer of these functions than formerly, they are still a vital form of voluntary organization. They still offer and people still choose to utilize services such as counseling centers, schools, adoption services, hospitals, summer camps, social centers, colleges, old-age homes, day-care centers, soup kitchens, and rehabilitation centers. Other voluntary organizations such as Boy Scouts, YWCA, and Alcoholics Anonymous are not related to a single religious group but emphasize a religious orientation.

Some authors suggest that this segregation of functions does not necessarily mean a decline in religion's influence but means that religion's influence has become indirect, exercised mainly through individuals' values and attitudes; by shaping individuals' values and attitudes, religion has an indirect influence on their work behavior, voting patterns, leisure-time activities, educational choices, patterns of consumption, and marriage and family life (Parsons, 1963). Nevertheless this change toward segmentation of institutional functions, even if not evidence of decline of religion, does have other implications for the location of religion, which we will discuss later in this chapter.

Evaluation

Although the commonsense evaluation by intellectuals and the general populace seems to be that religion in modern society has declined in significance, there is no clear-cut evidence supporting this point. Three main problems exist with theories about secularization as religious decline: level of analysis, dimensions of religion, and historical claims (Robertson, 1974:49). **Level of analysis** refers to whether the theory focuses on the individual, group, or societal expressions of religion. Opinion poll data are at the level of individual belief; evidence about civil religious practices (as described in Chapter 6) is generally at the societal level. Evidence at one level of analysis often contradicts evidence from another level. Individuals seeking religious experiences may be increasing, for example, while denominational attendance figures are dropping.

The second problem area, that of **religious dimensions**, refers to the specific aspects of religion that theories include or exclude as representative of religion. Theories of religious change need to specify why a given indicator should be accepted as relevant or important. As shown in Chapter 4, considerable disagreement exists in sociology about how to use the concept of religiosity in research. Any study that points to the increase or decrease of "religiousness" must justify its specific indicators and concepts. Existing evidence on church attendance, assent to traditional items of belief, and church membership are not very reliable measures of religiosity. Furthermore, it is extremely difficult for theories of decline to overcome the limitations of their (implicit or explicit) substantive definitions: To the extent that religion is equated with traditional cultural expressions (i.e., church-oriented religiosity), *any* change from that pattern will appear as a decline.

Third, the historical time frame or **historical claims** of decline must also be specified. If secularization means decline of religion in "recent times," it is necessary to establish a historical basis for comparison with earlier times. Exact comparable data are unfortunately not available for earlier periods, but careful historical analysis is useful in delineating developments in the religious situation. If a theory specifies level of analysis, justifies its indicators of religion, and clarifies its time frame, it can be a useful interpretation of religious change. Many theories of religious decline, however, attempt to generalize from limited indicators to a sweeping trend (Glasner, 1977:112).

Secularization as Religious Transformation

An alternative interpretation of the contemporary religious situation is that the change is not a decline but rather a transformation. Accordingly the decline of historical religious organizations is but one part of a larger transition. Theories that view secularization as transformation rather than decline are based upon functional, very inclusive definitions of religion. Two prominent theories of religious transformation that we will consider are those of Bellah and Luckmann.

Bellah's operative definition is that religion is "a set of symbolic forms and acts which relate man to the ultimate conditions of his existence" (Bellah, 1964:359). This definition becomes clearer as Bellah explores his hypothesis that the change is one of religious evolution. He emphasizes that it is not the religious person or the ultimate religious situation that changes; rather it is religion as *symbol system* that evolves.

Religious Evolution: Bellah
Evolution, according to Bellah (1964:358), is

a process of increasing differentiation and complexity of organization which endows the organism, social system or whatever the unit in question may be, with greater capacity to adapt to its environment so that it is in some sense more autonomous relative to its environment than were its less complex ancestors.[1]

[1]Quotations and the following synopsis are used by permission of the author and the American Sociological Association.

Bellah clarified that evolution is not inevitable, irreversible, or unidirectional; it does not imply that what results is necessarily "better." He characterizes five stages of historical patterns of religion: primitive, archaic, historic, early modern, and modern. Each stage can be described in terms of how this symbolic differentiation is accomplished, and each has a characteristic symbol system, style of religious action, religious organization, and social implications.

The capacity for symbolization distinguishes religious from prereligious humans or animals. Religious symbolization makes possible a "differentiation between experiences of the self and the world which acts upon it" (Bellah, 1964:361). Thus imaging the "ultimate conditions of existence" also results in symbolizing personal identity.

Primitive Religion. The simplest form is exemplified by the religion of the Australian aborigines. The symbol system of primitive religion is a mythical world. Myths serve as paradigms for the detailed features of the actual world, physical and social. Primitive religious action consists of the enactment of ritual, in which participants become identified with the mythical beings represented. The organization of primitive religion comprises no separate social structure because there are no distinctive religious roles; religious roles are fused with other important roles along lines of age, sex, and kin-group membership. Although there are innovative aspects to the performance of myths and rituals, overall the effect of primitive religion is to promote the solidarity of the society. Primitive religious life is experienced as fixed; it offers little leverage from which to change the world.

Archaic Religion. A more complex form of religion is illustrated by the religions of much of Africa and Polynesia, as well as some American Indian religions. The key characteristic distinguishing archaic from primitive religion is the development of religious cults with gods, priests, worship, sacrifice, and sometimes divine kingship. The religious symbol system is similar to that of primitive religion. Mythical beings are more objectified and are seen as actively influential and controlling the human and natural world; that is, the mythical beings have become gods. The basic world view is, like that of primitive religion, monistic (i.e., viewing religious reality as all part of a single reality), but archaic religion is more differentiated and hierarchical. The mythology is often developed into a vast cosmology in which all beings are located. Archaic religious action emphasizes the distinctions between humans as subjects and gods as objects, necessitating communication systems such as prayer and sacrifice. Archaic religious organization is still generally merged with other parts of the social structure. As in primitive religion, individual and society are interpreted in terms of a divinely instituted cosmic order. Thus change-oriented impetus is minimized, and religion has a strong social control function.

Historic Religion. The development of the next stage is relatively recent— within historic time. Examples are the major "world religions" such as Christianity, Buddhism, Judaism, Hinduism, and Islam. The key characteristic distinguishing historic religion from its predecessors is the development of cosmological **dualism,** referring to the image of two realms: One is the human world, and the other a higher realm of universal reality. The empirical world of everyday human life is seen as subordinate or less real. At this stage, the concept of the supernatural develops. The transcendent deities of historic religions also contribute to the universalism of these religions through the image of all humans being responsible to the supernatural deity (or deities) rather than individually relating to a particularistic cult.

Religious action in historic religions is characterized by the pursuit of salvation. The cosmological dualism of the symbol system encourages individuals to seek salvation by orienting themselves to the higher spiritual reality. Unlike earlier stages of religion, historic religions promote rejection of the empirical world of natural and human beings. Devaluation of the empirical world and empirical self results in an emphasis upon a true, responsible self, which can surmount the fundamentally less real world of mere sensory impressions. The main feature of the social organization of historic religion is the development of differentiated religious collectivities (i.e., the social form that theories of religious decline identify as "religion"). The cosmological dualism of the symbol system is expressed in the social realm, with the religious hierarchy claiming special status. Emergence of a specialized religious elite and differentiated religious organizations creates problems of legitimation; elements of the social structure that were simply coextensive with religion in archaic religion must be specifically legitimated by religious organizations. The social implications of historic religions are related to this differentiation; possibilities of tension, conflict, and change emerge, based upon the development of evaluation standards for acts that political authorities cannot control. Thus religion develops its dual capacity as a legitimator of the status quo and as impetus for social dissent and change.

Early Modern Religion. Bellah's characterization of this stage is based upon the case of the Protestant Reformation, which several sociologists have considered a prototype of a new mode of religion. Although the case of Protestantism is well developed, other great traditions such as Roman Catholicism and Islam may be undergoing transitions to this stage in recent years. The foremost characteristic of early modern religion is the collapse of the hierarchical structuring of both the empirical and transcendental worlds. While early modern religion is still dualistic, it does not emphasize rejection of "this" world but focuses on a direct relation between the individual and transcendent reality.

Religious action in early modern religion is identified with the whole of life. The world is accepted, not as "good" but as a valid sphere to work out the will of God. Collapse of the hierarchical structure applies to religious organizations, too. The motto of "priesthood of all believers" illustrates this leveling theme. Early modern religions are hardly "open-minded" or pluralistic; they utilize clear distinctions between right and wrong, good and evil, saved and damned. The social implications of this transition include the institutionalization of social change as the attempt to realize religious values. The outcome, according to Bellah, is the image of the self-revising social order, expressed in a voluntaristic and democratic society.

Modern Religion. Although the modern situation may be only part of a transition to a new stage, it is nonetheless clearly different from historic and early modern religions. The key feature of this difference is the collapse of the dualism that characterized those earlier stages. This does not, however, signal a return to the monism of primitive and archaic religion. According to Bellah (1964:371), "it is not that a single world has replaced a double one but that an infinitely multiplex one has replaced the simple duplex structure. It is not that life has become again a 'one possibility thing' but that it has become an infinite possibility thing." In the modern situation, religion is no longer the monopoly of explicitly religious groups. Although traditional historic religions still inform modern religion, they have no control because every fixed position has become open to question.

An especially important feature of Bellah's evolutionary scheme is its linkage of the structural differentiation of religion with the process of individuation. Historic religions "discovered" the self; early modern religions enabled a greater acceptance of the self; and modern religion represents an even greater emphasis upon the autonomy and responsibility of the self. According to Bellah, modern religion is characterized by an image of the dynamic multidimensional self, able (within limits) to continually change both self and the world. The mode of action implied by this image is one of continual choice, with no firm, predetermined answers, and the social implications of modern religion include the image of culture and personality as perpetually revisable. Bellah notes, however, that whether the freedom allowed by this perspective will be realized at the social rather than purely individual level remains to be seen (Bellah, 1964:374). This is a critical issue to which Thomas Luckmann, another theorist of religious transformation, speaks more strongly.

Church-Oriented Religion as Peripheral: Luckmann
Drawing upon similarly broad historical material and an even broader definition of religion, Luckmann proposes that the specialization of religion into a single institution is only one social form of religion. The characteristics of the institutional specialization of religion include the emergence of specifically religious organizations (e.g., churches), the standardization of doctrine (e.g., in a creed), and the differentiation of religious roles—especially the emergence of religious specialists (e.g., the clergy). This development corresponds approximately to Bellah's notion of historic religion. The clear distinction between religion and society is possible only if religion is differentiated in special social institutions, as in this social form of religion (Luckmann, 1967:66, 67).

Luckmann accepts the idea that church-oriented religion has declined in influence and notes that the vestigial strength of historic religion in modern societies lies among the peripheral members of society (i.e., those least involved in the major institutions of the public sphere). He cites figures showing women to be more involved in church-oriented religion than men; however, working women tend to resemble the church orientation of men more than nonworking women do. According to Luckmann (1967:39), "the decrease in traditional church religion may be seen as a consequence of the shrinking relevance of the values, institutionalized in church religion, for the integration and legitimation of every-day life in modern society" (used by permission).

While this form is declining, religion itself is transforming into a new social form. A main feature of this new social form is personal choice: The individual constructs a private system of meanings, choosing from a wide assortment of religious representations (which include traditional religious representations). Such individual religiosity receives no significant support from the primary public institutions (e.g., the spheres of work, education, law, politics); it is virtually totally "privatized"—supported by and relevant to relations in private life such as the family, social clubs, and leisure-time activities (Luckmann, 1967:103–105).

Luckmann asserts that the emerging "invisible" social form of religion does not register on most standard surveys of religiosity. Survey research methodology typically measures only the degree to which respondents agree or disagree with traditional Western religious items (e.g., supernatural beliefs, moral norms, and other elements of church-oriented religion) or with identifiable alternative belief systems. A methodology that aims at discovering each individual's operative personal meaning system is necessarily very complex, and the empirical data are not readily quantifiable (Luckmann, 1973). Some promising methodological insights come from recent studies of ritual and language use in nontraditional religious groups in Western societies. These studies suggest that expressions of nonchurch religiosity are rich and varied. The scientific study of religion is, however, still far from being methodologically able to grasp a general view of individual structures of personal meaning. There is much evidence of nonchurch religiosity, but the exact nature of this mode is unclear.

Like Bellah, Luckmann identifies autonomy as one of the central themes of modern religiosity; however, Luckmann is less optimistic about its significance. He suggests that individual autonomy has been redefined to mean the absence of external restraints and traditional limitations in the private search for identity. Themes of modern religiosity (e.g., self-expression and self-realization) characterize this quest. Nevertheless the institutions of the public sphere have real power over the individual; performance of one's roles in these spheres must conform to institutional requirements. Thus autonomy is limited to the private sphere. By endowing the increasing subjectivity of human existence with a sacred quality, the new social form of religion supports the functioning, power, and control of public sphere institutions without explicitly legitimating them (Luckmann, 1967:109–115).

Comment

Although the conclusion that religion is undergoing irrevocable decline appears simplistic and overstated, the conclusion that religion is undergoing a "mere" transformation may also be misleading. The social location and significance of religion (including nonchurch religion) in contemporary society suggest that important social changes have occurred. Some of these changes have apparently resulted in such massive, qualitatively different patterns of relationships and meaning that religion, among other institutions, is profoundly affected. Evidence suggests that religion may be adaptable and vital in such numerous social forms that decline of its traditional forms does not spell its demise. Other changes described by some theories of secularization, however, are substantial and significant. It appears that major changes in the relationship of the individual to society have occurred, and any examination of the nature of religious change must be linked with an understanding of other major changes in the structure of society.

Religious Change and Societal Change

The secularization thesis implies several processes of societal change. Although these processes are interrelated, four general themes are emphasized in theories of secularization: institutional differentiation, competing sources of legitimacy, rationalization, and privatization. These interpretations of societal changes suggest changes in the nature and location of religion but do not necessarily imply decline. They only emphasize significant aspects of religious change.

Institutional Differentiation

Institutional differentiation refers to the process by which the various institutional spheres in society become separated from each other, with each institution performing specialized functions. For example, religious functions are focused in special "religious" institutions, separate from other institutions such as educational, political, and economic. Differentiation is a neutral concept, but it is cited as evidence both by theorists of religious decline and theorists of religious transformation. The contrasting image behind the concept of differentiation is that in simpler societies, the beliefs, values, and practices of religion directly influence behavior in all spheres of existence, and religion is diffused throughout every aspect of the society. Workers might pray over their tools at the beginning of each workday, and an intragroup conflict might be expressed in a religious ritual. In complex societies, by contrast, each institutional sphere has gradually become differentiated from others. The division of labor in complex societies is similarly differentiated, with specialized roles for each different function. In a highly differentiated social system, the norms, values, and practices of the religious sphere have only *indirect* influence on other spheres such as business, politics, leisure-time activities, education, and so on (Parsons, 1971:101). This means that religion influences these other areas through the personally held and applied values and attitudes of people who are active in each sphere, rather than directly through specifically religious institutions such as the church.

Some theorists point to differentiation as evidence of religious decline. They interpret the facts that religion is not diffused throughout the society and that specifically religious institutions have limited control over other institutional spheres as evidence of religion's diminished strength and viability. Particularly important is the loss of control over the definition of deviance and the exercise of social control (Wilson, 1976:42). During the Middle Ages, the churches defined and prosecuted deviant behavior, exercising social control both through informal measures (e.g., confession or community ostracism) and formal measures (e.g., church courts). In most modern societies, however, the churches have no such direct control. Courts are more independent, and laws are the province of specialists. Medical institutions have similarly acquired much power over social control, defining deviance as "sick" and calling medical social control measures "therapy." The net effect of this differentiation is that separate institutional specialists *compete* for areas of control that previously were mainly church prerogatives. While religious institutions still proclaim their definitions of deviance and use some measures of social control, their influence is limited in most modern societies.

Most of the evidence supporting the hypothesis of increasing institutional differentiation is from historical studies. Other evidence can be drawn from conflict between institutional spheres over control of a given function. For example, recent court conflicts over civil disobedience and euthanasia involved competing jurisdictional claims by representatives of several institutional spheres (Barkan, 1979; Fenn, 1978). Different institutions also compete for control over the definitions of health, illness, and healing, as the Extended Application at the end of this chapter illustrates. These contemporary issues exemplify the process of delineating the boundaries of institutional differentiation.

Implications for the Individual. There are two important implications of extensive institutional differentiation: one for the situation of the individual, and one for the larger society. For the individual, the process of differentiation involves a conflicting development. On the one hand, differentiation appears to go hand in hand with the discovery of the self—the unique individual within society. As the capsule description of Bellah (1964:361) suggests, religion has been an important factor in the increased awareness of and emphasis upon the individual. On the other hand, differentiation results in segregation of the individual's various roles. A woman's role as mother is not considered relevant to her role as mayor; a man's role as religious believer is not considered relevant to his role as corporate manager.

Specialization in the division of labor extends not only to the separation of institutional spheres but also to specialization of roles within each sphere. One is not merely a "factory worker" but, more specifically, the one who turns the third bolt on the left side of the object coming down the assembly line. Each institutional sphere dictates its own expectations of the individual so that he or she should become an effective performer of that role. Requirements of institutional functioning, however, often conflict with the individual's personal goals, preferences, or needs. The role of advertising account executive may require the individual to wear certain kinds of clothes, to eat and drink in certain kinds of places, to have tact, to lie, to flatter, to be self-effacing, polite, or even obsequious in order to please clients and keep accounts (good examples of such role requirements are found in Berger, 1964, and Terkel, 1975).

Role requirements of occupations vary, but all tend to exclude qualities that do not contribute to achieving the goals of the organization. Values such as moral qualms or self-realization are not necessarily negated; they are simply relegated to another institutional sphere and considered irrelevant to the job. We will discuss these developments as we find them implied in other processes. The key point is that the individual may experience a conflict between the needs and goals of the self and the demands of these social roles (see Simmel, 1959, 1971).

Implications for Society. Similarly the processes of differentiation contribute to society's difficulty in mobilizing the commitment and efforts of its members.

Values from one separate sphere do not readily motivate behavior in another. Why should one vote in an election, serve in the army, or work hard on the job? In societies with relatively little institutional differentiation, behavior in work, politics, and social or military service is often motivated by values from other spheres—family, community, religion, and tradition. In contemporary society, the main motivating force in public spheres appears to be the promise of certain levels of consumption—that is, a material standard of living (Fenn, 1974:148).

The process of differentiation is not inexorable. There appear to be limits to the effectiveness of specialization. Some workplaces are experimentally reducing job specialization, with hopes of increasing worker motivation. Even such experiments, however, are dictated by the criteria of the economic sphere; their goal is not to make work meaningful but to increase productivity. Nevertheless the process of differentiation has important implications for the location of religion in contemporary society. The effective criteria of public institutional spheres—notably the economic—are separate from the values of the private sphere.

Religion (whether defined substantively or functionally) is relegated to the private sphere, a development detailed further in this chapter. The individual's desire for meaning and belonging must be pursued in the private sphere. Apparently the same differentiation that makes possible the "discovery of the self" also frees the institutions of the public sphere to ignore or counteract the autonomy of individuals under their control. The tension between the demands and needs of institutions at the societal level and the demands and needs of individuals makes this an important issue in both the sociology of religion and sociology in general.

Competing Sources of Legitimacy

Legitimacy, as we defined it in Chapter 6, refers to the basis of authority of an individual, group, or institution, by which they can expect their pronouncements to be taken seriously (Fenn, 1978: xiii). Legitimacy is not an inherent quality of individuals, groups, or institutions but is based upon the *acceptance* of their claims by others. If an individual proclaims "It is absolutely imperative for Americans to reduce their consumption of gas and oil by 15 percent," on what basis does this person claim to be taken seriously? Such a statement by the president of the United States would be based on a different source of legitimacy than the same statement by a spokesperson for the Union of Concerned Scientists, the editor of *Newsweek*, the National Council of Churches, or, for that matter, a Chicago elevator operator.

The location of religion in contemporary society reflects societal changes in the bases of legitimacy. Relatively stable societies typically have stable sources of legitimacy. The key criterion in such societies is usually traditional authority such as the inherited authority of the patriarch or king. Institutional differentiation often produces a different kind of authority: the authority of the holder of a specialized role of "office." Claims to be taken seriously are based not upon who one is but upon what position one holds. The authority of a judge, for example, is based upon the role rather than the person.

Religion legitimates authority indirectly in traditional societies by its pervasive interrelationship with all aspects of society. Myth and ritual support the seriousness of all spheres of life. The chief, priest, or matriarch can speak with authority because their roles correspond to or reflect the authority of divine beings. Historic religions legitimate authority more directly, as shown in Chapter 7. Such historic religions as Christianity, Islam, and Judaism have similarly given authority to pronouncements on education, science, economic policy, law, family life, sport, art, and music. Whether directly or indirectly invoked, the images and symbols of the sacred are a source of legitimacy (Fenn, 1978:xiii). The taken-for-granted quality of religion as a source of legitimacy characterizes all of these earlier societal situations.

Conflicting Sources of Authority. The main feature of legitimacy in contemporary society is that the differentiation process has resulted in competition and conflict among the various sources of legitimacy of authority. As Bellah (1964) suggests, historic and early modern religions experienced such competition to a limited extent. The beginnings of differentiation of religious from political institutions meant that religious institutions could come in conflict with political institutions. Historically the churches could authoritatively evaluate whether the state was engaged in a "just" war and could authoritatively criticize business practices they judged as "usurious" (i.e., charging unfair interest rates on loans). In contemporary society, by contrast, religious institutions must actively compete with other sources of legitimacy. Personal, social, and political authority are more uncertain.

This competition for legitimacy can be seen in a number of issues in recent years. Civil disobedience over the war in Vietnam and over civil rights was often based upon a different source of authority than that of the prevailing legal or political ones. Civil disobedience often claimed religion or higher human values as the basis for conflict with civil authorities. Sometimes court events involve a clash of several different sources of legitimacy. In one recent court case, claims were made from legal, medical, parental, and religious bases of authority. A young person had been comatose for months and "as good as dead" in the common-sense view. Her body was kept alive by technological intervention, and eventually her parents sought legal permission to terminate the "extraordinary" measures of keeping her body alive. No single authority held uncontested legitimacy. The court case was complicated. Medical experts gave their opinions on the medical definitions of death. Legal experts raised issues of the legal rights and guardianship of comatose patients. Theological experts offered briefs on the borderlines of life and death, and the girl's father made a thoughtful personal statement about his request. The relevant issue is not merely the uncertainty of the outcome but that the court is the arena in which medical, legal, religious, and parental figures vied to have their statements taken seriously (Fenn, personal communication).

Pluralism. One particular source of this uncertainty of legitimacy is pluralism, referring to a societal situation in which no single world view holds a monopoly. This is an especially important feature of the American and Canadian religious scenes (see D. Martin, 1978:1–99, for a sophisticated description of factors related to secularization in nonpluralistic as well as pluralistic societies). Historic religions were characteristically monolithic: They established *the* world view of their society and had a monopoly over the ultimate legitimation of individual and collective life. Where alternative views coexisted with the dominant one, they were absorbed and coopted or effectively suppressed and segregated. Examples of absorption include the incorporation of early monasticism into church-controlled monastic orders, or the development of sects within Hinduism. The alternative world views of medieval Jews among Christians and Zoroastrians (i.e., Parsees) among Hindus were no threat to the monopolies of these dominant world views because the minority religions were effectively suppressed and segregated (Berger, 1967:134, 135).

Pluralism is sometimes used in a narrower sense to describe the political or societal tolerance of competing versions of truth. Highly pluralistic societies such as the United States, Canada, and Australia typically have several diverse groups with competing world views. By contrast, Spain and Russia exemplify a generally monopolistic situation. Between these two polar types, however, there is much variation. In England and Scandinavian countries, there is an official state church but relatively high tolerance of minority positions. A more rigid situation exists in the Netherlands, Northern Ireland, and Lebanon; while there is "official" tolerance at the societal level, there is little intergroup tolerance. In the Netherlands, the least volatile of the three, most aspects of society are divided into three mutually exclusive "columns": Roman Catholic, Reformed, and neo-Calvinist. Political parties, mass media, youth clubs, and schools are all divided according to these religious lines. All three columns are given political and societal recognition, but there is little intergroup mingling (Laeyendecker, 1972; Moberg, 1961).

Berger emphasizes that pluralism, in both this limited sense and in the broader sense previously described, is a key factor in the secularization process. Where world views coexist and compete as plausible alternatives to each other, the credibility of all is undermined. The pluralistic situation relativizes the competing world views and deprives them of their taken-for-granted status (Berger, 1967:151). A farm family in Spain (where only approximately 0.1 percent of the population is non-Catholic, most of whom live in the subcultural province of Catalonia) takes the Roman Catholic world view for granted (cf. Almerick, 1972:462). It is the world view of their friends, relatives, and neighbors and it is a part of everyday life. Although members of the community may vary considerably in piety or religious activity, non-Catholic world views are probably literally inconceivable.

In a pluralistic situation, by contrast, no single world view is inevitable. In the United States, a committed Roman Catholic's neighbors are Baptist, Jewish, Unitarian, Lutheran, atheist, and Zen Buddhist. The government and the society do not (formally, at least) give favorite legitimacy to any of these world views, nor does anyone's god accommodate anybody's quandary by sending down a lightning bolt to get rid of all the "wrong" believers. If people wish to protect the belief that their world view is uniquely true, they must isolate themselves from alternative world views. In American society, especially in relatively urban settings, that is not easy to do. On the job, in school, through the media, working for a political party or a social "cause," or even playing softball—and increasingly in neighborhoods, social clubs, and parties—Americans are exposed to others who hold different world views from their own. The impact of the pluralistic situation is thus that the various world views in society also compete for legitimacy. No single view has such uncontested legitimacy that a person expressing it authoritatively could be certain of being taken seriously (Berger, 1967:151).

Religious pluralism, in the broadest sense of the term, is not like having a choice between Rotary and Kiwanis. The pluralism of world views is qualitatively different from a pluralism of affiliations or associations because the taken-for-granted quality of any one world view is undermined by pluralism. Differentiation made it possible to conceive of religion as an entity separate from other institutional spheres. Pluralism, furthermore, made it possible to conceive of religions; the very concept implies a stance of some distance, a meaning system that one does not personally believe (Hammond, 1974:119, 120).

Pluralism and Legitimacy in the United States. The evidence supporting this interpretation of social change is fairly strong, at least in the United States; but we need to remember that pluralization is a process that is neither inexorable nor complete. In colonial America, the principles of pluralism and religious tolerance were established, but colonial society was far from the pluralistic mode of contemporary society. It was essentially Protestant and adamantly Christian. The principle of religious liberty, together with the growing multiplicity of religious views, pressed the government and especially the courts to resolve conflicts. The courts needed moral answers to resolve legal questions, yet the increasing ethno-religious diversity of the country made it impossible for the courts to resort to the language and legitimacy of orthodox Protestantism. In 1879, the Supreme Court had to decide whether polygamy (i.e., plural marriage) would be legally permitted if it were part of a religious group's (i.e., Mormons') practices (*Reynolds* v. *United States*, 98 U.S. 145, 1879). The court decided against making "religious" exceptions to "the law of the land" (Hammond, 1974:129–130).

Similar conflicts arose over whether to allow exemptions on religious grounds from national ceremonies (e.g., saluting the flag) and military service, release time from public schools for religious instruction, prayer in public schools, taking prohibited drugs for religious purposes, and so on (see Manwaring, 1962). It would be a mistake to see these conflicts as merely church-state issues; the very *process* of their resolution reflects the pressure of an increasingly pluralistic situation, in which no single religious world view is granted legitimacy. Note the change between the language of cases in 1892 and 1965:

Church of the Holy Trinity v. *United States*, 143 U.S. 226, 1892:
Mr. Justice Brewer wrote that events in our national life "affirm and reaffirm that this is a religious nation." Deciding that a statute prohibiting importing aliens for labor was not intended to prevent a church from hiring a foreign Christian minister, the Court quoted with approval two earlier judicial opinions stating that "we are a Christian people, and the morality of the country is deeply ingrafted upon Christianity" and "the Christian religion is a part of the common law of Pennsylvania."

United States v. *Seeger*, 380 U.S. 163, 1965:
In a conscientious objection case, the Court determined that "belief in relation to a Supreme Being" (thus exemption from military service) shall be determined by "whether a given belief that is sincere and meaningful occupies a place in the life of its possessor parallel to that filled by the orthodox belief in God of one who

clearly qualifies for the exemption." Exemption is not limited to monotheistic beliefs. Mr. Justice Clark noted the prevalence of a "vast panoply of beliefs," thus Seeger's beliefs qualified as "religious" and he was exempted (cited in Hammond, 1974:130, 131).

One general impact of pluralism and differentiation is to create a problem of legitimacy for both the individual and the society. The problem of legitimacy at the societal level involves the society's very basis for authoritative decision making and its grounds of moral unity or integration. At the individual level, the problem of legitimacy makes the individual's meaning system more precarious, voluntary, and private.

Problems at the Societal Level. In a pluralistic situation, world views and authoritative claims compete; this results in the diffusion of sources of legitimacy among many agents in society. These competing claims may appeal to sacred or quasi-sacred sources of authority, even if not using explicitly religious symbols (Fenn, 1978:45). A good example is, again, the courts. Hammond suggests that the pluralistic situation creates problems of defining order (because no monolithic world view exists to authoritatively define it), but the social situation still needs order. Legal institutions are then called upon to establish and interpret a uniform order, and the result is a constellation of legal institutions with a "decided religio-moral character" (Hammond, 1974:129). Thus the hypothesis of secularization is connected with the issue of civil religion (i e , the national expression of unity, as discussed in Chapter 6). According to this interpretation, the courts are trying to articulate a basis for moral unity where no such foundation is given by specifically religious institutions. Some sociologists view the civil religion as attempting to overcome problems of legitimate authority and societal integration in American society.

The problem of legitimacy results from the collapse of a societal shared conception of order (Wilson, 1976:100; Wilson specified "transcendent" order, but the collapse of any shared world view has equivalent results). What some people decry as "secularity" is not the result of lost belief followed by immoral behavior; first lost is the overall sense of moral community and consensus (literally "thinking and feeling together"). Without agreement on the way to live together, claims of moral authority make no sense (MacIntyre, 1967:54).

This problem affects both individual and societal decision making. How is it possible for human values to determine public policy in a pluralistic society? Is the role of religion in political decision making reduced to that of one more interest group vying with opposing interest groups? Or is it even possible for a pluralistic society to agree on human values at a societal level? The obvious examples of religious groups asserting themselves on a national level have typically been issues of legislating what might be called "private morality"—homosexuality, abortion, pornography, divorce, gambling, or drinking. Less publicized but still important have been the efforts to apply religious values to decision making on "public morality"—civil rights, the Vietnam War, arms proliferation, and the human environment.

The difficulties of reaching a consensus on values at the societal level in a pluralistic society are illustrated by the issues involved in developing a national energy policy for America. The energy situation could be viewed as merely the conflict of competing interests: producers versus consumers, producers versus environmental protection groups, voters versus major campaign contributors, the United States versus other nations, and so on. Policy decisions could reflect a juggling of these interests according to relative power, influence, technological expertise, financial muscle, or political pressure. Nevertheless human values have also been raised: fair distribution of scarce resources, concern for the "have-nots," human health and safety, responsibility to future generations, and responsibility in international relations. None of these interests or values specifies the exact outcome of any policy decision, but the specific factors accepted as relevant in the decision-making process do make a difference. Is consensus on values necessary or even possible? And if so, does the society consider human values relevant or important to decisions in the public sphere?

Unstable Sources of Legitimacy: Fenn. Fenn's analysis of secularization raises similar points, but he considers civil religion as only one critical but unstable phase in the process. Fenn begins by defining secularization as a process of dealing with uncertainty or ambiguity of boundaries between the sacred and the profane. It involves conflict among groups, individuals, and the nation. It both disturbs and clarifies the sources of legitimacy of social and political authority (Fenn, 1978:xvii, 55).

The first stage is the *differentiation of religious roles and institutions*. This is the earliest development chronologically, but it is also continuous. Differentiation of roles and institutions is exemplified in Western society by the development of cults (e.g., mystery cults or shamanic cults in archaic religion), churches (i.e., historic religion), and denominations (i.e., early modern religion). The increased complexity of modern societies implies this differentiation. Whereas Bellah's evolutionary scheme focuses upon the development of different expressions of religion, Fenn's analysis emphasizes the extent to which certain changes are qualitatively different. He suggests, for example, that in what Bellah calls "early modern" and "modern" religion, the very concept of "religion" becomes problematic.

The second step in Fenn's scheme is the *demand for clarification of the boundary between religious and secular issues*. This step is illustrated by the conflict between Mormons and civil authorities over polygamy. The demand for clarification may produce a desire for some general, overarching symbols to which all competing groups can subscribe.

Fenn's third stage is the *development of generalized religious symbols or ideology*. The set of generalized religious symbols is often in the form of an ideology. Indonesian President Sukarno developed an ideology (the Panch Shila) to try to bridge the conflict between Hindu and Moslem ethno-religious subcultures of that country. The nationalist ideology included generalized religious symbols, which if accepted might have unified conflicting elements of the society (see Geertz, 1973:193–233). The generalized symbols may take the form of a civil religion such as America developed in the nineteenth century (Fenn, 1978:32–40). This third step is typically unstable. Dissident minorities attack the generalized symbol system, especially its "inappropriate" uses of religious symbols. This conflict is illustrated by the anti-Vietnam War dissidents, who objected that wartime political uses of both civil and particular religious themes were inauthentic. That era's proliferation of court cases over civil disobedience further illustrates the problems of legitimacy inherent in a conflict of world views.

The conflict results in two seemingly disparate situations in Fenn's fourth stage: the *development of minority and idiosyncratic definitions of the situation*, together with increasingly *secularized political authority*. On the one hand is pressure to desacralize the political authority—for example, removing any ideological notions of what is "good" from decision making and replacing them with criteria such as due process and technical procedures (Fenn, 1972:27; Hammond, 1974). On the other hand, challenging the civil religious synthesis results in spreading access to the sacred. Thus individuals and groups develop their own particular (i.e., "idiosyncratic") views and symbols for which they claim the same seriousness as recognized religions. Individual and group claims to social authority multiply as the uncertainty of boundaries becomes evident. As Fenn (1978:55) states, "Secularization increases the likelihood that various institutions or groups will base their claims to social authority on various religious grounds, while it undermines the possibility for consensus on the meaning and location of the sacred."

Some interesting examples of the ambiguities at this stage can be seen in recent court cases. The use of peyote (a hallucinogen) by some American Indians has had a long tradition. The Native American church, instituted in 1918, is a **syncretic religion**—a new religion formed in the fusion of beliefs and practices of two or more previously separate religions. This church ties together themes from American Indian religions and incorporates peyotism in its ritual. In 1962, a group of Navajos using peyote in their religious ceremony was arrested and convicted under a California law prohibiting possession of peyote. The California Supreme Court overturned the conviction, however, granting the Indians immunity under the First Amendment of the Constitution, which guarantees free exercise of religion (*People* v. *Woody*, 394 P 2d813, 1964).

The courts were somewhat more pressed on the religious freedom issue when individuals and groups in the larger culture began to use hallucinogens for religious purposes. A number of "psychedelic churches" (e.g., the Church of the Awakening and the League of Spiritual Discovery, both founded in the mid-1960s) have tried to establish their constitutional immunity for the religious use of drugs (mainly marijuana, peyote, and mescaline). The best-known case on this issue was in the mid-1960s, when Dr. Timothy Leary was convicted and sentenced to thirty years in jail and $40,000 in fines for illegal possession of marijuana. Dr. Leary, a researcher of psychedelic drugs, claimed that marijuana use was an integral part of his religious practice. On appeal, the court upheld the conviction, commenting that Leary's religious use of marijuana was occasional, private, and personal. The court declared a "compelling state interest" in drug prohibition:

> It would be difficult to imagine the harm which would result if the criminal statutes against marijuana were nullified as to those who claim the right to possess and traffic in this drug for religious purposes. For all practical purposes the anti-marijuana laws would be meaningless, and enforcement impossible. . . . We will not, therefore, subscribe to the dangerous doctrine that the free exercise of

religion accords an unlimited freedom to violate the laws of the land relative to marijuana (*Leary* v. *United States* 383f.2d841, 1967).

This kind of conflict illustrates the lack of moral unity and problems of legitimacy characteristic to the fourth step in Fenn's analysis. Similar cases involving idiosyncratic perspectives include conflict over whether Transcendental Meditation (TM) should be allowed in the schools, whether faith healers or Scientologists could be banned as fraudulent, or whether to allow movements with strong political overtones (e.g., Black Muslims) the prerogatives of religious organizations (for a synopsis of some of these cases, see Burkholder, 1974, and Pfeffer, 1974; see also *The Annals of The American Academy*, Nov., 1979).

Two contrary tendencies are found in Fenn's fifth step. One is the *separation of the individual from corporate life,* discussed more fully later in this chapter. The other tendency is varying degrees of group *pressure toward integrating personal value systems with activities in the public sphere*—the world of work, politics, law, and so on. This tendency, detailed in Chapter 5, is expressed in different modes of religious organization: church, sect, denomination, cult. Each mode has a characteristic stance toward the integration of value systems. At one extreme is satisfaction with minimal integration (e.g., groups that consider their values irrelevant to the public sphere). At the opposite pole are groups seeking totalistic solutions; these would include seemingly secular ideologies as well as overtly religious totalism (Fenn, 1978:64–82).

Secularization both disturbs and clarifies the bases of social authority. It is disturbing because it undermines the ability of society to maintain belief in a symbolic whole that transcends the separate identities and conflicting interests of society's component parts (Fenn, 1978:8). Pluralism and institutional differentiation are generally important factors in this process because they break down the overarching world view—the symbolic whole. These processes make it impossible to achieve a new firm source of societal integration and legitimacy. At the same time, however, they increase the likelihood that people will need and seek this symbolic whole.

Problems at the Individual Level. Pluralism, as suggested, undermines the taken-for-granted quality of the world view. The individual's own meaning system receives less social support and becomes precarious, voluntary, and private. This too can produce conflict for the individual. Pluralism increases personal ambiguity: What am I to believe? How am I to act? On what basis can I decide?

A good example of the widespread conflict and doubt created by religio-cultural pluralism is the issue of abortion. At the societal level, the main issue is whether to legally permit abortion and, if so, under which circumstances. Thus societal resolution requires response to conflicting legal, biological, religious, and social claims. At the individual level, however, the issue includes personal decisions: Is it right for me to have an abortion? What shall I teach my children about abortion? And how shall I respond if my friend or daughter wants an abortion? Religious pluralism contributes directly to the quandary. Some religions teach that life begins at the moment of conception; others allow that intrauterine life (i.e., the developing fetus) is qualitatively different from life after birth. Accordingly the former view would equate abortion with killing, while the latter might allow abortion but counsel that it is still not a desirable action. Many other religious groups hold still different interpretations in good conscience.

There is little consensus even within religious groups. A 1972 survey of American Christians found that only 10 percent of members in theologically liberal Protestant churches (e.g., Congregationalists) were "unconditionally" opposed to abortion; however, those who rarely attended church were even less likely to oppose abortion (7 percent) than those who attended regularly (12 percent) or those who attended very frequently (33 percent). Among Roman Catholics, for whom the church's official position is strongly opposed to abortion, only 32 percent were unconditionally opposed to abortion. Church attendance was a similarly important factor, with 17 percent of infrequent attenders, 34 percent of regular attenders, and 50 percent of very frequent attenders opposed to abortion. Overall, unconditional opposition to abortion was least among liberal Protestants (10 percent), moderates such as Presbyterians (21 percent), and conservatives such as American Baptists (25 percent). More Roman Catholics and fundamentalists (e.g., southern Baptists and various sects) were opposed—32 percent and 39 percent respectively (Petersen and Mauss, 1976:247). There is similar variation within groups in their acceptance of abortion under certain extenuating circumstances such as threatened health of the mother, pregnancy resulting from rape, and probable deformity of the fetus. The problem for many individuals, then, is that while the decision is often defined as a moral issue, there is profound disagreement over the "good" path. Whatever the individual chooses, there is no massive social support for that decision.

Personal value decisions are important, but a more critical issue at the individual level is the impact of the problem of legitimacy for personal *identity,* which (as developed in Chapter 3) is influenced and supported by religion. The individual's world view is an important element of personal identity (Luckmann, 1967:70). But one need not go so far as Luckmann, who equates personal identity with religiosity, to appreciate the connection between religion and identity. The individual's subjective meaning system legitimates that person's hierarchy of goals, values, and norms. What happens, then, if this key part of the individual's identity is undermined? This problem of legitimacy of the self is related to the process of "privatization" discussed later in this chapter.

Rationalization

Several theories relate secularization to the process of **rationalization,** the process by which certain areas of social life are organized according to the criteria of means-ends (or functional) rationality. This linkage was a central thread in the works of Weber (1947; 1958a), who viewed a special form of rationality as the outstanding characteristic of modern society.

The key characteristic of modernization, according to Weber, is increasing emphasis upon functional (i.e., means-ends) rationality (note, however, that Weber used the concept of rationality in several ways, giving rise to some ambiguities in his theories; see Luckmann, 1977:16, 17). In traditional societies, for example, a farmer prepares the soil for planting in a certain way because "that's the way it's always been done" (i.e., traditional behavior); such orientations are extremely resistant to change. By contrast, the modern farmer is more likely to consider alternative and new methods, judging each according to rational criteria such as relative productivity, costs versus benefits, and appreciation of land values. Although Weber's concept of rationality may be useful in understanding the place of religion in contemporary society, we must avoid an overrationalized conception of human action.

Rationality and Modernization. According to Weber, modern Western society has a "rationalized" economy and a concomitant special "mentality." A **rational economy** is functionally organized, with decisions based upon the reasoned weighing of utilities and costs. The **rational mentality** involves openness toward new ways of doing things (in contrast with traditionalism) and readiness to adapt to functionally specialized roles and universalistic criteria of performance. Although these forms of rationality originated in the economic order, they have extended into political organization and legal order—the modern state. Weber argued that religious motives and legitimations played a central role in bringing about this form of organization and mentality—for example, by the development of universalistic ethics (i.e., the norm of treating all people according to the same generalized standards) and by the development of religious drive for rational mastery over the world. Nevertheless this rationality, once a part of societal structure, became divorced from its historical origins and acquired an impetus of its own (Weber, 1947, 1958a).

Weber closed his early essay on the Protestant ethic (1958a) with an almost prophetic evaluation of possible outcomes from the process of rationalization. He observed that the rationally organized order of modern society presents itself to the individual as an overwhelming force. All people engaged in the extensive system of market relationships are bound by the norms of functional rationality. This is exemplified by the great difficulty of establishing alternative economic arrangements, as countercultural communes have discovered. The conditions of the modern economic order have become an "iron cage" of instrumentality, which in Weber's opinion was far from desirable:

> No one knows who will live in this cage in the future, or whether at the end of this tremendous development entirely new prophets will arise, or there will be a great rebirth of old ideas and ideals, or, if neither, mechanized petrification, embellished with a sort of convulsive self-importance. For of the last stage of this cultural development, it might well be truly said: "Specialists without spirit, sensualists without heart"; this nullity imagines that it has attained a level of civilization never before achieved (Weber 1958a:182).

Weber's analysis suggests that the differentiation process alone does not account for important changes in contemporary society. Rationalization specifies the direction of differentiation: Differentiation proceeds according to the criteria of means-ends rationality. Businesses can (and many do) specialize tasks according to nonrational criteria. Nevertheless the main thrust of organization in business (and increasingly in other spheres such as schools, government, churches, and other voluntary organizations) is to extend the criteria of functional rationality: effectiveness, efficiency, cost-benefit analysis, and specialization of tasks. While differentiation produced separate norms appropriate to each institutional domain, rationalization of public sphere institutions means that nonfunctional values (e.g., kindness, honesty, beauty, or meaningfulness) are generally irrelevant to action within these institutions. The ethical regulation of an impersonal rational organization is thus impossible (Weber, 1958a:331).

If modern society is indeed moving in the direction of increasing functional rationality, this process implies problems at two levels: the location of individual meaning and belonging; and a conflict between corporate control and values versus personal autonomy and values. Personal meaning is not only relegated to the private sphere but is also undermined by the dominant rationality of other spheres. Rationalized medical practice, for example, does not deal with the "meaning" of childbirth. It is more functional to treat the woman's and child's bodies as objects to be manipulated. Personal meaning, satisfaction, and emotions in giving birth are not overtly denied by the medical process, but they are subordinated to "rational" criteria of efficiency and medical management. The individual seeking to apply meaning to personal experiences is in a weak situation relative to the powerful institutions for which individual meaning is irrelevant.

Disenchantment of the World. Another feature of rationalization undermines the individual's personal sense of meaning and belonging: Weber called it **"disenchantment"** of the world, referring to the process by which things held in awe or reverence are stripped of their special qualities and become "ordinary." Protestantism thus brought about much disenchantment of what Roman Catholicism had held in awe (Berger, 1967:111), emptying the believer's world of angels, saints, shrines, holy objects (e.g., candles, blessed water, and oil), holy days, and elaborate sacraments. Rational science also promotes disenchantment, explaining natural phenomena without reference to nonnatural categories of thought. Phenomena previously attributed to miracles are reinterpreted by rational science as natural (e.g., "spontaneous remission of disease"). The key feature of the rationalization process is not so much the particular explanations of phenomena but the *belief* that all phenomena *can* be rationally explained (Weber, 1958a:139).

Thus rational science undermines other ways of knowing. The process of rationalization results in a dichotomy between "serious" and "nonserious" interpretations (rational explanations being serious and other forms of explanation nonserious). The cognitive style appropriate to modern bureaucratic structures in the public sphere and utilized in science, medicine, law, and so on, is not amenable to the cognitive style of religion— which, by contrast, allows reference to a transcendent, empirically nonverifiable realm and allows undifferentiated "experiencing" as a valid way of knowing. The rational cognitive style of modern public institutions has filtered down to everyday life, though it is not consistently or pervasively applied there. Consequently not only is one's everyday knowledge more restricted to rationally knowable items but the world itself is indeed transformed. The way in which people think of the world becomes distinct from the way in which they think of themselves and each other (Gellner, 1974:196). The process of rationalization means that the rational mode of cognition applies to those institutional spheres that "really matter" (i.e., are serious); other modes of cognition (e.g., fantasy, play, religion) are treated as frills of private life (i.e., as nonserious).

According to Bell (1977), this disjunction between the norms of rationality and the principles of self-realization or human rights is inherent in the very nature of society. He postulates three realms in society, the norms of which can be radically antagonistic. In the *techno-economic realm* of modern Western societies, the key principles are functional rationality and efficiency. By contrast, the *polity* typically emphasizes norms of equality, participation, and human rights; whereas the *culture* is characterized by desire for self-realization and self-fulfillment. Bell suggests that usual use of the concept of secularization is confused because it fails to distinguish social and cultural change. Social change is characterized by secularization—institutional differentiation and rationalization. A separate process, profanation, describes cultural change, especially disenchantment of the world. Bell argues that if these are indeed separate realms, it is possible for religion to gain new sources of vigor in the cultural realm without undoing changes in the social realm (Bell, 1977; also see B. Wilson, 1979).

Rationalization does not necessarily mean that people are generally more rational than in the past. Some evidence exists that superstition and folk religion are widespread elements in highly industrialized societies. A 1968 study in the area of London found a core of approximately 8 percent of respondents who strongly believed in superstitious rituals (e.g., avoiding ladders, knocking on wood, and throwing salt); approximately 23 percent strongly believed in astrology; some 60 percent believed in premonitions; and 30 percent believed in "ghosts or spirits that can sometimes be seen or sensed by people." The proportionately greater amount of superstitious interpretation of events among women and working-class persons apparently reflects these believers' relative lack of control over the events of their lives. While rational modes of cognition are increasingly dominant among the strata of modern society that feel in control of their lives and their world, nonrational modes may increasingly reflect other stratas' sense of loss of control (Abercrombie et al., 1970).

This situation on the individual level may therefore reflect societal conflict between the extension of corporate control and the degree of individual autonomy. The modern economic situation is characterized by the increasing power and scope of **corporate actors** in conflict with the power and rights of individuals. The corporate actor is one who fills a role in an institution; the role, rather than the individual, is part of the corporate world (Fenn, 1978:66), and the corporate role is functionally rational in the institutional area. There is little or no integration of the meaning of institutional roles into a subjective meaning system for the individual actor. This lack of integration does not disturb the business or political worlds; the individual is still controlled by the corporate norms. It does not matter in a teddy bear assembly line who (or why someone) attaches the eyes; all that matters is that the role is satisfactorily performed.

Increasing anonymity of functionally specialized roles makes the individual replaceable. The corporate actor is also less responsible as a person, able to claim, "I didn't do anything wrong; I was only doing my job." Individuals may consequently segregate "rational" institutional norms in their consciousness, compensating for their lack of autonomy in the public sphere by a somewhat illusory sense of autonomy in the private sphere (Luckmann, 1967:96, 97; also see Fenn, 1978:81, 82, on the legitimation of the corporate actor's nonresponsibility).

Privatization

Privatization is the process by which certain differentiated institutional spheres (e.g., religion, family, leisure, the arts) are segregated from the dominant institutions of the public sphere (e.g., economic, political, legal) and relegated to the private sphere. This segregation means that the norms and values of the private sphere are irrelevant to the operations of public sphere institutions (Berger, 1967:133). It also implies that the functions of providing meaning and belonging are relegated to institutions of the private sphere. The hypothesis of privatization is directly related to the previously discussed processes of differentiation, pluralization, and rationalization. Differentiation creates separate institutional spheres, in which formerly pervasive institutions such as religion and family are compartmentalized. Pluralization contributes to the complexity of society and makes it difficult, if not impossible, to speak of cultural consensus. And rationalization of the economic (and by extension, the politico-legal) institutional spheres renders the functions of meaning and belonging irrelevant in public institutions.

Whereas differentiation, pluralization, and rationalization all refer to conditions in the larger society, privatization primarily describes the residual category of self. Privatization implies that the individual finds sources of identity increasingly only in the private sphere. Concomitants of personal identity are a sense of order, an interpretation of reality, a system of meaning, and the integration of oneself into a larger community (see Mol, 1976:9–15). The individual finds fewer sources of identity in public sphere institutions, largely because the order obtaining in this sphere is functional rationality. All that contributes to making, maintaining, or changing personal identity is located in the private sphere. The individual's very self is privatized.

On the one hand, privatization apparently promotes some of the personal freedoms enjoyed by many in modern society. One freedom is the extent to which one's reference groups (i.e., those whose opinion of one "counts" in shaping one's behavior) are not imposed by kin or neighborhood but are more freely chosen. On the other hand, privatization apparently results in problems of meaning and integration for many individuals. These problems may be reflected in the relatively widespread quest for holistic world views (as expressed by many alternative health movements, agrarian communes, contemporary religious movements, and some strands of parapsychology). Holistic perspectives such as these express a desire for integrating all aspects of life, gaining a sense of wholeness in social, physical, psychic, and spiritual life.

Privatization implies problems in legitimating oneself. Identity becomes problematic. Sources of order, meaning, and community have been undermined; all have become increasingly voluntary and uncertain. Luckmann (1967:99) suggests that this voluntary quality contributes to a sense of autonomy in the private sphere, perhaps making up for the individual's lack of autonomy in institutions of the public sphere:

> Once religion is defined as a "private affair" the individual may choose from the assortment of "ultimate" meanings as he sees fit—guided only by the preferences that are determined by his social biography.

An important consequence of this situation is that the individual constructs not only his personal identity but also his individual system of "ultimate" significance (used by permission).

This self-selected construction is, according to Luckmann, the contemporary social form of religion. While church-oriented religion continues to be one of the elements that some people choose for their constructions, other themes from the private sphere (e.g., autonomy, self-expression, self-realization, familism, sexuality, adjustment, and fulfillment) are also available in a supermarket of "ultimate" meanings (Luckmann, 1967:100–114; see also Fenn, 1978:xii, on identity and privatization).

Critiques of Contemporary Society

Luckmann (1967:115–117) raises a critical note in a "postscript" when he observes the discrepancy between the subjective autonomy of the individual in modern society and the objective autonomy of the major institutions of the public sphere. He wonders if the removal of nonfunctionally rational considerations from these institutions has not contributed to the dehumanization of the social order. The irony, then, would be that privatized religiosity, by sacralizing the increasing subjectivity of the individual, supports this dehumanization; by withdrawing into privatized religious expressions, this new mode of religiosity fails to confront the depersonalized roles of the public sphere. If this is true, modern forms of religion do not have to legitimate society directly—they support it indirectly by motivating retreat into the private sphere.

A similarly pessimistic projection is drawn by Habermas (1975:117–130), who observes serious problems of legitimation and motivation in modern societies. He proposes a process of "communicative ethics" to overcome the inability of nonrational criteria to evaluate behavior in the public sphere and to motivate individual commitment. At the same time, however, Habermas is pessimistic about the prospect of a societal organization that involves such great cleavage between individuals' corporate roles and their inner, identity-seeking selves. He asks whether this might portend the "end of the individual."

Another possible outcome is advanced by Robertson, who focuses upon the process of **individuation** rather than privatization. Individuation refers to the process by which the individual and his or her concerns come to be seen as distinct from the social group and its concerns. For example, Bellah's stages of religious evolution include increasing complexity of the larger society and increasing individuation. Robertson's synthesis of themes from Weber, Durkheim, and Simmel likewise emphasizes the twin processes of individuation (especially the quest for individual autonomy) and societalism (i.e., the growth in societal power over individual members). He suggests that the individuation process has proceeded so far that large-scale institutions of the public sphere cannot easily resist it. Some emerging religious movements of recent years, he suggests, may prompt a new mode of relationship between the individual and society (Robertson, 1977:305; 1978:180; 1979).

Extended Application: The Secularization of Health and Healing

Health and the process of healing have been greatly secularized in Western societies. For the purposes of this essay, *secularization* means the removing of belonging- and meaning-providing elements from an institutional area (i.e., healing). To say that the Western medical system is secularized is to suggest that medical treatment in the context of that system is not related to any larger framework of meaning or general order. By extension, this implies that religion (a meaning system) is generally not related to Western medicine. The Western medical system, while allowing other sources to project meaning for health and illness, generally denies that meaning is related to medical problems or their resolution. The process by which the institution of healing became secularized illustrates a number of the concepts we have discussed.

Differentiation

Western medicine has gradually differentiated itself from other institutions. Traditionally healing was interwoven with numerous other institutional domains, notably the family and religion. Long before there was any distinctive occupation of medicine, healing was the function of mothers and other nurses, herbalists, folk healers (e.g., persons with a special gift for setting bones), religious persons, midwives, diviners, and so on. Although the institutional differentiation of medicine proceeded especially rapidly in the last century, its roots can be traced at least as far back as early Greek and Persian medicine. Characteristics of this differentiation include the development of a distinctive body of knowledge, a corps of specialists with control over this body of knowledge and its application, and public acknowledgement (or legitimacy) of the specialized authority of medical specialists.

A body of specialized medical knowledge existed before the Greeks (as it does in even relatively "primitive" societies), but Greek physicians emphasized a rationalized approach to medicine: observation, description, generalization, and prediction. Although Greek medicine was based upon relatively naturalistic categories, it was interpretive and related health and illness to social, psychological-spiritual, and environmental aspects of the patient's life. Hippocratic physicians believed that health was based upon harmony of the "humors" (i.e., blood, phlegm, black bile, and yellow bile) and upon the pneuma (i.e., "spirit") and social and climatic environment. There were several competing schools of medical knowledge such as the dogmatists, the empiricists, the aesclepiades, the methodists, and the pneumatists, each holding alternative interpretations of health and illness (Freidson, 1970:13, 14). Although such physicians enjoyed some respect, they were essentially small clusters of masters and apprentices, and their influence was generally limited to the social elite.

The specialized occupation of "doctor" did not develop until the Middle Ages. Healing in this period, however, was highly supernaturalized. The church attempted to control healing because the power to heal was believed to come from spiritual sources, either evil or good. Nonclerical healing was severely limited. The Lateran Council of 1215 (which represented the apex of church power in the Middle Ages) forbade physicians from undertaking medical treatment without calling in ecclesiastical advice. Healing that took place outside clerical jurisdiction was suspect of having been aided by the devil. The two main groups of healers thus suspect were Jewish doctors and "white" witches (typically women). Jewish (and, in small numbers, Moorish) physicians kept their ancient medical lore alive throughout the Middle Ages, while the dominant European medical knowledge was a stagnant form of late Greek medicine (i.e., Galenism). Therefore Jewish physicians were sought by the wealthy, to the disgust of Christian clergy who proclaimed (for example) that "it were better to die with Christ than to be cured by a Jew doctor aided by the devil" (cited in Szasz, 1970:88).

The masses, however, were served by an assortment of folk healers such as white witches—members of the community who used herbs, potions, magic, charms, and elements of pre-Christian religions to cure disease and ward off evil influences (see Ehrenreich and English, 1973). They served as midwives and were often consulted for advice about personal problems as well as magic. These healers were a special target of the Inquisition in several countries. A papal bull (i.e., official writ), the *Malleus Mallificarum* (1486), became a manual for witch hunts. The *Malleus Mallificarum* (Sprenger and Kramer, 1948) singled out women healers as especially dangerous:

> All witchcraft comes from carnal lust, which in women is insatiable . . . Wherefore for the sake of fulfilling their lusts they consort with devils . . . it is sufficiently clear that there are more women than men found infected with the heresy of witchcraft . . . And blessed be the Highest Who has so far preserved the male sex from so great a crime.

Similarly witch hunts in Protestant countries (e.g., England and New England) considered the "good" witch to be especially dangerous (Szasz, 1970:89).

The specialized occupation of doctor developed largely through the establishment of university medical schools and the later state regulation of credentials for physicians and creation of medical guilds. This specialization also had the effect of legitimating the increasing monopoly of physicians against the claims of other healers. University medical schools, which were heavily under church control, could control the body of knowledge and interpretive framework of medicine. Thus when the church declared that "if a woman dare to cure without having studied, she is a witch and must die," it was legitimating only its own controlled version of medicine and the medical occupation (Szasz, 1970:91). Church-recognized physicians were often called upon to identify and certify witches. Nevertheless the formally recognized physicians were unable to command a monopoly over healing services, largely because the state of their craft did not inspire public confidence.

Rationalization

The preeminence of the modern medical profession has its roots in the rationalization and further differentiation begun in the Renaissance and proceeding rapidly since about 1850. This rationalization occurred mainly in two spheres:

the application of rational science to medical discoveries, and the rational organization of the profession. The rationalization of medical knowledge meant increasing reliance on scientific methods of discovery and utilization of technology and technique. Careful observation and systematic recording, dissection and autopsies, and pharmacological experiments contributed to the formal knowledge of the field, whereas some of these methods had been previously forbidden by church authorities. Technological developments such as the invention of the microscope and stethoscope also were a part of this rationalization process. Especially important was the discovery, in the latter part of the nineteenth century, that specific agents (e.g., bacteria) caused specific diseases (Freidson, 1970:16). Access to specialized knowledge and specialized technologies uniquely "qualified" the physician.

The increasing rationalization of medical knowledge led to a focus on *disease*, a biophysical entity, rather than on *illness*, the complex social, psychological, and spiritual situation of the sick person (Kleinman, 1978). Rational medicine has a built-in tendency toward treating the human body as an object rather than a person. This narrow biological determinism promotes the image of the physician as active and powerful, the client as passive and objectlike. The sick person must give up control of his or her own body and depend upon the benevolence and knowledgeability of the professional (Young, 1976:18, 19).

Rational organization within the medical profession went hand in hand with the rationalization of medical knowledge. Thus as knowledge and technical skill became more specialized, physicians' areas of expertise became more compartmentalized. A medical group today often consists of doctors in ten or more separate specializations. As physicians divided specialties among themselves, they also consolidated their control and prestige by annexing and subordinating a number of potentially competing occupations such as nursing, pharmacy, and medical technology.

Other competitors such as midwives and bone-setters were effectively driven out of practice and their functions taken over by the medical profession (Freidson, 1970:52). In America, one approach to medicine (called "allopathy") gained a monopoly over medical practice, education, and licensing. This monopoly has been so complete as to exclude from legitimacy most competing medical approaches. Important alternative medical approaches such as homeopathy, osteopathy, chiropractic, and naturopathy—each positing different interpretations of causes and treatments of illness—have been effectively subordinated or suppressed by the monopoly of allopathic medicine (Wardwell, 1972).

The dominant medical system has also effectively reduced the legitimacy of actions of other "encroaching" institutional areas such as religion and the family. In 1967, the pastor of First Church of Religious Science was found guilty of illegal practice of medicine for treating members' "emotional and weight problems" with hypnosis—judged by the court to be an appropriate procedure only for medical therapy (cited in Szasz, 1970:91). Other religious groups have experienced similar problems. Although Christian Science practitioners have gradually worked around legal difficulties with their religious healing, the Founding Church of Scientology has been under considerably greater medical and legal attack (see Burkholder, 1974).

Various courts have similarly overruled religious or moral objections to medically "required" procedures. Jehovah's Witnesses believe that blood transfusions are forbidden by Scripture, but the courts have generally upheld the medical authorization of transfusions, even for unwilling recipients (*U.S.* v. *George*, 239 F. Supp. 752, 1965). Medical authority supersedes parental authority in decisions presumed to determine life or death (precedent cases in 1952, 1962, and 1964 are cited in Burkholder, 1974:41). Even in instances where medical ability to prevent death is doubtful, greater legitimacy is given to medical rather than parental authority. In 1977, for example, a Massachusetts court ordered that parents of a child dying of leukemia submit the child to medically prescribed chemotherapy, rather than to a less unpleasant (but also less respectable) naturopathic therapy.

Legitimation and Social Control

The result of these processes of differentiation and rationalization (together with the efforts of the interested parties—the physicians themselves) is that the medical profession today has an officially approved monopoly over the definition of health and illness and the treatment of persons defined as "sick" (Freidson, 1970:5). A good case could, in fact, be made that the church authority of the Middle Ages was undermined first by legal institutions, which, in turn, were undermined by the medical institution. The medical profession has become a key legitimating agency in Western societies and thus has a major role in social control.

Medicalization of Deviance. Society must deal with individuals who differ significantly from socially established norms. The concept of **social control** refers to all of the mechanisms a society uses to try to contain its members' behavior within those norms: deterrents, incentives, rewards, and punishments. Whether the society punishes the individual depends largely upon its determination of the individual's responsibility for the deviant behavior. A person who fails to go to work for two weeks is likely to be fired, but if it is determined that the absence resulted from sickness, the person will probably be exempted from normal obligations of work. At the same time, however, a person who is permitted to take the "sick role" is obliged to try to get well, cooperate with medical help, and act appropriately "sick" (Parsons, 1972).

The key issues in understanding social control are definition of deviance, determination of responsibility, and administration of punishment. Religious, legal, and medical institutions have served as significant agents of social control in all three aspects. The definition of deviance is a particularly important aspect because the norms by which deviance is defined are themselves socially constructed. The definition essentially depends upon the social group's idea of what is "normal" (Becker, 1963). If a society defines noncompetitive or unobtrusive behavior as the norm, any individual who is competitive or stands out is likely to be considered deviant. Deviance is a product of the group that labels it.

Religious, legal, and medical institutions have all contributed to the definition of deviance in society. For example, "Thou shalt not steal" defines a religious norm; stealing is a sin. Legal systems define similar norms of behavior, and violation of the norms is a crime. Medical systems also define what is normal or desirable behavior; deviance is sickness. But the relative weight of religious, legal, and medical institutions in defining deviance has shifted. As the Middle Ages waned and these three institutions became increasingly differentiated, the religious organizations still held greatest influence in defining societal deviance. This preeminence continued into the eighteenth century, but in America and France (and later other European countries), the legal mode of defining deviance gained ascendancy. In America, the increasing preeminence of the legal definitions was promoted by pluralism (as previously noted) and by increasing rationalization of the nation-state.

The significance of legal definitions of deviance has waned somewhat in the twentieth century, and medical definitions of deviance have gained preeminence. This shifting balance is clearly reflected in the 1954 precedent-setting court case *Durham* v. *United States*, 214 F 2d, 863, which decided that "an accused is not criminally responsible if his unlawful act was the product of a mental disease or mental defect." Abe Fortas, the court-appointed defense in this case and later a Supreme Court justice, stated, "Psychiatry is given a card of admission [into the courtroom] on its own merits, and because of its own competence to aid in classifying those who should be held criminally responsible and those who should be treated as psychologically or emotionally disordered" (cited in Szasz, 1970:317). The shift in balance favoring medical definitions of deviance corresponds chronologically with the period of rapid professionalization of medicine, when medical discoveries and technology proceeded rapidly and public faith in science and medicine was increasing.

The appeal of medical definitions of deviance over legal or religious definitions is understandable. Religious definitions appear too nonrational and, in a religiously pluralistic country, they lack society-wide acceptance. Legal definitions, while more rational, appear to hinge too greatly upon human decisions — the judgment of twelve ordinary citizens on a jury, for example. Medical definitions of deviance, by contrast, appear more rational and scientific.

The concept of sickness, however, far from being a neutral scientific concept, is ultimately a *moral* one, establishing an evaluation of normality or desirability (Freidson, 1970:208). A wide range of disapproved behavior has been defined by the medical profession (especially its psychiatric branch) as sick: alcoholism, homosexuality, promiscuity, drug addiction, arson, suicide, child abuse, and civil disobedience (see Conrad and Schneider, 1980). The seeming rationality of medical diagnosis thus masks the evaluative process. Jurisdiction of medicine over these behaviors does not depend upon medical *knowledge* of their causes or cures, for medicine is no better able to cure alcoholism or homosexuality than can religion or law. The preeminence of medical definitions is based upon the popular and juridical *acceptance* of medical authority (Bittner, 1968; Freidson, 1970:251–253).

Social Control and Power. The labeling of deviance is an issue of legitimacy on another level, for the power to define sickness and to label someone "sick" is also the power to discredit that person. If a person's mental health is called into question, the rest of society does not have to take that person seriously. During the Vietnam War, a physician refused to train medical personnel for the U.S.

Army, claiming that his religious conscience compelled him to refuse this service. The army insisted that his compulsions were psychological rather than religious (cited in Fenn, 1978:57). By raising doubt about his psychological health, the army was able to evade his religious dissent as well as his legal claim to protection under the First Amendment.

Control over the definition of deviance also produces power in the other aspects of social control: certifying deviance. The societal acceptance of medical definitions of deviance gives the medical profession power to certify individual cases as sick or well. If a back disorder is a legitimate basis for taking the "sick role" (thus to be excused from work or to claim insurance), a physician is the appropriate agency for certifying a valid claim. Similarly when homosexuality was a legitimate basis for denying citizenship (1952–1979), psychiatrists were given the power to certify that a homosexual should be thus denied (see Szasz, 1970).

Having certified that a person is deviant, the agency of social control must then deal with the offender. Religious responses to deviance include counseling, moral indignation, confession, repentance, penance, and forgiveness. Legal responses include parallel actions such as legal allegations against the offender, confession, punishments, "rehabilitation," and release with or without the stigma of a "record." In the medical model, the process entails other parallels: diagnosis and therapy. The process of reintegrating the deviant individual into the social group is "therapy," which for even relatively minor deviance involves a form of social control (e.g., getting a young mother "back on her feet" so she can resume her family responsibilities). The social control functions of therapy are clearly evident in its grossest forms such as the mental hospitalization of political dissidents (Medvedev and Medvedev, 1971; similar use of medical definitions for political purposes in the United States are exemplified by the treatment of Ezra Pound and General James Walker; Freidson, 1970:246; also see Turner, 1977b).

Social control may seem more pleasant or humane when the deviance is treated as sickness rather than as crime or sin, but the potency of the control agencies is just as great. There is some evidence that the informal stigma (i.e., negative reputation adhering to the individual even after "cured") attached to imputed mental illness is even greater than legal or religious stigma (cf. Phillips, 1963; 1967). Certain medically defined deviance can permanently spoil the individual's identity (cf. Goffman, 1963).

A further reason for the greater power of medical agencies of social control is their apparent rationality and scientific base. These qualities appeal to people in modern society, with their need for a mode of social control that works in a pluralistic, diverse culture. That apparent rationality and scientific base is, however, belied by medicine's inability to "cure" most deviance and by its culture-bound definitions of deviance.

Privatization: The Place of Meaning and Belonging in the Treatment of Illness

A foremost characteristic of the institution of medicine in modern Western societies is that it has divorced the function of curing disease from the functions of providing meaning and belonging to the sick person. The medical institution has limited itself to the cure of disease (a biophysical entity) and the physical tending of the diseased person. The meaning- and belonging-providing functions of healing are treated as relatively unimportant and are relegated to the private sphere institutions of family and religion. Thus if a person has cancer, the physician diagnoses a "malignancy" and uses surgery, radiation, or chemotherapy. The "disease" is an abnormal mass of cells in the body. The physician typically does not address, however, the person's *illness:* what cancer means to the person, how it is experienced, how it affects the person's life, feelings, and personal relationships (Kleinman, 1973, 1978). There is some recognition of problems of meaning for cases of "mental illness," but their treatment is also segregated in separate institutions with separate specialists. Most physicians, however, see the provision of meaning as totally unrelated to the cause or healing of medical problems.

Since a high percentage (roughly half) of patients' visits to physicians are for nonspecific complaints (i.e., for which no clear biophysical basis can be found), it appears that illness (i.e., the social and psychological problems of the person) needs as much attention as the disease or biophysical difficulties (Kleinman, 1978:63). For example, if a thirty-three-year-old mother of five children goes to a physician complaining of pains in her legs and increased difficulty with chronic asthma but no biophysical basis for the leg pain is found, what is the physician's response? The doctor may say there is nothing wrong with her legs and nothing to be done for her, or decide that her trouble is "all in her head" and prescribe placebos (i.e., pretend pills) or antidepressant drugs; or the physician may refer her to a specialist for illnesses that are "all in the head." The physician treats her physical problems as fundamentally unreal and inappropriate for medical attention.

Folk Healing. The hypothetical example just given contrasts with an actual case study of treatment for illness by a Puerto Rican spiritist in New York. The following is the researcher's account of the treatment:

> Background: The medium, here called Julia, and the client in this case were neighbors in the same building, and this incident was part of an ongoing therapeutic relationship between the two. The client (I shall call her Nilda) is in her early 30s and has five children. In the course of the last 12 years she has had relationships with several men, each lasting a number of years. After one of these relationships terminated, Nilda was hospitalized in a mental institution and her children placed in a home. She subsequently underwent periodic hospitalizations for asthma, during which times the children either returned to the home or were cared for by relatives. After her last marriage broke up, Nilda was again hospitalized in a mental institution, but at the time of this séance (several years later) she had established a new relationship with a man who wished to marry her. The couple has been together almost a year. Lately, however, Nilda had experienced pains in her legs in addition to her usual asthma.
>
> [When the researcher entered, Julia told her she was giving Nilda's apartment a "spiritual cleaning" in order to work on Nilda. Julia was washing the floor with water, ammonia, and probably other things like perfumes.] After putting the pail and mop in the corner of the living room, she took out a dish with incense and put it in the center of the room.
>
> Julia's husband then entered, and Julia asked him for cigars. He distributed

them, and everyone began smoking. Julia began blowing smoke on her husband and exorcising him so that he could leave. Julia explained that a priest [spirit] protects her husband and the priest does not get along with the Madama, who is her [spirit] protector. . . .

After her husband left, Julia began fumigating Nilda with cigar smoke. She then put a glass of water on the floor and began playing records of songs in honor of saints. She began to dance and clap and brought out a doll representing the Madama [one of several powerful Spirits invoked by spiritists]. She placed the doll and a vase of water on the phonograph and began exorcising herself, throwing the evil influences into the water [that is, tapping her hands on the edge of the vase after running her hands over the back of her head and shoulders].

Afterward she took the spirit of the Madama and began to cry and speak in a slightly different voice, saying that people are envious of Nilda. Although the Madama did not say why they are envious, people want Nilda's children to be taken back to a home. This will not happen, said the Madama, while she is at her side. Nothing will happen to her. Nevertheless, people want Nilda to go crazy so that the children will be taken away for good.

When Nilda returned, Julia rubbed *agua florida* on Nilda's forehead, back of the head, and legs, depositing the evil influences (*mala influencia*) in the vase. She did the same to the researcher and then served everyone black coffee [a drink attractive to good spirits].

Comment: Here we see in context the use of many of the paraphernalia of spiritist treatment . . . The spiritual cleaning of the apartment before the session, as well as the cigar smoke and containers of water, rids the apartment and the participants of the *fluido* of wayward spirits. For attracting favorable spirits, incense, *santero* songs, *agua florida*, and black coffee were used. Julia's Madama doll was also taken from the altar during the seance to help the spirit manifest herself.

The description . . . exemplif[ies] an exorcism in treatment of *envidia* [misfortune caused by unexpressed envy of one's associates] (as diagnosed by the Madama). The medium, as the Nun, first took the noxious spiritual influences adhering to Nilda onto herself and then made Nilda attractive to favorable spirits with *agua florida* and black coffee.

. . . The medium, after expressing some of Nilda's anxieties (about going crazy and having her children taken away from her), gave her reassurance that none of these fears would come to pass because she had good protection beside her. The reader will note that Nilda's fears were phrased as coming not from her but from outside sources —"people" want her children taken away, "people" want Nilda to go crazy. . . . this phraseology is common in spiritist treatment and is antithetical to psychiatric procedure. . . . [because it acknowledges the fears but does not make the patient responsible for them] (Harwood, 1977:97–99; used by permission).

This example of folk healing illustrates the combination of the meaning-providing functions with therapeutic practices. The patient is helped by the symbolic interpretation of her problems and by the specific symbols of power provided for her to deal with those problems. The symbol system allows her to express the anxieties and fears that may have been part of the basis of her pain. It explains her problems and suggests a course of action; thus it restores order to experiences that seemed disordered. The healer was also acting in the role of neighbor, reaffirming the patient's relationships with her community. By restricting itself to attending to disease, Western "scientific" medicine is unable or unwilling to reach patients' problems of the meaning of their situation and is thus less able to heal illness.

Medical Systems and Meaning. All medical systems, from "scientific" Western medicine to Eskimo shamans, from the Chinese revolutionary medical system to Mexican curanderos, perform similar functions. The four major functions of medical systems are: *construction of the illness experience; cognitive organization and management of the illness experience; healing practices per se; and management of death.*

Construction of the illness experience involves giving symbolic form (i.e., meaning) to the illness (Kleinman, 1973:160–161). Each culture attaches different meanings to different biological situations; members learn how to feel, experience, and interpret the illness itself. Cultural meanings define some physical situations as illness. Our culture has generally defined pregnancy as illness, and obviously pregnant women are expected to retreat from worldly roles and take the sick role, seeking medical supervision of their condition; in other cultures, pregnancy is not considered a matter of medical concern at all. Another example is the extent to which the culture considers it appropriate for the sick person to experience and express pain. There is wide variation in cultural responses to pain (Zborowski, 1958). Illness is not simply a biophysical fact, but, through symbolic interpretation, is shaped into a human experience.

Medical systems apply interpretive models to an illness by naming it. Diagnosis is not merely a prelude to healing; it is part of the healing process itself because, in naming the illness, the healer helps the sick person to make sense of what is happening. Labeling illness helps to restore order. Medical diagnoses are **transformative processes**, changing behavioral or biophysical expressions (i.e., signs) into "symptoms"—socially understandable indicators of a specific category of illness (Young, 1976:13, 14). In this transformation, some signs are discarded or recede in importance; others are expanded or elicited. The symptoms are not, therefore, simple products of the illness itself but are *socially* constructed, fitting into preexisting socially available categories of meaning. Diagnosis, for example, transforms several expressions of general discomfort or specific pain and descriptions of personal habits into symptoms of an ulcer—a category of conditions understandable to most persons in modern societies (but for which no equivalent may exist in other societies).

The Western medical system, in contrast with traditional (folk) healing systems, has severely truncated these meaning-providing aspects. Construction of the illness experience is viewed as trying to get the patient to cooperate with the medical regimen (i.e., patient management). Diagnosis is viewed as mere biophysical classification, often mediated by much technological intervention (e.g., blood tests, urinalysis, electrocardiograms, etc.). The focus of Western medicine is on the curative practices themselves—prescription of medicines, application of bandages and sutures, surgery, transfusions, radiation therapy, diet regimens, exercise, rest, and so on. By contrast, traditional (folk) healers emphasize the explanation of illness. A study comparing shamans (i.e., *tangkis*) with Chinese and Western-style doctors in Taiwan, found that shamans not only spent more time with each patient but also spent a much greater proportion of that time explaining the disease and treatment to patients (Kleinman, 1978:64).

Management of death is another function that is truncated in Western medicine. The medical profession has almost exclusive social authority to define death. Even though an ambulance attendant may know that a patient is "dead on arrival," a medical authority is required to pronounce the person dead. Further, the definition of death is socially constructed. Even rational Western medicine applies the definition of death differently according to the social situation. For example, a ninety-year-old man is much more likely than a five-year-old to be pronounced dead and receive no extraordinary efforts to keep him alive (Glazer and Strauss, 1965; Sudnow, 1967). Although the medical profession has gained authority to define death and to control its usual social setting, it has generally avoided the problem of what dying *means* or how the dying person and family feel about the process of dying. Unlike traditional medical systems, modern medicine does not address these problems of meaning. Instead, the meaning-providing functions are segregated and relegated to separate agencies, usually the family and religious representatives. And when these agencies are weak or absent, the meaning-providing functions are often denied altogether.

All medical systems have a repertoire of legitimations for therapeutic failure. A group using faith healing might say, "The healing does not seem to have worked, probably because we did not have enough faith." Most traditional (folk) healing involves legitimations that link the illness with some larger order or social situation. The legitimation might explain, "This illness is a chastisement from the gods; unless we change our ways, our healing efforts will not work."

Rational medicine, on the other hand, is less willing to link biophysical disease to nonphysical situations, though this is changing somewhat with the discovery of the biophysical effects of social environment such as stress, conflict, sense of threat, rapid social change, and sense of powerlessness (see Kiely, 1972; Wolff, 1962). By contrast, theodicies (as described in Chapter 2) are in-stitutionalized religious legitimations for suffering and death, giving meaning to the experiences of illness or dying. Western medicine, however, has generally relegated these meaning-providing aspects of healing to the private sphere. The net effect is to undermine the meaning-providing aspects, to make them a less real part of treatment. As far as the medical system is concerned, the provision of meaning by the family or religious group is something extraneous to treatment of the sick or dying person.

Because Western medicine is focused upon the curing of "disease" rather than healing of illness, the provision of meaning is privatized and undermined. Secularized medicine is generally unable to deal with illness, the complex of perceptions and experiences of the sick person. One critic, who speaks from both a medical and anthropological background, suggests that Western physicians should be trained to treat sickness in the context of the patient's culture and psychology (Kleinman, 1978:68). While such attentiveness to the illness experi-ence would probably produce a more humane treatment of patients, it is doubtful that it would satisfy the patient's desire for meaning. The Western medical paradigm is based upon some presuppositions that cannot be readily reconciled with the belief systems of many patients, especially in a culturally and religiously pluralistic society. While physicians could be taught to respect the beliefs and values of, for example, Jehovah's Witnesses (a worthwhile task), it is improbable that this would overcome physicians' evaluation that their own paradigm is superior.

Thus the conflict is a basic one: The Western medical paradigm denies the validity of other paradigms, including the interpretive ones provided by religion, family, and the ethnic community. The secularization of health and healing is the process by which the Western medical system has come to conclude and defend that health, illness, or dying have no real meaning other than the biophysical realities determinable by empirical, rational means. Provision of meaning is allowed to institutions of the private sphere, as voluntary and purely subjective interpretations, only so long as that interpretive scheme does not interfere with biophysical treatment of the disease.

Summary

Theories of secularization figure importantly in contemporary sociology of religion, but there is little agreement about the meaning or significance of the concept. One interpretation views religion as undergoing a massive, irreversible decline. While this perspective meshes with the popular perception of overall religious decline, empirical evidence supporting the thesis is neither clear-cut nor conclusive. Nevertheless this perspective can point to important areas of religious decline.

Another interpretation of the contemporary religious situation is that the change does not represent decline but transformation. According to this perspective, religion has undergone a transformation in which its church-oriented modes of expression have declined, while other modes have gained ascendancy. Both Bellah's and Luckmann's interpretations of religious transformation emphasized that the emerging social forms of religion are more individual oriented and eclectic. Yet the conclusion that religion has undergone a "mere" transformation may be misleading.

The social location and role of religion (including nonchurch religion) in contemporary society suggest that important social changes have occurred. These changes have apparently resulted in qualitatively different patterns of relationships and meanings. Religion, as well as other institutions, has been profoundly affected by larger changes in society. While religion appears adaptable and vital in its numerous social forms, these larger changes raise some important questions about the continued ability of religion—and other institutions of the private sphere—to influence other important aspects of society. Particularly apparent is that major changes in the relationship of the individual to society have occurred, and any examination of the nature of religious change must be linked with an understanding of other major changes in the structure of society.

The secularization paradigm is particularly important because of its implications for the relationship between the individual and society. Several interpretations of this relationship are represented in the key themes of religious change theories: institutional differentiation, competing sources of legitimacy, rationalization, and privatization. Assessing these projections about the individual-to-society relationship is one of the important research tasks of modern sociology of religion.

Analysis of the secularization of health and healing illustrates these processes. Western medicine has become highly differentiated from other institutions, and specialized physicians have gained effective monopoly over healing services. Medicine has also become increasingly rationalized, both in the content of medical knowledge and practice and in the organization of the profession. Medicine has gained ascendancy over legal and religious institutions in legitimation and social control, as evidenced by the medicalization of deviance. Finally, elements of meaning and belonging in the treatment of illness have been privatized; they are considered irrelevant to medical practice and relegated to private sphere agents such as the family. These processes in one institutional sphere illustrate some of the broader issues raised by the secularization thesis.

Recommended Readings

Articles

Robert N. Bellah. "Religious Evolution." *American Sociological Review* 29 (3), 1964:358–374; reprinted in Robertson (1969) reader and Bobbs-Merrill reprints.

Roland Robertson. "Religious and Sociological Factors in the Analysis of Secularization." In A. Eister, ed. *Changing Perspectives in the Scientific Study of Religion*. New York: Wiley, 1974:41–60.

Larry Shiner. "The Concept of Secularization in Empirical Research." *Journal for the Scientific Study of Religion* 6, 1967:207–220; reprinted in Faulkner (1972) and Newman (1974) readers.

Books

Peter Berger. *The Sacred Canopy: Elements of a Sociological Theory of Religion*. Garden City, N.Y.: Doubleday, 1967. Berger analyzes the impact of rationalization, privatism, and especially pluralism upon traditional religious meaning systems.

Richard Fenn. *Toward a Theory of Secularization*. Society for the Scientific Study of Religion, Monograph 1, 1978. Fenn's theory, while not well integrated, raises important issues of the relationship between the process of secularization and civil religion, emerging religious movements, and legal consternation over what is "religious."

Thomas Luckmann. *The Invisible Religion: The Problem of Religion in Modern Society*. New York: Macmillan, 1967. Luckmann's essay explores the changing social bases of religion, suggesting that modern society's chief mode of religiosity is a privatized "invisible religion."

David Martin. *A General Theory of Secularization*. New York: Harper & Row, 1978. Martin's analysis emphasizes patterns of church-state relations in explaining secularization. His model incorporates factors such as pluralism versus monopolism, church-state relations and civil religions, and internal versus external perceived sources of opposition—in interpreting a wide range of cross-cultural and historical examples.

Bryan Wilson. *Contemporary Transformations of Religion*. London: Oxford University Press, 1976. Originally presented as a lecture series, this book develops Wilson's analysis of secularization. Particularly interesting is his interpretation of whether contemporary religious movements counteract or promote further secularization.

Epilogue

Weber closed his work on the Protestant ethic with an almost prophetic statement, wondering if society were heading toward the ultimate nullity of a totally rationalized, disenchanted world. In the preceding chapter on secularization, we explored this and related theses about the future of religion. Following Weber and Durkheim, we have used our examination of religion to provide a picture of the modern world and the individual's place in it.

Events of recent years make the sociology of religion a particularly helpful approach to understanding this relationship between individual and society. In the second half of the twentieth century, just as some observers were predicting that religion was declining and would virtually disappear, new religious movements arose among the very sectors of society that were supposed to be most secularized. The new religious movements highlight a number of questions about the future of religion: Do they presage new forms of individual-to-society relationship? Do they highlight individual autonomy, or are they new forms of authoritarianism? Do they represent religion's potential for bringing about social change, or are they so privatized that they exemplify the disempowerment of individuals in modern society? These questions remain to be addressed by further sociological research.

Similarly the issue of religion's role in modern societal coherence is critical. Studies of civil religions, nationalism, political messianism, and church-state relations in modern and modernizing societies will be useful to our understanding of this issue. We need to know more about fundamental processes such as legitimacy and authority in the context of modern societies. Contemporary sociology of religion has the potential to contribute to our understanding of these important topics.

Although these themes suggest that our focus must be broader than the narrow, institutionally specific sociology of religion, much is yet to be learned from the study of church-oriented religion. Religious organizations continue to be important in the lives of many individuals; their membership, organization, and basis of social support make religious institutions perhaps the most important kind of voluntary association in the United States, and their direct and indirect influences in society are still worth studying. In addition to official religion and religiosity, however, sociologists also need to study nonofficial religion and religiosity. We have been too quick to accept the official model of religion in our research (just as sociology of medicine uncritically accepted the medical profession's definition of health and illness as the basis of its approach). More importantly, the sociology of religious institutions needs to ask larger questions. Rather than focus on religious organizations (e.g., parishes or denominations) as ends in themselves, we must ask: Of what larger phenomenon is this an example? The model of religious collectivities presented in Chapter 5 illustrates such a broader perspective. Thus the concepts of church and sect can be seen as broad developmental models of *any* group in particular kinds of tension with its social environment.

Sociology has strived for an objective approach to social reality. But sociologists of religion, while guided by this ideal, sometimes find themselves uncomfortable with its implications. Specifically, we cannot assume the superiority or necessity of religious world views; at the same time, however, we wonder about the direction society would take if it were utterly nonreligious. Without higher sources of authority for appeal, is legitimacy in modern society to be based upon raw power and domination? What becomes of human freedom in the face of powerful public sphere institutions, especially those of modern scope such as huge multinational corporations, which are effectively free of normative constraints? There is no necessary religious "solution" to these issues, but the sociology of religion is uniquely poised to raise them.

Doing a Literature Search in the Sociology of Religion

Students who are preparing term papers or theses will find these resources especially useful.

1. The main journals and yearbooks in the sociology of religon are:
   Annual Review of the Social Sciences of Religion.
       The Hague, 1977 to date.
   Archives de Sociologie des Religions.
       Paris, 1956 to date. Many articles in English.
   International Yearbook for the Sociology of Religion.
       Koln-Opladen, 1965–1975.
   Journal for the Scientific Study of Religion.
       U.S.A., 1961 to date.
   A Sociological Yearbook of Religion in Britain.
       London, 1970 through 1975.
   Review of Religious Research.
       U.S.A., 1959 to date.
   Social Compass.
       The Hague and Louvain, 1953 to date. Most articles in English.
   Sociological Analysis.
       U.S.A., 1939 to date.
   Also, *Current Sociology* (International Sociological Association) has occasional entire issues with annotated bibliographies on religion.
   Other sometimes useful periodicals are religious journals such as *Commentary, Commonweal, Christianity and Crisis,* and *Cross Currents.*

2. These journals are indexed or abstracted in:
   Religion Index (after 1977), previously *Index to Religious Periodical Literature; Social Sciences Index,* previously *Social Science and Humanities Index; Sociological Abstracts.*

3. Newspapers with frequent good religious coverage include:
   New York Times, indexed in *New York Times Index.*
   National Catholic Reporter, indexed in *Catholic Periodical and Literature Index.*

4. Bibliographies, Dictionaries, and Encyclopedias:
   Bibliographic Index; an index of compiled bibliographies.
   Encyclopaedia Brittanica; includes good coverage of religious history.
   Encyclopedia of American Religions (2 volumes), 1978, ed. J. Melton.
       Wilmington, Delaware: Consortium.
   The Oxford Dictionary of the Christian Church, 1958, ed. F. L. Cross. London: Oxford.

   Remember too that a good source of references is the bibliography of a book or article on the specific topic, such as the bibliography of this text. Bibliographies in journal articles are generally even more current than references in books.

5. Unpublished papers.

Serious students in the sociology of religion should attend the meetings of the professional associations and obtain copies of unpublished papers presented at these meetings. These papers are usually abstracted in a booklet available to registrants or in *Sociological Abstracts*. Professional associations have reduced student rates for membership and conference registration.

Especially recommended are the meetings of:

The Society for the Scientific Study of Religion.

The Religious Research Association.

These two group meet jointly, usually in October; check the current issues of *Journal for the Scientific Study of Religion* or *Review of Religious Research* for program announcements.

Association for the Sociology of Religion; meets jointly, usually in August, with the Society for the Study of Social Problems and the American Sociological Association; check *Sociological Analysis* for program announcements.

Film Resources

The Bible Belt: A CBS White Paper—The Politics of the Second Coming. Canadian Broadcasting Company, 1972, 90 minutes, color.
  Examines the rise of fundamentalist Protestant sects in Western Canada during the 1920s and 1930s and their impact on Canadian politics then and now.
Black Muslims Speak From America. BBC/Time/Life, 1969, 33 minutes, black and white.
  Interviews with seven young Black Muslims about their discontent and their beliefs. Somewhat dated (applies to their more militant nationalist, antiwhite period) but very informative.
Essene. Zipporah, 1972, 86 minutes, color.
  A Frederick Wiseman cinema vérité documentary of monastic life; no narration.
The Gospel According to St. Matthew. CCM Films/Macmillan, 1964, 136 minutes, black and white.
  Portrays Jesus as a compassionate leader of radical social reform.
Hare Krishna. KEI Productions, 1973, 52 minutes, color.
  The Krsña Consciousness movement in America. Devotees in several locations discuss their philosophy and practices.
The Hasidim. Vedo Films, 1972, 29 minutes, color.
  Film sequences of synagogue, home, school, and neighborhood of Lubavitcher Hasidim in New York.
Holy Ghost People. McGraw-Hill, 1968, 53 minutes, black and white.
  Describes beliefs and practices of a snake-handling Pentecostal church and shows candid shots of congregation during service, including snake handling and glossolalia. Dramatic ending when the leader is bitten by a rattlesnake.
The Hutterites. National Film Board of Canada, 1964, 28 minutes, black and white.
  Documentary (without shooting restrictions) of life in a Hutterite colony in western Canada (see also a more recent color documentary, *Hutterites,* Canadian Broadcasting Company).
The Jesus Trip—The Search for Spiritual Values. BBC/Time/Life, 1972, 35 minutes, color.
  Portrayal of early years of Jesus movement, their proselyting and communal life.
The Long Search. BBC/Time/Life, series of 13 videotapes, 1977, 52 minutes each, color.
  A documentary on world religions and new religions, narrated by Donald Eyre (who is irritatingly obtrusive in several instances). Especially useful are: *Orthodox Christianity: The Rumanian Solution,* which is very useful for illustrating rich symbolism and ritual, the pervasiveness of religion in people's lives, and the place of religion in one Communist country; and *African Religion: Zulu Zion,* which focuses on new religions in South Africa, emphasizing the importance of dreams, ancestors, and place. Other useful films in the series include *Protestant Spirit, U.S.A.; Catholicism;* and *Judaism.* The film on *Alternate Lifestyles in California* is disappointingly shallow.

Lord of the Universe. TVTV, 1973, videotape, 30 minutes, color.
> A not very sympathetic documentary on the Divine Light Mission of Guru Maharaj Ji.

Louise. WGBHTV, 1974, 30 minutes, color.
> Focuses on a black Baptist in the rural South. Part of a 12-film series, *Religion in America.* Other especially recommended titles in the series include: *Meeting in the Air* (about a pentecostal service) and *Lubavitch* (about Hasidic Jews).

Martin Luther King: A Man of Peace. Journal Films, 1968, 30 minutes, color.
> Shows portions of sermons, speeches, and interviews with Martin Luther King, Jr., linking his philosophy of nonviolent resistance with biblical themes.

Meditation: Yoga, T'ai Chi, and Other Spiritual Trips. Document Associates, n.d., 22 minutes, color.
> Observations of three practices and interview with Alan Watts.

Minorities: In the Name of Religion. Coronet Films, 1972, 16 minutes, color.
> On the history and present problems of religious persecution and discrimination in America.

The New Klan. Corinth Films, 1978, 58 minutes. color.
> Vivid images of the contemporary Ku Klux Klan. Useful for discussing symbols and rituals in a quasi-religious secret society.

Occult: X Factor or Fraud. Documentary. n.d., 22 minutes, color.
> Observes part of a black mass, a New York City psychic dimensions center, moving-candle ritual, and other occult phenomena.

One Way. Stephen La Roque, 1978, 50 minutes, black and white.
> A delightful and not particularly nasty satire on "seekers" in various new religious sects and cults. Focuses on a group with remarkable resemblance to est.

People, Power and Change. University of Minnesota, 1968, 28 minutes, color.
> Linked to Gerlach and Hine's (1970) book, discusses the structure of social movements using Black Power and Protestant neopentecostal movement as examples. Visually appealing but too preoccupied with "teaching" authors' points.

Religion and Politics. WCBS-TV/Holt, Rinehart & Winston, 1969, 30 minutes, black and white.
> C. Eric Lincoln discusses the role of religion in social protest of blacks in this country, focusing on the period 1945–1954.

A Time for Burning. McGraw-Hill, 1966, 56 minutes, black and white.
> Documents the actual events in Omaha, Nebraska, in 1965 when the pastor of an all-white Lutheran congregation suggested interchurch visitation with Negro congregations. Shows the intensity of the situation and polarization of members. Somewhat too long and slow-paced for classroom use but realistic portrayal of issues. Some students think the issues are out of date, but whether they are is in itself an interesting topic.

To Find Our Life. University of California in Los Angeles, 1969, 65 minutes, color.
> Huichol Indians on a ritual journey to obtain peyote; ritual use and reactions. A sympathetic portrait of this syncretic native American religion.

Triumph of the Will. McGraw-Hill, 1936, 120 minutes, black and white.
> A Nazi propaganda piece documenting the Sixth Party Congress in 1934. Very useful for discussing the nature of ritual, political messianism, and whether movements like Nazism under Hitler are "religion."

The Ultimate Trip. NBC, EE, 1970, 32 minutes, color.
> Jesus People discuss their "trip" and new life. Refers to early stages of the Jesus movement.

Welcome to Holyland. Glen Farber, videotape, 25 minutes, color.
> A fascinating look at an American shrine of popular religion, its patrons and creators.

References

Abercrombie, Nicholas, John Baker, Sebastian Brett and Jane Foster
  1970 "Superstition and religion: The god of gaps." Pp. 93–129 in D. Martin and M. Hill (eds.), Sociological Yearbook of Religion in Britain. Volume 3. London: SCM.
Aberle, David
  1962 "A note on relative deprivation theory as applied to millenarian and other cult movements." Pp. 209–214 in S. Thrupp (ed.), Millennial Dreams in Action. The Hague: Mouton.
  1966 The Peyote Religion Among the Navaho. Chicago: Aldine.
Abramson, Harold
  1973 Ethnic Diversity in Catholic America. New York: Wiley.
Ahlstrom, Sidney
  1972 A Religious History of the American People. New Haven: Yale University Press.
  1978 "From Sinai to the Golden Gate: The liberation of religion in the Occident." Pp. 3–22 in J. Needleman and G. Baker (eds.), Understanding the New Religions. New York: Seabury.
Alfred, Randall
  1976 "The church of Satan." Pp. 180–202 in C. Glock and R. Bellah (eds.), The New Religious Consciousness. Berkeley: University of California Press.
Allon, Natalie
  1973 "Group dieting rituals." Society 10, 2:36–42.
Almerick, Paulina
  1972 "Spain." Pp. 459–477 in H. Mol (ed.), Western Religion: A Country by Country Sociological Inquiry. The Hague: Mouton.
Alston, John P.
  1972 "Review of the polls." Journal for the Scientific Study of Religion 11, 2:180–186.
AmaraSingham, Lorna Rhodes
  1978 "The misery of the embodied." Pp. 101–126 in J. Hoch-Smith and A. Spring (eds.), Women in Ritual and Symbolic Roles. New York: Plenum.
Anderson, Alan and Raymond Gordon
  1978 "Witchcraft and the status of women—the case of England." British Journal of Sociology 29:171–184.
Annals of the American Academy of Political and Social Science
  1979 Volume 446: The Uneasy Boundary: Church and State.
Anthony, Dick and Thomas Robbins
  1975 "From symbolic realism to structuralism." Journal for the Scientific Study of Religion 14:403–414.
  1978 "The effect of detente on the rise of new religions: The Unification Church of Reverend Sun Myung Moon." Pp. 80–100 in J. Needleman and G. Baker (eds.), Understanding the New Religions. New York: Seabury.
Aron, Raymond
  1968 Main Currents in Sociological Thought. Volume 1. Tr. R. Howard and H. Weaver. Garden City, N.Y.: Doubleday.
Atchley, Robert
  1980 The Social Forces in Later Life. Belmont, Calif.: Wadsworth.

Bahr, Howard
  1970 "Aging and religious disaffiliation." Social Forces 49:59–71.
Bainbridge, William S.
  1978 Satan's Power: A Deviant Psychotherapy Cult. Berkeley: University of California Press.
Balch, Robert W. and David Taylor
  1976 "Salvation in a U.F.O." Psychology Today 10:58–66.
  1977 "Seekers and saucers: The role of the cultic milieu in joining a U.F.O. cult." American Behavioral Scientist 20, 6:839–860.
Barkan, Steven
  1979 "Religion and courts in crisis." Unpublished paper presented to Association for the Sociology of Religion.
Barker, Eileen
  1977 "Inside the Unification Church: Followers of the Reverend Sun Moon in Britain." Unpublished paper presented to Fourteenth Conference Internationale de Sociologie Religieuse.
Barkun, Michael
  1974 Disaster and the Millennium. New Haven: Yale University Press.
Barnett, Homer G.
  1957 Indian Shakers: A Messianic Cult of the Pacific Northwest. Carbondale: Southern Illinois University Press.
Barrett, David
  1968 Schism and Renewal in Africa. Nairobi: Oxford University Press.
Barrett, Leonard
  1974 Soul Force: African Heritage in Afro-American Religion. Garden City, N.Y.: Doubleday.
Beach, Stephen
  1977 "Religion and political change in Northern Ireland." Sociological Analysis 38, 1:37–48.
Becker, Howard
  1932 Systematic Sociology on the Basis of the Beziehungslehre and Gebildelehre of Leopold Van Wiese. New York: Wiley.
  1963 Outsiders: Studies in the Sociology of Deviance. New York: Free Press.
Beckett, J. C.
  1966 A Short History of Ireland. London: Hutchinson.
Beckford, James
  1975a "Religious organization." Current Sociology 21, 2.
  1975b The Trumpet of Prophecy: A Sociological Study of the Jehovah's Witnesses. New York: Halsted-Wiley.
  1978a "Accounting for conversion." British Journal of Sociology 29, 2:249–262.
  1978b "Cults and cures." Unpublished paper presented to Ninth World Congress for Sociology, Research Committee for the Sociology of Religion.
Bell, Daniel
  1976 The Cultural Contradictions of Capitalism. New York: Basic Books.
  1977 "The return of the sacred? The argument on the future of religion." British Journal of Sociology 28, 4:419–449.
Bellah, Robert N.
  1964 "Religious evolution." American Sociological Review 29, 3:358–374.
  1967 "Civil religion in America." Daedalus 96:1–21.
  1970 "Christianity and symbolic realism." Journal for the Scientific Study of Religion 9, 2:89–96.
  1973 Emile Durkheim on Morality and Society. Chicago: University of Chicago Press.
  1974 "American civil religion in the 1970's." Pp. 139–160 in R. Richey and D. Jones (eds.), American Civil Religion. New York: Harper & Row.
  1975 The Broken Covenant: American Civil Religion in Time of Trial. New York: Seabury.
  1976 "New religious consciousness and the crisis of modernity." Pp. 333–352 in C. Glock and R. Bellah (eds.), The New Religious Consciousness. Berkeley: University of California Press.
  1978 "Religion and legitimation in the American Republic." Society 15:16–23.
Benedict, Ruth
  1934 Patterns of Culture. Boston: Houghton Mifflin.
Bennett, David
  1969 Demagogues in the Depression. New Brunswick, N.J.: Rutgers University Press.

Berger, Bennett M.
1969 "The new stage of American man—almost endless adolescence." New York Times Magazine, November 2, 1969:32,33.

Berger, Peter
1958 "Sectarianism and religious sociation." American Journal of Sociology 64:41–44.
1961 The Noise of Solemn Assemblies: Christian Commitment and the Religious Establishment in America. Garden City, N.Y.: Doubleday.
1964 The Human Shape of Work. New York: Macmillan.
1967 The Sacred Canopy: Elements of a Sociological Theory of Religion. Garden City, N.Y.: Doubleday.
1969 A Rumor of Angels: Modern Society and the Rediscovery of the Supernatural. Garden City, N.Y.: Doubleday.
1974 "Second thoughts on substantive versus functional definitions of religion." Journal for the Scientific Study of Religion 13:125–134.

Berger, Peter, Brigitte Berger and Hansfried Kellner
1973 The Homeless Mind: Modernization and Consciousness. New York: Random House.

Berger, Peter and Thomas Luckmann
1963 "Sociology of religion and sociology of knowledge." Sociology and Social Research 47:417–427.
1966 The Social Construction of Reality: A Treatise in the Sociology of Knowledge. Garden City, N.Y.: Doubleday.

Berger, Peter and D. Nash
1962 "Church commitment in an American suburb—an analysis of the decision to join." Archives de Sociologie des Religions 13:105–120.

Berger, Stephen
1971 "The sects and the breakthrough into the modern world: On the centrality of the sects in Weber's Protestant ethic thesis." Sociological Quarterly 12:486–499.

Bird, Frederick
1978 "Charisma and ritual in new religious movements." Pp. 173–189 in J. Needleman and G. Baker (eds.), Understanding the New Religions. New York: Seabury.
1979 "The pursuit of innocence: New religious movements and moral accountability." Sociological Analysis 40, 4:335–346.

Birnbaum, Norman
1973 "Beyond Marx in the sociology of religion?" Pp. 5–70 in C. Glock and P. Hammond (eds.), Beyond the Classics? Essays in the Scientific Study of Religion. New York: Harper & Row.

Birnbaum, Norman and Gertrud Lenzer (eds.)
1969 Sociology and Religion: A Book of Readings. Englewood Cliffs, N.J.: Prentice-Hall.

Bittner, Egon
1968 "The structure of psychiatric influence." Mental Hygiene 52:423–430.

Borker, Ruth
1978 "To honor her head: Hats as a symbol of women's position in three evangelical churches in Edinburgh, Scotland." Pp. 55–73 in J. Hoch-Smith and A. Spring (eds.), Women in Ritual and Symbolic Roles. New York: Plenum.

Bouma, Gary D.
1973 "Beyond Lenski: A critical review of recent 'Protestant ethic' research." Journal for the Scientific Study of Religion 12, 2:141–155.

Brazier, Arthur
1969 Black Self-Determination: The Story of Woodlawn Organization. Grand Rapids: Eerdmans.

Briggs, Kenneth
1979 "Women and the Catholic Church," New York Times, Dec. 16.

Brittan, Arthur
1977 The Privatised World. London: Routledge & Kegan Paul.

Bromley, David and Anson D. Shupe
1979a "Moonies" in America: Cult, Church and Crusade. Beverly Hills, Calif.: Sage.
1979b "The Tnevnoc cult." Sociological Analysis 40, 4:361–366.

Brotz, Howard
1964 The Black Jews of Harlem. New York: Free Press.

Bumpass, Larry and James Sweet
  1970   "Differentials in marital instability, 1970." American Sociological Review 37:754–766.
Burke, Kenneth
  1935   Permanence and Change. New York: New Republic.
  1953   A Rhetoric of Motives. Englewood Cliffs, N.J.: Prentice-Hall.
Burkholder, John Richard
  1974   "The law knows no heresy: Marginal religious movements and the courts." Pp. 27–52 in I.
          Zaretsky and M. Leone (eds.), Religious Movements in Contemporary America. Princeton,
          N.J.: Princeton University Press.
Burnham, Kenneth
  1978   God Comes to America: Father Divine and the Peace Mission Movement. Boston: Lambeth.
Calley, Malcolm
  1965   God's People: West Indian Pentecostal Sects in England. London: Oxford University Press.
Campbell, Colin
  1971   Toward a Sociology of Irreligion. London: Macmillan.
  1977   "Clarifying the cult." British Journal of Sociology 28, 3:375–388.
  1978   "The secret religion of the educated classes." Sociological Analysis 39, 2:146–156.
Campbell, Ernest Q. and Thomas F. Pettigrew
  1959   Christians in Racial Crisis: A Study of Little Rock's Ministry. Washington, D.C.: Public
          Affairs Press.
Carmody, Denise
  1979   Women and World Religions. Nashville: Abingdon.
Castenada, Carlos
  1968   The Teachings of Don Juan: A Jacqui Way of Knowledge. Berkeley: University of California
          Press.
Cherry, Conrad
  1969   "Two American sacred ceremonies." American Quarterly 21:739–754.
Clark, Elizabeth and Herbert Richardson (eds.)
  1977   Women and Religion: A Feminist Sourcebook of Christian Thought. New York: Harper &
          Row.
Clark, S. D.
  1948   Church and Sect in Canada. Toronto: University of Toronto Press.
Clarke, Aidan
  1967   "The colonisation of Ulster and the rebellion of 1641." Pp. 189–203 in T. W. Moody and F. X.
          Martin (eds.), The Course of Irish History. Cork: Mercier.
Clayton, Richard and James Gladden
  1974   "The five dimensions of religiosity: Toward demythologizing a sacred artifact." Journal for
          the Scientific Study of Religion 13, 2:135–143.
Cleage, Albert B., Jr.
  1967   The Black Messiah. New York: Sheed and Ward.
Cohn, Norman
  1970   The Pursuit of the Millennium: Revolutionary Millenarians and Mystical Anarchists of the
          Middle Ages. New York: Oxford University Press.
Coleman, James S.
  1956   "Social cleavage and religious conflict." The Journal of Social Issues 12:44–56.
Coleman, John A.
  1970   "Civil religion." Sociological Analysis 31:67–77.
Conrad, Peter and Joseph W. Schneider
  1980   Deviance and Medicalization: From Badness to Sickness. St. Louis: Mosby.
Cooper, Lee R.
  1974   " 'Publish' or perish: Negro Jehovah's Witnesses' adaptation in the ghetto." Pp. 700–721 in
          I. Zaretsky and M. Leone (eds.), Religious Movements in Contemporary America.
          Princeton, N.J.: Princeton University Press.

Coser, Lewis
  1973 "The militant collective: Jesuits and Leninists." Social Research 40, 1:110–128.
  1974 Greedy Institutions: Patterns of Undivided Commitment. New York: Free Press.
Cox, Harvey
  1965 The Secular City. New York: Macmillan.
Crapanzano, Vincent and Vivian Garrison (eds.)
  1977 Case Studies in Spirit Possession. New York: Wiley.
Cross, Robert D.
  1958 The Emergence of Liberal Catholicism in America. Cambridge: Cambridge University Press.
Cross, Whitney
  1965 The Burned-Over District: The Social and Intellectual History of Enthusiastic Religion in Western New York, 1800–1950. New York: Harper & Row.
Culpepper, Emily
  1978 "The spiritual movement in radical feminist consciousness." Pp. 220–234 in J. Needleman and G. Baker (eds.), Understanding the New Religions. New York: Seabury.
Cutler, Donald R. (ed.)
  1968 The Religious Situation: 1968. Boston: Beacon.
Daly, Mary
  1973 Beyond God the Father. Boston: Beacon.
  1978 Gyn/Ecology: The Meta-ethics of Radical Feminism. Boston: Beacon.
D'Antonio, William V. and Frederick B. Pike (eds.)
  1964 Religion, Revolution and Reform: New Forces for Change in Latin America. New York: Praeger.
Davidson, Laurie and Laura Kramer Gordon
  1979 The Sociology of Gender. Chicago: Rand McNally.
Davis, David Brian
  1960 "Some themes of counter-subversion: An analysis of anti-Masonic, anti-Catholic, and anti-Mormon literature." Mississippi Historical Review 48, 2:205–224.
Davis, Kingsley and Wilbert Moore
  1945 "Some principles of social stratification." American Sociological Review 10:242–249.
Demerath, N. J., III
  1965 Social Class in American Protestantism. Chicago: Rand McNally.
Deren, Maya
  1970 Divine Horsemen. The Voodoo Gods of Haiti. New York: Chelsea House.
Desroche, Henri
  1962 Marxisme et Religions. Paris: Presses Universitaires de France.
  1969 "Socialism and the sociology of Christianity." Pp. 215–225 in N. Birnbaum and G. Lenzer (eds.), Sociology and Religion. Englewood Cliffs, N.J.: Prentice-Hall.
Dollard, John
  [1937] Caste and Class in a Southern Town. Garden City, N.Y.: Doubleday.
  1949
Dougherty, Molly C.
  1978 "Southern lay midwives as ritual specialists." Pp. 151–164 in J. Hoch-Smith and A. Spring (eds.), Women in Ritual and Symbolic Roles. New York: Plenum.
Douglas, Mary
  1966 Purity and Danger: An Analysis of Concepts of Pollution and Taboo. London: Routledge & Kegan Paul.
  1970 Natural Symbols: Explorations in Cosmology. New York: Random House.
Downton, James V.
  1979 Sacred Journeys: The Conversion of Young Americans to Divine Light Mission. New York: Columbia University Press.
Ducey, Michael H.
  1977 Sunday Morning: Aspects of Urban Ritual. New York: Free Press.

Durkheim, Emile
  1938 The Rules of the Sociological Method. Chicago: University of Chicago Press.
  [1897] Suicide: A Study in Sociology. Tr. J. A. Spaulding and G. Simpson. Glencoe, Ill.: Free
  1951 Press.
  [1893] The Division of Labor in Society. Tr. G. Simpson. New York: Free Press.
  1964
  [1915] Elementary Forms of the Religious Life. Tr. J. W. Swain. New York: Free Press.
  1965
  [1898] "Individualism and the intellectuals." Tr. S. Lukes. Political Studies 17:14–30.
  1969
Dynes, Russell
  1955 "Church-sect typology and socio-economic status." American Sociological Review 20,
      5:555–560.
Earle, John, Dean Knudsen and Donald Shriver
  1976 Spindles and Spires: A Re-Study of Religion and Social Change in Gastonia. Atlanta: John
      Knox.
Ehrenreich, Barbara and Dierdre English
  1973 Witches, Midwives and Nurses: A History of Women Healers. New York: Feminist Press.
Eisenstadt, S. N.
  1969 "The Protestant ethic thesis." Pp. 297–317 in R. Robertson (ed.), Sociology of Religion.
      Baltimore: Penguin.
Eisenstadt, S. N. (ed.)
  1968 The Protestant Ethic and Modernization: A Comparative View. New York: Basic Books.
Eisenstadt, S. N. and Stein Rokkan (eds.)
  1973 Building States and Nations. Beverly Hills, Calif.: Sage.
Eister, Allan (ed.)
  1974 Changing Perspectives in the Scientific Study of Religion. New York: Wiley.
Elazar, Daniel
  1976 Community and Polity: Organizational Dynamics of American Jewry. Philadelphia: Jewish
      Public Service of America.
Eliade, Mircea
  1958 Rites and Symbols of Initiation: The Mysteries of Birth and Rebirth. New York: Harper &
      Row.
  1959 The Sacred and the Profane: The Nature of Religion. Tr. W. R. Trask. New York: Harcourt,
      Brace & World.
  1964 Shamanism: Archaic Techniques of Ecstasy. Tr. W. R. Trask. New York: Pantheon.
Elkind, David
  1964 "Age changes in the meaning of religious identity." Review of Religious Research 6, 1:36–
      40.
Ellwood, Robert S., Jr.
  1973 One Way: The Jesus Movement and Its Meaning. Englewood Cliffs, N.J.: Prentice-Hall.
  1978 "Emergent religion in America: An historical perspective." Pp. 267–284 in J. Needleman
      and G. Baker (eds.), Understanding the New Religions. New York: Seabury.
  1979 Alternative Altars: Unconventional and Eastern Spirituality in America. Chicago: Univer-
      sity of Chicago Press.
Elzey, Wayne
  1975 "Liminality and symbiosis in popular American Protestantism." Journal of the American
      Academy of Religion 43:741–756.
Fabian, Johannes
  1974 "Genres in an emerging tradition: An anthropological approach to religious communica-
      tion." Pp. 249–272 in A. Eister (ed.), Changing Perspectives in the Scientific Study of
      Religion. New York: Wiley.
Faulkner, Joseph E., ed.
  1972 Religion's Influence in Contemporary Society. Columbus, Ohio: Charles Merrill.

Faulkner, J. E. and Gordon DeJong
1966 "Religiosity in 5-D: An empirical analysis." Social Forces 45:246-254.
Fauset, Arthur H.
1944 Black Gods of the Metropolis. Philadelphia: University of Pennsylvania Press.
Fenn, Richard
1972 "Toward a new sociology of religion." Journal for the Scientific Study of Religion 11, 1:16–32.
1974 "Religion and the legitimation of social systems." Pp. 143–161 in A. Eister (ed.), Changing Perspectives in the Scientific Study of Religion. New York: Wiley.
1978 Toward a Theory of Secularization. Monograph Series 1. Storrs, Conn.: Society for the Scientific Study of Religion.
Festinger, Leon
1957 A Theory of Cognitive Dissonance. Palo Alto, Calif.: Stanford University Press.
Festinger, Leon, Henry W. Riecken and Stanley Schachter
1956 When Prophecy Fails. New York: Harper & Row.
Feuerbach, Ludwig
[1841] The Essence of Christianity. Tr. G. Eliot. New York: Harper & Row.
1957
Fichter, Joseph
1951a Dynamics of a City Church. Chicago: University of Chicago Press.
1951b Southern Parish. Chicago: University of Chicago Press.
1954 Social Relations in the Urban Parish. Chicago: University of Chicago Press.
1975 The Catholic Cult of the Paraclete. New York: Sheed and Ward.
Fischler, Claude
1971 "Astrology and French society: The dialectic of archaism and modernity." Pp. 281–293 in E. Tiryakian (ed.), On the Margin of the Visible. New York: Wiley.
Flora, Cornelia Butler
1976 Pentecostalism in Colombia. Rutherford, N.J.: Fairleigh Dickinson University Press.
Frazier, E. Franklin
1974 The Negro Church in America. New York: Schocken.
Freidson, Eliot
1970 Profession of Medicine. New York: Dodd, Mead.
Freund, Peter
1969 "A conceptual framework for the analysis of conversion." Unpublished doctoral dissertation, New School for Social Research, New York.
Friedl, Ernestine
1975 Women and Men: An Anthropologist's View. New York: Holt, Rinehart & Winston.
Fukuyama, Yoshio
1961 "The major dimensions of church membership." Review of Religious Research 2:154–161.
Gallup Poll
1975 Religion in America: 1975. Princeton, N.J.: Gallup International.
1976a "Americans taking up religious, spiritual experimentation." Princeton, N.J.: Gallup International. See also New York Times, November 18, 1976.
1976b Religion in America. 1976. Princeton, N.J.: Gallup International.
1978 Religion in America, 1977–78. Princeton, N.J.: American Institute of Public Opinion.
Gallup Poll and Princeton Religion Research Center
1978 The Unchurched Americans. Princeton, N.J.: Gallup International.
Gallup Poll/Social Surveys, Limited
1968 International Survey of Religious Beliefs: 1948–1968. Princeton, N.J.: Gallup International.
Gardner, Hugh
1978 The Children of Prosperity. New York: St. Martins.
Garrett, William R.
1975 "Maligned mysticism: The maledicted career of Troeltsch's third type." Sociological Analysis 36, 3:205–223.

Geertz, Clifford
1957 "Ritual and social change: A Javanese example." American Anthropologist 59:23–54.
1963 "The integrative revolution: Primordial sentiments and civil politics in the new states." Pp. 105–157 in C. Geertz (ed.), Old Societies and New States. New York: Free Press.
1964 "Ideology as a cultural system." Pp. 47–76 in D. Apter (ed.), Ideology and Discontent. New York: Free Press.
1966 "Religion as a cultural system." Pp. 1–46 in M. Banton (ed.), Anthropological Approaches to the Study of Religion. London: Tavistock.
1973 The Interpretation of Cultures. New York: Basic Books.
Gellner, Ernest
1974 Legitimation of Belief. Cambridge: Cambridge University Press.
Genovese, Eugene
1974 Roll, Jordan, Roll: The World the Slaves Made. New York: Pantheon.
Gerlach, Luther
1974 "Pentecostalism: Revolution or counter-revolution." Pp. 669–699 in I. Zaretsky and M. Leone (eds.), Religious Movements in Contemporary America. Princeton, N.J.: Princeton University Press.
Gerlach, Luther and Virginia Hine
1968 "Five factors crucial to the growth and spread of a modern religious movement." Journal for the Scientific Study of Religion 7, 1:23–40.
1970 People, Power, and Change: Movements of Social Transformation. Indianapolis: Bobbs-Merrill.
Glanz, David and Michael Harrison
1977 "Varieties of identity transformation: The case of newly Orthodox Jews." Unpublished paper presented to Israeli Sociological Association.
Glasner, Peter E.
1977 The Sociology of Secularisation: A Critique of a Concept. London: Routledge & Kegan Paul.
Glazer, Barney G. and Anselm L. Strauss
1965 Awareness of Dying. Chicago: Aldine.
Glazer, Nathan
1957 American Judaism. Chicago: University of Chicago Press.
Glazer-Malbin, Nona
1976 "Housework." Signs 1:905–922.
Glock, Charles Y.
[1962] "On the study of religious commitment." Research Supplement, Religious Education 57, 4.
1965 Reprinted in C. Glock and R. Stark, Religion and Society in Tension. Chicago: Rand McNally.
1973 "On the origin and evolution of religious groups." Pp. 207–220 in C. Glock (ed.), Religion in Sociological Perspective. Belmont, Calif.: Wadsworth.
Glock, Charles Y. (ed.)
1973 Religion in Sociological Perspective. Belmont, Calif.: Wadsworth.
Glock, Charles and Robert Bellah (eds.)
1976 The New Religious Consciousness. Berkeley: University of California Press.
Glock, Charles, Benjamin Ringer and Earl Babbie
1967 To Comfort and to Challenge: A Dilemma of the Contemporary Church. Berkeley: University of California Press.
Glock, Charles and Rodney Stark
1966 Christian Beliefs and Anti-Semitism. New York: Harper & Row.
Glock, Charles and Robert Wuthnow
1979 "Departures from conventional religion: The nominally religious, the nonreligious, and the alternatively religious." Pp. 47–68 in R. Wuthnow (ed.), The Religious Dimension: New Directions in Quantitative Research. New York: Academic Press.
Goffman, Erving
1961 Asylums. Garden City, N.Y.: Doubleday.
1963 Stigma: Notes on the Management of Spoiled Identity. Englewood Cliffs, N.J.: Spectrum.
Goldenberg, Judith
1974 "Epilogue: The coming of Lilith." Pp.341–343 in R. Ruether (ed.), Religion and Sexism. New York: Simon & Schuster.

Gonzalez-Wippler, Migene
   1975   Santería: African Magic in Latin America. Garden City, N.Y.: Doubleday.
Goode, Erich
   1967   "Some critical observations on the church-sect dimension." Journal for the Scientific Study
          of Religion 6:69–77. Followed by commentaries, N. J. Demerath and Allan Eister, pp. 77–90.
Gordon, David
   1974   "The Jesus People: Identity synthesis." Urban Life and Culture 3, 2:159–178.
Gorsuch, Richard and D. Aleshire
   1974   "Christian faith and ethnic prejudice." Journal for the Scientific Study of Religion 13:281–
          307.
Gouldner, Alvin
   1976   The Dialectic of Ideology and Technology. New York: Seabury.
Gray, Robert and David O. Moberg
   1977   The Church and the Older Person. Grand Rapids: Eerdmans.
Greeley, Andrew
   1963   Religion and Career: A Study of College Graduates. New York: Sheed and Ward.
   1964   "The Protestant ethic: Time for a moratorium." Sociological Analysis 25:20–33.
   1971   Why Can't They Be Like Us?: America's White Ethnic Groups. New York: Dutton.
   1972a The Denominational Society: A Sociological Approach to Religion in America. Glenview,
          Ill.: Scott, Foresman.
   1972b Unsecular Man: The Persistence of Religion. New York: Schocken.
   1974   Ecstasy: A Way of Knowing. Englewood Cliffs, N.J.: Prentice-Hall.
   1975   The Sociology of the Paranormal: A Reconnaissance. Beverly Hills, Calif.: Sage.
   1976   "The 1975 H. Paul Douglass lecture: Council or encyclical?" Review of Religious Research
          18:3–24.
   1977   The American Catholic: A Social Portrait. New York: Basic Books.
   1979   "Towards a secular theory of religious behavior." Unpublished paper presented to Ameri-
          can Sociological Association.
Green, Robert W. (ed.)
   1959   Protestantism and Capitalism: The Weber Thesis and Its Critics. Boston: Heath.
Greil, Arthur
   1977   "Previous disposition and conversion to perspectives of social and religious movements."
          Sociological Analysis 38, 2:115–125.
Habermas, Jurgen
   1971   Knowledge and Human Interests. Boston: Beacon.
   1975   Legitimation Crisis. Tr. T. McCarthy. Boston: Beacon.
Hadden, Jeffrey K.
   1969   The Gathering Storm in the Churches: The Widening Gap Between Clergy and Laymen.
          Garden City, N.Y.: Doubleday.
Hall, John R.
   1979   "The apocalypse at Jonestown." Unpublished paper presented to the American Sociological
          Association.
Hamilton, Charles
   1972   The Black Preacher in America. New York: William Morrow.
Hammond, John L.
   1979   The Politics of Benevolence: Revival Religion and American Voting Behavior. Norwood,
          N.J.: Ablex.
Hammond, Phillip
   1974   "Religious pluralism and Durkheim's integration thesis." Pp. 115–142 in A. Eister (ed.),
          Changing Perspectives in the Scientific Study of Religion. New York: Wiley.
   1976   "The sociology of American civil religion: A bibliographical essay." Sociological Analysis
          37, 2:169–182.
Hammond, Phillip and Robert Mitchell
   1965   "The segmentation of radicalism—the case of the Protestant campus ministries." American
          Journal of Sociology 71:133–143.
Happold, F. C.
   1970   Mysticism. Baltimore: Penguin.

Hargrove, Barbara
    1978   "Integrative and transformative religions." Pp. 257–266 in J. Needleman and G. Baker (eds.), Understanding the New Religions. New York: Seabury.

Harris, Louis and Associates
    1975   The Myths and Reality of Aging in America. Washington, D.C.: National Council on the Aging.

Harrison, Michael
    1974a "Preparation for life in the Spirit: The process of initial commitment to a religious movement." Urban Life and Culture 2:387–414.
    1974b "Sources of recruitment to Catholic pentecostalism." Journal for the Scientific Study of Religion 13:49–64.
    1975   "The maintenance of enthusiasm: Involvement in a new religious movement." Sociological Analysis 36, 2:150–160.

Harrison, Paul
    1959   Authority and Power in the Free Church Tradition. Princeton, N.J.: Princeton University Press.

Harwood, Alan
    1977   Rx: Spiritist as Needed: A Study of a Puerto Rican Community Mental Health Resource. New York: Wiley.

Hawthorne, Harry
    1955   The Doukhobors of British Columbia. Vancouver: University of British Columbia Press.

Heilman, Samuel C.
    1976   Synagogue Life: A Study in Symbolic Interaction. Chicago: University of Chicago Press.

Heirich, Max
    1977   "Change of heart: A test of some widely held theories about religious conversion." American Journal of Sociology 83, 3:653–680.

Herberg, Will
    1960   Protestant-Catholic-Jew: An Essay in American Religious Sociology. Garden City, N.Y.: Doubleday.

Hermassi, Elbaki
    1978   "Politics and culture in the Middle East." Social Compass 25, 3–4:445–464.

Hertel, Bradley and Hart Nelsen
    1974   "Are we entering a post-Christian era?: Religious beliefs and attendance in America, 1957–1968." Journal for the Scientific Study of Religion 13:409–419.

Hill, Herbert
    1973   "Anti-Oriental agitation and the rise of working-class racism." Society 10, 2:43–54.

Hill, Michael
    1973a The Religious Order: A Study of Virtuoso Religion and Its Legitimation in the Nineteenth Century Church of England. London: Heinemann.
    1973b A Sociology of Religion. New York: Basic Books.

Hobsbawm, Eric J.
    1959   Primitive Rebels. Manchester: Manchester University Press.

Hoch-Smith, Judith and Anita Spring (eds.)
    1978   Women in Ritual and Symbolic Roles. New York: Plenum.

Hoge, Dean R. and David A. Roozen (eds.)
    1979   Understanding Church Growth and Decline, 1950–1978. New York: Pilgrim.

Holloman, Regina A.
    1974   "Ritual opening and individual transformation: Rites of passage at Esalen." American Anthropologist 76:265–280.

Holt, John
    1940   "Holiness religion: Cultural shock and social reorganization." American Sociological Review 5:740–747.

Hood, Ralph
    1973   "Religious orientation and the experience of transcendance." Journal for the Scientific Study of Religion 12, 4:441–452.
    1976   "Conceptual criticisms of regressive explanations of mysticism." Review of Religious Research 17, 3:179–188.

Houtart, François
   1977   "Theravada Buddhism and political power—construction and destruction of its ideological function." Social Compass 24, 2/3:207–246.
Hyman, Paula
   1973   "The other half: Women in the Jewish tradition." Response: A Contemporary Jewish Review 8, 18:67–76.
Isichei, Elizabeth
   1967   "From sect to denomination among English Quakers." Pp. 161–181 in B. Wilson (ed.), Patterns of Sectarianism. London: Heinemann. Also, "Organization and power in the Society of Friends, 1852–59," pp. 182–212.
Jackson, John and Ray Jobling
   1968   "Towards an analysis of contemporary cults." Pp. 94–105 in D. Martin (ed.), Sociological Yearbook of Religion in Britain. Volume 1. London: SCM.
Jacquet, Constant H. (ed.)
   1976   Yearbook of American and Canadian Churches. Nashville: Abingdon.
Jahoda, Gustav
   1969   The Psychology of Superstition. London: Allen Lane.
James, William
   [1902] The Varieties of Religious Experience. New York: New American Library.

Jamison, A. Leland
   1961   "Religions on the Christian perimeter." Pp. 162–231 in J. W. Smith and A. L. Jamison (eds.), The Shaping of American Religion. Princeton, N.J.: Princeton University Press
Johnson, Benton
   1961   "Do holiness sects socialize in dominant values?" Social Forces 39: 309–316.
   1963   "On church and sect." American Sociological Review 28:539–549.
   1971   "Church-sect revisited." Journal for the Scientific Study of Religion 10:124–137.
   1977   "Sociological theory and religious truth." Sociological Analysis 38, 4:368–388.
Johnson, Doyle Paul
   1979   "Dilemmas of charismatic leadership: The case of the People's Temple." Sociological Analysis 40, 4: 315–323.
Johnson, Weldon T.
   1971   "The religious crusade: Revival or ritual?" American Journal of Sociology 76, 5:873–880.
Jolicoeur, Pamela and Louis L. Knowles
   1978   "Fraternal associations and civil religion: Scottish Rite Freemasonry." Review of Religious Research 20, 1:3–22.
Jones, R. Kenneth
   1975   "Some sectarian characteristics of therapeutic groups." Pp. 190–210 in R. Wallis (ed.), Sectarianism: Analyses of Religious and Non-Religious Sects. London: Peter Owen.
   1978   "Paradigm shifts and identity theory: Alternation as a form of identity management." Pp. 59–82 in Hans Mol (ed.), Identity and Religion. London: Sage.
Jules-Rosette, Bennetta (ed.)
   1979   The New Religions of Africa. Norwood, N.J.: Ablex.
Kanter, Rosabeth Moss
   1972   Commitment and Community: Communes and Utopias in Sociological Perspective. Cambridge: Harvard University Press.
Kearl, Michael
   1980   "Time, identity, and the spiritual needs of the elderly." Sociological Analysis 41, 2:172–180.
Kersevan, Marko
   1975   "Religion and the Marxist concept of social formation." Social Compass 22, 3/4:323–352.
Kiely, W. F.
   1972   "Coping with severe illness." Pp. 105–118 in S. Lipowski (ed.), Advances in Psychosomatic Medicine: Psychosocial Aspects of Physical Illness. Basel: Karger.
Kiev, Ari (ed.)
   1964   Magic, Faith, and Healing: Studies in Primitive Psychiatry Today. Glencoe, Ill.: Free Press.

274   References

Kim, Byong-Suh
  1977 "Ideology, conversion and faith maintenance in a Korean sect: The case of the Unified Family of Reverend Sun Myung Moon." Koreans in America: Korean Christian Scholars Journal 2:8–59.
Klapp, Orrin
  1969 Collective Search for Identity. New York: Holt, Rinehart & Winston.
Kleinman, Arthur
  1973 "Some issues for a comparative study of medical healing." International Journal of Social Psychiatry 19, 3/4:159–165.
  1978 "The failure of Western medicine." Human Nature (November): 63–68.
Knudsen, Dean, John Earle and D. W. Shriver
  1978 "The conception of sectarian religion: An effort at clarification." Review of Religious Research 20, 1:44–60.
Kroll-Smith, Stephen
  1980 "Testimony as performance." Journal for the Scientific Study of Religion 19, 1:16–25.
Kuhn, Thomas S.
  1970 The Structure of Scientific Revolutions. Chicago: University of Chicago Press.
Laeyendecker, Leo
  1972 "The Netherlands." Pp. 325–363 in H. Mol (ed.), Western Religion: A Country by Country Sociological Inquiry. The Hague: Mouton.
Lakoff, Robin
  1975 Language and Woman's Place. New York: Harper & Row.
L'Alive D'Epinay, Christian
  1969 Haven of the Masses: A Study of the Pentecostal Movement in Chile. London: Lutterworth.
Lanternari, Vittorio
  1963 The Religions of the Oppressed: A Study of Modern Messianic Cults. Tr. L. Sergio. New York: Alfred Knopf.
Laumann, Edward O.
  1969 "The social structure of religious and ethno-religious groups in a metropolitan community." American Sociological Review 34:182–197.
Lavender, Abraham (ed.)
  1977 A Coat of Many Colors: Jewish Sub-Communities in the United States. Westport, Conn.: Greenwood.
Lebra, Takie Sugiyama
  1972 "Millenarian movements and resocialization." American Behaviorial Scientist 16, 2:195–217.
Lee, Robert and Martin Marty (eds.)
  1964 Religion and Social Conflict. New York: Oxford University Press.
Lemert, Charles
  1975 "Defining non-church religion." Review of Religious Research 16, 3:186–197.
Lenski, Gerhard
  1963 The Religious Factor: A Sociological Study of Religion's Impact on Politics, Economics and Family Life. Garden City, N.Y.: Doubleday.
Lerner, Max
  1937 "The Constitution and the Court as symbols." Yale Law Journal 46:1290–1319.
Levine, Daniel H. (ed.)
  1979 "Religion, the church and politics in Latin America." Journal of Interamerican Studies and World Affairs.
Lewis, I. M.
  1971 Ecstatic Religion: An Anthropological Study of Spirit Possession and Shamanism. Harmondsworth, England: Penguin.
Lewy, Guenther
  1974 Religion and Revolution. New York: Oxford University Press.
Lifton, Robert J.
  1963 Thought Reform and the Psychology of Totalism. New York: Norton.
Lincoln, C. Eric
  [1961] The Black Muslims in America. Boston: Beacon.
  1973
  1974 "The power in the black church." Cross Currents 14, 1:3–21.

Lipset, Seymour M
    1959   Political Man. Garden City, N.Y.: Doubleday.
    1963   "Three decades of the radical right: Coughlinites, McCarthyites, and Birchers." Pp. 373–446 in D. Bell (ed.), The Radical Right. Garden City, N.Y.: Doubleday.
Lofland, John
    1966   Doomsday Cult: A Study of Conversion, Proselytization and Maintenance of Faith. Englewood Cliffs, N.J.: Prentice-Hall.
    1977   "Becoming a world-saver revisited." American Behavioral Scientist 20, 6:805–818.
London Sunday Times Insight Team
    1972   Northern Ireland: A Report on the Conflict. New York: Vintage.
Longhurst, John E.
    1962   The Age of Torquemada. Lawrence, Kans.: Coronado.
Luckmann, Thomas
    1967   The Invisible Religion: The Problem of Religion in Modern Society. New York: Macmillan.
    1973   "Comments on the Laeyendecker et al. research proposal." Pp. 55–68 in The Contemporary Metamorphosis of Religion?: Acts of the 12th Conference Internationale de Sociologie Religieuse. Lille, France: CISR.
    1977   "Theories of religion and social change." Annual Review of the Social Sciences of Religion 1:1–28.
McAvoy, Thomas
    1957   The Great Crisis in American Catholic History, 1895–1900. Chicago: Henry Regnery.
McClelland, David C.
    1961   The Achieving Society. Princeton, N.J.: Princeton University Press.
McCoy, Charles S.
    1964   "The churches and protest movements for racial justice." Pp. 37–54 in Robert Lee and Martin Marty (eds.), Religion and Social Conflict. New York: Oxford University Press.
McCracken, J. L.
    1967   "Northern Ireland, 1921–1966." Pp. 313–323 in T. W. Moody and F. X. Martin (eds.), The Course of Irish History. Cork: Mercier.
McCready, William and Andrew Greeley
    1976   The Ultimate Values of the American Population. Beverly Hills, Calif.: Sage.
MacEoin, Gary
    1974a "Irish Catholicism. What Protestant Christians fear." Cross Currents 23:397–417.
    1974b Northern Ireland. New York: Holt, Rinehart & Winston.
McGuire, Meredith B.
    1972   "Toward a sociological interpretation of the Underground Church movement." Review of Religious Research 14, 1:41–47.
    1974   "An interpretive comparison of elements of the pentecostal and Underground Church movements in American Catholicism." Sociological Analysis 35, 1:57–65.
    1975   "Religion and socio-economic change in western Ireland." Pp. 225–252 in Religion and Social Change: Acts of the 13th Conference Internationale de Sociologie Religieuse. Lille, France: CISR.
    1977   "Testimony as a commitment mechanism in Catholic pentecostal prayer groups." Journal for the Scientific Study of Religion 16, 2:165–168.
    1981   Control of Charisma: A Sociological Interpretation of the Catholic Pentecostal Movement. Philadelphia: Temple University Press.
MacIntyre, Alisdair
    1967   Secularisation and Moral Change. London: Oxford University Press.
McKown, Delos B.
    1975   The Classical Marxist Critiques of Religion: Marx, Engels, Lenin, Kautsky. The Hague: Martinus Nijhoff.
McNamara, Patrick H. (ed.)
    1974   Religion American Style. New York: Harper & Row.
Maduro, Otto
    1975   "Marxist analysis and the sociology of religion." Social Compass 22, 3–4:305–322.
    1977   "New Marxist approaches to the relative autonomy of religion." Sociological Analysis 38, 4:359–367.

Malinowski, Bronislaw
[1925] "Magic, science and religion." Pp. 17–92 in Magic, Science and Religion and Other Essays.
1948 New York: Free Press.
Manwaring, David
1962 Render unto Caesar: The Flag Salute Controversy. Chicago: University of Chicago Press.
Martin, Bernard (ed.)
1978 Movement and Issues in American Judaism: An Analysis and Sourcebook of Developments since 1945. Westport, Conn.: Greenwood.
Martin, David A.
1962 "The denomination." British Journal of Sociology 13, 2:1–14.
1965 Pacificism: An Historical and Sociological Study. New York: Schocken.
1969 The Religious and the Secular. New York: Schocken.
1978 A General Theory of Secularization. New York: Harper & Row.
Marty, Martin
1970a "The occult establishment." Social Research 37:212–230.
1970b The Righteous Empire: The Protestant Experience in America. New York: Dial.
1974 "Two kinds of two kinds of civil religion." Pp. 139–160 in R. Richey and D. Jones (eds.), American Civil Religion. New York: Harper & Row.
1976 A Nation of Behavers. Chicago: University of Chicago Press.
Marty, Martin, Stuart Rosenberg and Andrew Greeley
1968 What Do We Believe?: The Stance of Religion in America. New York: Meredith.
Marx, Gary T.
1967 "Religion: Opiate or inspiration of civil rights militancy among Negroes?" American Sociological Review 32, 1:64–72.
1969 Protest and Prejudice. New York: Harper & Row.
Marx, Karl
[1844] "Contribution to the critique of Hegel's philosophy of right." Pp. 43–59 in T. B. Bottomore
1963 (ed.), Early Writings. New York: McGraw-Hill.
Marx, Karl and Frederick Engels
1964 On Religion. New York: Schocken.
Maryknoll Fathers (eds.)
1957 Daily Missal of the Mystical Body. New York: P. J. Kennedy.
Maslow, Abraham
1964 Religions, Values and Peak-Experiences. New York: Viking.
Mayrl, William
1976 "Marx' theory of social movements and the church-sect typology." Sociological Analysis 37, 1:19–31.
Mead, George Herbert
1918 "The psychology of punitive justice." American Journal of Sociology 23:577–602.
Medvedev, Z. and R. Medvedev
1971 A Question of Madness. New York: Alfred Knopf.
Menendez, A. J.
1973 The Bitter Harvest: Church and State in Northern Ireland. Washington, D.C.: Robert B. Luce.
Merton, Robert K.
1957 Social Theory and Social Structure. Glencoe, Ill.: Free Press.
Miller, Walter M., Jr.
1959 A Canticle for Liebowitz. New York: Harold Matson.
Mintz, Jerome
1977 "Brooklyn's Hasidim." Natural History 86:46–59.
Mirbt, Carl Theodor and [anonymous]
1943 "Ultramontanism." Encyclopaedia Brittanica 22:675–677.
Moberg, David
1961 "Social differentiation in the Netherlands." Social Forces 39:333–337.
1962 The Church as a Social Institution: The Sociology of American Religion. Englewood Cliffs, N.J.: Prentice-Hall.

Mol, Hans J. (ed.)
 1972   Western Religion: A Country by Country Sociological Inquiry. The Hague: Mouton.
 1976   Identity and the Sacred. New York: Free Press.
Moodie, T. Dunbar
 1975   The Rise of Afrikanerdom. Berkeley: University of California Press.
 1978   "The Afrikaner civil religion." Pp. 203–228 in H. Mol (ed.), Identity and Religion. London:
        Sage.
Moody, Edward
 1971   "Urban witches." Pp. 280–290 in J. Spradley and D. McCurdy (eds.), Conformity and
        Conflict: Readings in Cultural Anthropology. Boston: Little, Brown.
 1974   "Magical therapy: An anthropological investigation of contemporary Satanism." Pp. 355–
        382 in I. Zaretsky and M. Leone (eds.), Religious Movements in Contemporary America.
        Princeton, N.J.: Princeton University Press.
Mooney, James
 1965   The Ghost-Dance Religion and the Sioux Outbreak of 1890. Chicago: University of Chicago
        Press.
Morgan, Barbara
 1976   "As God sees us." New Covenant. June, 1976:8–11.
Morioka, Kiyomi and William H. Newell
 1968   The sociology of Japanese Religion. International Studies in Sociology and Social An-
        thropology 6. Leiden: Brill.
Murvar, Vatro
 1971   "Messianism in Russia: Religious and revolutionary." Journal for the Scientific Study of
        Religion 10, 4:277–338.
Myerhoff, Barbara
 1974   The Peyote Hunt: The Sacred Journey of the Huichol Indians. Ithaca, N.Y.: Cornell Univer-
        sity Press.
 1978   "Bobbes and Zeydes: Old and new roles for elderly Jews." Pp. 207–244 in J. Hoch-Smith
        and A. Spring (eds.), Women in Ritual and Symbolic Roles. New York: Plenum.
Needleman, Jacob and George Baker (eds.)
 1978   Understanding the New Religions. New York: Seabury.
Nelsen, Hart M. and Anne Kusner Nelsen
 1975   The Black Church in the Sixties. Lexington: University of Kentucky Press.
Nelson, Benjamin
 1949   The Idea of Usury: From Tribal Brotherhood to Universal Otherhood. Princeton, N.J.:
        Princeton University Press.
Nelson, Geoffrey
 1969   Spiritualism and Society. New York: Schocken.
Newman, William M. (ed.)
 1974   The Social Meanings of Religion. Chicago: Rand McNally.
Niebuhr, H. Richard
 1929   The Social Sources of Denominationalism. New York: Meridian.
Noonan, John T., Jr.
 1965   Contraception: A History of Its Treatment by Catholic Theologians and Canonists. Cam-
        bridge: Harvard University Press.
O'Brien, Conor Cruise
 1974   States of Ireland. London: Granada.
O'Connor, Edward
 1971   The Pentecostal Movement in the Catholic Church. Notre Dame, Ind.: Ave Maria Press.
O'Dea, Thomas
 1957   The Mormons. Chicago: University of Chicago Press.
 1961   "Five dilemmas in the institutionalization of religion." Journal for the Scientific Study of
        Religion 1:30–39.
O'Dea, Thomas and Renato Poblete
 1970   "Anomie and the 'quest for community': The formation of sects among the Puerto Ricans of
        New York." Pp. 180–200 in T. O'Dea (ed.), Sociology and the Study of Religion. New York:
        Basic Books.

Oden, Thomas
1972 The Intensive Group Experience: The New Pietism. Philadelphia: Westminster.
"Orthodox Eastern Church."
1943 Encyclopaedia Brittanica 16:938–942.
O'Toole, Roger
1976 "Underground traditions in the study of sectarianism: Non-religious uses of the concept 'sect'." Journal for the Scientific Study of Religion 15, 2:145–156.
Parsons, Anne
1965 "The pentecostal immigrants: A study of an ethnic central city church." Journal for the Scientific Study of Religion 4:183–197.
Parsons, Talcott
1944 "The theoretical development of the sociology of religion." Journal of the History of Ideas 5:176–190.
1951 Religious Perspectives of College Teaching in Sociology and Social Psychology. New Haven: Hazen Foundation.
1963 "Christianity and modern industrial society." Pp. 33–70 in E. Tiryakian (ed.), Sociological Theory, Values and Socio-cultural Change. Glencoe, Ill.: Free Press.
1969 "Family and church as 'boundary' structures." Pp. 423–429 in N. Birnbaum and G. Lenzer (eds.), Sociology and Religion. Englewood Cliffs, N.J.: Prentice-Hall.
1971 "Belief, unbelief and disbelief." Pp. 207–245 in R. Caporale and A. Grumelli (eds.), The Culture of Unbelief. Berkeley: University of California Press.
1972 "Definitions of health and illness in the light of American values and social structure." Pp. 107–127 in E. G. Jaco (ed.), Patients, Physicians and Illness. New York: Macmillan.
Parsons, Talcott, Edward Shils, Kaspar D. Naegele and Jesse R. Pitts
1961 Theories of Society: Foundations of Modern Sociological Theory. New York: Free Press.
Paul, Lois
1978 "Careers of midwives in a Mayan community." Pp. 129–150 in J. Hoch-Smith and A. Spring (eds.), Women in Ritual and Symbolic Roles. New York: Plenum.
Peters, Victor
1971 All Things Common: The Hutterite Way of Life. New York: Harper & Row.
Petersen, Donald and Armand Mauss
1973 "The cross and the commune: An interpretation of the Jesus People." Pp. 261–280 in C. Glock (ed.), Religion in Sociological Perspective. Belmont, Calif.: Wadsworth.
Petersen, Larry R. and Armand Mauss
1976 "Religion and the 'right to life': Correlates of opposition to abortion." Sociological Analysis 37, 3:243–254.
Pfeffer, Leo
1974 "The legitimation of marginal religions in the United States." Pp. 9–26 in I. Zaretsky and M. Leone (eds.), Religious Movements in Contemporary America. Princeton, N.J.: Princeton University Press.
Phillips, Derek L.
1963 "Rejection: A possible consequence of seeking help for mental disorders." American Sociological Review 28:963–972.
1967 "Identification of mental illness: Its consequences for rejection." Community Mental Health Journal 3:262-266.
Pilarzyk, Thomas
1978 "The origin, development, and decline of a youth culture religion: An application of sectarianization theory." Review of Religious Research 20, 1:23–43.
Poll, Solomon
1969 The Hasidic Community in Williamsburg: A Study in Sociology of Religion. New York: Schocken.
Pope, Liston
1942 Millhands and Preachers. New Haven: Yale University Press.
Priesand, Sally
1975 Judaism and the New Woman. New York: Behrman.
Raab, Earl (ed.)
1964 Religious Conflict in America. New York: Doubleday.

Report of the National Advisory Commission on Civil Disorders
1968 New York: Bantam.
Richardson, James
1979a "From cult to sect: Creative eclecticism in new religious movements." Pacific Sociological Review 22, 2:139–166.
1979b "People's Temple and Jonestown: A corrective critique and comparison." Unpublished paper presented to Society for the Scientific Study of Religion.
Richardson, James (ed.)
1977 Conversion and Commitment in Contemporary Religion. American Behavioral Scientist 20,6.
1981 The Deprogramming Controversy: Sociological, Psychological, Legal and Historical Perspectives. New Brunswick, N.J.: Transaction.
Richardson, James, Mary Harder and Robert B. Simmonds
1978 Organized Miracles: A Sociological Study of a Jesus Movement Organization. New Brunswick, N.J.: Transaction.
Richey, Russell and Donald Jones (eds.)
1974 American Civil Religion. New York: Harper & Row.
Robbins, Thomas
1977 " 'Deprogramming' the 'brainwashed': Even a moonie has civil rights." The Nation 224, 8:238–242.
Robbins, Thomas and Dick Anthony
1972 "Getting straight with Meher Baba." Journal for the Scientific Study of Religion 11, 2:122–140.
1979 "Cults, brainwashing, and counter-subversion." Annals of the American Academy of Political and Social Science 446 (November): 78–90.
Robbins, Thomas, Dick Anthony and Thomas Curtis
1975 "Youth culture religious movements: Evaluating the integrative hypothesis." Sociological Quarterly 16, 1:48–64.
Robbins, Thomas, Dick Anthony, Madeleine Doucas and Thomas Curtis
1976 "The last civil religion: The Unification Church of the Reverend Sun Myung Moon." Sociological Analysis 37, 2:111–125.
Robbins, Thomas, Dick Anthony and James Richardson
1978 "Theory and research on today's 'new religions'. " Sociological Analysis 39, 2: 95–122.
Robertson, Roland
1967 "The Salvation Army: The persistence of sectarianism." Pp. 49–105 in B. Wilson (ed.), Patterns of Sectarianism. London: Heinemann.
1970 The Sociological Interpretation of Religion. New York: Schocken.
1974 "Religious and sociological factors in the analysis of secularization." Pp. 41–60 in A. Eister (ed.), Changing Perspectives in the Scientific Study of Religion. New York: Wiley.
1977 "Individualism, societalism, worldliness, universalism: Thematizing theoretical sociology of religion." Sociological Analysis 38, 4: 281–308.
1978 Meaning and Change: Explorations in the Cultural Sociology of Modern Societies. New York: New York University Press.
1979 "Religious movements and modern societies: Toward a progressive problemshift." Sociological Analysis 40, 4:297–314.
Robertson, Roland (ed.)
1969 Sociology of Religion. Hammondsworth, England: Penguin.
Robinson, John
1974 "A song, a shout, and a prayer." Pp. 213–235 in C. E. Lincoln (ed.), The Black Experience in Religion. Garden City, N.Y.: Doubleday.
Robinson, John A.
1963 Honest to God. Philadelphia: Westminster.
Roebuck, Julian and Robert Quan
1976 "Health care practices in the American deep South." Pp. 141–161 in R. Wallis and P. Morley (eds.), Marginal Medicine. New York: Free Press.
Rokeach, Milton
1960 The Open and Closed Mind. New York: Basic Books.

Roof, Wade Clark
  1978   Commitment and Community: Religious Plausibility in a Liberal Protestant Church. New York: Elsevier.
Rose, Richard
  1971   Governing Without Consensus. London: Faber and Faber.
Ruether, Rosemary
  1975   New Woman/New Earth. New York: Seabury.
Ruether, Rosemary (ed.)
  1974   Religion and Sexism: Images of Women in Jewish and Christian Traditions. New York: Simon & Schuster.
Russell, Letty Mandeville (ed.)
  1976   The Liberating Word: A Guide to a Nonsexist Interpretation of the Bible. Philadelphia: Westminster.
Ryan, Joseph
  1978   "Ethnoscience and problems of method in the social scientific study of religion." Sociological Analysis 39, 3: 241–249.
Ryder, Norman
  1973   "Recent trends and group differences in fertility." Pp. 57–68 in C. Westhoff (ed.), Toward the End of Growth: Population in America. Englewood Cliffs, N.J.: Prentice-Hall.
Sacks, Karen
  1974   "Engels revisited: Women, the organization of production and private property." Pp. 207–222 in M. S. Rosaldo and L. Lamphere (eds.), Woman, Culture and Society. Stanford, Calif.: Stanford University Press.
Samuelsson, Kurt
  1964   Religion and Economic Action. New York: Harper & Row.
Sargant, William
  1957   Battle for the Mind. Garden City, N.Y.: Doubleday.
Schmitt, David
  1973   The Irony of Irish Democracy. Lexington, Mass.: Heath.
Schneider, Louis and Sanford M. Dornbusch
  1957   "Inspirational religious literature: From latent to manifest functions of religion." American Journal of Sociology 62:476–481.
Schumann, Howard
  1971   "The religious factor in Detroit: Review, replication and reanalysis." American Sociological Review 36, 1:30–48.
Schweitzer, Albert
  1936   Indian Thought and Its Development. Boston: Beacon.
Shaffir, William
  1974   Life in a Religious Community: Lubavitcher Chassidim in Montreal. Toronto: Holt, Rinehart & Winston.
  1978   "Witnessing as identity consolidation." Pp. 39–57 in H. Mol (ed.), Identity and Religion. London: Sage.
Shannon, William V.
  1963   The American Irish. New York: Macmillan.
Shapiro, Deanne
  1974   "Factors in the development of black Judaism." Pp. 254–272 in C. E. Lincoln (ed.), The Black Experience in Religion. Garden City, N.Y.: Doubleday.
Sheehy, Michael
  1969   Is Ireland Dying? Culture and the Church in Modern Ireland. New York: Taplinger.
Shils, Edward and M. Michael Young
  1953   "The meaning of the coronation." Sociological Review 1:63–81.
Shiner, Larry
  1967   "The concept of secularization in empirical research." Journal for the Scientific Study of Religion 6:207–220.
Shupe, Anson, Roger Spielmann and Sam Stigall
  1977   "Deprogramming: The new exorcism." American Behavioral Scientist 20, 6:941–956.

Simmel, Georg
  1906 "The sociology of secrecy and of secret societies." American Journal of Sociology 11:441–498.
  1955 Conflict: The Web of Group Affiliations. Glencoe, Ill.: Free Press.
  [1906] Sociology of Religion. New York: Philosophical Library.
  1959
  [1908] On Individuality and Social Forms. Chicago: University of Chicago Press.
  1971
Simms, J. G.
  1967 "The restoration and the Jacobite war." Pp. 204–216 in T. W. Moody and F. X. Martin (eds.), The Course of Irish History. Cork: Mercier.
Simpson, George E.
  1965 The Shango Cult of Trinidad. Puerto Rico: University of Puerto Rico Press.
  1978 Black Religions in the New World. New York: Columbia University Press.
Sizer, Sandra
  1979 Gospel Hymns and Social Religion: The Rhetoric of Nineteenth Century Revivalism. Philadelphia: Temple University Press.
Sklare, Marshall
  1971 America's Jews. New York: Random House.
Sklare, Marshall and Joseph Greenblum
  1967 Jewish Identity on the Suburban Frontier. New York: Basic Books.
Slater, Philip
  1966 Microcosm: Structural, Psychological and Religious Evolution in Groups. New York: Wiley.
Smith, Huston
  1965 The Religion of Man. New York: Harper & Row.
Spillers, Hortense J.
  1971 "Martin Luther King and the style of the black sermon." Black Scholar 3, 1:14–27.
Spiro, Melford
  1966 "Religion: Problems of definition and explanation." Pp. 85–126 in M. Banton (ed.), Anthropological Approaches to the Study of Religion. London: Tavistock.
  1970 Kibbutz. New York: Schocken.
Sprenger, Reverend J. and H. Kramer
  [1400] Malleus Mallificarum. Ti. M. Summers. London: Pushkin Press.
  1948
Stark, Rodney and Charles Glock
  1968 American Piety: The Nature of Religious Commitment. Berkeley: University of California Press.
  1969 "Prejudice and the churches." Pp. 70–92 in C. Glock and E. Siegelman (eds.), Prejudice, U.S.A. New York: Praeger.
Stauffer, Robert E.
  1974 "Radical symbols and conservative functions." Unpublished paper presented to Society for the Scientific Study of Religion.
Steeman, Theodore M.
  1975 "Church, sect, mysticism, denomination: Periodological aspects of Troeltsch's types." Sociological Analysis 36, 3:181–204.
Steinberg, Stephen
  1965 "Reform Judaism: The origin and evolution of a 'church movement'." Journal for the Scientific Study of Religion 5:117–129.
Straus, Roger
  1979 "Religious conversion as a personal and collective accomplishment." Sociological Analysis 40, 2:158–165.
Streiker, Lowell and Gerald Strober
  1972 Religion and the New Majority: Billy Graham, Middle America and the Politics of the 70's. New York: Association Press.
Strommen, Merton (ed.)
  1971 Research on Religious Development. New York: Hawthorne.

Sudnow, David
  1967   Passing On: The Social Organization of Dying. Englewood Cliffs, N.J.: Prentice-Hall.
Swanson, Guy E.
  1968   "Modern secularity: Its meaning, sources, and interpretation." Pp. 801–834 in D. R. Cutler (ed.), The Religious Situation, 1968. Boston: Beacon.
Swatos, William, Jr.
  1975   "Monopolism, pluralism, acceptance, and rejection: An integrated model for church-sect theory." Review of Religious Research 16, 3:174–185.
  1979   Into Denominationalism: The Anglican Metamorphosis. Monograph Series 2. Storrs, Conn.: Society for the Scientific Study of Religion.
Szasz, Thomas S.
  1970   The Manufacture of Madness. New York: Dell.
Talmon, Yonina
  1966   "Millenarian movements." Archives Europeenes de Sociologie 7, 2:159–200.
Tawney, R. H.
  1926   Religion and the Rise of Capitalism. New York: Harcourt Brace.
Taylor, P. A. M.
  1966   Expectations Westward: The Mormons and the Emigration of Their British Converts in the 19th Century. Ithaca, N.Y.: Cornell University Press.
Terkel, Studs
  1975   Working. New York: Random House.
Thomas, Michael and C. C. Flippen
  1972   "American civil religion: An empirical study." Social Forces 51:218–225.
Thompson, E. P.
  1968   The Making of the English Working Class. Harmondsworth, England: Penguin.
Thompson, William Irwin
  1967   The Imagination of an Insurrection: Dublin, Easter, 1916. New York: Harper & Row.
Tippett, Alan R.
  1973   "The phenomenology of worship, conversion and brotherhood." Pp. 92–109 in Walter Clark (ed.), Religious Experience: Its Nature and Function in the Human Psyche. Springfield, Ill.: Charles Thomas.
Tiryakian, Edward A.
  1974   "Toward the sociology of esoteric culture." Pp. 257–280 in E. Tiryakian (ed.), On the Margin of the Visible. New York: Wiley.
Tobey, Alan
  1976   "Summer solstice of the Happy-Healthy-Holy Organization." Pp. 5–30 in C. Glock and R. Bellah (eds.), The New Religious Consciousness. Berkeley: University of California Press.
Touraine, Alain
  1977   Self-Production of Society. Chicago: University of Chicago Press.
Towler, Robert and Audrey Chamberlain
  1973   "Common religion." Pp. 1–27 in M. Hill (ed.), Sociological Yearbook of Religion in Britain. Volume 6. London: SCM.
Troeltsch, Ernst
  [1931] The Social Teachings of the Christian Churches. Volumes 1 and 2. Tr. O. Wyon. New York:
  1960   Harper & Row.
Truzzi, Marcello
  1972   "The occult revival as popular culture: Some random observations in the old and nouveau witch." Sociological Quarterly 13: 16–36.
  1974a "Definition and dimension of the occult: Towards a sociological perspective." Pp. 243–255 in E. Tiryakian (ed.), On the Margins of the Visible. New York: Wiley.
  1974b "Witchcraft and Satanism." Pp. 215–222 in E. Tiryakian (ed.), On The Margins of the Visible. New York: Wiley.
Turnbull, Colin
  1961   The Forest People. New York: Simon & Schuster.
Turner, Bryan
  1977a "Class solidarity and system integration." Sociological Analysis 38, 4:345–358.
  1977b "Confession and social structure." Annual Review of the Social Sciences of Religion 1: 29–58.

Turner, Victor
    1969   The Ritual Process. Chicago: Aldine.
    1974a Dramas, Fields, and Metaphors. Ithaca, N.Y.: Cornell University Press.
    1974b "Metaphors of anti-structure in religious culture." Pp. 63–84 in A. Eister (ed.), Changing Perspectives in the Scientific Study of Religion. New York: Wiley.
    1979   "Betwixt and between: The liminal period in 'rites de passage'." Pp. 234–243 in E. Vogt (ed.), Reader in Comparative Religion: An Anthropological Approach. New York: Harper & Row.

Tyler, Lawrence
    1966   "The Protestant ethic among Black Muslims." Phylon 27: 5–14.

Underhill, Evelyn
    1961   Mysticism. New York: Dutton.

Utrecht, Ernst
    1978   "Religion and social protest in Indonesia." Social Compass 25, 3–4:395–418.

Van Gennep, A.
    1960   The Rites of Passage. Tr. M. Vikedom and G. Coffee. Chicago: University of Chicago Press.

Varga, Ivan
    1975   "Is religion a political factor? Is politics a religious factor?" Pp. 465–491 in Religion and Social Change: Acts of the 13th Conference Internationale de Sociologie Religieuse. Lille, France: CISR.

Vecsey, George
    1979   "233,144 left U.S. Catholic Church in year." New York Times, July, 17.

Verdesi, Elizabeth Howell
    1976   In But Still Out: Women in the Church. Philadelphia: Westminster.

Vlachos, Evan
    1975   "Apocalyptic strains and the potential for utopian movements in the United States." Unpublished paper presented to Society for the Scientific Study of Religion.

Vonnegut, Kurt, Jr.
    1963   Cat's Cradle. Baltimore: Penguin.

Waardenburg, Jacques
    1978   "Social development and Islamic religious tradition." Unpublished paper presented to 9th World Congress of Sociology.

Wach, Joachim
    1944   Sociology of Religion. Chicago: University of Chicago Press.

Walker, Andrew and James S. Atherton
    1971   "An Easter pentecostal convention: The successful management of a 'time of blessing'. " Sociological Review 19, 3:367–387.

Wallace, Anthony
    1956   "Revitalization movements." American Anthropologist 58: 264–281.
    1957   "Mazeway disintegration: The individual's perception of socio-cultural disorganization." Human Organization 16:23–27.

Wallace, Ruth
    1975   "Bringing women in: Marginality in the churches." Sociological Analysis 36, 4:291–303.

Wallis, Roy
    1973   "A comparative analysis of problems and processes of change in two manipulationist movements: Christian Science and Scientology." Pp. 407–422 in Contemporary Metamorphosis of Religion?: Acts of the 12th Conference Internationale de Sociologie Religieuse. Lille, France: CISR.
    1974   "Ideology, authority and the development of cultic movements." Social Research 41: 299–327.
    1977   The Road to Total Freedom: A Sociological Analysis of Scientology. New York: Columbia University Press.
    1978   The Rebirth of the Gods?: Reflections on the New Religions in the West. Belfast: Queen's University New Lecture Series 108.

Wardwell, Walter
    1972   "Orthodoxy and heterodoxy in medical practice." Social Science and Medicine 6:759–763.

Warner, W. Lloyd
   1953   American Life: Dream and Reality. Chicago: University of Chicago Press.
   1961   Family of God: A Symbolic Study of Christian Life in America. New Haven: Yale University Press.
Washington, Joseph
   1964   Black Religion: The Negro and Christianity in the United States. Boston: Beacon.
   1972   Black Sects and Cults. Garden City, N.Y.: Doubleday.
Weber, Max
   [1920–21] From Max Weber: Essays in Sociology. Tr. and ed. H. H. Gerth and C. W. Mills. New
   1946   York: Oxford University Press.
   [1925] The Theory of Social and Economic Organization. Tr. A. M. Henderson and T. Parsons.
   1947   New York: Oxford University Press.
   [1920–21] The Religion of China. Tr. H. H. Gerth. New York: Free Press.
   1951
   [1920–21] Ancient Judaism. Tr. H. H. Gerth and D. Martindale. New York: Free Press.
   1952
   [1904] The Protestant Ethic and the Spirit of Capitalism. Tr. T. Parsons. New York: Scribner.
   1958a
   [1920–21] The Religion of India. Tr. H. H. Gerth and D. Martindale. New York: Free Press.
   1958b
   [1922] The Sociology of Religion. Tr. E. Fischoff. Boston: Beacon.
   1963
   [1925] Economy and Society. Volume 3. Ed. G. Roth and C. Wittich. New York: Bedminster.
   1968
Weigert, Andrew and Darwin Thomas
   1969   "Religiosity in 5-D: A critical note." Social Forces 48: 260–263.
Weil, Andrew
   1973   The Natural Mind. Boston: Houghton Mifflin.
Weisberger, Bernard
   1958   They Gathered at the River: The Story of the Great Revivalists and Their Impact upon Religion in America. Boston: Little, Brown.
Welter, Barbara
   1966   "The cult of true womanhood: 1820–1860." American Quarterly (Summer), Part I:151–174.
Westhues, Kenneth
   1973   "The established church as an agent of change." Sociological Analysis 34, 2:106–123.
   1976   "The church in opposition." Sociological Analysis 37, 4:299–314.
Westin, Alan
   1964   "The John Birch Society." Pp. 239–268 in D. Bell (ed.), The Radical Right. Garden City, N.Y.: Doubleday.
Westley, Frances
   1978a "The cult of man: Durkheim's predictions and new religious movements." Sociological Analysis 39, 2:135–145.
   1978b "The cults of man." Unpublished doctoral dissertation. Montreal: Concordia University.
Whyte, J. H.
   1971   Church and State in Modern Ireland. Dublin: Gill.
Wiesel, Elie
   1960   Night. New York: Pyramid.
Williams, Melvin D.
   1974   Community in a Black Pentecostal Church: An Anthropological Study. Pittsburgh: University of Pittsburgh Press.
Wilmore, Gayraud S., Jr.
   1972   Black Religion and Black Radicalism. Garden City, N.Y.: Doubleday.
Wilson, Bryan R.
   1970   Religious Sects. New York: McGraw-Hill.
   1976   Contemporary Transformations of Religion. London: Oxford University Press.
   1979   "The return of the sacred." Journal for the Scientific Study of Religion 18, 3:268–280.
Wilson, Bryan R. (ed.)
   1967   Patterns of Sectarianism: Organization and Ideology in Social and Religious Movements. London: Heinemann.

Wilson, John F.
   1979   Public Religion in American Culture. Philadelphia: Temple University Press.
Wilson, William J.
   1978   The Declining Significance of Race. Chicago: University of Chicago Press.
Wimberley, Ronald
   1976   "Testing the civil religion hypothesis." Sociological Analysis 37:341–352.
   1979   "Continuity in the measurement of civil religion." Sociological Analysis 40, 1:59–62.
Wimberley, Ronald, Thomas Hood and C. M. Lipsey
   1976   "The civil religion dimension: Is it there?" Social Forces 54:890–900.
Wimberley, Ronald, Thomas Hood, C. M. Lipsey, Donald Clelland and M. Hay
   1975   "Conversion in a Billy Graham crusade: Spontaneous event or ritual performance."
          Sociological Quarterly 16:162–170.
Winter, Gibson
   1961   The Suburban Captivity of the Churches. Garden City, N.Y.: Doubleday.
Wolff, Harold G.
   1962   "A concept of disease in man." Psychosomatic Medicine 24, 1:25–30.
Wood, James R.
   1970   "Authority and controversial policy: The churches and civil rights." American Sociological
          Review 35, 6:1057–1069.
Woodward, C. Vann
   1957   The Strange Career of Jim Crow. New York: Oxford University Press.
Worsley, Peter
   1968   The Trumpet Shall Sound: A Study of "Cargo" Cults in Melanesia. New York: Schocken.
Wuthnow, Robert
   1976a "Astrology and marginality." Journal for the Scientific Study of Religion 15, 2:157–168.
   1976b The Consciousness Reformation. Berkeley: University of California Press.
   1978   "Religious movements and the transition in world culture." Pp. 63–79 in J. Needleman and
          G. Baker (eds.), Understanding the New Religions. New York: Seabury.
Yinger, J. Milton
   1946   Religion in the Struggle for Power. Durham, N.C.: Duke University Press.
   1957   Religion, Society and the Individual. New York: Macmillan.
   1963   "The 1962 H. Paul Douglass lectures, I. Religion and social change: Functions and dysfunc-
          tions of sects and cults among the disprivileged." Review of Religious Research 4, 2:65–84.
   1970   The Scientific Study of Religion. New York: Macmillan.
Young, Allan
   1976   "Some implications of medical beliefs and practices for social anthropology." American
          Anthropologist 78:5–24.
Zablocki, Benjamin
   1971   The Joyful Community. Baltimore: Penguin.
Zald, Mayer
   1970   Organization Change: The Political Economy of the Y.M.C.A. Chicago: University of
          Chicago Press.
Zaretsky, Eli
   1976   Capitalism, the Family and Personal Life. London: Pluto Press.
Zaretsky, Irving and Mark Leone (eds.)
   1974   Religious Movements in Contemporary America. Princeton, N.J.: Princeton University
          Press.
Zborowski, M.
   1958   "Cultural components in response to pain." Pp. 256–268 in E. G. Jaco (ed.), Patients,
          Physicians and Illness. New York: Free Press.
Zeldin, Mary-Barbara
   1969   "The religious nature of Russian Marxism." Journal for the Scientific Study of Religion
          8:100–111.
Zetterberg, Hans
   1952   "The religious conversion as a change of social roles." Sociology and Social Research 36,
          1:159–166.

Author Index

Abercrombie, Nicholas, 85, 242
Aberle, David, 38, 121
Abramson, Harold, 32
Ahlstrom, Sidney, 135, 188, 190
Aleshire, D., 163
Alfred, Randall, 87
Allon, Natalie, 71
Almerick, Paulina, 233
Alston, John P., 80
AmaraSingham, Lorna Rhodes, 98
Anderson, Alan, 100
Anthony, Dick, 16, 34, 38, 39, 59, 63, 123, 144, 179, 188
Aron, Raymond, 216
Atchley, Robert, 56
Atherton, James, 66

Bahr, Howard, 56
Bainbridge, William, 87
Baker, George, 143
Balch, Robert, 39, 63, 124
Barkan, Steven, 230
Barker, Eileen, 112
Barkun, Michael, 36, 37, 38, 39, 123
Barnett, Homer, 38
Barrett, David, 210
Barrett, Leonard, 204
Beach, Stephen, 169, 198
Becker, Howard, 109, 164, 248
Beckett, J. C., 169, 170, 171, 172, 175
Beckford, James, 36, 61, 63, 64, 66, 124, 127, 130, 143, 144
Bell, Daniel, 190, 242
Bellah, Robert, 10, 16, 18, 76, 83, 121, 142, 147, 149, 151, 152, 153, 154, 157, 158, 179, 180, 224, 225, 227, 230, 232, 256
Benedict, Ruth, 149
Bennett, David, 160
Berger, Bennett, 51
Berger, Peter, 6, 10, 16, 18, 22, 23, 26, 28, 29, 30, 35, 41, 46, 47, 48, 55, 59, 61, 65, 109, 112, 121, 133, 230, 233, 234, 241, 243, 256
Berger, Stephen, 193
Bird, Frederick, 34, 142
Birnbaum, Norman, 15, 19, 190
Bittner, Egon, 249
Borker, Ruth, 94

Bouma, Gary, 193
Brazier, Arthur, 211
Briggs, Kenneth, 92
Brittan, Arthur, 48
Bromley, David, 63, 112
Brotz, Howard, 209
Bumpass, Larry, 53
Burke, Kenneth, 61, 81
Burkholder, John Richard, 238, 247, 248
Burnham, Kenneth, 209

Calley, Malcolm, 123
Campbell, Colin, 76, 108, 117
Campbell, Ernest, 202
Carmody, Denise, 93
Castenada, Carlos, 13
Chamberlain, Audrey, 83, 85
Cherry, Conrad, 151
Clark, Elizabeth, 97
Clarke, Aidan, 170
Clayton, Richard, 83
Cleage, Albert B., Jr., 209
Cohn, Norman, 38, 39
Coleman, James S., 159, 161, 163, 180, 186
Coleman, John A., 157
Conrad, Peter, 249
Cooper, Lee, 210
Coser, Lewis, 117, 164
Cox, Harvey, 48
Crapanzano, Vincent, 86
Cross, Robert, 166
Cross, Whitney, 123
Culpepper, Emily, 86

Daly, Mary, 92, 93, 100
D'Antonio, William, 186
Davidson, Laurie, 90
Davis, David Brian, 63
Davis, Kingsley, 148
DeJong, Gordon, 83, 104
Demerath, N. J., III, 118, 185
Deren, Maya, 204
Desroche, Henri, 190
Dollard, John, 91
Dornbusch, Sanford, 84
Dougherty, Molly, 103
Douglas, Mary, 54, 96, 151, 162

Subject Index